EURASIAN LEGAL SYSTEMS IN A WORLD OF TRANSITIONS

Cultures juridiques et politiques
Vol. 20

Cultures juridiques et politiques Vol. 20

Les conceptions du pouvoir, du droit et de l'ordre se réfèrent inévitablement à l'ensemble du système de représentations qu'est la culture de chaque société. Toute forme de culture ayant donc nécessairement une dimension politique et juridique, la collection « Cultures juridiques et politiques » publie des travaux, tels que des thèses, synthèses de recherches, ouvrages collectifs et actes de colloques, se proposant de faire connaître les systèmes politiques et juridiques des pays européens, d'évaluer les grandes tendances des processus d'intégration politique et d'harmonisation juridique en cours dans l'Union européenne et d'éclairer les interférences entre le politique, le juridique et les autres aspects « culturels » dans le contexte de ces processus.

REMUS TITIRIGA, HYE-HWAL SEONG,
ZHULDYZ SAIRAMBAEVA, PIERRE CHABAL (eds.)
with the collaboration of Louis-Philippe GRATTON

EURASIAN LEGAL SYSTEMS IN A WORLD OF TRANSITIONS

ECONOMIC PROSPERITY OR DISPARITY, AND THE RETURN OF POLITICS IN INTERNATIONAL LAW

PETER LANG
Lausanne - Berlin - Bruxelles - Chennai - New York - Oxford

Funding was provided by :
- in Korea : the Inha University Legal Institute, the Inch'eon Bar Association
- in France : the JURISCOPE center in Poitiers, the LEXFEIM research center of Le Havre University
- in Kazakhstan : the Departement of International Law of Al-Farabi Kazakh National University
- in Europe : the SEFACil Foundation

Published by Peter Lang Éditions scientifiques internationales - P.I.E. SA, Brussels, Belgium
www.peterlang.com , info@peterlang.com

ISSN 2235-1078
ISBN 978-3-0343-4822-5 eprint
ISBN 978-3-0343-4824-9 ePub
D/ 2023/5678/54
ISBN 978-3-0343-4823-2 eBook
DOI 10.3726/b21528

Bibliographic information published by "Die Deutsche Nationalbibliothek". "Die Deutsche Nationalbibliothek" lists this publication in the "Deutsche National-bibliografie"; detailed bibliographic data is available on the Internet at <http://dnb.d-nb.de>.

CIP available at the British Library and the Library of Congress.

This book is dedicated
to all colleagues and friends from Eurasia
whose trust and kindness
are the keys to understanding who we are,
culturally as well as intellectually.

Books by Pierre Chabal also edited and published with Peter Lang

In the series *Cultures juridiques et politiques*

Eurasian legal systems in a world of transitions: Economic prosperity or disparity, and the return of politics in international law, Brussels, Peter Lang, 2023, 385 pages

Eurasian challenges to international economic law: New developments after Brexit and in the context of the Covid-19, Brussels, Peter Lang, 2022, 342 pages

The challenge of change in the legal and political systems of Eurasia and the New Silk Road, Brussels, Peter Lang, 2020, 314 pages

On the European and Asian origins of legal and political systems: Views from Korea, Kazakhstan and France, Brussels, Peter Lang, 2018, 298 pages

Mutations de société et réponses du droit: Perspectives franco-asiatiques comparées, Brussels, Peter Lang, 2017, 280 pages

Le régionalisme et ses limites: Regards croisés franco-kazakhs, Brussels, Peter Lang, 2016, 183 pages

In the series *International Issues*

L'Organisation de coopération de Shanghai et la construction de « la nouvelle Asie », Brussels, Peter Lang, 2016, 488 pages

Concurrences interrégionales Europe-Asie au 21e siècle, Brussels, Peter Lang, 2015, 393 pages

In the series *New International Insights*

The Completion of Eurasia ? Continental convergence or regional dissent in the context of "historic turns", Brussels, Peter Lang, 2023, 558 pages

Evolving regional values and mobilities in global contexts: The emergence of new (Eur)Asian regions and dialogues with Europe, Brussels, Peter Lang, 2020, 386 pages

Cross-border exchanges: Eurasian perspectives on logistics and diplomacy, Brussels, Peter Lang, 2019, 396 pages

*

Also by Pierre Chabal

La coopération de Shanghai: conceptualiser la « nouvelle Asie », Liège, Presses universitaires de Liège, 2019, 306 pages

**

Table of contents

Part II
Legal, political and economic impact on commercial institutions (EAEU, EU …) and cooperation agreements (Silk Roads …)

Acknowledgements

Remus TITIRIGA, Hye-Hwal SEONG,
Zhuldyz SARAIMBAEVA, Pierre CHABAL,
Louis-Philippe GRATTON

The InHa[1] University Law School, its Legal Institute, its Big Data Centre, all located on the InHa University main campus in Inch'eon (South Korea), in association with the Inch'eon Bar Association, hosted the 6th international conference devoted to comparative regional legal issues of Eurasia. The conference organisers express their sincere thanks to these institutions in Korea as well as to supporting institutions in other countries, namely the Lexfeim Research Centre in Law of Université Le Havre Normandie, the Institut Caennais de Recherche Juridique of Université Caen Normandie, the Juriscope Centre of Poitiers University as well as the Sefacil Foundation, France, and the Department of International Law of the Faculty of International Relations at Al-Farabi Kazakh National University in Almaty.

The three-day schedule of the conference could be considered short for the participants who enjoyed every minute and thank the organisers, or very long to the main InHa organiser, professor Hye-Hwal Seong, whom all colleagues thank whole-heartedly. Such an international conference can only come about through a series of plural good wills, as human beings are not only "social animals" (Aristotle) but above all "cooperative animals" (Seong). The organisers wish to thank also professor Tai-Uk Chung, who was the host of the 3rd seminar in InHa in 2017, and a key to the success of the 2023 edition. The Law School Dean Young-Jin Jung was the overall responsible person, professor Won-Oh Kim generously supported the very fact that the conference could take

1 The spelling InHa, with an upper-key H, comes from the original setting of the University being f[o]unded in **In**ch'eon city with large donations at the turn of the 50s from Korean settlers in **Ha**waï.

place. Ms Kyung-Min Im of the InHa Legal Institute and Ms Hyun-Hye Kim of the Administrative Office proved invaluable contributors.

This conference organisers are happy to say once more how aware they are of the thriving encouragement received from all institutions named above as well as from numerous well-wishing colleagues as intellectual partners. Colleagues in Korea have trusted distant partners without a trace of hesitation. Colleagues in Kazakhstan have offered their participation from the onset when they hosted the very first international and interregional seminar in 2014. Colleagues from Romania, China, Russia, Spain and Canada have embarked upon the adventure not always with a life-vest but always safe-reaching their changing ports of call. These solid academic friendships, that now extend well over a decade, are a telling indication that Eurasia is in the making, and is virtually realised in terms of academic and human dimensions.

Indeed, the fact that is has taken only a decade, since the 1st joint conference in 2014 in Almaty, for the original bilateral (Kazakhstan, France) and trilateral cores (with Korea) to have extended to four additional countries (China, Russia, Spain, Canada) is indeed an achievement, both institutionally and intellectually, looking at legal issues in Eurasia while mobilising all three sub-regions: Central Asia, East Asia, West Europe. We have been analysing "the new Eurasia", in all its dimension, and we have done so through six books, all six published in Belgium, first in French (two) then in English (four), and offering to the readers about 200 texts written by about 50 colleagues.

To our knowledge, such a broad trilateral approach is indeed an undisputable reality stemming from our international seminars.

We hope that these publications are a just tribute for all support received.

Welcoming address

Young-Jin JUNG

Dean
InHa University Law School

How best to open such a fine book that originates in a thriving conference held in the Law School that I head in InHa University in Inch'eon, South Korea? Most probably by stating simply and sincerely that it is a pleasure to welcome you all to the 6th Kazakh-Franco-Korean International Law Conference and its resulting book.

As the Dean of the law school, it is indeed my pleasure to congratulate both the organisers and the participants for this pointed and *au fait* conference that addresses critical legal issues of the Eurasian world today. This conference brought together legal experts from France, Kazakhstan, China, Russia, Spain and Korea to discuss and explore Eurasian legal systems in a world in transition in terms of economic prosperity or disparity, and the return of politics in international law.

We are living in an era of unprecedented change, where rapid technological advancements, demographic shifts, and environmental challenges are presenting complex legal and ethical issues, which require our collective expertise, knowledge, and skills to navigate effectively through them. As legal scholars and practitioners, we recognise the significant role that legal systems play in shaping the future of our societies. Legal systems provide the foundation for social stability, political governance, and economic development.

This conference consisted of four sections which feature an impressive line-up of determined legal scholars and practitioner. The conference provided and the book will provide us with a strong opportunity to seek and deepen our understanding of the critical legal and political issues that affect us all. And by publishing the results of this conference, we are now able to share our insights and experiences with the wider international community.

On behalf of InHa Law School, I would like to thank professor Hye-Hwal SEONG for his untiring and good-hearted efforts in preparing for this conference. Well done!

Foreword

Won-Oh KIM

Director
The Institute for Legal Studies and AI·Data Law Centre
InHa University

The Legal Institute at InHa University is happy to welcome professors Zhuldyz Sairambaeva, Pierre Chabal and Hye-Hwal Seong who made every effort to ensure that the international conference joining our three countries and beyond could be held safely despite various kinds of difficult circumstances. I express again, opening this book, my deepest gratitude to all participants and chapter authors.

The conference held in May 2023 and the ensuing book feature three countries and beyond these, four more countries as the momentum has picked up from the launching meetings of 2014, 2016 and 2017. The conference that started in Kazakhstan in 2014 was held in France in 2016, and in Korea in 2017 ended the first cycle. And the second cycle, which started in 2019 in Kazakhstan and 2021 in France, has concluded with a two-day conference in Korea on 11 and 12 May 2023.

Let us emphasise that it is meaningful of the efforts invested that such a rotating international conference should have consistently met and be published over the span of a decade, regularly, every two years, to share research results, and discuss the future of Eurasian legal systems in depth.

With the end of the COVID-19 pandemic, we indeed looked forward to a return to our daily lives, which is what this 2023 meeting represented after the 2021 one had to be held online. However, the outbreak of the Russian special operation in Ukraine presented another challenge for the international community. Sanctions against Russia did not have only the effect of isolating a country. In addition, it triggered a global food and energy security crisis and increased tensions between the US and China. Moreover, trade restrictions on food and energy are impacting the implementation of the Treaty on the Eurasian Economic Union (EAEU) and the Regional Comprehensive Economic Partnership (RCEP). With the arrival of the new Cold War era, the role of cooperative organisations in regional security, such as the Collective Security Treaty Organisation (CSTO) and the Shanghai Cooperation Organisation (SCO), is being re-examined.

The present book sheds light on these issues, especially in its parts I, II and III.

Part IV of this book draws attention, beyond the crisis caused by war, to equally important issues to do with the 4th industrial revolution. Problems of data monopoly, personal information infringement, surveillance and censorship based on artificial intelligence and data are key evolutions to which the international community must respond in the near future. T The InHa Institute for Legal Studies established in 2020 the AI·Data Law Centre in order to focus on legal issues related to artificial intelligence and data. The chapters that make up part IV of the book are of particular interest to the AI·Data Law Centre, that is becoming a hub for research on artificial intelligence and data laws in the countries represented in this book.

This book is impressive, not only since it brings together 23 scholars from 8 institutions in 6 countries after the InHa Law School meeting, but also since it promotes cooperation and provide opportunities for joint research.

Preface

Gwan-Ju AN

Chairman
Inch'eon Bar Association

The Bar Association which I represent offers again its congratulations to the organisers of the May 2023 conference in InHa Law School and now co-directors of the book published from the presentations of last Spring. Only six years after the previous research meeting in InHa University on 2017, colleagues met again and as impressively as last time conducted two days of thorough discussions.

It is said that this rotating conference started with the proposal of professor Pierre Chabal of the University of the Havre in Normandy, back in 2013–2014. To me, Normandy is mainly the symbol of the"Normandy landings" during World War II. The Normandy landings were a decisive operation to end the Second World War. Ending the war marks the beginning of peace. Normandy is a symbol of peace. I believe that professor Chabal's academic conference was a declaration of peace that no more wars should occur on this planet.

This declaration of peace has reached Al-Farabi University in Kazakhstan, the birthplace of the great philosopher Al-Farabi, whose philosophy is still being passed down to generations. The desire for peace and freedom in these two countries has reached InHa University Law School, located at the eastern end of the continent, beyond the Tianshan Mountains. InHa University Law School pursues justice.

I wondered today why professors from different countries, nations, cultures, languages, and universities gathered here. I believe there is only one reason for this. It is to create a world where universal values such as peace, freedom, and justice, pursued by humanity beyond such differences and ethnic boundaries, are alive and well.

The current world is said to be unstable in terms of commercial communities and security. I hope this academic conference has provided an alternative to this situation, as echoed in this book. We also live in the age of artificial intelligence and Chat GPT. However, we should not forget that all the roots of human thoughts are based on cultures created 2000–3000 years ago. I am endlessly envious and proud of professors who study and discuss such topics. I believe the continual development and progress of the world to be based on such efforts.

General introduction

Remus TITIRIGA

Professor, Law School, InHa University

This introduction briefs the main contents of the book. It aims to act as "intellectual appetiser" for whetting the reader's readiness to digest its contents. The book gathers contributions about recent developments in Eurasia, especially over the past two years as a previous conference and book date back to 2021. During this tumultuous period, the defining event was the "special military operation" projected by Russia into Ukraine, from 22 February 2022 onwards. Paradoxically, no paper analyses this military operation as such. However, in the filigree of its pages, chapters deal with the outcomes of this unprecedented (at least since 1945) European war.

As the reader is about to confirm for herself or himself, the essential contribution of the book is to focus on conflicting dynamics between construction and deconstruction in international and regional relations. It is also to highlight the legal and regulatory challenges created by new technological developments in IT, AI, and data protection, globally and in Eurasia.

The book structure covers four main parts. **Part I** deals with the *Challenges and turmoil in the region: when conflictual dynamics take over from Covid and jeopardise the context of cooperation.* The recurrent theme here is the multidimensional crisis, that the world experiences today and its missing answers. The crisis originates either from ideologies of the old past (Moscow as Third Rome) or from actions or competition of great powers threatening the security globally or locally, or even from the inner core of the modern technological society (the problem of waste and its ecological impact).

It begins with Élise Frêlon's chapter about the origin of the history of Moscow as the Third Rome, that is an ideological and religious justification of Russian imperialism over the centuries. It proves that the historical dimension of *l'histoire longue* is necessary, as expected, to make sense of the present.

The book continues with Philippe Gast's analysis about the inability of international governance institutions such as the UN to answer to global environmental, energetic, economic, or social challenges and, most of all, security threats represented, among others, by Russian and Chinese action demands. The author proposes an agenda for reforming the global system of rules and institutions.

Kuralay Baizakova and Fatima Kukeyeva examine the risks and opportunities confronting Kazakhstan's foreign policy in light of the geopolitical turbulence of 2022 in Eurasia. In doing so, they not only browse through the classic security challenges for Central Asia's largest territory but they also point to the novel ones associated with the clearly more unilateral role that Russia has embarked upon, at least in the west of the continent.

Sagyngaliy Aidarbayev examines the systemic crisis of modern international law and its mechanisms (unveiled once again by the armed conflict of Russia into Ukraine), which seems unable to ensure international peace and security. The suggestion to reform the world security system is an old one but the author contextualises it as and inasmuch as necessary.

Confronted with the same problem of peace and security resulting from his evaluation that the world of the 21st century has entered into an era of hegemonic competition, Tai-Uk Chung is proposing a statute of Permanent Neutrality for the Korean peninsula as a solution for a post-unification moment, when that comes.

Yesbol Omirzhanov, Almagul Tusupova, and Binur Bertayeva consider that the Russian "special military operation" in Ukraine has changed the geopolitical attitudes of many countries and weakened regional initiatives such as the Eurasian Economic Union (EAEU) or even the Collective Security Treaty Organisation (CSTO). According to them, an answer to security and peace challenges in the region suggests a revival and upgrade within the new context of the idea proposed early in the 20th century: the Greater Turkestan. A union of Central Asian countries, a confederation of Turkic-speaking states, would include countries of Central Asia, Azerbaijan, and Turkey.

The last chapter deals with global security from a long perspective of global sustainability for human life on our planet. Young-Geun Chae examines the possibilities of transforming the current Linear Economy concerning waste (aligning the acts of "produce, consume and then throw away") into a Circular Economy (composed of a closed loop of regeneration, where materials are endlessly repaired, reused, refurbished, and recycling), thus saving raw materials, reducing CO2 emissions and reducing the ecological imprint of humanity. Since raw material supply chains and waste flows are global, such a circular economy imposes changes on a worldwide scale.

Part II of the book deals with *the Legal, political, and economic impact on commercial institutions (EAEU, EU…) and cooperation agreements (Silk Road,…)*. The focus here is on the economy, considered either as a contributing factor for cooperation (through international instruments or approaches such as OECD, EAEU, WTO, and Singapore Convention) or as a disruptive factor, able to break cooperation on a global level (Western sanctions toward Russia) or local level (the problem of Comfort Women vs. the relations between South Korea and Japan).

In this respect, Ilya Lifshits examines the global tax reform (transboundary taxation) legally imposed under the auspices of the OECD. He underlines radical changes in taxing multinational enterprises (cross-border taxation) within multiple pillars. The first pillar of this reform is income taxation, while the second is the introduction of a minimum global corporate tax. Such changes will emerge with the new multilateral Convention in 2023, and the international community will move toward an international tax regime, replacing the old tax-avoidance schemes.

Remus Titiriga examines the sanctions (mostly Western) related to Russian military actions in Ukraine. Regardless of the outcome of the War in Ukraine, the economic, political, and demographic damage from the sanctions (and the War itself) will have a particular effect on Russia. However, the indirect impact of sanctions has spread evenly and touched Europe and countries such as Japan, Korea, and Taiwan, which, for example, rely on LNG as their primary energy source. Western sanctions (especially by the US) against Russia are here to stay, as they also deter China from geopolitical competition and the South China Sea and Taiwan security.

The chapter by Zhuldyz Sairambaeva and Madina Nurtai compares the customs protection of intellectual property rights within the Eurasia Economic Union (EAEU) with that of the European Union. The more rigorous EU mechanisms for combating counterfeiting and its adequate customs protection could inspire the EAEU solutions (by extending customs protection to intellectual property items such as patents, industrial designs, utility models, selection achievements, and integrated circuit layouts).

Zulfiya Baimagambetova and Assem Akhmetova analyse the WTO Dispute Resolution from the perspective of the international experience and prospects for Kazakhstan, a country that acceded to the Organisation in 2015. The authors review the WTO dispute resolution mechanisms, analyse the problems that Kazakhstan may face in using these mechanisms, and offer recommendations for improving the state's participation in the WTO dispute resolution, in the near and medium-term future.

Sung-Kee Hong examines the normalisation of South Korea-Japan relations in light of the Comfort Women Agreement of 2015 and the 2018 Supreme Court of Korea ruling on compensation for the forced labour. According to him, the provision of the initial 1965 Property and Claims Settlement Agreement covers the situation of comfort women. Moreover, the issue of comfort women is a typical case of sovereign immunity of a foreign state (here, Japan). Even if sovereign immunity were put aside, any decision favouring Korea against a foreign state (Japan) would be unenforceable and only a nuisance to the cooperation between South Korea and Japan.

Guillermo Palao analyses the 2018 UN Convention on International Settlement Agreements Reached as a Result of Mediation (or "Singapore Convention") and considers that it represents a real opportunity for Korea or any other countries of Eurasia to resolve international trade disputes and, as such, contribute to the further development of international trade and naturally also to region-building.

Part III of the book, *Legal and political impact on security institutions (SCO, CSTO …): expansion, "centration" or deconstruction of great ensembles?*, focuses on the regional turmoil and its impact on regional institutions. Once again, we have a chapter focusing on the security challenges et threats (emigration or the late military action of Russia), but this time as destabilissing factors for regional (Central Asian or European) institutions and Organisations which require constructive answers.

Klara Makasheva and Leila Delovarova address the migration issues in Central Asia. While the coordination and regulation of migration processes fall globally within the sphere of UN agencies (ILO, IOM, UNHCR), Central Asian regional organisations (CIS, EEU, Almaty Process, SCO, CICA) are considered from a comparative perspective as agents trying to tackle the problem efficiently. This case-study brings substance to the far broader discussion of the gradual invention by Central Asia of its own sub-regional security.

Zhulduz Baizakova's contribution asks whether the Collective Security Treaty Organisation (CSTO) can support the Caspian region's collective security requirements. The author considers that the CSTO would remain on the side-line of the Caspian and Central Asian geopolitics. At the same time, Moscow, which was instrumental in the Organisation's creation, would focus its attention elsewhere (the War in Ukraine being the expression of such far-away interest). To what extent the Caspian Sea can remain a militarily neutral space is fundamentally questioned.

Philippe Lagrange examines the future role of The Organisation for Security and Cooperation in Europe (OSCE) concerning the Ukraine crisis. The author considers that, given the military crisis among two of its members (Russia and Ukraine), it may be appropriate to review the functioning of the OSCE and some aspects of its politico-military approach to security. Moreover, the OSCE's economic, environmental, and human dimensions remain as relevant as ever and merit further development.

Gulmira Mashimbayeva's chapter examines the security in Central Asia in light of the institutional architecture of the Collective Security Treaty Organisation (CSTO) and that of the Conference on Interaction and Confidence Building Measures in Asia (CICA). The evaluation of the author is that the existing associations need to be able to guarantee the region's security, but naturally through a capacity (yet to be fully tested) to overcome and solve open crises..

Leila Delovarova and Alibek Yermekov evaluate the prospect of the Shanghai Cooperation Organisation (SCO) for development and enlargement within the new conditions of a multipolar world. According to the authors, the Organisation is actively evolving both by a continental enlargement of membership and by the transformation of its role as a diplomatic platform in solving regional problems, answering global challenges, and determining a new system of international relations.

Bakhyt Uderbayeva evaluates the legal security aspects of the Caspian region concerning the Russia-Ukraine conflict. On many occasions over the last year, Russia fired missiles at Ukraine from the Caspian Sea. A legal loophole in the current documents regulating the legal status and mode of use of the Caspian Sea does not contain norms prohibiting such missile launches. However, there is a risk of retaliations against the riverain

States. Hence, these countries should call on Russia to respect the peaceful status of the Caspian Sea and stop missile attacks from its waters.

Pierre Chabal asks whether regional institutions, in general, are meant to last or to become simple constructs. According to him, four types exist between formalised institutional and human social dimensions. These relations institutions-humans are either parallel dynamics, consequential dynamics, diachronic dynamics or chronological dynamics. In light of this, the author considers regional institutionalisation as a dynamics that turns neighbours into partners and modern regions developed around the concept of good neighbourhoods. Henceforth partnerships have come to replace the notion of alliances; alliances are narrowing down to military arrangements (NATO, CSTO, …), whereas regional economic arrangements (EU, EAEU, …) become open in time, membership, and scope.

Part IV of the book is about *Artificial Intelligence and Big Data*. The common trend of this final part of the book is the global challenge created by Artificial Intelligence, Big Data, or cybertechnologies and imposing urgent regulatory answers on the national levels (for example, in China, France, or South Korea).

Louis-Philippe Gratton examines China's artificial intelligence and algorithms regulations and their regional and international commerce implications. While addressing national concerns, this regulation can bring forth a new potential consequence: introducing legal biases into the architecture of the technology (China, for instance, has employed this approach to promote the Core Socialist Values through laws and regulations). The author examines the compatibility of such Chinese national measures with international commercial treaties.

Bing Chen examines the transformation of antitrust regulation in China concerning Digital Platforms development. The article examines the legal frame of the recent (24 June 2022) Revised Anti-Monopoly Law ("the RAML"), which provides adequate supervision of the platform economy.

In his chapter, Young-Soon Kim evaluates the possibility of taxing Artificial-Intelligence robots. The author considers the current wave of innovation related to AI, which might lead to the displacement of workers. Since tax policies should promote both innovation and social welfare, it might be necessary to tax companies or individuals using robots and automation instead of workers. The revenue generated from this tax could, in turn, fund retraining or re-education programs for displaced workers.

Amandine Cayol examines insurance as an instrument in the face of increased cyber risks. The paradigmatic case is the regulatory framework recently adopted in France in this area, which tries to reconcile the need to protect the interests of companies' victims of cyber-attacks and ensure better visibility of cyber risk.

Soo-Mee Lee analyses Korean patent-law reforms needed to accommodate the growth of Artificial-Intelligence-generated inventions. Since the traditional patent laws do not cover AI-generated inventions, the advancements in AI left the legal frame unable to catch up. The author explores the issues of invention, authorship, and the requirements of traditional patent and copyright laws when dealing with AI-generated works and proposes reforms to The Korean Patent Law to tackle such challenges.

Finally, Hyun-Jin Kim examines whether data in general could lie through the bias introduced by generative artificial intelligence. She explores the origins of bias in AI, presents several milestone cases, discusses the problems arising from such biases, and proposes potential solutions to mitigate their negative consequences. She emphasises the importance of addressing AI bias and the need for collaboration among technology developers, users, policymakers, and society.

*

To round up, the book chapters, overall, reflect the complex texture and the multiple dimensions of a Eurasian and Global crisis. Threats and challenges are intermingled and developing on multiple treads, requiring sophisticated answers within a new vision and with new instruments or integrative perspectives. The present book achieves its role of a wake-up call brilliantly. It offers both a diversity and a coherence of views as to what the most substantial challenges are for Eurasia. Its "legal" approach is wide, keeping abreast of historical, cultural, socio-economic dimensions, as well as proving up-to-date details of *droit positif*, i.e., the latest legislative and jurisprudential development. Its contexts span three vast sub-regions of the continent, each with a distinct legal culture, origins of its legal systems and capacities of those systems to respond to societal and international evolutions.

***

Part I

Challenges and turmoil in the region: When conflictual dynamics take over from Covid and jeopardise the context of cooperation

Introduction

Sung-Kee HONG
Korea

Pierre CHABAL
France

Looking at the context of recent evolutions in Eurasia, whether judicial or other evolutions, Part I of the book broadly reviews some embedded traits of the continent, its history, its shifting values and its essential crises, in order to make out a "portrait" of the situation in the contemporary scenery. It also opens up windows on material evolutions, from economic to geostrategic ones, so that the perspective is not "just" a historical or "historic" one but rather a broadly contextual one.

From oldest times (Élise Frêlon), the cultural anchor of Eurasia has been, since Greek and Roman antiquity, a dual one, if not an ambiguous one. The "Third" Rome – Moscow – thus represents from the 16th century, not a centre distinct and opposed to the previous two (Rome, Constantinople) but a link and a bond between West (Europe) and East (Eurasia). The issue of a "Eurasia" is thus, almost by definition, a trans-border and trans-continental one. The question of the definition or of the coherence of Eurasia is therefore one that is ill-posed if it suggests an impossibility of a Eurasian "entente". It is on the contrary very aptly posed if it suggests that there are many more reasons for Eurasia to be one day "completed" rather than dwell on its present crises.

Not only in time (Frêlon) but also in space (Philippe Gast), Eurasia is caught up in its own, intrinsic complexity, on account of the Russian factor. Here, the idea of a "Republic of Eurasia" (Frêlon - after Aristotle) can be uttered again if it is suggested (Gast) that more democracy must be applied to the United Nations governance. Democracy (over excess of authority) for Eurasia, a classic *moto*, should be tested for its likeliness and acceptability for all. Thus, from the principles of political philosophy to the realities of modern governance, Eurasia is indeed a testing ground for modern political evolutions because it has been for so long already the cradle of so many histories of political thought.

The questioning of Eurasian dynamics (Kuralay Baizakova, Fatima Kukeyeva), for instance its veering from Russia to other main partners, is logically one that begins at the heart of Eurasia - that is among Central Asian countries -, notably in Kazakhstan. The suspension of Russia's territory for transits is both limiting movements of goods and promoting alternative routes. Negatively, tensions are mounting. Positively, windows of opportunity open up for Kazakhstan: maritime connections and China's neighbourhood mean that on the continental scale, the country is being confirmed as a link-corridor from East and Southeast Asia to the west of the continent, until Europe.

The necessity to deeply reform the international system of governance (Gast) is examined further (Sagyngaliy Aidarbayev), from the procedural perspective, with the view that such a reform of the post-cold war system of monopolarity (USA) will necessarily put Eurasia at the centre of the stage, be it through the China-Russia bipolarity or be it via the Eurasian version of a West-East *summa divisio* of sorts. To be sure, procedures are "revealing", they are a telling indication that mentalities and facts come together to effect change in a system upon which international relations are built, lastingly but not irrevocably, as they must show a dual capacity to stabilise and adapt.

Stability in Eurasia (Tai-Uk Chung) depends on the capacity to solve a number of situations of tensions, above all in Korea, in Afghanistan, in Ukraine, around Taiwan, … Innovations here point to the setting up of novel peace regimes, that is, in the case of Korea, a regime of "perpetual" … neutrality as a suggestion of a solution for a post-unification eventuality. After over one century and more of the "idea" of neutrality being aired for the Korean peninsula, unrealised as Korea was dominated and dependent, the 21st century, dealing with a considerably reinforced Korea, is likely at that moment when neutralisation and neutrality should be coming about, to "complete" the post-war necessity for peace, stability and the contribution of the *whole* of East Asia to the completion of Eurasia.

Diachronically (Yesbol Omirzhanov, Almagul Tusupova, Binur Bertayeva), today's debate and dynamics around Central Asia and a possible Central Asia Union (suggested by N. Nazarbayev in 1992) echoes the past debate and dynamic of a Turkestan located in the heart of Eurasia.

This Turkestan – after being a Chinese one until the late 18th century, than a Russian one from the 19th century – as still today a "pivot" of Eurasia, is becoming an alternative (for the building of the continent) to the existing Eurasian Economic Union, should the latter flounder, notably on account of a possible and suggested "Kazakh-exit" from the EAEU (another such possible "exit" being that of Armenia from the CSTO – *Cf.* Part III of the book).

Awareness is increasing (Young-Geun Chae), at least at both ends of the Eurasian continent, as to the need to sustain the economy by recycling it. Provided that the model incentive from Europe could reach East Asia across the continent, Eurasia as a whole would prove the forebearer of "circularising" economies away from polluting linearity. For now, the most advanced and promising models are, within the European Union, that of the Netherlands, and, in East Asia, that of South Korea. The context of this new awareness is of course that the New Silk Road are undergoing deep change from logistics to green logistics.

The reader no doubt upon completing her or his reading of part I of the book will be able to keep a broad view and perspective in mind, before addressing the more sectoral issues of the other three parts of the book.

Moscow, the third Rome[1]

Historical and legal origins of a spiritual and temporal translation of the Roman Empire (15th–16th centuries)

Élise FRÊLON
France

In 1755, Jean-Jacques Rousseau[2] believed that, for a perpetual peace to avail, a special role should be given to the Roman emperor and to the Russian emperor in the framework of the European Republic.

This "European" recognition of a Russian emperor in the 18th century stands in stark contrast to today's ignorance of the existence of Moscow's Third Rome, especially in the European Union (as a European Republic has not merged).

Our purpose will not be to question the causes[3] of this dogmatic ignorance, but to restore the historical memory of a legal reality, initiated in the 15th century. In short, what does it matter which *terminus ad quem*[4] the Roman Empire had, let us return to its *terminus a quo*.

---

1 There is a colossal bibliography on this subject. A good overview can be found in the collection "Da Roma alla terza Roma". *Documenti e studi*, directed by P.A. Catalano and P. Siniscalco. But in France, the historiography is extremely poor.

2 J.J. Rousseau, "Discours sur l'origine et les fondements de l'inégalité parmi les hommes", *Œuvres complètes…, III*, Paris, 1964, p. 576 and following.

3 P.A. Catalano, Professor of Roman Law Emeritus at La Sapienza (Rome), together with other academics, has been working for several decades on the theme: "Da Roma alla terza Roma". He believes that the Rousseauist model was rejected by the dominant bourgeoisie after the demise of the "resurrected Romanity" [Marx, Engels] of the Jacobins and Napoleon. As a result, bourgeois historiography has developed an ideology of the "end of the Roman Empire", whose function is to exalt contemporary national states.

4 Thus, according to a simplistic view, the Roman Empire with Rome as its capital ended in 476, conquered by the Germans; the Roman Empire with Constantinople

The foundation of Rome – the year zero[5] of the Romulan City – in accordance with the auspices of Jupiter, is famous (Varro, Titus Livius). Jupiter then gave the Roman people an eternal empire over the whole world, but on the strict condition that they always carry out Justice. Empire and Justice[6] are therefore inseparable.

At this date, at the beginning of the City, the empire was already established. Indeed, historically, by convention, three Roman eras would have succeeded each other: kingship (753 BC), republic (509 BC), empire (27 BC). Nevertheless, legally, the initial and perpetual empire (in Latin, *imperium*[7]) is, by the will of the people, acquired successively by kings, consuls and princes[8].

In addition to perpetuity, the empire has the attribute of universality: from the time of the emperor Caracalla (edict of 212), all the peoples of the earth, wherever they have established their civilisation, belong to the empire of Rome, *orbi* if not *urbi*.

Since time immemorial, and for ever[9], the city (in Latin, *urbs*) of Rome is not the heart of the empire, but its head (in Latin, *caput*), its capital. And the fact is that if Rome was not built in one day, centuries of territorial expansion have necessitated the doubling of its capital.

This is the reason for the foundation[10] of Constantinople, the City (in Greek, *polis*) by Emperor Constantine in 330, also called the New

---

as its capital ended in 1453, conquered by the Turks; and the Roman Empire with Moscow as its capital ended in 1917 with the Bolshevik revolution.

5 Converted to the Gregorian calendar, the original year is 753BC.

6 It is on Justice (*ars boni et aequi*) – and not on force – that the imperial edifice rests. For a better understanding of Justinian's *"iuris religiosissimus"* formula, see the article by L. Hecketsweiler, "Observation sur la dévitalisation de la formule en droit", *Le droit international.* Aspects politiques, J. Bouineau (ed.), 2014, 44 pages.

7 R. Monier, *Petit vocabulaire de droit romain*, Paris, 1934, v° "imperium", " Supreme power of command which, after having originally belonged to the king, was then exercised by the superior magistrates and, from Augustus, by the emperor ".

8 Augustus, renewing the Roman republic in this way, founded the principate and not the empire: he was the prince holder of the imperium and not the emperor (except for a language convention).

9 Rome is no longer the capital of the temporal empire of the Caesars, but it remains the capital of the spiritual empire of the Popes.

10 On the site of the Greek city Byzantium, Constantine created a new Rome from scratch on the institutional model of the old one.

Rome[11]. From the spiritual point of view, the second – Christian, takes precedence over the old – pagan (Jupiterian), so that Constantine's act of foundation surpasses that of Romulus. From the material point of view, the coexistence of the two capitals, Rome and the New Rome, implies a distinction within the empire, dividing it into Western (with Rome as capital, Latin-speaking) and Eastern (with the New Rome as capital, Greek-speaking).

Remarkably, the founder of the new Rome, Constantine, was the first Christian[12] Roman emperor (conversion in 320). As early as 381, the Second Ecumenical Council of Constantinople declared the bishop of Constantinople to be second in the universal episcopal hierarchy, immediately after the bishop of Rome, "because Constantinople is the second Rome"[13].

In the 11th century (1054), the Christian faith was split into two religions: Western and Eastern, Catholic and Orthodox, with the Pope, Bishop of Rome, and the Patriarch of Constantinople as spiritual leaders. As a result of the schism, the two Romes, old and new, were to be rivals. It should be noted that neither emperor, of Rome or Constantinople, assumed spiritual leadership of their portion of the empire.

Still in chronological order, one and then the other of these capitals were taken by invaders: Germans (in 476) and Ottomans (in 1453). However, both parts of the empire survived: the western one by the imperial renovation in Aix-la-Chappelle (Aachen) (800), and the eastern one by the imperial translation to Moscow.

This is the origin of this translation – the second: from the new Rome to the third Rome – which legally questions the Romanists, and historically the historians of law. What is it technically? This is what we will briefly explain, preferring this legal and historical approach to the political and ideological one[14].

---

11 It is true that Constantinople was founded on the site of Byzantium, but the empire remained Roman and was not designated as Byzantine (an apocryphal formula).

12 After him, there is no more deification of the person of the emperor.

13 Quote reported by J. Rosenblum, "Les trois Romes", *Bulletin de l'association Guillaume Budé*, n° 3, 1971, pp. 383–394.

14 The formula "Moscow third Rome" for some expresses Russia's claims to the status of a great world power; for others it wants to justify the dominant position of the Moscow Patriarchate. To rationally assess this notion in the current Ukrainian conflict, cf. the words of J.F. Colosimo, collected by G. Malaurie in *Historia*, May 2022.

To do this, and even if it sometimes seems inextricable, it is necessary to distinguish the spiritual order from the temporal order. In the Roman legal system, divine order and human order coexist. By nature, the former takes precedence over the latter insofar as God takes precedence over man. In the 16th century, Moscow welcomed the perpetuity and universality of the Roman Empire, which was assumed by both the patriarch (spiritual empire, I) and the tsar (temporal empire, II). The symbolism of the two-headed eagle[15] testifies to this.

I. The Patriarch, Head of the Roman (Orthodox) spiritual empire

The church of Constantinople was first rallied by Kiev, before Moscow (first mention of this city in 1147), In 988, Kiev's prince (Vladimir) and his people (Slavic) were baptised after an agreement with the two Eastern co-emperors Basil II and Constantine VIII. A metropolitan and bishops have since been appointed for the people of Kiev by the Patriarch of Constantinople. In 1326, the Metropolitan of Vladimir, also a city spiritually attached to Constantinople, moved to Moscow.

At the date of the fall of the second Rome (1453), the separation had been consummated for several centuries between the Church of the West and the Church of the East (1054). In 1439, however, at the Council of Florence, Easterners came to the West to seek help against the Turks, even accepting a new union of the Churches, and putting an end to the schism. Among the Easterners are legates, the Emperor (John VIII) and the Patriarch of Constantinople. Upon their return, their people received them as apostates. The Russian representative to the Council, the Greek Isidore of Kiev, was also among the delegation.

---

15 Originally single-headed, the eagle is a major Roman symbol that accompanies the legions in their defence of the territorial limits (lat. *limes*) of the empire. From the dynasty of Palaiologos as princes of the new Rome – Constantinople (1261), the eagle is represented as two-headed. About a century later, this double-headed eagle is also associated with the Holy Roman Empire (renovation of the Western Empire). Finally, in 1472, the date of the marriage of the niece (Zoe) of the last prince of the Palaiologos dynasty, Constantine XI, with the Russian Prince Ivan III, it is the third Rome that is adorned with this heraldic figure. Translation is thus made in Russia of a symbol certainly Roman but in its oriental version.

When Isidore returned, he was disowned and driven out by Prince Vasily II, according to whom the ancient faith could not be corrupted by Rome. What is more, this prince alone appointed, without appointment of the patriarch of Constantinople, the metropolitan of Moscow (1448). The faith of Constantinople thus compromised (he had accepted the union with the Latins), there remained only the faith of Moscow. God's vengeance was not long in coming (invasion of 1453). The Turks having put an end to the second Rome, the third could begin. From that date, the only important Orthodox country not to suffer the Muslim yoke, Russia posed as a defender of Orthodoxy and Christianity.

In favour of this role, an old apostolic claim was resumed: originally invented for the church of Constantinople, according to which the apostle Andrew, elder brother of Peter (the first bishop of Rome) had been on mission to the Scythians. He blessed the future City of Kiev and declared that, in the distant future, Russia would maintain the true faith. So that the Russian Orthodox religion would be purer than the "Byzantine" Orthodox religion, itself purer than the Catholic religion.

And it is indeed the spiritual translation of the empire (of faith) that is first at stake in the famous marriage in 1472 of Zoe Palaiologos, niece of the last Eastern emperor Constantine Palaiologos (he died in besieged Constantinople in 1453). She married Ivan III (the Great), son of Vasily III, Prince of Russia. Diplomatically, the Pope wanted this princely union to be a symbol of the union between the Catholic Church and the Russian Orthodox Church. The bride was thus escorted to Moscow by a legate, to whom Ivan III refused entry into the City. Sophia, also taking sides against the prelate, sent him back to his Roman penates. Symbolically, Constantinople rejected Rome (schismatic) and married Moscow (Orthodox). In passing, Ivan obtained from his wife (as a dowry) the title of basileus which, in Greek, designated the emperor of Constantinople and the coat of arms of the double-headed eagle.

Twenty years later (1492), the same Ivan IIIs, was proclaimed: "new Emperor Constantine of the new Constantinople"[16]. This unprecedented title was due to the new Russian Orthodox liturgical calendar. The stakes are therefore spiritual before being temporal. The second half

---

16 "Constantine the Great founded the new Rome, St. Vladimir baptized Russia, and now Ivan III is the new emperor of the new Constantinople – Moscow", J. Rosenblum, *art. cit.* "The Three Romes".

of the fifteenth century is bathed in an eschatological fear of the end of the world. For, in 1492, prophetically, the seventh millennium since creation. had to be completed. Thus the paschal comput tables, both Greek and Russian, were completed in 1492. That same year, the world having not stopped, the Metropolitan of Moscow, Zosimus, established an Easter canon for the 8th millennium. It is in this canon that Moscow is proclaimed not the third Rome but the new Constantinople.

The formula of the "third Rome" came somewhat later, in 1523[17], under the pen of the monk Philoteus (see below). If the transfer is expressly designated, then it is the spiritual and not temporal transfer of the Empire (i.e., the transfer of the Church): "of the Apostolic Church which from Rome and Constantinople was transferred to the blessed city of Moscow; [and which] alone sheds upon the world a light clearer than the sun."[18].

In 1598, such a Moscow church, transferred from Rome and Constantinople, obtained its own patron: Jeremiah II, the patriarch of Constantinople[19], accepted the creation of a Moscow[20] patriarchate and installed the first in this function: Job. Addressing Tsar Feodor (son of Ivan IV the Terrible), he recognised in his turn[21] without naming it, Russia third Rome and this also for expressly spiritual reasons:

"Old Rome fell because of the heresy of Apollinarius[22], the second Rome, that is, Constantinople, was taken by the children of Hagar, the infidel Turks, but your great kingdom of Russia, O pious tsar, has surpassed them in piety, and all the pious kingdoms are gathered in yours; you are under heaven the only one to proclaim yourself the Christian tsar of all the universe, of all Christians."[23]

---

17 Not all authors agree on the exact date of the letters.

18 L. Poliakov, *Moscow troisième Rome, Les intermittences de la mémoire historique*, Paris, 1989.

19 In 1453, the Turks had accepted that their patriarch should remain in Constantinople, provided that he kept a low profile.

20 Until then there were only Eastern patriarchates.

21 It takes up without possible ambiguity the epistolary turns of Philotée.

22 Christological heresy about the nature of Christ (human body and soul but divine spirit). Note that the Council of Nicaea (325), which recognised the Trinity, was presided over by Constantine.

23 Quoted by P. Kuzenkov, "The Third Rome from eschatology to political myth", available online:https://mospat.ru/fr/authors-analytics/8mos6649.

The Russian patriarch and tsar were not rivals, quite the contrary: they both assumed responsibility for renewing the Roman Empire, both in its spiritual dimension and in its temporal dimension.

II. The Tsar, head of the Roman (Eastern) temporal empire

The first idea of a city that would succeed that of Constantinople as the capital of the Eastern Roman Empire, the basically unformulated idea of a third Rome, seems to date back to Tsar[24] Simeon of Bulgaria (reigned 893–927), whose capital Preslav was in his time compared to Constantinople. Above all, he would have tried by arms "to deprive the Byzantine emperors of their titles at the same time as their throne"[25].

Yet, it was not until 1520 that the formula of the third Rome was adopted and used in Muscovy and attributed to Moscow. On this date, the monk of Pskov, Philotheus, addressed a missive letter[26] to the legate of Prince Vasily III. He is the first to literally express a third Rome. In a prophetic tone, he adds[27] that "two Romes have fallen, but the third remains standing and there will be no fourth. That is why the tsar[28] must take great care of his kingdom and rule it piously.". Moreover, a second letter describes the tsar as "the only prince of Christians."

The Metropolitan of Moscow, Daniel, ratified this eschatological doctrine, which benefited the Prince of Moscow, first Vasily III but even more so Ivan IV [the Terrible] later, crowned in 1547. This coronation[29]

---

[24] As for the title, Simeon I the Great is khan, then kneze and finally tsar.

[25] L. Poliakov, *op. cit.* in particular, pp. 33–37.

[26] "Against astronomers". In terms of sources, there are more than 80 handwritten versions of this letter!

[27] "I would also like to say a few words about the present kingdom of our prince; on earth he is the only prince of Christians, the guide of the Apostolic Church which from Rome and Constantinople was transferred to the blessed city of Moscow; It alone spreads over the world a light clearer than the sun. Know the pious man: all Christian empires have collapsed, only one remains standing according to the books of the prophets, and that is that of the Russians.", L. Poliakov, *op. cit.*

[28] The original term should be clarified, before translation, because the first mention of a tsar in Russia is traditionally attributed to Ivan IV [the Terrible] and not to his father Vasily III.

[29] In this regard, cf. M.K. Schaub, "« Les couronnements des tsars en Russie du XVIe au XVIIIe siècles. Essai d'historiographie. », *La royauté sacrée dans le monde chrétien,*

particularly depicts the appropriation by the Russian prince of the oriental imperial symbolism (called "Byzantine", imported by his grandmother Zoe Palaiologos). The young prince received the title of tsar[30] and borrowed from the basileus of the second Rome all the details of the ceremony. The imperial office was sanctified, with Ivan vowing to reign on the throne of Moscow "as David and Solomon reigned on the throne of Jerusalem, and Augustus, and Constantine and Theodosius on the throne of Rome"[31].

IIn particular, the tsar was dressed in a short cape and an oriental-made jacket which were said[32] to have been given by Konstantin Monomakh (1042–1055) to Muscovite Vladimir Monomakh (1113–1125).

More generally, the ceremony performed the rites in force for the coronations of the emperors of the Palaiologos dynasty (completed in 1453). Some authors[33] acknowledge that The Book of Ceremonies, the main manual of imperial ceremonies in Constantinople compiled by Emperor Konstantin Porphyrogenitus (died 959) in the 10th century, is known and used in Moscow in the 15th and 16th centuries. Even more certainly, it is established that the Treatise on the Offices of the pseudo-Kodinos, a code of imperial ceremonies whose main part seems to have been written in the early 15th century, was translated and disseminated in Russia at the beginning of the 16th century. So that, temporally, the emperor of Moscow was now enthroned in the manner of the emperor of Constantinople.

The imperial succession of the second Rome – Constantinople – to the third Rome – Moscow – was all the more assertive because during the same 16th century, the Holy Roman Emperors (resulting from the Carolingian imperial renovation) also aspired to the timelessness and universality of the Roman Empire, and strove to mobilise the papacy in this direction.

A. Boureau and C.S. Ingerflom (eds.), Paris, 1992. By the same author, « Le couronnement des tsars, XVIe-XVIIIe siècles ; état de la question et perspectives de recherches. », *Revue des études slaves*, 1989, pp. 391–401.

30 Needless to say, this term of tsar is an alteration of the surname of Caesar, Roman imperial titulature par excellence. See infra note 29.

31 Quoted by L. Poliakov.

32 Sometimes the legend rubbed shoulders with the official story.

33 I. Kataev, E.V. Brsov, quoted by M.K. Schaub, art. cit.

As for the exercise of power, it is partly based – in theory[34] – on the text of Agapetus (6th century), known in Russia since the 11th century, *On the divine nature of the emperor and his function.* Metropolitan Macarius in particular, who performed the coronation of Ivan IV, of whom he was the tutor, used this text in his desire to sanctify the monarch.

The crowned tsar is the emperor in arms, acclaimed by his warriors and the protector of the Church, which recognises his power in his kingdom. In this capacity, in 1557, he asked the patriarch of Constantinople in exile to recognise his title of tsar. In 1561, the latter, the Patriarch of Constantinople, designated the first Tsar Ivan IV "universal head of Christendom". For him, no doubt, not the union[35] but the conversion of the other churches. In 1598, Patriarch Jeremiah of Constantinople, in his enthronement of Patriarch Job of Moscow, in turn stated that: "Moscow is the third Rome and the last, surpassing in piety all the ancient empires and its tsar is the only Christian prince in the universe."

Like a Constantine holding council at Nicaea (325), Ivan IV also held council in Moscow (1551–1552), a council known as the hundred chapters ("Stoglav") in order to solve the problems of the Russian Orthodox Church. The rites and the Russian Orthodox liturgy were approved and definitively fixed. Once canonised in this way, they became so many symbols, *a contrario*, of the errors into which all the other Catholic and Orthodox Churches had sunk.

*

In conclusion, in the 16th century, spiritually and temporally, Moscow is designated as the third capital of the Roman Empire, the third Rome, above all by default of the first (Rome) and the second (Constantinople).

---

34 To this political theory are added various narratives more mythical than historical but very popular. For example, The Tale of the Princes of Vladimir, (late fifteenth century), makes the genealogy of the tsars of Moscow, direct descendants of Rurik, himself a direct descendant of Prus, legendary brother of the emperor Augustus sent from Rome to the banks of the Vistula to organise this part of the Roman world.

35 "To the Jesuit Anthony Possevino who came to Moscow in 1582 to propose the union of the Churches he replied that the Russians had received the Christian faith before the Latins, when the Apostle Andrew, brother of the Apostle Peter, came to our country before going to Rome", quoted by L. Poliakov, *op. cit.*, p. 36.

Even more than the double-headed eagle, the phoenix belongs to the symbolism of the Roman Empire (used by the emperor and the pope). Also, eschatologically, it is just not possible – in view of the founding prophecies of eternity and universality – for Rome to cease to exist. Thus, in the 15th and 16th centuries, in the context of the capture of Constantinople by the Turks, translation is undoubtedly obvious, whose divine and human necessity can escape us in the 21st century.

Opportunely, the city of Moscow took advantage of this necessity and was thus promoted to capital: its patriarch and its prince were recognised spiritual and temporal leaders of the empire once again "reoriented".

Nevertheless, *in terminus ad quem*, it should be noted that the last "tsar of all Russias" so called was assassinated in 1918. As for the last Patriarch of Moscow "and of all Russias", Kirill, he was elected in 2009 and is still in office[36]. But neither Moscow, nor Constantinople, nor Rome is today the capital of a Christian state. Perhaps, however, this is a *sine qua non* condition for the construction of a "European republic" and, even more so, for the "perpetual peace" that JJ Rousseau called for.

---

36 Perpetuity and universality are divine attributes, not human ones. It is perhaps in this perspective that we must understand the perpetuity and universality of the Church (spiritual dimension of the Empire) and, *a contrario*, the successive falls of the Empire (in its temporal dimension). In addition to the Patriarch of Moscow, to this day, the Patriarch of Constantinople (Bartholomew I, appointed in 2019) and the Bishop of Rome (Francis, appointed in 2013) are still in priestly activity. Only the recognition by the State of Christianity as the official religion is lacking.

Growth and decline (*décroissance*): For a balanced global governance

Philippe GAST
France

For some years already, a series of crises has intensified, threatening peace, even humanity and the biosphere as a whole. Whereas after WWI a certain global consciousness emerged from the League of Nations, and also later with the UN after WWII, but is clear that nowadays a global consciousness is a vital necessity for humanity, with the climate change particularly. It is obvious that UN in its current structure is unable to solve the present problems, whether in terms of their environmental, energetic, economic or social dimension. Even for the maintenance of peace, its main founding objective, as illustrated by the war in Ukraine, where the international prohibition on resorting to war except in the event of aggression against its territory by a state[1] has been clearly flouted by Russian neo-colonialist imperialism[2] and the Chinese attitude, rejecting the decisions of the International permanent Court of Arbitration prosecuted by Philippines because of colonisation of rocky islands in the south China sea[3].

The non-respect of the UN charter threatens humanity with a WWIII which, if it triggered a nuclear war, would annihilate suddenly all humanity and even a large part of the terrestrial biosphere (the use of more than

1 UN Charter

2 Even though war crimes have been committed by Russians, as the UN commission of inquiry found in march 2023 : see https://news.un.org/fr/story/2022/09/1127701 …even crimes against humanity : see https://information.tv5monde.com/info/direct-guerre-en-ukraine-16-mars-2023

3 See Patrick Saint Paul article "La Cour Permanente d'arbitrage désavoue Pékin" in Le Figaro, 2016.07.12

15,000 nuclear weapons would reduce the earth to a radioactive space where very few forms of life could survive).

We see that crises generate a violence that "globalises" (I) and that can be rescinded only by a radical "reformation" of the UN (II)

I. Crises generate a violence that is becoming global

The multi contemporising crisis of today (A) suggest that they have been caused by a spreading oligarchic avidity (B)

(A) The multi contemporising crisis

Several contemporary crises, such as climatic change, although they may be contested by some politicians (at least as to their cause – the greenhouse effect – Trump rely), though, on scientific certainty such as the undeniable shrinking of the glaciers and the rise in sea level[4].This climatic change worsens the water crisis due to global warming. Water becomes scarce, even in the south of Europe, even more in sub-tropical areas (Africa, India, Australia, South America, aggravated by massive equatorial deforestation as in Brazil).

The rise in food prices is amplified by the energetic crisis[5]. The search for new energies and agricultural growth requires raw materials (to manufacture solar panels and other wind turbines panels with electronic, digital elements – rare earths – but also fertilisers whose prices increase also. These elements are interdependent as energy, water, rare earths and metals, fertilisers, and impact agriculture as industry – mostly digital industry.)

---

4 See the different report of the UN IPCC (GIEC) :

https://www.google.com/search?client=firefox-b-d&q=rapport+du+giec+en+fran%C3%A7ais+pdf+2023

And specially the Resumé of the 6th report of synthesis from the IPCC: https://report.ipcc.ch/ar6syr/pdf/IPCC_AR6_SYR_SPM.pdf

5 The energy is one of the first need of a civilization, as the discovery of fire in prehistorical times showed, then the coal energy during the industrial revolution, then oil on 20th century with the nuclear one etc., energy that will be necessary to desalinate sea water in dry areas, (but also necessary for circular economy by recovering raw materials from waste such as rare earths and metals through recycling that has become essential.).

These ecological upheavals (and their impact, such as the rise of the oceans) and the economic upheavals already cause mass migrations. Social and political crises will revive economic and military imperialisms for the control of these commodities, in particular for the benefit of oligarchies, which is already at work through the failed globalisation since the GATT and the WTO. It is therefore urgent to move towards an economy of shorter circuits (producer-consumer) and cyclical circuits (systematic recycling of used goods and materials[6]), with mileage/kg taxes (to reduce transport of goods) and taxes on exchanges (abolition of fiduciary money, allowing the monitoring of monetary exchanges and their taxation), as solution to fight oligarchic greed (and one global money would be fare, against monetary dumping!).

(B) Crisis caused by oligarchic avidity

In parallel with these social crises caused by climate-related migration flows and wars that generate misery increasing poverty[7], the number of billionaires in the world grows faster: most of the world's capital is held by a reduced number of people whose lifestyle boosts this entropy (the rich consume ever more – private jets, yachts, …). This economic oligarchy at the origin of this globalisation (allowing multinationals to buy from poor countries at low cost products that are sold on[89] in the West at a high price), placing their dividends in tax havens (Singapore), bribing totalitarian regimes to prevent socio-political claims (Bangladesh, China, Africa…)[10]

---

6 EU regulation in 2019.

7 Even if the global standard of living – increase in wealth and PIB – seems to be parallel the creation of the WTC.

8 https://www.banquemondiale.org/fr/news/press-release/2021/10/27/global-wealth-has-grown-but-at-the-expense-of-future-prosperity-world-bank PRESS RELEASE NO.: 2022/23/ENR: "Indeed, while indicators such as gross domestic product (GDP) have traditionally been used to measure economic growth, the report demonstrates that whether growth is sustainable requires consideration of natural capital, human capital and produced capital."

9 1 % of the world's population owns nearly 50 % of the world's capital, according to Credit Suisse (cited by https://www.inegalites.fr/La-repartition-du-patrimoine-dans-le-monde)

10 As Maurice ALLAIS, first French Nobel Prize in economy, had already denounced in 1989 in "*Globalization: destruction of jobs and growth*" published in 1990 (cf Edition Clément Juglard, Paris 1999), leads to millions of unemployed in the West and

As Pericles suggested in his concept of democracy, the possibility that the majority interest and therefore the majority will (implemented by the *isonomos* in the Agora of Athens, ancestor of the Swiss *votation*) imposes itself on minority interests (oligarchy: government of a few) in view of the "happiness of all" referred to in the preamble to the Declaration of Human Rights of 1789, who deduced freedom (there is no happiness without freedom), equality (there is no freedom without equality: freedom without restriction leading to the law of the strongest and therefore to an oligarchy that confiscates freedom for its benefit – the law is made for those who do it-): majority sovereignty.

On the contrary, oligarchies rule. The WTO seems to be their tool. Through multinationals that impose mono-production (ores, oil, uranium, copper, cocoa, coffee, rice, soy …) to poor regions of the world (yet regions rich in population potential, minerals and others), in order to control production markets and populations that are then dependent on them (monopolies of GMO – Monsanto / Bayer for example- that product sterile seeds through international patents for example, following the colonial "India Company"). These multinationals are often based in tax havens, evading their profits from the redistribution of democratic taxes (Western countries are trying to remedy this, especially in Europe where there is an obligation to denounce the bank accounts of other non-resident nationals – even Switzerland has decided to do so). Yet, some States remain "grey", such as the UK (Anglo-Norman havens) or the USA (Delaware). Outside the West, tax havens escape these rules (yet, it would be easy to tax digitised exchanges every time they leave or enter a tax haven!)[11].

---

semi-slaves in totalitarian countries -Uighurs in labour camps-, strengthening the financial – and military – power of the latter -China, Turkey-, associated with multinational trade companies based in compliant tax havens (Singapore..) "Globalization can only generate instability, unemployment, injustice, disorder and misery of all kinds everywhere, and it can only ultimately prove disadvantageous for all peoples. (…) Widespread globalisation is neither inevitable, necessary nor desirable. Globalisation, it cannot be stressed enough, only benefits multinationals. They make huge profits from it." Quoted by

http://www.liberation.fr/futurs/2010/10/11/deces-de-maurice-allais-prix-nobel-liberal-et-protectionniste_685598

11 After the Opium War where the British wanted to impose the trade then prohibited in China (to compensate for the large trade deficit of the import of tea with this country and which also induced the theft by the English of tea plants – a thousand-year-old

Yet, new approaches are possible, following Gandhi's fight against British imperialist monopolies. The king of Bhutan conceived, in dialogue with the Dalai Lama[12], an alternative concept the GDP (GDP echoes the "[13]grow and multiply" of the Jewish Torah[14] but is a danger for the ecology due to growing and multiplying energy consumption). The GNH (Gross National Happiness) was then picked up by Nobel Prize in Economics Stiglitz who theorised it as Gross Domestic Happiness (GDH), mentioned in the 2008 Stiglitz report commissioned by N. Sarkozy, that stressed the danger of limiting oneself to GDP, giving illusions. For instance, traffic jams can be positive for GDP as they indicate consumption and therefore production; yet have a negative impact on the environment and drivers[15]. The same goes for education and health. They have a high cost for the State but over time they are productive as they enable millions of citizens to obtain wealth-creating skills.[16]

---

monopolistic beverage of China – which they grew in Darjeeling and Ceylon to free themselves from these imports).

12 One of the fundamental concepts of Buddhist philosophy is the interdependence of phenomena: if man destroys his environment, he destroys himself.

13 The 4th King of Bhutan put in the place of the Gross Domestic Product in the democratic Constitution that he established in 1972 in his country, in relation to the Dalai Lama his great friend: Gross National Happiness which covered four criteria: growth and economic development, conservation and promotion of Bhutanese culture, safeguarding the environment and promoting sustainable development and responsible good governance.

14 Genesis 9:7 (Ecumenical Translation of the Bible, TOB, Cerf, Paris, 1989). Who opposes the idea of renunciation present in Christian monasticism in application of the precepts of Christ "If you want to be perfect, sell what you have, give it to the poor and you will have a treasure in heaven. Then come, follow me" (Mt19:21–30 Ib.). Renunciation which is also present in Indian thought: "Meditating with delight on the Supreme Soul, sitting, needing nothing, inaccessible to any sensual desire" (Lois de Manou tr. Loiseleur deslongchamps, ed. d'aujourd'hui, Paris, 1976: ch. 6: 49) where the Sanskrit term Nir-vana designates the end, the absence of any aspiration (breath-desire) as is repeated throughout chapter 4 of the Avadhuta Gita of Dattareya -son of one of the Vedic poetsAtri- cf. tr. and ed. Janki Parikh, 2015 warsawa (ISBN No. 978 198 10 6148 8, pp. 65–75). Concept particularly developed in Buddhism which is presented as a final spiritual state (cf "The first teaching of the Buddha" tr. Dr. Rewata Dhamma, Ed. Claire Lumière1997, ISBN n° 978 2 35454 057 9, p. 107).

15 Even we know that a gross of 2 % of GDP makes the unemployment decrease, which is of course a good thing

16 Published on 11 September 2009 and whose conclusions can be summarised in 5 points: (1) Refer to income and consumption rather than production. (2) Take into account wealth at the same time as income and consumption. (3) Focus on the household perspective. (4) Give greater importance to the distribution of income,

This economics Nobel Prize report convinced the OECD, which on 24 May 2008 began to use this index of Gross Domestic Happiness (GDH) based on eleven criteria: income, housing, employment, health, security, community life, governance, education, environment, personal satisfaction, balance between work and family life.[17] These criteria echo fundamental rights set out in the Preamble to the 1946 French Constitution, still in force in our positive law.

Another economist, Jean Gadrey, suggests to complete this GDH with a GCH (Gross Collective Happiness). According to him, the GDH taken in isolation "is oriented towards individual well-being, and not towards what could be called the quality of a society". In particular, a measure concerning the social security coverage of the inhabitants or the income of the richest compared to that of the poorest should be added.[18] Yet, it can be included in the GDH, since in the end, it is the individual who benefits (while being careful not to make an average that would stifle categorical difficulties. The DGH must therefore be measured by social category.)

However, in these approaches, growth still appears to be an important and always desirable criterion, whereas from the point of view of Gandhi or the Dalai Lama there is a search for balance that could be characterised as a project of financial growth for the poor and "degrowth" (decline) for the rich, all while respecting the environment and plant and animal biodiversity.

A minimum of material comfort is necessary for human fulfilment (Bentham, late 18th century). Inner happiness, yet, does not depend on it: it is a psychological given and the key is liberation of desire. On the contrary, the unbridled race for possession, the desire to exist and to have sensations (mark of perpetual frustration) is the self-destructive factor of humanity. Of course, if it is a personal philosophical quest, legal structures can rebalance these facts: the growth of the poor and the decline of the rich, through[19]democratic taxation, which ensures a certain distribution of wealth, even within a liberal system. Indeed, the

---

consumption and wealth. (5) Broaden income indicators to include non-market activities.

17 http://tempsreel.nouvelobs.com/economie/20110527.OBS4039/le-bib-preferer-le-bonheur-a-la-richesse.html

18 The per capita poverty rate is 15.1 % in the United States, 6.9 % in Switzerland, 6.2 % in France, 1.16 % in Taiwan, 13.4 % in China, close to 14 % in Great Britain and 15.5 % in Germany: http://www.indexmundi.com/g/r.aspx?t=0&v=69&l=fr.

19 The "grow and multiply" of the Jewish Torah which will be taken over the Anglo-Saxon Protestant world in savage capitalism and the resulting globalisation

law could allow that, for example, the usufruct of a third of the capital of a company be managed by the collective of employees (making them benefit from the growth of the company by the distribution of a third of the profits)… and that the remuneration of the directors be voted not by a board of directors (cross-agreements with other directors of other companies, accomplices) but by the General Meeting of Shareholders (as in Switzerland).[20]

II. These crises can only be resolved through UN major reform

The general interest of humanity can only be managed by global governance through a radical reform of UN (A) based on democratic principles (B).

(A) The global balance of power resolved by UN reform for a true global governance

This requires legal monism whereby international law (in particular the 1948 Universal Declaration of Human Rights) is automatically enforced within States before their judges. It also necessitates the possibility for citizens to sue States before an international court (as is the case in European law).

The major crisis of energy, water, wars etc, can only be resolved with a global governance including real military international army (and decreasing national armies) to stop any war!

Recently (February 2022), in violation of the UN Charter, Russia deployed its special military operation in Ukraine,[21] despite the 1994

---

20 Even, provide that, in the event of the closure of a non-loss-making factory, the ownership of the factory would be transferred to the collective of employees in compensation for the loss of usufruct – dissuasion for relocations linked to social or fiscal dumping!

21 The imperialist pretext of pan-Slavism (imperialist myth – like Hitler's pan-Germanism in his time – because contrary to the will of the Slavic peoples of Eastern Europe, who freely joined EU and NATO) and the negation of the Ukrainian nation invoked by Putin, holds all the less since it is President Yeltsin (Putin's mentor) who is at the origin of the break-up of the USSR. Indeed, it was he who declared the independence of Russia from the USSR and that this was followed by the other republics let us remember!

Budapest Memorandum signed by the USA, Great Britain and Ukraine, in exchange for the latter's denuclearisation. The signatories, including Russia, undertook to respect Ukraine's borders.[22,23] Clearly, the 2022

But the mistake of the former Soviet republics liberated from Russian imperialism at their independence, was not to expel the Russians (as do the Algerians who expelled the French during their independence) who can even though these Russians had been settled by Russia or the USSR (Tatars deported by Stalin and replaced by Russians in Crimea, or Kaliningrad etc.) ask to be attached to Russia .. Similarly, the expulsion from Ukraine, of the Moscow clergy under the orders of Kyrill and his friend Putin (both ex-KGB), appears to the majority of Ukrainians as indispensable because this clergy does espionage and denunciation (in the occupied zones) for the benefit of Moscow.

.https://www.france24.com/fr/europe/20220307-l-invasion-russe-remet-en-cause-la-loyaut%C3%A9-de-l-%C3%A9glise-orthodoxe-ukrainienne-envers-moscou

.https://www.tdg.ch/pretre-espion-propagandiste-la-vie-secrete-du-chef-de-leglise-russe-en-suisse-766374038310

.https://www.lefigaro.fr/flash-actu/ukraine-perquisition-dans-un-monastere-de-kiev-soupconne-de-liens-avec-moscou-20221122

22 Treaty on the Non-Proliferation of Nuclear Weapons, signed at Budapest on 5 December 1994 :

https://archive.wikiwix.com/cache/index2.php?url=https%3A%2F%2Ftreaties.un.org%2Fdoc%2FPublication%2FUNTS%2FVolume%25203007%2FPart%2Fvolume-3007-I-52241.pdf%2Findex.html#federation=archive.wikiwix.com&tab=url

1. The Russian Federation, the United Kingdom of Great Britain and Northern Ireland and the United States of America reaffirm their commitment to Ukraine, in accordance with the principles set forth in the Final Act of the Conference on Security and Cooperation in Europe, to **respect its independence and sovereignty and its existing borders.**

2. The Russian Federation, the United Kingdom of Great Britain and Northern Ireland and the United States of America reaffirm their obligation to refrain from the threat or use of force against the **territorial integrity or political independence** of Ukraine, and that none of their weapons be used against Ukraine, except in self-defence or otherwise in accordance with the provisions of the Charter of the United Nations. [...]

3. Ukraine, the Russian Federation, the United Kingdom of Great Britain and Northern Ireland and the United States of America will consult in the event of a question arising with respect to the commitments set out above. This Memorandum shall be applicable upon signature.

See UN Treaty Series: I. Nos. 52234–52254 VOLUME 3007 2014 Annex A – Annex A https://www.google.com/search?client=firefox-b-d&q=memorandum+de+budapest

23 https://www.google.com/search?client=firefox-b-d&q=M%C3%A9morandum+de+Budapest+de+1994&sa=X&ved=2ahUKEwi22oXz4o74AhWD4YUKHW0ZAc44FBDVAnoECCMQAQ&biw=1536&bih=703&dpr=1.25

Russian operation in Ukraine not only violates this Memorandum but can be qualified as aggression against the USA and the UK who were also party to the agreement. Furthermore, war in the form of an outright attack is prohibited by the UN Charter; and any territorial dispute must be settled by the International Court of Justice in La Hague.[24]

---

[24] **Article 1:** The purposes of the United Nations are:

1. To maintain international peace and security and, to this end: to take effective collective measures to prevent and remove threats to the peace and **to suppress any act of aggression or other breach of the peace**, and to effect, by peaceful means, in conformity with the principles of justice and international law, adjustment or settlement of disputes or situations, of an international character, likely to lead to a breach of the peace;

2. To develop friendly relations among nations based on respect for the principle of **equal rights and self-determination** of peoples [...]

Article 2: The United Nations and its Members, in pursuit of the purposes set forth in Article 1, shall act in accordance with the following principles: [...]

3. **Members of the Organisation shall settle their international disputes by peaceful means** in such a way that international peace and security and justice are not endangered.

4. Members of the **Organisation shall refrain in their international relations from the threat or use of force against the territorial integrity** or political independence of any State or in any other manner inconsistent with the purposes of the United Nations. »

Article 33: 1. The parties to any dispute the prolongation of which is likely to threaten the maintenance of international peace and security **shall seek a solution** first and foremost through negotiation, inquiry, mediation, conciliation, arbitration, **judicial settlement**, recourse to regional agencies or arrangements, or other peaceful means of their choice. 2. The Security Council shall, if it deems it necessary, invite the parties to settle their dispute by such means.

Article 41: The Security Council may decide what measures not involving the use of armed force shall be taken to give effect to its decisions, and may invite Members of the United Nations to implement such measures. **These may include the complete or partial interruption of economic relations and rail, sea, air, postal, telegraphic, radio and other means of communication, as well as the severance of diplomatic relations.**

Article 42: If the Security Council considers that the measures provided for in Article 41 are inadequate or have proved to be inadequate, it may take **any action it deems necessary** for the maintenance or restoration of international peace and security. Such action may include demonstrations, blockade measures and other operations carried out by air, naval or land forces of Members of the United Nations.

The consequence should be the immediate and automatic suspension of an aggressor country from all UN institutions for violation of the international social contract (Articles 5 and especially 6 of the UN Charter[25]). This, however, must be proposed by the Security Council – unanimously[26] – and Russia can block the process which is a frustration[27] and calls for reform.[28] The situation is one where a minority or even a single State can block the process of global governance (as is the case and weakness of the EU). Without a radical reform of the UN (also integrating into the Security Council countries with at least one tenth of the world population -India-) and allowing any veto to refer the decision to the General Assembly (where, too, each country should have the weight of its population – as should be done for the EU!) no lasting peace is possible![29] But these reforms must be democratic to protect majority interest!

Article 51: Nothing in the present Charter shall affect the inherent right of individual or collective self-defence in case of armed attack against a Member of the United Nations until the Security Council has taken the necessary measures to maintain international peace and security. https://www.un.org/fr/about-us/un-charter/full-text

25 **Article 5: A Member of the United Nations against which preventive or enforcement action has been taken** by the Security Council may be suspended by the General Assembly, on the recommendation of the Security Council, **from the exercise of the rights and privileges inherent in membership. The exercise of these rights and privileges may be restored by the Security Council.**

Article 6: **If** a Member of the Organisation persistently violates the principles of the present Charter, **it may be expelled** from the Organisation by the General Assembly on the recommendation of the Security Council.

26 This rule of unanimity is an institutional danger for both the UN (as in EU): when a blockage appears, the resolution would then have to be transmitted to the UN General Assembly (or the parliament for the EU) which would then have the last word.

27 Including WIPO and the global dissemination of patents, because it means letting dictatorships have access to international patents.

28 Same thing in European law: it would be desirable for any Member State that does not respect the EU treaties to be immediately suspended from decision-making bodies (parliament, council, commission) and European rules (financial support, subsidies, free movement of goods and people…) until a possible expulsion!

29 It would also be necessary to avoid any return to war, that there be a gradual disappearance of national armies replaced by a single military force attached to the UN to enforce peace and avoid any conflict between States (and therefore the disappearance of nuclear weapons, which have become useless)… with an integrated command of

(B) The necessity of a democratic governance

Indeed, the action of the UN can only be effective by respecting the democratic principle enunciated by Pericles: liberty, equality, majority interest emanating from the majority will, supplemented by the separation of powers (Montesquieu) to avoid totalitarian excesses.

What is true at the level of local institutions must also be true for the UN and continental intermediary institutions (the Swiss Confederation has shown the way for the EU etc. with the federal principle – principle of subsidiarity in the EU but not always respected by the technocracy of standards – and the vote).

Thus, the three functions described by Aristotle: the legislative, the executive and the judicial must be separated organically and each must respond to the democratic principle of election. There can be no direct democracy without representative democracy, that alone can organise it. Thus, at least a supreme magistrate should be elected by direct universal suffrage (and then in turn appoint the magistrates of the supreme court) – as is the head of the executive (who then appoints his government); and the president of the legislature (possibly on a basis of recognised competence). Any elected representative should be removable by a recall vote.[30]

Such a representative democracy serves essentially to enable direct democracy, that is the expression of the majority will: to organise the demands of the populations for voting, referendum of citizens' initiative, and not to confiscate power during the duration of their mandate, as is the case if there is no vote.

*

---

these national armies initially pending this definitive replacement (as should also be done at EU level).

30 Doctorate in law (theoretical training) and professional practice (10years for example in a court) for the candidate magistrate; doctorate in economics, political science or military arts etc. and professional practice (10 years for example) in a public or private company for the candidate for the executive; a doctorate in communication, political science for a candidate for the presidency of the legislature and experience as a deputy (10 years).

In conclusion, certainly this ideal vote is difficult to set up at the global and continental level. Yet, with the current means of communication, internet voting is possible with some technical guarantees: national embassies could be replaced by UN offices that would make the census and issue a biometric digital identity card and could ensure the votes.

Risks and opportunities for Kazakhstan's foreign policy in the context of modern geopolitical changes[1]

Kuralay BAIZAKOVA, Fatima KUKEYEVA
Kazakhstan

The events of 2022 in Eurasia changed the geopolitical reality in the world. Kazakhstan's foreign policy faces a number of political and economic issues, both general and country-specific and, indeed, the terms "new geopolitics" or "new geopolitical reality" appear in official discourses of the country's politicians and in academic circles.

The geopolitical and geo-economic conditions for the realisation of Kazakhstan's foreign policy (KFP) require, from the scientific and expert community, a comprehensive analysis of the situation, the proposal of constructive ideas and forecasts on KFP strategy in the context of these new geopolitics.

This chapter's main purpose, based on the analysis of Kazakhstan's foreign policy changes in the main vectors, is to identify the risks and the new opportunities for Kazakhstan's strategy in the new geopolitics. In order to identify the influence of geopolitical realities on Kazakhstan's foreign policy principles, it is necessary to analyse the historical, political and economic narrative of the main leading players, in the Central Asian region as a whole and in Kazakhstan in particular.

As to theory and methodology, the chapter's problematics are investigated through the prism of various theories that, more or less, explain the foreign policy of the state in changing geopolitical conditions: the theory of geopolitics, rational choice and dependence/interdependence, etc.

---

1 This research IS funded by the Science Committee of the Ministry of Science and Higher Education of the Republic of Kazakhstan (Grant No. BR18574168).

Theory of geopolitics. Within the framework of the geopolitics theory, the issue of revising the basic principle of Kazakhstan's foreign policy is raised. The growing polarisation of the international system, differences in expert assessments of Kazakhstan's multi-vector foreign policy could actualise this problem. In Kazakhstan's political discourse there is a dispute about the historical choice of a priority of a foreign partner. On the one hand, there are calls to continue the systematic process of Eurasian integration, on the other hand, to ensure the independence of the economy and politics from the influence of a large neighbour.

In the context of recent world's events, Kazakhstan needs to understand, evaluate and even anticipate the potential conditions for possible geopolitical changes in its immediate geographical environment. At the same time, geopolitical analysis can predict changes in the balance of power in the international system.

The theory of interdependence considers the relationship of states in the "centre-periphery" plane. According to this theory, for developing countries, the neighbourhood with a more developed state creates unequal relations, that lead to economic, political and other types of dependence. To analyse the factors influencing the building of relations in the new geopolitical situation, we propose to turn to the theory of interdependence through the prism of "core-periphery", which will reveal new trends in relations between the Kazakhstan-Russia and the Kazakhstan-China dimension.

The theory of a small economy or small states considers, among many questions, the problem of their relations with their neighbours. The analysis of Russian and Chinese vectors in Kazakhstan's foreign policy shows that Astana acts as a small economy. The large economies / powers use the "bigger-smaller" approach to Kazakhstan. A larger state is able to influence the international system. A small/medium state has the capacity for a certain level of systemic presence and influence.

The analysis also used the theory of *soft power*, which enables us to consider the relations between civil societies at the level of "people-to-people".

The *theory of securitisation and the regional security complex* makes it possible to identify Kazakhstan's national interests and regional and non-regional states in the new geopolitics.

The theory of rational choice pays special attention to the stats's choice in the foreign policy strategy, based on its priorities and interests, that can be achieved through certain mechanisms of action. In the context of the new geopolitics, Kazakhstan's leadership builds its foreign policy, striving to maintain a strong / positive position of the state on the world stage and expanding tasks, develop effective mechanisms for responding to new geopolitical/geo-economic risks, challenges and threats.

I. Changes in the priorities of Kazakhstan's foreign policy

In order to analyse the risks and opportunities of Kazakhstan's foreign policy in the new geopolitical reality, it is logical to analyse the changes in the priority areas in order to identify the risks and opportunities for the state.

The Russian vector. In the new conditions of international relations, the Russian vector should be analysed through the prism of the risks of bilateral / multilateral cooperation. "Shared risks" determine the rational choice, geopolitical interest and dependence/interdependence of partner states, allies. General risks are both economic and political in nature, as well as directly related to security issues.

Indicators of these risks are the factors of Moscow's pressure on Astana. (i) *The first indicator* is Kazakhstan's membership in the Eurasian Economic Union (EAEU). Since 2022, more and more experts have called the EAEU a "toxic organisation" for Kazakhstan. Due to anti-Russian sanctions, as a result war in Ukraine since 24 February 2022. Economists note the impact of sanctions on EAEU countries. Goods produced by foreign companies on the territory of Russia have ceased to enter Kazakhstan, production links between extractive (in the territory of Kazakhstan) and manufacturers (in the territory of Russia) enterprises have been broken.

Sanctions are a blow to the technological development of certain industries in Kazakhstan. So, technological products, engineering goods, components for agricultural machinery, etc. imported from Russia. The business of Kazakhstan suffers largely because its logistics are tied to Russia. Kazakhstan exports most of its oil products through Russian ports, including the port of Novorossiysk.

In July 2022 Kazakhstan's president Tokayev instructed to establish new ways of supplying oil bypassing Russia, including by sea. Kazakhstan has never been a maritime country, but "now it's a different time," he said. In March 2023, Kazakhstan carried out the first test shipment of its oil through the Caspian Sea to Azerbaijan. Oil from the Kashagan field in the northern part of the Caspian Sea was delivered to the port of Aktau, from where it went to Baku. As part of the first batch, 6,900 tons of crude oil were loaded[2].

Thus, the economies of Kazakhstan and Russia in the EAEU are poorly integrated and in many cases remain at the level of relations between small and large economies. Kazakhstan, as an open economy, is included in almost all Russian integration projects, and therefore more dependent on the Russian economy.

(ii) The allied relations of the Kazakhstan with Russia should be considered as the *second risk indicator*[3]. In the new Kazakhstan Foreign Policy Concept 2020–2030, relations with Russia are defined as allied. Despite the strategic partnership, allied relations presuppose not only common economic interests, but also common views on political problems. The geopolitical factor is the dominant one in allied relations, when the allies are considered as a continuation of the territorial base for negotiations in peacetime and actions in the event of a war[4].

Issues of historical memory and ideology (language policy) are not conducive to strengthening bilateral relations. Statements of Russian officials and semi-officials, as well as media people on issues of territories in a historical context, the issue of an independent language policy, etc. cause a negative reaction from the Kazakh public.

There are two main negative trends for Kazakhstan in the Russian media: nationalist and neo-imperial. The first is connected with the thesis about the oppression of Russians in Kazakhstan. The second, neo-imperial, trend emerged after 2014 in connection with the events in Ukraine. According to this approach, Kazakhstan is "leaving Russia". Yet,

---

2 Kazakhstan sent oil to alternative Russia for the first time by way of the Caspian Sea (Казахстан впервые отправил нефть альтернативным России путем через Каспийское море). – URL: https://www.forbes.ru/finansy/486383-kazahstan-vper vye-otpravil-neft-al-ternativnym-rossii-putem-cerez-kaspijskoe-more

3 "On the Concept of Foreign Policy of the Republic of Kazakhstan for 2020 – 2030" (О Концепции внешней политики Республики Казахстан на 2020 – 2030 годы). 09.032020. – URL: https://www.akorda.kz/ru/legal_acts/decrees/o-koncepcii-vnesh nei-politiki-respubliki-kazahstan-na-2020-2030-gody

4 Russia and the problem of allied relations in international politics (Россия и проблема союзнических отношений в международной политике), 05.03.2022. – URL: https://vm.ric.mil.ru/Stati/item/385451/

at the official level, this thesis is not supported. There is also a negative trend for Russia in the Kazakh media. The authors of the article agree with the characterisation of this trend as "anti-colonial discourse with a touch of Russophobia"[5].

Moscow's actions violate the basic principles of the alliance, such as mutually beneficial cooperation, equal rights and protection of the national interests of all members.

An example is Moscow's desire to present sanctions as a common problem for EAEU member states, which requires a response from the organisation[6]. But Kazakhstan's Ministry of Foreign Affairs stated that the country is not conducting any negotiations on "consolidated measures of the EAEU countries in response to the sanctions."

(iii) The next indicator should be considered Kazakhstan's membership in CSTO. Russia's military operation in Ukraine has prompted Kazakhstan academic and civil society to question the country's membership in the CSTO, which is seen as limiting Kazakhstan's sovereignty. Civil society activists are calling for a referendum on membership in the CSTO.

Within the framework of the CSTO, Kazakhstan is considered the closest ally of Russia after Belarus, so Moscow expected some kind of support from Astana in the military conflict with Ukraine[7]. President Tokayev speaking on 21 June 2022 at the Qatar Economic Forum stated that "the territorial integrity of countries should prevail"[8].

At a plenary meeting of the St. Petersburg International Economic Forum with the participation of President Putin, President Tokayev stated that Kazakhstan would not recognise the independence of the so-called

---

5 Russia and Kazakhstan: what interferes with the cooperation of neighbours (Россия и Казахстан: что мешает сотрудничеству соседей). URL: https://regnum.ru/news/polit/2552206.html

6 Kazakhstan dispersed from Russia in the reply of EEU to sanctions of the West (Казахстан разошелся с Россией в ответе ЕАЭС на санкции Запада), 06.11.2021. URL: https://central.asia-news.com/ru/articles/cnmi_ca/features/2021/06/11/feature-03

7 See: T. Umarov. Too neutral ally. Whether waits for Kazakhstan the fate of Ukraine (Умаров Т. Слишком нейтральный союзник. Ждет ли Казахстан судьба Украины). – URL: https://carnegieendowment.org/politika/87625

8 In Conversation with President Tokayev. – URL: https://www.youtube.com/watch?v=eoJesrRMdHg

"DNR" and "LNR"[9]. The Astana official statements testify the desire to pursue an independent security policy, while remaining legitimate for Western partners and acceptable to its own citizens.

Kazakhstan's military doctrine provides cooperation with both the CSTO and the SCO, as well as in NATO PFP. In 2022, the Ministry of Defence developed a draft on amending Kazakhstan's Military Doctrine, that provides the use of troops in "in crisis situations"[10].

However, the main problem that erodes bilateral relations is Russia's inability to become a model for Kazakhstan. Russia does not demonstrate an attractive development model for Kazakhstan.

Taking into account these and other factors, Kazakhstan's foreign policy structures are faced with the main problem of determining the spheres of manifestation of allied relations with Moscow and their borders.

II. Kazakhstan foreign policy in the context of the new geopolitics: The Chinese vector

In Kazakhstan's Foreign Policy Concept 2020–2030, relations between Kazakhstan and China are defined as a "comprehensive strategic partnership." The status of a strategic partner unequivocally enhances the role and significance of relations. Thus, Kazakhstan's participation in the Belt and Road Initiative (BRI) allows not only to realise the transport potential of the country, but also to enter the Asia-Pacific markets.

In the context of a changing geo-economy, Kazakhstan's President seeks not only to preserve the achievements, but also to shift the economic agenda in a new direction. At the meeting of the Kazakh-Chinese Business Council, President Tokayev urged the parties to focus on the development of the "new economy" based on innovation and high-tech production and elements of Industry 4.0. "We are interested in

---

9 Tokayev: Kazakhstan doesn't recognise "quasi-public" DPR and LPR (Токаев: Казахстан не признает «квазигосударственные» «ДНР» и «ЛНР»). – URL: https://rus.azattyq.org/a/tokaev-o-priznanii-lnr-i-dnr/31903400.html

10 Kazakhstan intends to radically change its military doctrine by the end of 2022 (Казахстан намерен кардинально изменить свою военную доктрину до конца 2022 года). – URL: https://kaztag.kz/ru/news/kazakhstan-nameren-kardinalno-izmenit-svoyu-voennuyu-doktrinu-do-kontsa-2022-goda

creating joint innovative enterprises, technology parks and IT centres with Chinese companies," he emphasised[11].

The use of this asset will depend on the answers to problems of bilateral cooperation: Sinophobia sentiments in Kazakhstani society, the issue of transboundary rivers, migration and demographic components, increased dependence on Chinese investments and loans, the land issue, etc. Yet, the Chinese leadership does not dramatise the presence of anti-Chinese sentiments in Kazakhstan.

In the context of Kazakhstan's search for a diversification of development strategy within the framework of various forms of bilateral and multilateral cooperation, Beijing is strengthening the development of cooperation within the framework of the SCO. Under the SCO security umbrella, Kazakhstan has strengthened its security commitments not only with Russia, but also with China, that is a guarantee that certain security challenges associated with the unstable and politically tense situation in Central Asia will not escalate.

The growing role of China in the Central Asian region is evidenced by the SCO summit held in Samarkand (2022). The meeting showed that international security still remains at the top of the organisation's agenda. Xi Jinping's visit to Astana and his supports of Kazakhstan's position on regional and international issues, showed a real picture of the current situation between SCO member countries: "No matter how the international situation changes, we will continue to strongly support Kazakhstan in defence of independence, sovereignty and territorial integrity, … categorically oppose the interference of any forces in the internal affairs of [the] country"[12]. Clearly, this statement was addressed to Moscow.

However, at the present stage, the economic component of the SCO is being overwhelmed by the rapidly growing influence of the Belt and Road Initiative. Recognising the great opportunities, we should also analyse the

---

11 Tokayev: We are interested in creation of the joint innovative ventures with the Chinese companies (Токаев: Мы заинтересованы в создании совместных инновационных предприятий с китайскими компаниями). – URL: https://www.businessfm.kz business>tokaev-my-zainteresovany-v-sozdanii-sovmestnyh-innovacionnyh predpriyatij-s-kitajskimi-kompaniyami

12 Xi Jinping: the Kazakh-Chinese relations came for new historical start (Си Цзиньпин: казахско-китайские отношения вышли на новый исторический старт). – URL: https://ru.sputnik.kz/20220914/-si-tszinpin-kazakhsko-kitayskie-otnosheniya-vyshli-na-novyy-istoricheskiy-start-27583287.html

risks for Kazakhstan. In the context of SCO expansion, Astana may find itself under the strongest influence of the PRC, the main regional player in CA. It will be problematic to maintain a balance between the main players: Beijing and Moscow.

The Russian weakening as a result of economic sanctions and war in Ukraine could have a long-term effect. Beijing's political ambitions will increase while maintaining the existing trends, expressed in Russia's insufficient economic influence on Kazakhstan and the Central Asian region as a whole.

III. Foreign policy of Kazakhstan in the context of the new geopolitics: Kazakhstan-Central Asia

In the new geopolitical conditions, the issue of Central Asian regionalisation is being updated. For a long time, relations among regional countries were characterised by a low level of cooperation and regular disputes, including trade wars, border disputes, and disagreements over the management and use of water and energy.

Thus, Kazakhstan intends to strengthen its leading position in the region. This thesis is indicated in Kazakhstan's Foreign Policy Concept 2020–2030 as a strategic goal. Astana intends to give a strategic character to cooperation with regional states. Usually, this practice was applied to world and regional powers. The strategic partnership involves expanding multilateral dialogue and cooperation, as well as promoting the expansion of multilateral ones in Central Asia.

The Kazakhstan Foreign Policy Concept focus is shifting from the country vector to the regional one. This can become a real foreign policy asset for the country if leadership means being a model and example for regional states, setting certain standards and pace of development in the process of Central Asia 2.0.

Astana's policy of closer cooperation with CA states has economic and political reasons, **internal** and external. The first should include economic factors related to economic diversification problem. Shift from the resource-based economy is possible as part of strengthening cooperation within the region. The combined raw materials will allow to increase the subjectivity of the region as a whole and of each country in particular.

Cooperation and, in the future, integration becomes a factor in maintaining and strengthening the independence and Central Asian integration into the world economic community.

An important factor supporting economic regionalism is the requirement to strengthen it at the level of society, appealing to civilisational values.

External factors include Kazakhstan's interest in integrating the region for the unimpeded trade flow, investment, services and people through Central Asian countries. It could lead CA to become an important part of global production networks and supply chains. The modern trends in regionalisation form a qualitatively new space, where Central Asia is part of the global integration area and is influenced/pressured by regional and global powers.

Factors that may impede the implementation of President Tokayev Central Asian strategy are: imbalance in Central Asian countries development, unresolved border disputes, Turkmenistan's integration into regional processes, the lack of institutions and mechanisms aimed at jointly solving regional problems, including socio-economic tensions.

Thus, in the new geopolitical reality, Central Asia should become a priority for Kazakhstan's foreign policy. It will help to achieve one of the main tasks of Kazakhstan foreign policy strategy – leadership in the region.

IV. A window of opportunity for Kazakhstan's foreign policy

An analysis of changes in the main directions of Kazakhstan's foreign policy in the new geopolitics demonstrate the presence of factors both positive (opportunities, trends) and negative (risks and challenges). Despite the complexity of the situation, it is necessary to continue the analysis of the so-called. "windows of opportunity" for Kazakhstan's politics and economy.

Economic opportunities are related to the pace of implementation of target indicators for investment in fixed capital and attraction of foreign direct investment, as well as a number of other issues.

An analysis of Kazakhstan's economic assets demonstrates the open economy in the conditions of the anti-Russian sanctions can contribute to the integration of Kazakhstan into the global production chains. Kazakhstan could develop a new regionalism based not so much on a geographical as on a functional principle.

The analysis of "shared risks" within the EAEU also opens a "window of opportunity" for Astana, with Russia and Belarus under international sanctions and Armenia and Kyrgyzstan as small and debt-ridden economies. If withdrawal or suspension of membership in the EAEU is not possible now, then the activation of Kazakhstan's role in shaping the agenda is quite possible.

Analysing the "window of opportunity" it is necessary to identify the risks. Positive processes, as the relocation of certain businesses in Kazakhstan and the flow of qualified personnel, the formation of new transport and logistics corridors, contain certain risks that need to be minimised.

A window of opportunity has been opened to give drive to regional cooperation. Several factors contribute to this: changing geopolitics around Central Asia; strengthening the regional component in the foreign policy of Uzbekistan; relations among the key CA countries Kazakhstan and Uzbekistan are being strengthened; intensification of diplomatic meetings of CA countries' leaders, as a result of the "Central Asia-2.0" process appeared; the request of the Central Asian countries to develop more sustainable mechanisms for regional interaction.

Political opportunities. Building Kazakhstan Republic 2.0. The transit of power, coupled with geopolitical changes, allowed the Kazakh leadership to determine a new course for democratisation of the country's social and political course. President Tokayev emphasised that "Our course towards consistent democratisation in all spheres of life is irreversible – this is my principled position"[13].

The building the new Kazakhstan, striving for modernisation and democratisation, is the most important *window of opportunity.*

*

---

13 We shouldn't forget about a reverse side of democratization – the president (Мы не должны забывать об обратной стороне демократизации – президент). – URL: https://kapital.kz/gosudarstvo/110461/my-ne-dolzhny-zabyvat-ob-obratnoy-storone-demokratizatsii-prezident.html

In conclusion, in the context of geopolitical turbulence, Kazakhstan's foreign policy aces risks but also enjoys a "window of opportunity". The basis for effective risk management and for protecting the national interests and sovereignty of Kazakhstan is the preservation of the basic principle of Kazakhstan's foreign policy – multivectoralism.

Clearly, the multi-vector foreign policy requires adjustment due to the complicated global realities, constant turbulence and transformation of modern international relations. Otherwise, the risk is creating space for external players to interfere in the internal affairs and foreign policy of the state.

Risk management is based on the principle of balancing and diplomatic manoeuvring, which is made complex by the worsening of global and regional actors' relations around the region and Kazakhstan.

An effective use of the "window of opportunity" analysed will ensure the stability of Kazakhstan's positions at the regional and global levels, its consistency in promoting national interests, the evolution of the foreign policy in the context of tactical manoeuvres while maintaining the overall strategy.

The crisis of modern international law and of its mechanisms to provide international security

Sagyngaliy AIDARBAYEV
Kazakhstan

Humanity is presently experiencing an unprecedented crisis of international law and of its mechanisms to ensure international security. This is a turning point in the development of the system of international relations, a circumstance noted by many researchers. Civilisational, geopolitical and some other factors are called as the reasons for the emerging and growing crisis thus under examination here.

Many global threats unfold before the states – crisis of international security, financial and economic, environmental, demographic, migration crises, the crisis of the foundations of civilisation – politics, law, ethics, morality, culture, etc.[1] One of the main reasons for the deepening of all of these is the crisis of international law: "… the international legal system … is now plunged into a systemic global crisis."[2] According to the Chairman of the Constitutional Court of the Russian Federation V.D. Zorkin, at the St. Petersburg International Legal Forum 2016 "Humanity has never in its history faced a systemic military-political, economic, social, moral, legal crisis of such complexity and depth."[3]

1 Алферова Е.В. Кризис международного права: причины и пути выхода. https://cyberleninka.ru/article/n/krizis-mezhdunarodnogo-prava-prichiny-i-puti-vyhoda-obzor

2 Зорькин В.Д. Цивилизация права и развитие России. – 2-е изд., испр. и доп. – М.: Норма: ИНФРА-М, 2016. – 416 с. – С.406.

3 Зорькин В.Д. Доверие к праву – путь разрешения глобальных кризисов. Российская газета. М., 2016. 19 мая.

I. Chronological framework of the emergence of the crisis of international law and its nature: A variety of approaches

(A) Pro-Eastern approach

Researchers from different countries have been talking about the crisis of international law for many years. At the same time, they define the chronological framework of the emergence and development, as well as the socio-political and legal nature of this crisis in different ways.

For example, the president of the Centre for the Restoration of International Law, Goran Petronievich from Belgrade (Serbia), connects the beginning of the crisis of international law with the entry of the liberal-globalist system onto the historical stage in the 1970s of the twentieth century, and the complete collapse of international law connects liberal globalist system into neoliberal globalism in the 1990s. According to him, these processes coincided with the end of the Cold War and the collapse of one of the largest world powers – the Soviet Union. In turn, neoliberal globalism led to the emergence of a world monopolarity led by the USA, which led to the complete collapse of the already shaken international legal order of the bipolar system. This caused damage to the international legal mechanisms that made it possible to restore the international legal order after the Second World War.[4]

The carrier of monopolarity in the person of the United States and its allies is aware of its capabilities and the possibilities of its power, therefore force comes to replace law. As a result, the rule of law ("the force of law") is transformed into the "law of force". This violation of the international legal order has led to the widespread illegal behaviour of the holders of the "right of force". Military conflicts caused by various sanctions and general legal uncertainty while respecting the interests and needs of only one side have become an integral part of the globalist world order. Entire peoples, states and regions (the Balkans, the Middle East, North Africa, etc.) suffered from this social catastrophe. To this it should be added that the second decade of the 21st century is characterised by the return of some countries to the international political arena, which, together

---

4 Петрониевич Г. Последствия кризиса и необходимость восстановления международного права (22.06.2021). https://ru.valdaiclub.com/a/highlights/neobkhodimost-vosstanovleniya-mezhdunarodnogo-prava/

with their allies, set the goal of eliminating the negative impact of the neoliberal globalist monopoly and achieving their own prosperity. Such states that have completely broken the former monopolarity include the Russian Federation and China as world powers, as well as a large number of regional powers – Iran, Turkey, Brazil. The awareness by these, and after them by some other countries, of the need to strengthen the sovereignty of the state, destroyed over the past period, gives rise to a new world ideology of sovereignty, which is slowly but surely replacing globalism. Refusal to restore the world legal order inevitably leads to new world conflicts, the consequences of which cannot be foreseen. For the resumption of such a legal order, which will regulate relations between sovereign states or communities of states, the existing mechanism of the UN is a good basis. .[5] This is the position of one of the many researchers of the problem.

According to another researcher, the crisis of international law did not begin today, but from the moment of the destruction of the USSR and the "bloc" bipolar world system headed by its international leaders – the USSR and the USA. As a result, a strong blow was dealt to the Yalta-Potsdam agreements on state borders, which are the foundation of European stability. After the collapse of the USSR, the United States began quite openly to claim unconditional global superiority. Local and global conflicts have arisen in the world that violate the fundamental norms of international law regarding individual states and their citizens, formulated in the UN Charter, in various UN conventions and in the final documents of the Helsinki Conference on Security and Cooperation in Europe.[6] The author traces the chronology of these legal collisions and describes only a few of the most famous episodes of the many examples of the tragic events of the last 25 years of world history, when international law collapsed and was replaced by brute force, these are: Rwanda in 1994, the NATO war against Serbia "for Kosovo" in 1999, the war against Iraq in 2003 and against Libya in 2011, etc.[7]

---

5 Петрониевич Г. Там же.

6 Зорькин В.Д. Цивилизация права и развитие России. – 2-е изд., испр. и доп. – М.: Норма: ИНФРА-М, 2016. – С.274–275.

7 Алферова Е.В. Кризис международного права: причины и пути выхода. https://cyberleninka.ru/article/n/krizis-mezhdunarodnogo-prava-prichiny-i-puti-vyhoda-obzor

We have cited the opinions of representatives of science from the so-called "Eastern" bloc of states.

(B) Pro-Western approach

It would be correct and fair to quote the opinions of representatives of legal science and Western states. In this regard, we can be helped by the collection of materials of the annual conference, which was organised in 2016 in Latvia under the auspices of the European Association of International Law by the Graduate School of Law of the city of Riga and the Latvian Society of International Law. The initiators and editors of this conference entitled "How international law works in times of crisis". Professors J. Ulrich and I. Ziemele grouped all reports into four main areas – security, immunities, sustainable development and philosophical perspectives. It is in these areas, according to the editors, today international law faces acute problems and challenges. The general conclusion from the materials of this collection is that the international legal system contains norms and principles, concepts and mechanisms for regulating any events that challenge the international community.[8]

When comparing the approaches of representatives of "Eastern" and "Western" countries and regions, it is immediately evident that for representatives of the Western doctrine, the crisis of international law and its institutions does not look like something special. They very often qualify it as an everyday, everyday phenomenon that does not deserve any special attention.

For example, James Crawford in his report "Reflections on Crises and International Law" writes about this very casually: "If there were no international crises, many of us would not be international lawyers. We go around shouting "crisis" while trying to find it and sometimes seeing it when it's not there. We justify calling ourselves international lawyers by referring to some kind of international crisis that has affected us in one way or another.[9]"

---

8 How International Law Works in Times of Crisis. Edited by: George Ulrich, Ineta Ziemele. – Oxford University Press, 2019. 368 p.

9 James Crawford. Reflections on Crises and International Law. How International Law Works in Times of Crisis. Edited by: George Ulrich, Ineta Ziemele. Oxford University Press, 2019. pp. 10–18.

Another representative of the European doctrine of international law, Jean-Marc Sauve, reflecting on how international law functions during a crisis, notes that the European continent today is facing a multifaceted crisis that extends to several levels, forming a complex tangle that needs to be unravel, despite its indeterminate appearance. To solve this problem, he turns to the work of the philosopher Paul Ricoeur, who, in one of his lectures in 1986, noted the originality and diversity of the crises experienced by modern societies. In particular, in the medical, economic and political fields, there is traditionally nothing unexpected or disorderly in crises. They are a necessary, sometimes extreme stage in the course of events that come to an end, end. They indicate the state of human health, the degree of maturity of the economy or the degree of support for the political regime. At the same time, crises are orderly and understandable processes that determine the future. This is a very important moment when it is necessary to make a choice and make a constructive decision. They are not purely destructive, as they can also have purifying, soothing signs in cases where they pave the way for a new phase of growth or progress. As a result, economic crises form links between different cycles of expansion, and political crises accompany fundamental changes in society and are able, through the disruptions they create, to help establish a more just political order.[10]

Stephen Bowie analyses the issue of decision-making during a crisis in the aspect of international law through a case study based on the Chilcot report. It should be noted here that the British inquiry into the decision to intervene in Iraq is one of the longest and most comprehensive studies of the government's decision-making process. Thus, in the course of the investigation, the processes of providing legal advice, which were part of the decision of the British government to interfere in the internal affairs of Iraq, were studied in detail. Through this lens, the report examines what the investigation of general international law reveals in relation to the decision to intervene in the affairs of Iraq, and, more broadly, what illustrates the role of international law in decision-making in general. In particular, the report deals with the practical and ethical aspects of

10 Jean-Marc Sauvé. Reflections: How International Law Functions in Times of Crisis. How International Law Works in Times of Crisis. Edited by: George Ulrich, Ineta Ziemele. – Oxford University Press, 2019. pp. 291–318.

providing international legal advice to a government in a situation where fundamental principles of international law are violated.[11]

As we can see, the violation of the principles of international law is not something extraordinary for the representatives of these states.

II. Modern problems that testify to the crisis of international law

What problems of contemporary international law may indicate its crisis? The most important of them, in our opinion, are the following.

First, one of the main problems of international law has always been the lack of a single mechanism for its enforcement and application. Many decisions taken by international organisations and bodies are not binding and may be ignored by states. Sometimes even binding decisions are not implemented due to weak enforcement mechanisms.

Second, the frequent disregard of international legal norms by influential states in cases where these norms did not correspond to their political interests.

Third, internal inconsistency between some of the basic principles of international law (for example, the principle of the territorial integrity of the state and the principle of self-determination of peoples).

Fourth, insufficient adaptability of international law to new challenges and threats (for example, such as cybersecurity, global warming, cross-border migration). Some experts believe that international law is unable to solve these problems and requires serious modernisation.

Fifth, the growth of nationalistic tendencies and protectionism, which can lead to further weakening of international legal institutions and norms.

This is not a complete list of problems that testify to the crisis of international law, create serious challenges for it and its future development.

---

11 Stephen Bouwhuis. The Chilcot Report: International Law and Decision-Making in Times of Crisis. How International Law Works in Times of Crisis. Edited by: George Ulrich, Ineta Ziemele. Oxford University Press, 2019. pp. 273–366.

III. The origins of the crisis of international law in terms of doctrine

E.V. Alferova, having reviewed the views of various researchers on the problem of the crisis of modern international law, comes to the conclusion that the fundamental origins of the crisis of international law are explained by legal scholars in different ways:[12]

(1) the balance of power on the world stage, or the geopolitical balance, is changing; the doctrine of state sovereignty is undermined; subjects of international law become less stable;[13]
(2) the system of law and law enforcement does not have time to adapt to a too rapidly changing reality;[14]
(3) lack of a positive perspective, an image of a common human future;[15]
(4) "uncertainty of the prospects of some international entities (EU, CIS), inaction of a number of international organisations; institutional stagnation of the UN; the vulnerability of certain institutions in terms of legitimacy (international criminal tribunals); dominance of the concept of functionalism";[16]
(5) "the maniacal persistence of the United States and the EU countries to expand the content of a person's status at the expense of socio-economic and political rights and freedoms of the individual and citizen, adjust it to fictitious Western standards, plant them on all inhabited continents of the globe, as well as the passive role of the UN in the settlement of regional conflicts";[17]

---

12 Алферова Е.В. Кризис международного права: причины и пути выхода //https://cyberleninka.ru/article/n/krizis-mezhdunarodnogo-prava-prichiny-i-puti-vyhoda-obzor

13 Кустарев А. Кризис государственного суверенитета (Обзор новейших точек зрения западных политологов). Космополит. 2004. №16. С.166–170.

14 Зорькин В.Д. Кризис международного права: Современный контекст //https://www.globalaffairs.ru/articles/krizis-mezhdunarodnogo-prava-sovremennyj-kontekst/

15 Зорькин В.Д. Доверие к праву – путь разрешения глобальных кризисов: Лекция для участников Международного юридического форума (Санкт-Петербург, 19 мая 2016). Российская газета. 2016. 19 мая.

16 Толстых В.Л. Международное право и постмодернизм. Российское правосудие. М., 2012. № 9. С.7–14. (С.8).

17 Казанник А.И. Естественные права человека и кризис современного международного права. Вестник Омского ун-та. Сер.: Право. Омск, 2015. № 2 (43). С. 47–53. (С.53).

(6) extension to the sphere of international relations of the norms of Anglo-Saxon case law; competition of jurisdictions and court decisions,[18] etc.

Thus, the main causes of the crisis of international law are being studied by researchers.

IV. The crisis of international legal security mechanisms

(A) Crisis of the UN Security Council mechanism

Along with the crisis of modern international law, crisis phenomena have also affected its mechanisms for ensuring international security.

In the world, there are many international legal security mechanisms that have been created to ensure peace and security. All these mechanisms can be divided into universal, regional and bilateral. Of all these mechanisms, of course, universal and regional ones are of the greatest importance.

Among the universal international legal mechanisms for ensuring security, the UN mechanism occupies a special place. At the centre of this mechanism is such a power body as the UN Security Council, which has the right to make binding decisions. Chapter VII of the UN Charter empowers this body to take coercive measures to maintain or restore international peace and security. However, this body is not in a position to respond effectively to situations involving a breach of the peace, a threat to the peace, or an act of aggression.

It has been so many times. The latest example of this is the armed conflict between Russia and Ukraine that began on February 24, 2022 and which has already drawn all NATO countries into it. This is a large-scale conflict that could lead to the use of nuclear weapons, in which, on the one hand, the nuclear power (Russia) directly participates, on the other hand, indirectly (due to direct arms supplies to the second side of the conflict – Ukraine) three more world nuclear powers (United States of America, Great Britain, France).

---

18 Власенко Н.А. Кризис права: Проблемы и подходы к решению. Журнал российского права. М., 2013. № 8. С. 43–54. (С.46).

In such a most dangerous situation, the UN Security Council, which is the most universal and most effective mechanism for ensuring the peace and security of the United Nations, is inactive. What is the reason for such inaction?

The main reason is the weakness of the institutional mechanism. This disease could be called by the medical term "congenital heart disease" of the organisation.

Many researchers noted that when the UN was created in 1945, its Charter laid down the concept of special responsibility of the world powers (the five permanent members of the UN Security Council) for the entire architecture of the organisation, the post-war system of international relations and for the maintenance of international peace and security. . One of the most important manifestations of this concept in the Security Council was the principle of consensus of all five permanent members of the Council when making the most important decisions, primarily those related to the adoption of coercive measures relating to the maintenance of international peace and security. In other words, such decisions could be taken only in one case – if the majority of the members of the Council vote "for" provided that none of the five permanent members votes "against".

This guarantee, connected with the principle of consensus of all five permanent members of the Security Council, was supposed to prevent the possibility of a direct clash between them, as conceived by the drafters of the UN Charter. However, in reality, this norm practically acted as a reason for paralysis of the UN in all cases when the interests of the permanent members of the Security Council contradicted each other.

Indeed, in virtually any situation of international tension, the interests of the five permanent members of the Council necessarily came into conflict, which, as a result, led to blocking the work of the UN Security Council by voting against.

And today, as in many other similar cases, the most important world mechanism, designed to ensure the preservation and maintenance of international peace and security, is not able to function. On the Russian-Ukrainian armed conflict, the UN Security Council is not in a position to adopt a single resolution related to the use of coercive measures, since such a resolution will be blocked either by one member of the Council (Russia) or other members (USA, UK, France).

In this situation, it is good that China did not join any of the parties to the armed conflict. Otherwise, if China took the side of Russia, the world would be divided into two warring camps, and the prospects for a peaceful settlement of the conflict would worsen even more.

Thus, the most effective mechanism of the UN, designed to maintain and guarantee international peace and security, turned out to be once again (for the umpteenth time!) turned off.

(B) The need to reform the mechanism of the UN Security Council

Considering that the mechanism of the UN Security Council, laid down at the end of World War II by the Yalta-Potsdam agreements, is not able to function in modern conditions, many researchers believe that it needs to be reformed. The main obstacle to this mechanism is the principle of consensus, which needs to be either abolished or replaced. For example, one of the options for improving the consensus principle could be the "consensus minus 1" principle.

According to Goran Petronievich, President of the Centre for the Restoration of International Law, the existing UN mechanism is a good basis for the resumption of such a legal order, and in light of the changing world order, which is gradually sliding towards multipolarity, it is necessary to restore a system of clear and firm legal norms based on Centre the pre-existing legal order.[19] It should be borne in mind that when they talk about the reform of the UN, they mean, first of all, the reform of the UN Security Council.

The main reason for the crisis of the UN, its displacement to the periphery of international relations by regional organisations such as NATO, lies in the following:[20]

- the need for compliance by UN member states with the basic norms of international law;
- in serious improvement of legal categories;

---

19 Petronievich G. Ibid.

20 Гришаева Л.Е. Россия, ООН и крымские санкции. Экономический журнал. М., 2014. № 3 (35). С. 6–23. (С.6–7).

- elimination of obvious contradictions between the most important international legal norms;
- improving the very mechanism of crisis management (peacekeeping potential) and developing clear legal aspects of the use of force in international relations;
- preventive activities to prevent regional crises;
- careful planning and adequate application of sanctions imposed by the UN Security Council.

(C) Crisis of regional security mechanisms

Today, in the situation of the incapacity of the UN, the mechanism for applying sanctions has been applied within the framework of such a regional international organisation as NATO.

At the same time, the application of sanctions has acquired a mutual character: if on the part of NATO member states these sanctions are collective in nature, then on the part of Russia they are individual.

Among the regional security arrangements, the mechanism of the Organisation for Security and Cooperation in Europe (OSCE) occupies a special place. This mechanism is of particular importance, because both Russia and Ukraine participate in it.

At present, we can observe the crisis of all security mechanisms, which manifests itself in several aspects.

First, many international organisations, such as the UN, NATO and others, experience a lack of trust on the part of a number of states and the population. This is due to the fact that these organisations are not always able to respond quickly and effectively to crisis situations, and also to the fact that some states use their veto in the UN Security Council to block decisions that do not correspond to their political interests. .

Secondly, many international treaties are violated or not respected by some states, which undermines the credibility of international legal security mechanisms.

Thirdly, some states use unilateral actions that circumvent international law, which also undermines confidence in international legal security mechanisms. For example, the United States has withdrawn from the Paris Climate Agreement and intends to withdraw from the Intermediate-Range Nuclear Forces Treaty.

*

In conclusion, the crisis of international legal security mechanisms is a serious problem that needs to be addressed. The armed conflict between Russia and Ukraine, which began on February 24, 2022, exposed to the limit the crisis phenomena, both in the field of international law and in the field of ensuring international security.

The armed conflict in Ukraine exposed almost all existing systemic problems of international law. The crisis of modern international law and its mechanisms to ensure international security requires its speedy resolution. Otherwise, humanity will collapse.

A permanent neutrality for the Korean peninsula: Past and present

Tai-Uk CHUNG
Korea

The geostrategic position of the Korean peninsula has determined the geopolitical fate of the country. Korea has repeatedly undergone hardships when continental and maritime powers collide. The consequences have ranged to foreign rule, dependence or division throughout history.

The hope of the global village has faded. The world of the 21st century has entered the era of hegemonic competition again. Regarding the current situation on the Korean peninsula, many people are proposing neutrality, that is, permanent neutrality.

This chapter looks at how the confrontation among great powers developed on the Korean peninsula, and which suggestions of neutrality for Korea emerged. It discusses the appropriate neutralisation plan for the Korean peninsula.

I. Conflicts between continental and maritime powers in the Era of Imperialism

(A) The Sino-Japanese War: China vs. Japan and UK

Korea had been dependent on China for a long time. A vassal state of China, she formed a kind of collective security system according to the principle that a small country serves a large one and a large country protects a small one (事大字小). Japan, an ancient maritime power, had accepted the Chinese world order at times, but at times was at odds with China.

The East Asian order in the 19th century was reorganised by the advance of Western imperialism. China's Qing (清) dynasty fell into a semi-colonial state due to the Opium Wars. Qing lost Vietnam, which was a vassal state, to France, Myanmar to Britain, and Okinawa to Japan. Now, the only country where Qing exercised suzerainty was Korea. Japan was forcibly opened by the United States, but it soon succeeded in modernisation and industrialisation with the Meiji Restoration and aimed to advance into Taiwan, Korea, and Manchuria.

Meanwhile, of the continent, Russia was moving from north south. Russia's defeat in the Crimean War prevented its expansion in Europe and instead advanced into Asia. Russia pressured the weak Qing and the territory north of the Amur River was ceded, and then it acquired the Primorsky Krai, finally reaching the border with Korea. At the time, Britain, which was in confrontation with Russia on a global level, became vigilant about Russia's advancement.

The Qing Dynasty, nervous about the expansion of Japan and Russia, tried to strengthen its suzerainty over Korea. When a rebellion broke out in Korea (Imo Incident in 1882), Qing dispatched troops, purged the rebels. Qing continued to station troops in Korea and to dispatch officials to interfere in Korea's internal and external affairs.

The Korean court depended on the Qing Dynasty. However, a small number of reformers promoted the independence and enlightenment of Korea with the support of the Japanese legation (Gapsin Coup in 1884). However, the forces of the coup did not receive additional support from the Japanese government. Qing's Yuan Shikai (袁世凱) moved his forces quickly and subdued the ringleaders of the rebellion.

Meanwhile, Russia established a plan for the Trans-Siberian Railway and signed a Korea-Russia Treaty of Amity and Commerce in 1884. Russia began to consider dispatching warships to the Korean Peninsula when the situation in Joseon was shaken by the Gapsin Coup. These rumours provoked the British, who immediately occupied Geomundo (Port Hamilton) in 1885, an island in the southern sea of the Korean Peninsula. The Qing mediated between Russia and Britain. Thus, Russia provided an assurance that it would not advance into the Korean Peninsula, and Britain withdrew from Geomundo Island.

While the competition between China, Japan, Russia, and Britain intensified and the Qing Dynasty strengthened its suzerainty anew, some proposals for neutralisation of Korea were put forward. One of them was the idea of Yu, Gil-Jun (유길준), a representative intellectual of the late Joseon dynasty. His major concern was Russia's ambitions. At the same time, he was also wary of Japan's expansion. He insisted that, under the leadership of Qing, the relevant countries such as Britain, France, Japan, and Russia should convene and sign an agreement on the neutrality for Korea, which was modelled after Belgian neutrality (Treaty of London in 1839).

However, Qing, which exercised suzerainty over Korea, would not accept that idea as it would involve Japan or Russia in equal capacity. Instead, Qing only adopted the strategy that use foreign countries to control each other (以夷制夷), which encouraged Korea to establish diplomatic ties with various powers.

Japan accelerated preparations for the Sino-Japanese War in 1890 when Yamagata Aritomo (山縣有朋), who had real power in the Japanese army, became Prime Minister. He emphasised that the Korean peninsula was within Japan's interest line,

In 1894, the Donghak ("Eastern Learning") Rebellion broke out in Korea, and when the Korean government failed to suppress it and requested troops to be dispatched from the Qing Dynasty, Japan quickly dispatched more of its own army. The Donghak riots subsided. However, Japan somehow tried to find an excuse for war.

Britain was concerned about the Sino-Japanese War. They did not like a war between the two countries that would prevent Russia from going south. Accordingly, the British foreign minister, Kimberley, proposed the division and joint occupation of the Korean peninsula for both powers. At the same time, he also thought that in the event of a war, he would have no choice but to support Japan. Britain and Japan signed the Anglo-Japanese Treaty of Commerce and Navigation in 1894. This allowed Britain to recognise Japan as a potential ally.

Finally, Japan declared war on Qing and defeated the Qing army on land and at sea. In the end, Qing had no choice but to come to peace negotiations with Japan. The Shimonoseki Treaty was signed. Qing paid large reparations to Japan and further agreed to cede the Liaodong peninsula and Taiwan Island to Japan. Qing also pledged to confirm Korea's complete independence and to abolish the Chinese suzerainty over Korea. As a result, Korea was formally freed from the thousand year-long East Asian order ruled by China. However, this can be said to be the process by which Korea eventually became a protectorate of Japan.

(B) The Russo-Japanese War: Russia vs. Japan, UK, USA

After the Sino-Japanese War, Russia started to block Japanese expansion. Russia brought in France and Germany to pressure Japan. Japan had to return the Liaodong Peninsula to Qing, and even had to give up its claims to Lushun and Dalian.

As Russia's influence expanded, Korea became an arena of fierce rivalry between Russia and Japan. Japan killed the queen of Korea, the core of the pro-Russian political faction (Eulmi Incident in 1895), and the monarch of Korea fled to the Russian legation to seek protection.

The confrontation between Russia and Japan on the Korean peninsula was tentatively compromised with the Lobanov-Yamagata Agreement of 1896. Russia and Japan maintained the status quo in the balance of power. Moreover, the two countries agreed to station their troops on the Korean peninsula and establish a neutral zone in the event of additional dispatch. This neutral zone would be at the 39th parallel north latitude.

Russia accelerated their advance into Manchuria. When Germany pressed Qing for the murder of missionaries and occupied Jiaozhou Bay on the Shandong Peninsula, Russia gained the right to build a South Manchurian railroad and acquired the concessions in Lushun and Dalian on the Liaodong Peninsula. This came as a huge shock to Japan, where public opinion grew in favour of war.

As the confrontation between Russia and Japan intensified, the Korean king left the Russian legation in 1897 and declared the establishment of a Korean Empire. Afterwards, the constitution of Korea was promulgated in 1899. By declaring the independence of the monarchy, Korea sought to benefit from the principle of sovereign equality under international law.

When the outbreak of the Boxer Rebellion occurred in China in 1900, the situation in Northeast Asia escalated again. With dispatching troops through Manchuria, Russia used the rebellion as an opportunity to virtually occupy all the areas. Japan also sent the largest number of troops to form an allied force to suppress the Boxers, keeping Russia in check. Russo-Japanese faced a collision.

The Korean emperor King Gojong felt threatened by the possibility of a conflict between Russia and Japan and developed diplomacy to neutralise Korea. King Gojong instructed W. F. Sands, an American advisor to prepare a neutrality plan. Sands proposed a neutrality modelled after Belgium and urged to reform Korea's internal affairs, which required foreign loans. However, the US and UK governments did not approve Sands' efforts.

King Gojong himself developed neutralisation diplomacy. He made neutrality offers to Japan and the United States. Japan discarded the neutrality idea as being instigated by Russia. The United States was reluctant to intervene in Korean issues. King Gojong also tried the possibility of neutralisation through international organisations. He recognised the Universal Peace Conference in The Hague as an instrument for the peaceful settlement of international disputes and tried to send delegates to it. He also considered the possibility of a neutral zone in the International Humanitarian Law and acceded to the first Geneva Conventions (1864) in 1903.

Furthermore, shortly before the start of the Russo-Japanese War in 1904, King Gojong declared Korea's neutrality to Western countries. The US, UK, Germany, French sent an acknowledgment that the Declaration had been *received*. When Gojong saw this, he mistook it for Western countries *supporting* Korea's neutrality. However, Britain was on the side of Japan in the Russo-Japanese War through the Anglo-Japanese Alliance in 1902, and also the United States supported Japan through the Katsura-Taft Secret Agreement in 1905.

The Russo-Japanese War broke out and Japan defeated the Russian army in Manchuria and the Korea Strait. Japan and Russia signed a peace treaty under the mediation of the United States (Treaty of Portsmouth in 1905). As a result, Korea became a protectorate of Japan and was forcibly annexed in 1910.

II. Conflict between continental and maritime powers during the Cold War Era

(A) Divided Occupation of Korea: USA vs. USSR

With Japan's defeat in World War II, Korea again welcomed an opportunity for independence. However, the Korean peninsula was sacrificed in the geopolitical confrontation between the US and the USSR.

The original plan of the United States that defeated Japan was a trusteeship of four countries (US, UK, China, and Soviet Union) over Korea. In February 1945 in Yalta, the Allied Powers, who seized the victory of World War II, discussed the idea of post-war order. Roosevelt asked Stalin to participate in the war against Japan and proposed a trusteeship plan for the Korean peninsula. Stalin agreed.

Shortly after the US dropped atomic bombs on Japan, the Soviet Union declared war on Japan. While the US forces were in Okinawa in the Pacific Ocean, the Soviet forces had already swept through Manchuria and entered the northern part of the Korean peninsula. The United States wanted to protect Seoul and the Japanese islands from the Soviet advance and eventually proposed to the Soviet Union to divide and occupy Korea along the 38th parallel.

The idea of allied powers presiding over the Korean destiny was materialised in the Moscow Conference of Foreign Ministers in December 1945. An agreement was reached on the establishment of a unified Korean Provisional Government and a trusteeship up to five years by the four countries. However, there was no plan on how to form such a unified Provisional Government with Korea divided and occupied by the US and the USSR.

As a country that was divided and occupied after World War II, Austria in Europe can be cited as an example of achieving unification beyond the confrontation of the US and the USSR. As is well known, the Provisional Government established under the leadership of Karl Renner in Vienna, which was occupied by the Soviet Union at the time, won national support, and based on that, the proposal for a permanent neutrality was approved by the US and the USSR.

Koreans were not able to follow Austria's path. The real interest of the United States and the Soviet Union was in establishing governments friendly to their countries in their occupied parts of the Korean peninsula. Likewise, Korean political leaders were divided between the left and the right, and each depended on the US/Soviet military government in the South and North.

At the time of the founding of the country after liberation, there was no voice toward neutrality in Korean politics but an extreme division of the left and right. The claim of neutrality would be devalued as opportunistic and irresponsible by either side,

(B) Korean War: USA, Japan vs. USSR, China

The United States and the Soviet Union eventually failed to establish a unified Korean government. Instead, separate governments were established in South and North Korea. Afterwards, the US and Soviet troops withdrew from Korea and the military regime ended (1948), but the independence of South and North Korea was fragile. The two Koreas did not recognise each other as independent states. To South Korea, the North Korean regime was a rebel group, and vice versa. This logic of mutual negation would soon lead to war.

At the same time, in China, the Communist Party took control of the entire continent (1949) through the Chinese Civil War. Tens of thousands of Korean troops fought for the Chinese Communists and they later entered North Korea. The North Korean government began invading the South (1950) with the approval of Stalin and Mao. The military instructors dispatched from the Soviet Union guided the military strategy.

The US and the UN then intervened. The UN Security Council defined North Korea's invasion as a breach of the peace and resolved to impose military sanctions. The UN tried to secure troops from member states and set up a command headquarters within the UN, but the US did not agree. In the end, the name was the United Nations Command, but the command was held by the United States. The substance of the United Nations Command was the same as the US Far East Command, headquartered in Japan at the time. Also, during the Korean War, Japan served as a rear supply base for the US military.

The US forces repulsed North Korea and advanced beyond the 38th parallel, but retreated again below the 38th parallel due to the intervention of the Chinese Communists. The Korean War was a sort of proxy war between the two opposing camps of the world.

In the confrontation of the Cold War, South Korea and North Korea were incorporated into their respective camps. During the Korean War, South Korea transferred its military command to US commander MacArthur. Likewise, after the Chinese forces entered the war, the command of the North Korean forces was transferred to Peng De-huai (彭德怀), the commander of the Chinese forces. From a military standpoint, South and North Korea became protectorates of the confronting great powers respectively.

(C) Korean Armistice and Vietnam War: The US, Japan, and South Korea vs. USSR, China, North Korea

The Korean War ended with an armistice. Yet, US troops did not withdraw from South Korea. South Korea signed a mutual defence treaty with the United States, laying the groundwork for the stationing of US forces. The command of the Korean military, which was transferred to the United States during the Korean War, has not been fully restored. South Korea and the United States formed the ROK-US Combined Forces Command, which was commanded by a US general, and most units of the Korean army were under the operational command of the ROK-US Combined Forces Command.

The United States also urged South Korea to restore diplomatic relations with Japan. Although no military alliance has been created between Korea and Japan, the three countries have formed an organic military relationship through the distinct US-Japan alliance and the ROK-US alliance.

Chinese forces withdrew from North Korea in 1958. However, North Korea signed treaties of friendship and cooperation with both China and the Soviet Union in 1961. These two treaties provided for immediate military assistance from China and the Soviet Union in case North Korea is invaded by another country. In addition, important international issues should be discussed in advance. North Korea was formally not subordinate to China or the Soviet Union, but in practice, North Korea could not take military action on its own.

The Vietnam War broke out in the 1960s. In South Korea, the Park Chung-hee regime, which came to power through a military coup, actively proposed the dispatch of troops to Vietnam, expecting political recognition and economic aid from the United States. During the Vietnam War, South Korea dispatched nearly 50,000 troops a year, becoming the country that sent the most combat troops after the United States. As in the Korean War, Japan played a role as a military base-station in the Vietnam War. On the other hand, Vietnam's Ho Chi Minh forces received support from China and the Soviet Union, and North Korea also dispatched some troops, including the air forces.

As the Cold War confrontation deepened, the voice of neutrality could not be officially raised on the Korean peninsula. The US government only briefly considered neutrality for Korea as a post-Korean War armistice plan. In Korea, there were discussions about neutralisation among small opposition parties and scholars. But the permanent neutrality never become a meaningful agenda in Korean politics during the cold war period.

III. Dissolution of the Cold War: Isolation of North Korea

In the 1980s, Soviet Communist Party leader Gorbachev transformed the Soviet Union with reform and opening policies, eventually dissolving the Soviet system and ending the Cold War with the US "victory".

Amid these changes, the North Korean leader Kim Il-sung raised the neutralisation of the Korean peninsula as an official issue. For the 1987 summit between Soviet leader Gorbachev and US President Reagan, Kim Il-sung sent a proposal to resolve the Korean peninsula issue to Gorbachev, who forwarded it to President Reagan. Kim Il-sung proposed a confederation or federal system between North and South Korea, hoping that the Korean peninsula would become a neutral country and become a buffer zone for international relations.

The US and South Korea did not respond to this neutrality proposal. Instead, South Korea implements the so-called Northern Policy. In 1988, Seoul hosted the Olympics and invited the Soviet Union and China to participate. In 1990, South Korea established diplomatic relations with the Soviet Union and in 1992 with China. North Korea, which was put on the defensive, also actively worked to improve inter-Korean relations. Finally, in 1991, the Inter-Korean Basic Agreement was adopted, and both Koreas joined the United Nations at the same time. However, the United States and Japan were not active in improving relations with North Korea.

1n 1994, the North Korea's ruler Kim Il-sung died and the North Korean economic system began to collapse. North Korea suffered what will be recorded as one of the greatest famines of the 20th century. The country was thought to be about to collapse, and unification by absorption into South Korea was expected. The United States thought of a model of German reunification.

However, North Korea sought independent survival in isolation, which resulted in nuclear weapons development. China opposed North Korea's nuclear weapons, but did not neglect North Korea's collapse. China provided massive aid to North Korea. The Kim Dae-jung administration of South Korea successfully held a summit meeting with North Korea (2000) and pursued a policy of reconciliation and cooperation between the two Koreas, but it failed to attract a favourable response from the United States.

After the death of Kim Il-sung in July 1994, power was passed on to his son Kim Jong-il; later to his grandson Kim Jong-un, and the North Korean regime is muddling through a system crisis. The North Korean nuclear issue failed to find a solution, As North Korea succeeds in developing intercontinental ballistic missiles, military tensions between North Korea and the United States are rising. To make matters worse, peace on the Korean peninsula is getting farther away as the era of hegemonic competition between the US and China unfolds.

IV. The New Cold War era of the 21st century: The possibility of neutralising the Korean peninsula

The world is now witnessing a return to a new area of Cold War. In Europe, Russia invaded Ukraine in response to NATO's possible eastward movement, and in Asia, tensions between the US and China are deepening. China started global expansion with the One Belt, One Road policy, and the United States is attempting a containment policy. China is seeking to expand its maritime hegemony in the South China Sea and wants to maintain its dominion over Taiwan. In response, the United States insists on the compliance with international maritime laws and protect freedom of navigation, supporting Taiwan's independence and freedom.

In this situation, Korea is falling once again into a very difficult conundrum. Currently, many people are claiming a solution through the strengthening of the ROK-US-Japan military alliance. However, such a policy carries the risk of South Korea's possible involvement in the military confrontation between China and the United States. In the event of a military conflict between the United States and China, not only US troops stationed in Korea would be mobilised and the US military units in South Korea could be targeted by China.

Instead, this chapter proposes the neutralisation of the Korean peninsula. As we have already seen, the neutralisation of the Korean peninsula is not a new idea. It has been raised for Korea's survival and peace since at least the late 19th century, when continental and maritime powers collided on the Korean peninsula.

The classic principle of neutralisation is to ban all foreign military alliances and to ban foreign military presence and circulation. However, US forces are stationed in South Korea, and a ROK-US Mutual Defence

Treaty is still effective. North Korea also has a mutual military assistance treaty with China. These relationships cannot be dissolved all at once. It may cause another crisis caused by distrust and misunderstanding since the two Koreas are still in a state of armistice.

The neutralisation of the Korean peninsula should be understood as a gradual and step-by-step process. First, the wartime operational control over the South Korean military, which is currently held by the US military, will have to be returned to the Korean government. A militarily-dependent country cannot speak of neutrality.

The next step is to revise the Korea-US alliance and the North Korea-China alliance. South and North Korea must avoid getting involved in an armed conflict between the United States and China.

Eventually the Korean War Armistice Agreement must be replaced with a peace treaty. The peace treaty is to be signed by South Korea, North Korea, China and the United States, while Russia and Japan may participate as guarantors. Such a peace treaty would have to include the neutralisation of both South and North Korea.

And finally, the Korean peninsula should be made a nuclear-free zone, and the US army should withdraw or be turned into a kind of peacekeeping force.

*

In conclusion, some critics argue that neutrality between good and evil means cowardice. Yet, more often than not, neutrality means peace in between bad wars. The UN Charter is based on a distinction between good and bad wars but the United Nations' collective security, or police action, has rarely been conducted in accordance with the United Nations Charter. Neutrality prevents the spread of war and secures a safe zone. Neutrality helps to maintain peace and is consistent with the United Nations Charter.

At the end of the Joseon Dynasty, Korea's attempt to become a neutral country failed. At that time, Korea's national power was so insignificant that it could not become a meaningful player in the situation of Northeast Asia. However, today Korea is different from that time. If Korea declared neutrality, no great power would be able to ignore it as losing neutral Korea could mean losing hegemony in Northeast Asia.

Prospects of the "Greater Turkestan" idea in the wake of the EAEU's weakening

Yesbol OMIRZHANOV, Almagul TUSUPOVA,
Binur BERTAYEVA
Kazakhstan

In connection with the Russian "special military operation" in Ukraine, the geopolitical attitudes of many countries of the world have changed. In turn, political scientists began to speak of a possible failure of the Eurasian Economic Union (EAEU), of the Collective Security Treaty Organisation (CSTO) and of the possible emergence of new unions in the CIS territories.

This chapter analyses the situation in the post-Soviet space, the creation of a new regional union of Central Asian countries. It suggests that the time has come to implement the idea of a Greater Turkestan, proposed by Mustafa Shokay at the beginning of the 20th century. The main purpose here is to analyse the idea of strengthening the Organisation of Turkic States with the participation of the countries of Central Asia at a time of weakening of the EAEU. The chapter thus substantiates the implementation of the idea of Greater Turkestan, based on methods of system analysis, comparative analysis, as well as historical methods. It exposes the possibilities of implementing the idea of a Greater Turkestan in the current difficult geopolitical conditions.

I. The historical situation: A brief history of the origin and development of the idea of a "Greater Turkestan"

Towards the end of the 19th century, the idea of creating a unified state in Central Asia, in Turkestan, which is considered the centre of the Turkic world, came to the fore. The founders of the Greater Turkestan idea aimed to contribute to the strengthening of the Turkic world by creating a single strong state in Central Asia. Talking about a Greater Turkestan refers to the ideas of its spiritual leader M. Shokay.

«Aware of the multi-nationality of the peoples of Central Asia and Kazakhstan, M. Shokay saw real prospects for the consolidation of these peoples within the framework of a single political entity. Proof of this was the strong historical-ethnographic, economic and cultural tendencies towards unification, manifested in the mentality of the East. It was at the early stages of personality development that the political ideal of the state system of Turkestan as a federation of Turkic peoples was formed in the representation of M. Shokay»[1].

Shokav further suggested that "Turkestan is the land of the Turks. Turkestan has experienced a long period of deep crisis and decline. Part of the Turks moved to Asia Minor and founded the Ottoman Empire, which united most of the Muslim world under its banner, on the ruins of the Byzantine Empire. After the Amir Temur Age, a part of the Turks who remained in their homeland was divided into a few khanates, which based their independent existence only on personal pride".

This is saying that Turkestan is a part of three equal states in terms of ethnographic size, namely (a) Eastern (Chinese) Turkestan, which the Chinese changed to Xin-Jiang; (b) Western Turkestan (Russian, Soviet); (c) It is emphasised that it is Afghan Turkestan, which is called "Chahar vialet" (i.e., 4 provinces) and is divided into Badakhshan, Greater and Lesser Maymen and Andhoi provinces. Regarding the population, "The resident population of Turkestan consists of two unequal peoples – Turks and Tajiks. The first ones are known in Europe as "Kazakh", "Karakalpak", "Kyrgyz", "Turkmen", "Uzbek". They all speak the Turkic language common to all Turks from the Arctic Ocean to the Adriatic Sea[2]."

At the time when the Soviets came to power and carried out propaganda work on the idea that each nation should decide its own destiny, the Kokan autonomy was established on 28 November 1917 on the initiative of M. Shokay. The temporary government of the Kokan autonomy was formed, and M. Tynyshbayev was appointed as the Prime Minister,

---

1 Б.Сергазинов. Государственно-правовые взгляды М.Чокая: автореферат диссертации на соискание ученой степени кандидата юридических наук. А.: 2005. – С 15.

2 М.Шоқай. Түркістанның қилы тағдыры. А.: Жалын, 1992. 75 б.

and after his resignation, M. Shokay had come to this place. However, in January 1918, the government of worker-soldier deputies in Tashkent overthrew the autonomy, M. Shokay emigrated to a foreign country, and until the end of his life he was engaged in exposing the plight of Turkestan during the Soviet period to the Western public. In this regard, M. Shokay did not welcome the creation of several Soviet republics on the basis of national-territorial boundaries in the Central Asian space. Those Bolsheviks in this region "divide and rule!" He explained that he is following the policy[3].

There were supporters of Turkism among the Kazakh communists. T. Ryskulov and M. Kh. Sultan-Galiyev can be singled out among the communists on the communist platform who fought for the creation of a unified state of Turkestan. They tried to gain support from the Central Committee of the Russian Communist Party (Bolsheviks) while fighting against the chauvinistic influence of the local Russian communists. In the autumn of 1919, Muslim buro won a political victory in Turkestan, and all branches of power were taken over by Turkic representatives. Concerned about this, the Central Committee of the Russian Communist Party (Bolsheviks) organised the Turkic Commission in accordance with the resolution signed by Lenin on 8 October 1919, and sent it against the Muslim bureau. T. Ryskulov and other leaders of the Muslim bureau at first expressed great trust and hope in the Turkic Commission. But soon, the Muslim bureau headed by T. Ryskulov, who clearly felt the influence of the Turkic Commission, began to change its actions tactically. As a defensive ideology against the chauvinist interests and colonial policy of the Central Committee of the Russian Communist Party (Bolsheviks) and the Turkic Commission, the Turkic direction, that is, the idea of a whole Turkestan, was chosen.

As a way to implement it, the following two directions have been established: (1) by uniting the peoples living in Turkestan to the idea of "Turk", turning the republic into a republic of Turkic peoples from the legal point of view; (2) Forming separate national republics of the Turkic-speaking peoples inhabiting the republic and uniting them into the Turkic confederation[4]. Later, the founders were persecuted by Stalin,

---

3 М.Шоқай. Таңдамалы. А.: Қайнар, 1998. 1 том. – 21 б.

4 С.Шілдебай. 20 ғасырдың 1-ші жартысындағы Қазақстанның ұлт-азаттық қозғалысындағы түрікшілдіктің орны мен маңызы (тарихи

and the ideas of Turkism and Turkestan were pushed out of the scene of history thanks to the efforts of the communists.

II. The revival of the idea of a "Greater Turkestan" at the stage of post-Soviet development of Kazakhstan

However, in the period when the Soviet government was nearing its end, the Turkic idea and thoughts about Greater Turkestan began to rise again. On September 27–30, 1990, the congress of eastern peoples living in the USSR was held in Moscow. Khakassia, Yakutia, Azerbaijan, Tatarstan, Kazakhstan, Tajikistan, Uzbekistan, Bashkortostan, Gagauz Republic, Chechen-Ingushetia, Kyrgyzstan, Crimean Tatars, Nogais, RSFSR Representatives of social organisations and political parties of Orenburg, Omsk, Penza, Gorky regions took part[5]. At this meeting, for the first time, the Turkic-speaking peoples spoke openly about the violence against them, addressed the issues that should be resolved to the leaders of that time, and made their demands.

In March 1991, democratic political movements and parties in Central Asia united and formed the Central Asian Democratic Congress. It included political organisations such as Kazakhstan "Azat", "Zheltoksan", "Alash" along with Uzbekistan's "Unity" movement, the Democratic Party of Tajikistan, the Kyrgyz "Asaba" party and the Democratic Movement, and the Turkmen "Auzbirlik" movement[6]. On 25–26 May 1991, 13 political parties, movements and organisations from Central Asia and Kazakhstan became founders of the Democratic Congress Foundation which held its second meeting in Bishkek. In order to strengthen the foundation of the political union of the states, they made statements such as influencing the signing of a mutually beneficial economic agreement and the creation of voluntary cooperation of sovereign states on the basis of confederation of founding participants[7].

талдау): тарих ғылымдарының кандидаты ғылыми дәрежесін алу үшін дайындалған диссертацияның авторефераты. А.: 2001. – 21 б.

5 Ж.Бабалықов. ССРО-ны мекен ететін шығыс халықтарының құрылтайы. Азат. 1990 жыл қараша. 7 б.

6 Б.Дәрімбет. Азат қозғалысы. Алматы: Өркениет, 2001. 49 б.

7 Орта Азия мен Қазақстан Демократиялық Конгресінің мәлімдемесі. Азат. 1–15 маусым 1991. 2 б.

Within the framework of the Soviet policy, five republics divided into separate states, with their own independent structures and borders, could integrate with each other, create a common defence line, and form a common economic zone only by creating a confederation. Having fully understood this, the participants of the foundation put forward the creation of the "Greater Turkistan".

Among the leaders ofTurkic-speaking countries, only Abilfaz Elshibek, the President of Azerbaijan, said: "Our main aim is Turkic unity. It will be a new economic and cultural unity. There is no reason why such unity should not be possible. For this, a common dictionary should be created, a common encyclopaedia of history should be created. In this regard, first of all, cultural ties, and lastly, political ties should be strengthened"[8] [14, 2 б].

However, the authorities of Kazakhstan, closely connected with the Russian Federation; gave priority to the idea of creating a new union with Russia. The idea of creating a Eurasian economic union belongs to the First President of Kazakhstan, N. Nazarbayev. He announced it on 29 March 1994, during a lecture at M. Lomonosov Moscow State University. This idea was realised only after 20 years, the Treaty on the Eurasian Economic Union was signed on 29 May 2014 in the capital of Kazakhstan.

Before that, in 2010, Russia, Kazakhstan and Belarus formed the Customs Union. The agreement provided for the introduction of a single customs tariff for countries that are part of the union, as well as the elimination of internal customs duties. In 2011, the Free Trade Zone of the CIS was created. It included Armenia, Belarus, Russia, Ukraine, Kazakhstan, Kyrgyzstan, Moldova, Tajikistan and Uzbekistan (on special conditions).

The final stage of integration before the emergence of the EAEU was the creation of the Eurasian Economic Space, which provides "four freedoms": free movement of goods, capital, services and labour.

In addition to Kazakhstan, the EAEU includes Russia, Belarus, Kyrgyzstan and Armenia. According to the agreement, these undertake to conduct a coordinated economic policy: to levy the same customs tariffs on goods imported from outside the Union, and also to ensure the

---

8 Ә.Елшібек. Идеалымыз – Түрік бірлігі. Түрік бірлігі. 1992, №1. 2 б.

free movement of people, goods, capital and services within the Union. In addition, unified technical regulations for goods are established within the EAEU (member states do not have the right to establish their own regulations over the general list) and a coordinated macroeconomic, anti-monopoly and currency policy is implemented.

III. The perspective from Kazakhstan's multi-vectorial diplomacy

Kazakhstan, having followed and following a multi-vectorial approach in foreign policy, supported both the Eurasian Union just as the idea of Turkic unity. On 30 October 1992, at Turkey's president's initiative, Turgut Özal, the Turkic-Speaking States held their first Summit in Ankara[9]. Participants announced the establishment of political and economic unity. TURKSOY, the international organisation for the joint development of Turkic culture and art, a clear signature in world civilisation, was officially established on 12 July 1993 in Almaty. There, the Ministers of Culture of Azerbaijan, Kazakhstan, Kyrgyzstan, Turkmenistan, Turkey and Uzbekistan signed an international agreement on the establishment of the International Organisation of Turkic Culture. After that, the Turkic republics of the Russian Federation: Altai, Bashkortostan, Sakha (Yakutia), Republic of Tatarstan, Tuva and Khakas, as well as Gagauzia (Moldova) and the Turkish Republic of Northern Cyprus were admitted to TURKSOY as supervisory members[10].

On 3 October 2009, the Nakhchivan Agreement on the establishment of the Cooperation Council of Turkic-speaking countries was signed in Nakhchivan. According to this agreement, the Turkic-speaking countries agreed to cooperate not only on cultural cooperation, but also on security and peace of the region.

On 31 March 2021, the city of Turkestan was declared the spiritual capital of the Turkic world at the informal summit of the Cooperation Council of Turkic-speaking countries on the theme "Turkestan is the

9 Attended by Turgut Ozal, Abulfaz Elchibey, Islam Karimov, Nursultan Nazarbayev, Saparmurat Niyazov and Askar Akayev

10 Р. Ризуан. Түріксой ұйымы – түркі халықтарыны мәдениетінің бірлігі, 19.09.2019. Martebe.kz сайты. https://martebe.kz/

spiritual capital of the Turkic world”[11]. Indeed, the idea of Turkic unity has been well developed in the fields of culture, art, education and science but achievements in economic, political and military integration still were scarce. At this summit, Kazakhstan's Tokaev recalled the time needed to transform the Council of Cooperation of Turkic-speaking States into a full-fledged organisation: “It is obvious to everyone that the importance of the Turkic world in modern international politics has increased. We must express our position on regional and global issues. And our voice should be strong and clear.”

At the end of the summit, the leaders of the Turkic Council signed a declaration[12]. Clearly, Kazakhstan's President focuses about the development of political and economic cooperation with Turkic-speaking countries.

With the holding of the historic summit in Istanbul in November 2021, a new stage began for the Turkic states, which will be remembered as an important turning point for the Organisation, when the relations between the member states entered a new era of closer and comprehensive cooperation.

IV. The organisation of Turkic States

The transformation of the Turkic Council into the Organisation of Turkic States (OTS) and the adoption of its official doctrine under the name “Turkish Global Vision 2040” is a new impetus for the development of cooperation among Turkic-speaking countries. The members of the OTS are Turkey, Azerbaijan, Uzbekistan, Kazakhstan and Kyrgyzstan, with two Observers: Turkmenistan and Hungary. Special attention is attracted by Hungary, a country in which not only the linguistic identity of its main people is in doubt (previously its national doctrine was Turanism with an accent on Ugric, but in recent years it has begun to

---

11 Түркітілдес мемлекеттердің ынтымақтастық кеңесі бейресми саммитінің Түркістан Декларациясы, 31.03.2021. ҚР Президентінің ресми сайты. https://www.akorda.kz

12 А.Алиев. Тюрки всех стран, объединяйтесь… 14.04.2021//website TRT на русском. https://www.trtrussian.com

position itself as Turkic), but also differently from other participants is Christian, not Muslim[13].

The **doctrine "Turkic World Vision – 2040"** aims to develop a framework supporting the capacity of its members to address, individually and collectively, the challenges of our time. The existing spirit of cooperation will be harnessed to serve the fundamental objective of each Member State to raise the political, economic, social and cultural standards of their societies. Through cooperative mechanisms and joint projects, pooling of experiences and offering material and intellectual resources when needed, the Organisation will provide a robust and transparent platform of growing cooperation and solidarity.

This document covers all spheres of cooperation among members of the Organisation of Turkic States. It begins with Political and Security Cooperation. Political Cooperation Strengthen the regular mechanism of multilateral political consultations among the Member States on international and regional foreign policy issues of common interest and etc. Security Cooperation Build a network for cooperation and information sharing among the Member States to combat the threats of radicalisation, violent extremism, Islamophobia, xenophobia and terrorism, and to ensure border security.

The second block of cooperation is devoted to Economic and Sectoral Cooperation. Economic Cooperation Work towards achievement of free movement of commodities, capital, services, technologies and people among the Member States and includes the following areas: Transport and Customs, Information and Communication Technologies, Energy, Tourism, Health, Environment, Agriculture.

The third block is devoted to People-to-People Cooperation.[14] This document, according to experts, was compiled flawlessly from the point of view of international law and standards of the international community, since their principles are the basis of it. That is, the text of the document states adherence to "norms and principles of international law, including sovereign equality, territorial integrity and inviolability of internationally recognised borders and states". The overall idea of the

---

13 Х.Сидоров."Тюркский мир" и "русский мир": реалии и перспективы, 20.11.2021//website Idel.Реалии. https://www.idelreal.org/

14 Turkic World Vision. 2040. https://turkicstates.org/assets/pdf/haberler/turkic-world-vision-2040-2396-97.pdf

document is to strengthen regional and global cooperation, interaction with existing states and their associations[15].

V. The context post-2022: Questioning the EAEU interstate conflicts in the post-Soviet space as a new opportunity to implement the idea of "Greater Turkestan"

On 24 February 2022, Russia's "special military operation" in Ukraine began, after a period of concentration of Russian troops at the Ukrainian border and a crisis in relations between Russia and Ukraine.

Before the start of the war, Kazakhstan did not support the Kremlin's politicians on annexing part of the Ukrainian territory. On 22 February, Astana's Foreign Minister told journalists that "the issue of recognition for the Donetsk and Luhansk people's republics by Kazakhstan is not on the agenda"[16].

At the St Petersburg International Economic Forum (15–18 June 2022), Kazakhstan's Tokayev used the occasion to push back hard against territorial claims made on Kazakhstan by some Russian commentators, and to re-state his country's refusal to recognise Moscow-backed breakaway territories of Ukraine. "It has been calculated that if the right of nations to self-determination was realised in reality on the entire globe, over 500 or 600 states would emerge on Earth, instead of the 193 states that are currently part of the UN. Of course, that would be chaos," said Tokayev. "For this reason, we do not recognise Taiwan, or Kosovo, or South Ossetia, or Abkhazia. And in all likelihood, this principle will be applied to quasi-state entities, which, in our opinion, Luhansk and Donetsk are."[17]

Such behaviour of Kazakh politicians has its own explanations. After gaining independence, Russian state and public figures repeatedly openly

---

15 И.Хан. Тюркский мир на подъеме, "Русский мир" летит в пропасть. Как не повторить его ошибок? 15.11.2021 // Голос ислама.ru. https://golosislama.com/news.php?id=40268

16 Russia attempts to contrive appearance of support from Central Asian allies, 27.02.2022. website Eurasianet. https://eurasianet.org

17 Joanna Lillis. Kazakhstan-Russia frictions over Ukraine war go public, 20.06.2022. website Eurasianet. https://eurasianet.org

declared their territorial claims to Kazakhstan. In his essay "*Kak nam obustróit Rossíu?*", Alexander Solzhenitsyn called most of Kazakhstan's territory as a part of Russia, and many other Russian politicians continued to express similar ideas in recent years. The beginning of the war between Russia and Ukraine alarmed not only the population of Kazakhstan, but also its government.

Before the start of the war between Ukraine and Russia, the Eurasian Union was not particularly criticised, but after that, many experts openly declared that this Union was detrimental to Kazakhstan.

The well-known Kazakh economist Almas Chukin said in March 2022, a month after Russia's invasion of Ukraine, that "on the whole, the EAEU worked in favour of the strong." He summarised that over the past years, Russia has increased exports to Kazakhstan, but Kazakhstan to Russia has not. As a result, the negative balance of mutual trade amounted to 12 billion $/year. International business shifted the investment focus to the Russian Federation as the central market of the EAEU. Even warehouses of goods were centralised in the Russian Federation and the hubs were closed here. He also noted that "restrictive duties for foreign goods entering the EAEU made our life more expensive." As the main example, Chukin named automobile prices. As another expert Magbat Spanov explains, one of the biggest problems of the EAEU is its largely unilateral orientation[18].

The official government of Kazakhstan also does not deny the presence of negative factors in the Union. According to the Vice-Minister of Trade and Integration of Kazakhstan Zhanel Kushukova, the Union must ensure free access to the markets of its participants. However, Kazakh businessmen in the process of developing the Russian market, the largest in the EAEU, face various barriers. This is explained by the desire to protect the domestic market from competitors[19].

In turn, the heads of Turkic-speaking countries began to hold joint events frequently. The visits of the leaders of Turkic-speaking countries to each other also took place.

---

18 Никита Шамсутдинов. Зачем нужен Евразийский Экономический Союз, 08.09.2022. сайт Masa.Media. https://masa.media

19 М.Сарсенова. Жанель Кушукова: Барьеры в ЕАЭС как лакмусовая бумажка, 27.02.2023. website Капитал. https://kapital.kz/economic

The gathering of leaders in the Issyk-Kul Lake town of Cholpon-Ata on 21 July 2022, which was billed as a consultative meeting, was viewed as an opportunity for the region to pursue more integration and emerge from under the overbearing influence of neighbouring nations such as Russia and China. Kazakhstan's Tokayev said it was

> "extremely important to strengthen our unity and not to allow unnecessary competition with one another. (…) In this respect, the timely signing of the Treaty of Friendship, Good Neighbourliness and Cooperation for the Development of Central Asia in the 21st century is of particular importance. (…) We welcome the willingness of all parties to sign this historic treaty in the near future."[20]

On 11 November 2022, a summit of leaders of the Organisation of Turkic States was held in Samarkand, Uzbekistan, dedicated to the deepening of economic cooperation, improvement of transport corridors, food security and digitalisation among the five member states of the organisation (Azerbaijan, Kazakhstan, Kyrgyzstan, Turkey, Uzbekistan). The Samarkand summit was held under the motto "New era of Turkic civilisation: on the way to general development and prosperity".

During the extraordinary summit of the Organisation of Turkic States in Ankara (16 March 2023), Tokayev stated the importance of strengthening the cooperation of the Turkic world in the current geopolitical and economic situation in the world. "Our organisation has taken a worthy place in the international arena. Our countries need to bring political, economic and cultural interaction to a new level. This is one of the priority areas of Kazakhstan's foreign policy," Tokayev emphasised[21].

*

Analysing the current geopolitical situation in the world, we can conclude that the Idea of a Greater Turkestan can be implemented at the proper level in the near future. Of course, it will be a little different from what is was when proposed at the beginning of the 20th century,

---

20 Central Asia leaders' meeting fizzles as Tajiks, Turkmens refuse to sign treaty, 21. 07. 2022. website Eurasianet. https://eurasianet.org

21 *Президент Казахстана принял участие во внеочередном саммите Организации тюркских государств*
16.03.2023 // website Akorda. https://www.akorda.kz/

since today it is only possible to create a confederation of Turkic-speaking states, which includes not only the countries of Central Asia, but also Azerbaijan and Turkey. The idea of a Greater Turkestan has not come easy. It has evolved, supplemented by new ideas and will be implemented in the form of the Organisation of Turkic States. This organisation can eventually become a strong alliance that will serve the needs and aspirations of their people. It will become a platform for consultation and coordination among member states aimed at promoting peace, stability and security in their region and at the international level.

A Study on the transformation from the Linear Economy to a Circular Economy

Young-Geun CHAE
Korea

"Linear economy v. Circular economy" … As a solution to the global challenges of climate change and of loss in biodiversity, the transition to a circular economy is drawing attention around the world.[1] The linear economy model, which refers to the "take-make-waste" economy, has led to excessive consumption of resources and energy. The global population continues to grow rapidly, increasing demand for raw materials, while supplies are decreasing. The answer is to recognise that excessive consumption of resources is the root cause[2] and to minimise the use of resources and increase circulation within the economy. In a circular economy, waste does not exist and products are designed to be reused as long and intensively as possible, over and over again. Waste is the new raw material. If a product is broken, it will be repaired and if that is no longer possible, new products will be made from it. There is no longer the line of "produce, consume and then throw away". Instead, there is a closed loop of regeneration, where materials are restored by endless repair, reuse, refurbish, and recycle. This saves raw materials, reduces CO2 emissions and preserves the earth. It stimulates innovation, new business activities and employments. Smarter and more efficient use of resources will enable people to enjoy a prosperous life in a strong and sustainable economy.

1 "The biggest lever to push the circular industrial economy to the forefront may be a general perception that most of the topics jeopardizing world society, listed as the objectives of the UN Sustainable Development Goals … could be tackled simultaneously by the shift to a circular industrial economy." Walter R. Stahel, The Circular Economy: A User's Guide 90 (Routledge 2019).

2 It is estimated that 45 % of global CO2 emissions are due to the production of cars, clothing, food and other products that we use on a daily basis. In cities, the CO2 emissions from production of goods are higher than rural areas.

The current economy is deeply embedded in a linear economy. Economic actors, such as businesses, consumers, labourers, states are all segmented in the line of economic activities which consist of obtaining raw materials, manufacturing goods, consuming, transporting, financing, treating waste … Each specialised segment pursues its own efficiency and profitability. In most cases, "larger and more" is "better and higher" for their economic interest. Even for waste treatment plants, more waste means higher profit. For consumers this segmented linear economy brings convenience providing no hassle (purchasing goods and throwing them out). After all, huge amounts of materials are being extracted from the earth and the same amount are being incinerated or landfilled now. This is not sustainable.

This deeply embedded linear economy model is difficult to change. Traditional environmental policy addressed this matter from end-of-use material life by emphasising how to handle waste. Various policy tools were adopted. i/ In order to promote recycling of waste, government established as civic duty to separate recyclable waste and collecting system for those separated waste. ii/ The government adopted various policies to reduce waste, such as polluter paying waste charges, banning free plastic bags, getting rid of garbage cans in the public places, adopting an extended producer responsibility (EPR) regime … However, these end-of-life approaches could not really reduce waste. The effect of these policies is limited. The transition to a circular economy demands much more fundamental changes in the economy.

South Korea is natural-resource-poor, importing more than 90 % of its energy and resources. Nevertheless, it has developed a big manufacturing economy.[3] As a result, Korea's greenhouse gas emissions are the 8th largest in the world as of 2019, accounting for about 1.71 % of global emissions even if Korea's population accounts for only 0.7 % of the world's population. South Korea announced its plan to accomplish carbon neutrality by 2050. A circular economy can be an important instrument to tackle the climate crisis.

Since the Korean economy is highly dependent on imports, it frequently falls prey to the fluctuation of international prices of energy

3 The value added by the manufacturing sector as percent of GDP in 2021 was 25.46 %. For comparison, the world average in 2021 based on 157 countries is 12.32 %.

and resources. Therefore, a circular economy could be a good strategy to reduce its dependence on foreign natural resources as well.

I. Suggested alterations and transformations in the economic model

No single circular economy solution fits all. Transitions to a more circular economy require a holistic approach that involves a range of stakeholders and strategies. By focusing innovation, collaboration, and systemic change, it is possible to create a more sustainable and circular economy.

The method for transition requires, first, the redesigning of products and services, in order to reduce waste and increase reuse. It requires companies to design and develop products and services with no waste. Ideally, a circular product would be designed for indefinite reuse, created only with circular or sustainable materials, kept in useful life for as long as possible, and easy to disassemble into materials or components that can be brought back into a value-chain at the end of use at the highest possible value.[4] In true circularity, products and materials are indefinitely used and recirculated in a closed-loop system. This aims to redesign products to use less resource-intensive, single-use materials, and to prolong their use. The process can also enable the repurposing of products at end of use to deliver value beyond their first usage.

Second, at the use level, it is important to maximise the value delivered through the single use or multiple uses of a circular product or service in its original form. Products as a service or sharing platforms model would help maximise product utilisation. Product-use extension business-model such as maintenance or repair services, or reselling market would help multiple use of product.

Third, at the end of use, one would maximise the value delivered through multiple uses of a circular product or service in any form. This might include identifying circular uses for waste at end of use and repurposing it by recycling (or upcycling) as well as by creating or supporting a secondary materials market.

4 P. Lacy et al., The Circular Economy Handbook, 305 (2020)

Digitalisation would be much of help. The digital economy can be summed up as the economy based on digital technologies such as the internet of things, big data, blockchain and artificial intelligence. Innovative business models are rising, based on a closer relation with customers and mass customisation based on the smart applications. Numerous business activities are taking place on-line, reducing consumption of papers and off-line transportation. The use of new business models, such as product-as-a-service (selling the performance of goods instead of the goods themselves) or sharing economy models such as repair cafés, uber, or Airbnb encourage the long-term use and reuse of products. Accordingly, fewer products and fewer raw materials are demanded. New digital business models help maximise the efficiency of resource-use and lead to the decoupling of economic development and resource use.

We need to build circular supply chains. This involves changes to procurement, product specifications, and supply chain relations. This involves promoting collaboration and knowledge-sharing among stakeholders, including businesses, governments, and civil society organisations, and driving innovation and identifying new opportunities for circularity. This can involve sharing best practices, pooling resources, and co-creating solutions to common challenges. Research and development of new technologies and materials also support the circular economy. This involves public-private partnerships, academic research, and investment in start-ups and small and medium-sized enterprises. Innovation that reduces the costs of repairs and spare parts will boost the era of "R".[5] High volatility in commodity prices and the cost of labour can be drivers or obstacles for the eras of "R" and "D". Policymakers with a vision of the future can directly influence both factors through taxation.

A properly functioning circular economy does not depend only on the government and industry. Consumers, too, have a role. Choosing sustainable products must become the new standard. Consumers also contribute to a circular economy by using things longer, repairing them or taking them to the recycling shop. This behaviour can be stimulated

5 "The circular industrial economy manages the stocks of manufactured objects after the point of sale, which are controlled by the owner-users (called the era of 'R'), and the stocks of manufactured materials, controlled by economic actors recovering resources (called the era of 'D')." Walter R. Stahel, The Circular Economy: A User's Guide 16 (Routledge 2019).

by giving the circular economy a place in education and by conducting campaigns.

There are significant barriers that can make it challenging to promote a circular economy. First, lack of awareness and understanding. Many businesses, policymakers, and consumers may not be aware of the benefits of a circular economy or how to transition to circular business models. This can make it difficult to build support for policy tools and drive change.

Second, economic and political interests. The linear economy model is deeply embedded in the global economy, and there may be economic and political interests that resist the transition to a circular economy. This can include industries that rely on resource extraction and consumption, as well as political systems that prioritise short-term growth over long-term sustainability. Policymakers may face pressure from interest groups or may prioritise short-term economic interests over long-term sustainability goals.

Third, regulatory and legal barriers, existing regulations and laws may not support or may even hinder the transition to a circular economy. This can include regulations that favour resource extraction and consumption, or laws that make it difficult to implement circular business models.

Fourth, infrastructure and technological barriers. The transition to a circular economy may require significant changes to infrastructure, technology, and supply chains. This can be challenging, particularly in industries that have long-established systems and processes.

Fifth, financial barriers. The transition to a circular economy may require significant upfront investments in new technologies, infrastructure, and supply chains. This can be a barrier for small and medium-sized enterprises, as well as for governments and other organisations that may face budget constraints.

Lastly, cultural and behavioural factors. Cultural and behavioural factors can also be a barrier to implementing circular economy policy tools. For example, consumers may be resistant to change or may not prioritise sustainability when making purchasing decisions.

II. Circular Economy in the EU and the Netherlands

The EU and European countries are leading the way in this direction. The Netherlands is often even cited as a leader in the circular economy.

(A) Legislative Efforts of the EU

The European Union launched the European Green Deal in December 2019 and set a roadmap for transforming the EU into a climate-neutral and circular economy by 2050. The European Green Deal is the EU's flagship initiative for creating a more sustainable and low-carbon economy. The EU adopted many other initiatives aiming at reducing greenhouse gas emissions, protecting biodiversity, and promoting sustainable agriculture, among others.

The EU Circular Economy Action Plan is a key part of the Green Deal. The Action Plan is essential for achieving the Green Deal's objectives, as it seeks to reduce resource consumption and waste, while promoting a more efficient and sustainable use of resources. The Circular Economy Action Plan is a comprehensive policy framework that aims to transform the European economy into a circular and sustainable model, where resources are used more efficiently and waste is minimised. The Action Plan was adopted in March 2020 and is part of the EU's efforts to achieve its environmental and climate goals, as well as to boost competitiveness, innovation, and job creation.

The plan consists of many initiatives and measures such as proposals for the Waste Framework Directive, the creation of a sustainable products policy and a sustainable finance strategy, … and more.

The proposed EU waste legislation, the Waste Framework Directive includes the following. Frist, harmonised definitions and calculation methods for waste management, which will make it easier to compare data and monitor progress towards waste reduction targets. Second, binding waste reduction targets for Member States, including a target to reduce municipal waste generated per capita by 10 % by 2030 and to achieve a 55 % municipal waste recycling target by 2025 and a 65 % municipal waste recycling target by 2035. Third, schemes of extended producer responsibility (EPR) for certain products, which will require producers to take more responsibility for the environmental impact of their products throughout their lifecycle. Fourth, strengthened requirements for separate collection of waste, including separate collection of bio-waste by 2023, which will improve the quality of recycled materials and reduce the amount of waste sent to landfill. Fifth, stricter rules on hazardous waste, which will improve the management of hazardous waste and reduce the risk to human health and the environment.

In line with Better Regulation[6], the Commission will draft an impact assessment report in support of this revision to set out the options and assess their impacts. The adoption of revision of EU waste framework is planned in the second quarter of 2023.

The Sustainable Products Initiative (SPI) is a proposal by the EU to make products placed on the EU market more sustainable throughout their life cycle, from production to disposal. This policy will require manufacturers to design and produce more sustainable products that can be easily repaired, reused or recycled, and that contain a minimum amount of hazardous substances. The Sustainable Products Initiative aims to address the environmental impact of products by setting out minimum sustainability requirements, such as resource efficiency, durability, reparability, and recyclability, and by encouraging the use of more sustainable materials and production processes. The initiative also aims to promote the development of new business models, such as product-as-a-service and circular design, which can help reduce waste and increase resource efficiency. The Sustainable Products Initiative will cover a range of products, including electronics, textiles, furniture, and construction materials. The European Commission has been engaging with stakeholders through workshops and meetings to discuss the details of the initiative and gather feedback.

The Commission is expected to publish a legislative proposal for the initiative in 2023, which will then need to be approved by the EU Parliament and the EU Council.

A new regulatory framework for the circular economy also aims to prevent greenwashing. The European Commission is preparing the Green Claims Directive (GCD). This aims to crack down on greenwashing by regulating how companies substantiate and communicate their

---

6 The Better Regulation agenda requires evidence-based and transparent EU law-making based on the views of those that may be affected. https://ec.europa.eu/info/law/better-regulation/have-your-say/initiatives/13225-Environmental-impact-of-waste-management-revision-of-EU-waste-framework_en (2023.4.8.visit)

green claims. For the first time, legislation will oblige companies to make supporting evidence available alongside a green claim. The legislative proposal indicates that legal obligations would apply to all claims and labels displayed in products, services or companies in both physical and online points of sale across the EU single market. While the original aim was to oblige companies to substantiate their environmental claims using the Product Environmental Footprint (PEF) method, the Commission has now expanded its scope to regulate all types of green claims, including also those not covered by the PEF.

The EU is also supporting for sustainable and circular business models by various measures such as the creation of a platform for the exchange of best practices and the provision of funding and technical assistance for businesses transitioning to circular economy models. Overall, the EU Circular Economy Action Plan represents a significant shift in the EU's approach to resource management and sustainability, and is expected to have a significant impact on the European economy and the environment.

(B) The Netherlands

In 2016, the Dutch government launched its National Circular Economy Programme (NCEP), which aims to achieve a 50 % reduction in the use of primary raw materials[7] by 2030, compared to the baseline year of 2015, and fully circular economy by 2050.

In January 2017, in the Hague, 180 parties signed the Raw Materials Agreement (RMA) which sets out what is to be done to ensure that the Dutch economy can run on renewable resources. The agreement was signed by parties from both government and industry. The government and the signatories to the Raw Materials Agreement drew up five transition agendas, focusing on five sectors and value chains that are important to the economy but also have a high environmental burden. These are (1) plastics, (2) consumer goods, (3) manufacturing, (4) construction,[8] and (5) biomass and food. The agendas set out how these sectors can become circular by 2050, and what actions need to be taken.

---

7 Metals (including iron, aluminium, and copper, which are commonly used in construction, electronics, and transportation), fossil fuels (coal, oil, and gas), biomass (wood, crops, and waste materials), minerals (sand, gravel, and stone), plastics.

8 The construction sector accounts for 50 % of raw materials consumption in the Netherlands. A large proportion of our waste comes from demolition.

Thus, governments, industry and civil society organisations have joined forces to accelerate the transition to a circular economy. All actions that these partners work on are gathered in the Circular Economy Implementation Programme (CEIP) . The Programme provides an overview of circular economy developments and new activities that are being launched, and reports on the progress of activities that were already under way. Under this Programme, efforts are being made through five transitional agendas, ten cross-cutting themes and at regional level, with projects that yield valuable experience and lessons for central government policy and with the best combination of instruments.

The Circular Economy Implementation Programme included, for example, (1) lithium-ion batteries to be recycled at the end of their life; (2) the textile sector put Extended Producer Responsibility; (3) The Central Government Real Estate Agency and Rijkswaterstaat must make their operations circular by 2030. All government buildings constructed after 2018 must be energy neutral. As many recycled or recyclable materials and resources as possible will be used in the construction and redevelopment of real estate. The Implementation Programme will be updated regularly.

The Ministry of Infrastructure and Water Management will organise the annual National Circular Economy Conference at which stakeholders discuss progress with the circular economy. This might lead to adjustments to the Implementation Programme. Every two years, the Netherlands Environmental Assessment Agency (PBL) will publish a progress report. In the intervening years, an interim report will be issued. The findings and recommendations of the report may lead to adjustment of the implementation program. The Circular Economy Implementation Program has ten cross-cutting themes that play a role in each of the transition agendas. The country is also home to several innovative circular initiatives and has established a Circular Economy Hotspot to showcase these initiatives.

The transition to a circular economy in the Netherlands is being led by several government departments, each with their own specific areas of responsibility. The main department responsible for the circular economy is the Ministry of Infrastructure and Water Management, which is responsible for developing and implementing policies related to waste management, sustainable production, and resource efficiency.

III. Implication for South Korea

In 2021, South Korea announced the Korean Circular Economy Implementation Plan, and derived detailed policy tasks to promote the transition to a circular economy. Furthermore, in December 2022, the Circular Economy Transition Promotion Act was enacted to establish a legal basis for activating the transition to a circular economy. The National Assembly amended the preexisting the Framework Act on Resource Circulation and changed the title of the law to the Circular Economy Transition Promotion Act. This law reflects the global concerns on the sustainable economy and implementation of carbon neutrality and green growth goals. The revised law aims a sustainable circular economy by promoting efficient use of resources, restraining waste generation, and encouraging circular use in the entire process of production, consumption, and distribution of products.

The revised law defined the "circular economy" as "an eco-friendly economic system that minimises input of resources and energy by increasing the sustainability of products and establishing a circulation network of discarded resources." For implementation of the policy, the law (i) added the waste reduction rate as an indicator to the national circular economy goal setting, (ii) expanded the revenues of the circular economy special account so that local governments can more stably promote circular economy transition projects, (iii) extended the duration of the waste disposal charge to 2028, (iv) adopted the "circular use evaluation" system for products. The circular use evaluation system will consider (i) the use of recycled raw materials or eco-friendly materials and methods, (ii) the accessibility of repair, (iii) the possibility of circular use throughout the entire process, (iv) carbon emissions throughout the entire process.

The revised law advanced by improving its focus from waste to a more holistic approach, but in terms of policy tools it has still long way to go. The Ministry of Environment (MoE) is responsible for implementing the law. Currently, the MoE is the most enthusiastic within cabinet on this issue. However, the MoE has limitation in its administrative jurisdiction on adopting and implementing more effective policy tools. Obviously other government ministries such as the Ministry of Economy and Finance (MoEF) or the Ministry of Trade, Industry and Energy (MoTIE) which have broader authorities on economic policy-making are not as enthusiastic as the MoE. More effective transitional policy tools, such as taxation or government procurement rules could only be adopted with the support of the MoEF and of the MOTIE. The government itself should share the goal of circular economy inside and adopt coherent policy tools. Indeed, a circular economy is a more economic agenda.

The government should be active in spreading and sharing the goal of a circular economy among various stakeholders.[9] The strong expectation on economic growth and industrial development, which often come at the expense of environmental and social considerations is the biggest challenge which the transition faces. Thus, it is paramount to increase awareness and engagement among businesses and consumers, and to build more effective collaboration and partnerships among various stakeholders. The Korean government has to support the development of circular industries by providing financial incentives for companies that adopt circular business models and promoting the use of eco-friendly products through procurement policies. In addition, the government has to invest in research and development of new technologies and materials that support the transition to a circular economy.

*

In conclusion, to create a circular economy, changes are needed worldwide. This is due to the fact that raw material supply chains and waste flows are global. And not all waste products or materials end up within a country. Also, many businesses operate internationally. That's why the government needs to work with other governments in bilateral, regional and global settings.

---

9 An example of multistakeholder platforms in the Netherlands is the Platform for Accelerating the Circular Economy (PACE), with more than 40 members. The Netherlands also co-hosted the World Circular Economy Forum + Climate in April 2021. This global conference raised awareness about the circular economy in general, and the opportunities for the circular economy to help reach our climate goals in particular.

Part II

Legal, political and economic impact on commercial institutions (EAEU, EU …) and cooperation agreements (Silk Roads …)

Introduction

Sagyngaliy AIDARBAYEV
Kazakhstan

The second part of this book is entitled *Legal, political and economic impact on commercial institutions (EAEU, EU…) and cooperation agreements (Silk Road,…)*. Within this part, two groups of problematic issues are presented – issues of a global and issues of a regional nature. Among the global issues, the legal aspects of the global tax reform are considered; second, the geopolitical consequences of anti-Russian sanctions after the commencement of military operations in Ukraine. The second group of problems covers regional issues (Eurasia), subregional ones (EAEU, EU) and country-focused issues (Korea, Japan, Kazakhstan).

Chapters analyse various problems of resolving contentious issues. In particular, authors analyse the prospects for applying the WTO experience in resolving disputes for Kazakhstan, the opportunities that open up for Korea and all countries on the Eurasian continent as a result of the adoption of a new Convention on mediation, the prospects for the normalisation of Korean-Japanese relations in connection with the settlement of the issue of the payment of Japanese compensation for the forced labour of Korean women during World War II. A separate chapter is devoted to a comparative analysis of the advantages and disadvantages of customs protection of intellectual property rights within the EAEU and the EU.

In "Legal Aspects of the Global Tax Reform", Ilya Lifshits notes that the global tax reform, being developed from 2021 under the auspices of the OECD, should make a radical change in the approach to taxing multinational enterprises. The first pillar of this reform is the taxation of income, regardless of the physical presence of an international company in the tax jurisdiction, the second is the introduction of a minimum global corporate tax of 15 % of revenue. These changes suggest that the jurisdiction of origin of a multinational enterprise will be entitled to levy additional tax if the effective tax rate on the global profits of such an enterprise is less than the minimum corporate rate.

These changes were made to the new multilateral Convention in 2023. All these developments are the beginning of a major reform in the field of cross-border taxation, which should bring it into wider interaction with international law. The author concludes that after the implementation of the multilateral convention, the international community will move closer to the emergence of a new international tax regime, which is likely to replace the old tax avoidance schemes.

Remus Titiriga, in "Sanctions related to Russian military actions in Ukraine: consequences and future", suggest that Russia has lost the chance to become a superpower again and is turning into a regional power. Therefore, its chances to be more active in the international arena are rapidly decreasing. Regardless of the outcome of the war in Ukraine, the economic, political and demographic damage resulting from the sanctions (and the war itself) will have an effect on Russia at least for another generation.

The author states that the geopolitical situation in Europe after Russia's military aggression against Ukraine has completely changed, as the EU's energy dependence on Russian hydrocarbons has been reduced to a minimum. Changes that took place in Europe have caused energy problems around the world, especially in countries such as Japan, Korea and Taiwan, who rely on LNG as their main source of energy. R. Titiriga sums up that sanctions against Russia simultaneously serve as a deterrent for China in relation to the South China Sea and Taiwan.

The review of the second group of problems, which covers regional (Eurasia), subregional (EAEU, EU) and country (Korea, Japan, Kazakhstan) issues, should begin with the chapter by Zhuldyz Sairambaeva and Madina Nurtai "Customs protection of intellectual property rights within the Eurasia Economic Union and the European Union". The authors juxtapose and analyse the advantages and disadvantages of the customs protection of intellectual property rights within the EAEU and the EU. They believe that the customs legislation of the EU and the EAEU has many common features, both due to the presence of a single international legal framework, and in connection with the use of European experience in the EAEU.

The general conclusion is that, at the EU level, more effective methods of combating counterfeiting have been developed and an effective customs protection mechanism has been created. According to the authors, it is necessary to establish in the EAEU the application of the "ex officio" principle throughout the territory of the EAEU, which will allow initiating cases of administrative offenses and procedures for suspending the release of goods without including intellectual property objects in the customs register. In addition, it is advisable to extend customs protection to such intellectual property items as patents, industrial designs, utility models, selection achievements and integrated circuit layouts.

Three reports from the second group of reports, which have a general regional and country character, are devoted to different aspects of resolving international disputes.

Zulfiya Baimagambetova and Assem Akhmetova, in "Dispute Resolution in the WTO: International Experience and Prospects for Kazakhstan", note that from the moment of accession to the WTO in 2015 and until 31 March 2023, Kazakhstan was a party to one dispute as a defendant and as a third party in 35 trade disputes within the WTO. The authors review the WTO dispute resolution mechanisms, analyse the problems that Kazakhstan may face when using these mechanisms, and offer recommendations for improving the state's participation in the WTO dispute resolution mechanism.

The chapter provides a list of disputes in which Kazakhstan participated as a third party. It also substantiates the need to study the experience of other countries, argues the need for highly qualified specialists in the field of international law and trade policy for the country's effective participation in the WTO dispute resolution mechanism. The authors recommend that Kazakhstan actively use cooperation with countries that already have experience in the field of dispute resolution within the WTO, as well as strengthen its expert resource.

In "Normalising Korea-Japan Relations: Comfort Women Agreement and Forced Labour Compensation Judgment," Sung-Kee Hong reviews the 2015 Korea-Japan Comfort Women Agreement and the 2018 Supreme Court of Korea ruling on compensation for the forced labour of such women. In his opinion, the provision of the 1965 Property and Claims Settlement Agreement for a "full and final settlement" of "all claims by one State Party and its nationals against another State Party and its nationals" also covers the situation of comfort women.

Moreover, according to the author, the issue of comfort women appears to be a typical case of sovereign immunity. Even if sovereign immunity is excluded and the decision is in favour of the plaintiff against the state, it is almost impossible to enforce, so there is no need for the judiciary to cause disagreement with neighbouring countries with an unnecessary decision.

Indeed, one must agree with the view that the decision of the Supreme Court of the Republic of Korea - that Japanese colonial rule was illegal under the Korean constitution - is an unacceptable logic because it goes beyond the 1965 Property and Claims Settlement Agreement and ignored the 1965 Treaty on the Basic Relations between Korea and Japan. The illegality of colonial domination must be judged by the international law of that time, that is, the time of imperialism. The current domestic rules should not be used as a tool to interpret the illegality of colonialism. No domestic motive whatsoever can justify a domestic judicial decision that violates international law. In accordance with the Vienna Convention on the Law of Treaties of 1969, states must not violate treaty obligations under the guise of their constitutions.

The general conclusion of the author is that the deterioration of bilateral relations between Korea and Japan on this issue was mainly due to the fact that the Korean government shied away from taking appropriate measures. In conclusion, Korea, which is a party to the 1965 Property and Claims Agreement, should not unilaterally interpret or modify the treaty to the exclusion of Japan, which is the other party.

Guillermo Palao, in "Singapore Mediation Convention – An Opportunity for Korea", draws attention to the legal fragmentation of Eurasia and the lack of common international rules on the continent, which make it problematic to resolve international commercial disputes here, creating a high level of uncertainty and costs for the parties. In 2018, the UN Convention on International Settlement Agreements Reached as a Result of Mediation (Singapore Convention) was adopted, which slightly alleviates this problem, expanding the possibilities for alternative ways to resolve international commercial disputes in the Eurasia region. The Convention has been applicable since 12 September 2020. Not only states, but also international organisations of regional economic integration, can be parties to the Convention. Although the title of the chapter refers to an opportunity for Korea, the text refers to recommendations for all countries of Eurasia.

Prior to the adoption of the Singapore Convention, international mediation lacked such a contractual act that would promote mediation as a way to resolve international trade disputes. The author concludes that it is expected that the Singapore Convention will play a decisive role in facilitating mediation, which in turn, will contribute to the further development of international trade.

Thus, chapters in part II of the book give an idea of the state and dynamics of the Eurasian legal systems – both national and international (global and regional) – in the context of economic cooperation in the context of geopolitical changes.

Legal aspects of the global tax reform

Ilya LIFSHITS
Russia

Over decades after WWII, globalisation and the multilateral trade system failed to substantially influence national tax systems. International cooperations in the fiscal field were limited by double taxation issues and information exchange. Taxes remained almost an internal matter and states were reluctant to assume taxation commitments. Taxes remained the "Cinderella" of international law.

In the late 1980s, R. Martha wrote that international fiscal law was practiced by fiscalists who usually deny a role to international law[1]. Thirty years later, C. Braumann notes again that scholars of public international law have historically not paid attention to international tax law[2]. On the contrary, with international trade regime embracing the GATT and the WTO, or with the financial stability regime led by the IMF, no multilateral treaty existed between a substantial number of jurisdictions in the tax sphere. State tax measures could be challenged in national courts or in international courts belonging to other regimes: trade (WTO DSB), human rights (ECtHR), investment protection (investment tribunals).

This began to change after the 2007–2009 financial crisis. In 2014, the OECD plan addressing tax base erosion and taxable base shifting was approved (Addressing BEPS)[3]. This previously served as an "umbrella" that covered almost all international tax initiatives. Established in 2016

---

1 International Tax Law. Theory and Practice of Legislative Fiscal Jurisdiction by Rutsel Silvestre J. Martha. [Deventer: Kluwer. 1989. xxxii + 202 pp. ISBN 90-6544-416-5.] At 1.

2 Céline Braumann, Taxes and Custom: Tax Treaties as Evidence for Customary International Law, *Journal of International Economic Law*, 2020, 23, At 747.

3 OECD website: http://www.oecd.org/tax/beps/addressing-base-erosion-and-profit-shifting-9789264192744-en.htm (last accessed: April 15, 2023).

by the OECD and the G-20, This Inclusive Framework with a substantial number of participating jurisdictions has become a site not only for elaborating soft law recommendations on amending the national legal orders, but also as a treaty drafting body.

The Multilateral Convention to Implement Tax-Treaty-Related Measures to Prevent Base Erosion and Profit Shifting[4] was elaborated and signed over short periods by 100 jurisdictions. The unique international legal mechanism of this convention ensured amendment of 2000 double taxation agreements. More than 140 jurisdictions signed the Multilateral Convention on Mutual Administrative Assistance in Tax Matters[5] which created a global tax transparency regime.

This chapter covers the mode chosen by the international community to address digitalisation of the economy and globalisation. It describes the challenges of international taxation that had to be addressed (I), overviews the two pillars of the global tax reform (II and III) and presents the instruments of international law that will be used during the current changes (IV).

I. Digitalisation and taxation

In approving the "Addressing BEPS" plan, the participating states had to think about challenges for international taxation arising with regard to the digitalisation of the economy. The main aspect of the problem was in the specifics of digital services (for example app stores, online advertising, cloud computing, participative networked platforms[6]) that can be sold to customers remotely, i.e., without the supplier having to be physically present at the customer's location. Consequently, the provider of the digital services in the customer's jurisdiction (so-called marketing jurisdiction) may not establish a branch office, subsidiary or other site of presence. Thus, such providers may not create a permanent establishment in the marketing jurisdiction due to the double taxation treaties (DTT)

---

4 Ibid, https://www.oecd.org/tax/beps/multilateral-convention-to-implement-tax-treaty-related-measures-to-prevent-BEPS.pdf (last accessed: April 15, 023).

5 Ibid, https://www.oecd.org/ctp/exchange-of-tax-information/convention-on-mutual-administrative-assistance-in-tax-matters.htm (last accessed: April 15, 2023).

6 OECD (2015), *Addressing the Tax Challenges of the Digital Economy, Action 1 – 2015 Final Report*, OECD/G20, Base Erosion and Profit Shifting Project, OECD Publishing, Paris. At 58–62

currently in force; and the multinational entity (MNE) derives income from the marketing jurisdiction but is not obliged to pay a corporate tax there.

The situation when a state cannot impose corporate tax on the income of MNEs deriving from this state is perceived as unfair since revenue sourced from the state is treated as its national heritage in the contemporary world. As a result of such an injustice, states began implementing so-called digital taxes that obliged the customers to withhold taxes from the gross revenue due to digital service suppliers. Thus, the customers had to act as tax agents. However, the tax agent model could not be applied to customers who were physical persons due to ineffective tax administration. The outcome was found in the imposing of the obligation on digital companies to register as taxpayers in the marketing jurisdiction (so-called "landing" of the digital companies).

Multiple digital taxes have obviously become a significant obstacle hampering international trade. Moreover, the imposition of taxes on gross revenue contradicts the economic substance of business taxation, which should depend on the results of activities. Pistone noted that turnover taxation resulted in a new form of duplication of the tax burden, with considerable negative repercussions for business in cross-border relations[7]. Moreover, in response to digital tax initiatives, the US threatened to impose trade measures and revoked the bill once the agreement on the tax deal (see below) was reached.[8] Thus, widespread digital services, states' combat for the national tax base and uncoordinated implementation of the digital taxes have led to serious dangers for international trade. As a result, in 2021, an agreement on reforming the taxation of MNE was reached at the G7 level[9], and then at the G20

7 Pasquale Pistone, The Faltering Legitimacy of the Place of Physical Presence as a Tax Nexus for Active Income, in: Building Global International Tax Law Essays in Honour of Guglielmo Maisto Editor: Pasquale Pistone, IFBD, 2022, at 163

8 Joint Statement from the United States, Austria, France, Italy, Spain and the United Kingdom Regarding a Compromise on a Transitional Approach to Existing Unilateral Measures During the Interim Period Before Pillar 1 is in Effect, URL: https://home.treasury.gov/news/press-releases/jy0419 (last accessed: April 15, 2023).

9 G7 Finance Ministers & Central Bank Governors Communiqué, 5 June 2021, London, United Kingdom URL: https://home.treasury.gov/news/press-releases/jy0215 (last accessed: April 15, 2023).

level[10]. The OECD/G20 Inclusive Framework on Base Erosion and Profit Shifting has become an international body tasked with elaborating the details of the reform. This body announced that an agreement on the global tax reform was reached in October, 2021.[11]

According to the IF Statement, the proposed reform of taxation of multinational enterprises includes 2 Pillars.

The first of these elements provides unified rules for the inclusion of part of the revenue of multinational enterprises in the taxable base in the marketing jurisdiction, that is, it establishes a new principle of international taxation on the possibility of taxing the income of multinational enterprises by the state even without creating a Permanent Establishment in it.

The second element of the reform involves the introduction of a minimum corporate tax of 15 % of revenue, which opens a new page in solving the problem of tax competition among jurisdictions offering reduced or zero rates to divisions of multinational companies. The reform i/ was stimulated by the challenges associated with the widespread use of digital services, and ii/ is linked to the abolition of taxes on digital services. However, this is in fact a new taxation procedure for all international groups of companies (MNE), with some exceptions (see below).

This transformation of the international tax agenda has already been noted by researchers[12]. We will now look at both elements of the reform in more detail.

---

10 Third G20 Finance Ministers And Central Bank Governors Meeting | 9 -10 July 2021 – Communiqué, URL: http://www.g20.utoronto.ca/2021/210710-finance-press-release.html (last accessed: April 15, 2023).

11 Statement on a Two-Pillar Solution to Address the Tax Challenges Arising from the Digitalisation of the Economy – 8 October 2021 URL: https://www.oecd.org/tax/beps/statement-on-a-two-pillar-solution-to-address-the-tax-challenges-arising-from-the-digitalisation-of-the-economy-october-2021.htm (last accessed: April 15, 2023).

12 Ponomareva, Karina A. 2022. "New models of taxation of the income of international groups of companies: Analysis and prospects of use in Russia". *Vestnik of Saint Petersburg University. Law* 4: 1007–1021. https://doi.org/10.21638/spbu14.2022.411 (In Russian) at 1011.

II. International tax reform: Pillar I

The first fundamental element of the reform establishes a principle: taxation of revenue of multinational enterprises (MNE) in the jurisdiction where goods or services are used or consumed[13]. Thus, the new taxation rules will apply not only to digital, but to any goods and services, with the exception only of extractives and financial services[14].

Only 25 % of the profit exceeding 10 % of the revenue generated in the marketing jurisdiction will be taxed. The new rules apply to MNEs with a total revenue of more than USD 20 billion and only in cases when the revenue of a multinational enterprise in such a jurisdiction is more than EUR 1 million (for small jurisdictions with a GDP of less than USD 40 billion, this threshold has been lowered to USD 250 thousand). If, for example, an MNE in a marketing jurisdiction generates a revenue of USD 100 million and a profit of USD 22 million, then only USD 3 million will be taxed [(22 – 10 % x 100) x 25 %]. At that, for the tax paid in the marketing jurisdiction, the rules on the elimination of double taxation will be applied in the form of exemption from taxation of already-taxed profits. Or alternatively, depending of the DTT, it would be possible to credit the tax paid in the marketing jurisdiction from the tax payable in another jurisdiction with which an international Double Taxation Treaty has been concluded.

This provides for the introduction of a mandatory and legally binding mechanism for the prevention and resolution of disputes both in terms of avoiding double taxation of the amount of taxable profit (the so-called "Amount A") and in terms of the rules for determining the size of this amount[15]. There are plans to develop, sign and put into force the Multilateral Convention, which will provide for the procedure for determining the "Amount A", as well as the removal of unilateral measures – taxes on digital taxes and other similar measures[16]. The Convention should provide for a prohibition against introducing such measures in the future. This part of the Statement actually reflects the

---

13 Statement on a Two-Pillar Solution to Address the Tax Challenges Arising from the Digitalisation of the Economy – 8 October 2021 at 2.

14 Ibid. at 1.

15 Statement on a Two-Pillar Solution to Address the Tax Challenges Arising from the Digitalisation of the Economy – 8 October 2021 at 2.

16 Ibid., at 3.

deal that underlay the reform – the introduction of taxation in a market jurisdiction in exchange for the abolition of the digital services tax.

As of today, the provisions of the Multilateral Convention concerning the tax on digital services and other similar measures[17] have been published, as well as feedback from market participants on this project[18]. The draft contains two articles defining the scope of the concept of "Digital services tax or relevant similar measure" (Article 38 Paragraph 2 and Paragraph 3), as well as the obligation not to apply any such measures (Article 1). If a party to the Convention does apply the DST for any period, then it is no longer entitled to tax the amount of the profits distributed to that party under "Amount A" (Article 38 Paragraph 1). More than 30 reviews have been received for the project: criticism of the project mainly concerns the highly limited scope of the concept of DST. In addition, the proposed model of the consequences of violating the obligation not to apply DST has faced criticism – market participants consider the norm to be an ineffective provision when, in fact, the country gets a choice between applying DST or receiving a tax from "Amount A".

III. International tax reform: Pillar II

The essence of the second Pillar Element is to establish a minimum corporate tax of 15 %[19]. Introduction of the tax rate at the international level is a revolutionary development in international law. Never in history, have attempts been made at the international level to establish national rates of taxes, fees, customs tariffs, duties, constituting the source of income for a sovereign state and therefore are a very sensitive

---

17 PUBLIC CONSULTATION DOCUMENT Pillar One – Amount A: Draft Multilateral Convention Provisions on Digital Services Taxes and other Relevant Similar Measures 20 December 2022 – 20 January 2023, URL: https://www.oecd.org/tax/beps/public-consultation-document-draft-mlc-provisions-on-dsts-and-other-relevant-similar-measures.pdf (last accessed: April 15, 2023).

18 Tax challenges arising from digitalisation: Public comments received on the draft Multilateral Convention provisions on digital services taxes and other relevant similar measures under Amount A of Pillar One, URL: https://www.oecd.org/tax/beps/public-comments-received-on-the-draft-multilateral-convention-provisions-on-digital-services-taxes-and-other-relevant-similar-measures-under-amount-a-of-pillar-one.htm (last accessed: April 15, 2023).

19 OECD website, Statement on a Two-Pillar Solution to Address the Tax Challenges Arising from the Digitalisation of the Economy – 8 October 2021 at 4.

matter. Similar examples exist only in unions of states with a high degree of integration, for example, in the EU, where the directive sets a minimum value-added tax rate[20]. Yet, in the EU, Member States, by virtue of Founding Treaties, have committed themselves to comply with the prescriptions of legal acts of the EU, yet at the international level apart from the unions of states there is no legal instrument that could force states to introduce any universal tax rate in national law. It is not expected to introduce such an instrument as part of the tax reform. What then?

Instead of trying to force states to introduce a flat tax rate[21], which, apparently, would have been doomed to failure, a so-called *top-up tax* was invented. This is the tax that a parent company must pay on the income of a particular member of the group (such a member is called a *constituent entity*) provided that such income is taxed at a rate below the minimum corporate tax. This obligation is called the *Income Inclusion Rule*. If the constituent entity has not been taxed, the relevant jurisdiction has the right to deny deductions or require the equivalent adjustment to the extent the low tax income is not subject to tax. This rule is called the *Undertaxed payment rule*.

Both rules are linked to each other and form the *Global Anti-Base Erosion* (GloBE) Rules. These rules apply to groups of multinational enterprises with an annual income of EUR 750 million or more. Thus, this threshold is significantly lower than for the First Pillar.

To implement the second Fundamental Element of the reform, it was envisaged to develop model rules for implementation in national legal systems[22]. Such rules were developed on 14 December 2021, and comments to them with examples on 11 March 2022[23]. The rules include ten chapters, including provisions for allocation of top-up tax, and the

---

20 Council Directive 2006/112/ EC dated 28 November 2006 on the common system of value added tax. OJ L 347, December 11, 2006. pp. 1–118. Art 97: the standard rate may not be less than 15 %.

21 "…jurisdictions remain free to set their own tax rates or not to have corporate income tax system at all" Addressing the Tax Challenges of the Digitalisation of the Economy – Policy Note As approved by the Inclusive Framework on BEPS on 23 January 2019, At 2.

22 OECD (2021), *Tax Challenges Arising from the Digitalisation of the Economy – Global Anti-Base Erosion Model Rules (Pillar Two): Inclusive Framework on BEPS*, OECD, Paris, https://www.oecd.org/tax/beps/tax-challenges-arising-from-the-digitalisation-of-theeconomy-global-anti-base-erosion-model-rules-pillar-two.htm (last accessed: April 15, 2023).

23 OECD (2022), *Tax Challenges Arising from the Digitalisation of the Economy – Commentary to the Global AntiBase Erosion Model Rules (Pillar Two)*, OECD, Paris,

computation of global profit and tax. The chapter "Definitions" contains definitions of more than 150 terms.

IV. International law mechanism of the reform

Already at the previous stage of implementation of the "Addressing BEPS" project, a unique Multilateral Instrument[24] was applied: an international agreement that involves changing almost 2,000 bilateral agreements on the avoidance of double taxation[25]. The essence of the legal mechanism of this convention is as follows: each state is invited to either make a reservation on the non-applicability of certain provisions of the Convention, or choose one of the options for changing double taxation agreements specified in the Multilateral Instrument, then notify them of this to the Depositary of the Convention (and thus all other states with which such agreements are concluded), that is, to make a kind of choice from the international legal "menu". If another state chooses the same option for itself, then the bilateral agreement on the avoidance of double taxation among these states is deemed to be amended in accordance with the conditions contained in the Multilateral Instrument.

The current global tax reform under the auspices of the OECD provides for a specific mechanism that combines international treaties and soft-law recommendations in the form of model rules for changing national legal systems. Thus, the plans are to conclude a Multilateral Convention that will contain rules regarding six components of the reform: (1) determination of the "Amount A", (2) its allocation, (3) elimination of

---

https://www.oecd.org/tax/beps/tax-challenges-arising-from-thedigitalisation-of-the-economy-global-anti-base-erosion-model-rules-pillar-two-commentary.pdf; OECD (2022), *Tax Challenges Arising from the Digitalisation of the Economy – Global Anti-Base Erosion Model Rules (Pillar Two) Examples*, OECD, Paris, https://www.oecd.org/tax/beps/tax-challenges-arising-from-the-digitalisationof-the-economy-global-anti-base-erosion-model-rules-pillar-two-examples.pdf (last accessed: April 15, 2023).

24 Multilateral Convention to Implement Tax Treaty Related Measures to Prevent BEPS, text from the OECD website, URL: https://www.oecd.org/tax/treaties/multilateral-convention-to-implement-tax-treaty-related-measures-to-prevent-beps.htm (last accessed: April 15, 2023).

25 Multilateral Convention to Implement Tax-Treaty-Related Measures to Prevent Base Erosion and Profit Shifting: Functioning under Public International Law, Note by the OECD Directorate for Legal Affairs, URL: https://www.oecd.org/tax/treaties/legal-note-on-the-functioning-of-the-MLI-under-public-international-law.pdf (last accessed: April 15, 2023).

double taxation, (4) simplified tax administration process, (5) information exchange, (6) dispute prevention and resolution in a mandatory and binding manner between all jurisdictions, including allowances for developing countries. At that, the new Convention will change the existing bilateral agreements on the avoidance of double taxation in terms of the "Amount A", then the profits of groups of multinational enterprises (MNE) will be taxed in the market jurisdiction, regardless of the presence of a Permanent Establishment in it. The Convention will also apply to relations of country that are not bound by tax treaties, and as such, it will be the world's first multilateral tax convention to provide substantive taxation rules for a significant number of jurisdictions.

The new Multilateral Convention is envisaged to be supplemented by an Explanatory Statement that will contain "a description of the purpose of the Agreement and the operation of the rules and processes". Such an Explanatory Note will obviously not be an integral part of the Agreement and will be approved by the Inclusive Group (IF). Perhaps, this document will be provided with examples of the application of the new rules to facilitate understanding and application of the very casuistic rules of the reform. It is presumably intended that this Explanatory Note will play the role currently played by the OECD Commentary to the Model Tax Convention on Income and on Capital when the latter is applied.

In the 2021 Statement, the member states of the Inclusive BEPS Group stated their intention to develop model rules to amend the domestic legislation both within the first (in terms of new rights to tax the profits of MNEs)[26] and within the framework of the second component of the reform (regarding the Global Anti-Base Erosion Rules – GloBE)[27]. There are also plans to develop a model rule for amending bilateral tax agreements, as well as a commentary to it for implementing the Subject-to-Tax Rule (STTR)[28]. The law-making work plan also includes the signing of a Multilateral Instrument to facilitate the swift

26 For the Fundamental Pillar in July 2022 The OECD secretariat has developed a corresponding draft of 7 chapters and 10 annexes, see OECD (2022), *Progress Report on Amount A of Pillar One, Two-Pillar Solution to the Tax Challenges of the Digitalisation of the Economy, OECD/G20 Base Erosion and Profit Shifting Project*, OECD, Paris, https://www.oecd.org/tax/beps/progress-report-on-amount-aof-pillar-one-july-2022.pdf. (last accessed: April 15, 2023).

27 See above footnotes 22 and 23.

28 Statement on a Two-Pillar Solution to Address the Tax Challenges Arising from the Digitalisation of the Economy – 8 October 2021 at 7.

and consistent implementation of amendments to bilateral double taxation agreements[29]. Such an instrument means, apparently, a multilateral convention that will amend several thousand bilateral agreements on the avoidance of double taxation by analogy with the MLI discussed above, signed in 2017. Thus, the international legal reform mechanism provides for four types of actions: (1) signing of international conventions and commentaries thereto, (2) developing model rules for inclusion in national legislation, (3) developing a model text for amending bilateral agreements, (4) signing of a multilateral instrument for amending bilateral agreements.

The United Nations has also proposed a response to the challenges for international taxation associated with the widespread adoption of digital services. In 2021, the UN Model Convention was also amended in terms of digital services (Article 12B "Income from automated digital services")[30], providing for: (1) taxation of income from the sale of automated digital services at the place of residence of the beneficial owner of such income; (2) the possibility of establishing tax at the source of income at a rate established by agreement of the parties to the double taxation treaty (for example, 3 % or 4 % of the gross amount of income); (3) the right of the beneficial owner of income to require the state-source of income to tax its adjusted (qualified) profit at the national rate, while the adjusted profit is defined as 30 % of the annual profit received from the sale of digital services based on the profitability rate of the income owner. It should be recognised, therefore, that the approaches of the OECD and the UN to the taxation of digital services differ[31].

In principle, it should be noted that there has been competition between the OECD and the UN as international *fora* that should head global tax reform. African countries and China support strengthening the role of the UN in setting global tax policy, while European countries

---

[29] Ibid.

[30] Article 12B of the UN Model Tax Convention, as agreed by the Committee at its 22nd Session URL: https://www.un.org/development/desa/financing/document/article-12b-un-model-tax-convention-agreed-committee-its-22nd-session (last accessed: April 15, 2023).

[31] On comparison between the OECD and the UN initiatives: Ponomareva K.A. Digital Services Taxation in the Context of International Tax Agreements. *Actual Problems of Russian Law*. 2022;17(8):20–31. (In Russ.); see also PwC case study white paper: https://www.pwc.com/gx/en/tax/newsletters/tax-policy-bulletin/assets/pwc-un-tax-committee-adopts-article-12b.pdf (last accessed: April 15, 2023).

and the US are not inclined to create a parallel forum for global tax reform[32]. The advantages of the UN lie in its exceptional role as a universal and unique international organisation created to maintain international peace and security, but at the same time having a broad economic agenda, including to support developing countries. The OECD, firstly, has been a kind of "World Tax Organisation" for more than half a century, and, secondly, despite the obvious unrepresentativeness of its membership, it is making attempts to create various types of committees and groups of a more inclusive nature under its auspices.

At the end of December 2022, the UN General Assembly adopted a resolution to the effect that the UN is going to become the leading forum for organising international cooperation in tax matters[33]. In the resolution, the UN General Assembly places special emphasis on the interests of developing countries, notes the work of the OECD and the Inclusive Group on BEPS, but recognises the need to strengthen international cooperation through a more inclusive international forum[34]. The GA also decided to begin intergovernmental discussions in New York at the UN Headquarters that could lead to the development of international tax cooperation, and also instructed the UN Secretary General to prepare a report for the next 78th session of the GA with an analysis of all international legal instruments that address international tax cooperation, as well as outlining potential next steps[35].

*

In conclusion, global tax reform, in elaboration since 2021 under the auspices of the OECD, is about to bring radical changes to the century-based approach to the taxation of Multinational Enterprises.

---

32 Countries divided over UN tax role, International tax review, Josh White April 03, 2023, Available at:
https://www.internationaltaxreview.com/article/2bhiquh8utox5sltqdpfk/countries-divided-over-un-tax-role (last accessed: April 15, 2023).

33 UN General Assembly Resolution dated 30 December 2022. "Promotion of inclusive and effective international tax cooperation at the United Nations", United Nations General Assembly, A/RES/77/244.

34 Ibid, p. 1, preamble second indent; p. 3, preamble, first, fifth and sixth indents: para 1.

35 Ibid, paras 2, 3, 5.

The first pillar of this reform is revenue taxation irrespective of the physical presence of the international company in the marketing jurisdiction. Such presence has a special legal term –"permanent establishment" in Double Taxation Treaties and until now, permanent establishment has created the essential condition for business profits taxation in the host country. However, the current plan is to tax the revenue of an international company if it sells goods and services in a certain jurisdiction even if such company does not have permanent establishment there.

The second pillar is implementation of the global minimum corporate tax of 15 %. These changes suppose that the home jurisdiction of the Multinational Enterprise will have the right to impose top-up tax if the effective tax rate for the global profits of such enterprise is less than the minimum corporate rate. The BEPS Inclusive Framework states plan to implement these revolutionary changes in the new Multilateral Convention in 2023. All these developments are the beginning of the launch of a major reform in transboundary taxation that is set to bring it to wider engagement with international law.

A new level of tax cooperation will considerably enlarge the scale of tax authorities' contacts, and, following the implementation of the Multilateral Convention, the international community will approach the emergence of a new international tax regime[36]. This regime will likely push out "tricky and trendy" tax avoidance arrangements, since a tax base created in a certain state is now apprehended as a national heritage. The fair distribution of the tax base among jurisdictions in which Multinational Enterprises earn income has become a global public value. The states are prepared to take new tax commitments and we may expect that the rule of tax will consequently change the global economic order and international law.

Will Cinderella turn into a Queen?

36 Reuven Avi-Yonah, International Taxation, Globalization and the Economic Digital Divide, *Journal of International Economic Law*, 2023, 26, At 109.

The sanctions related to Russia's military action in Ukraine: Impact and future

Remus TITIRIGA
Korea

The paper examines Western sanctions against Russia (and its partners) concerning Russia's special military action in Ukraine. The article follows the succession of Western sanctions and their effect on Russia, and based on the sanction's place within the global Western interests and actions, elaborates a prognosis.

I. Sequence of sanctions adopted by the Western coalition against Russia

Western countries and other countries imposed sanctions on Russia[1] after it recognised the independence of its allied territories, the Donetsk and Luhansk People's Republics (DPR and LPR), on February 21, 2022, in a speech by Vladimir Putin[2].

---

1 Sanctions against individuals, companies, and officials in Russia have been applied by various countries since the beginning of the war in Donbas (February 2014). In addition, the United States, Canada, the EU, and other European countries (including Ukraine) have imposed sanctions against Crimea annexed by the Russian Federation. In turn, Russia introduced 2014 retaliatory sanctions against several countries, such as a ban on importing products from the EU, USA, Canada, and Norway.

2 The discussion of new sanctions began immediately after Russian President Vladimir Putin recognised the independence of the DPR and LPR (February 22, 2022). As a result, western countries and others began imposing limited sanctions on Russia immediately.

On February 24, 2022, Russia invaded Ukraine. The invasion received widespread international condemnation and Western countries[3] (a multilateral coalition regrouping more than 30 nations representing over 50 percent of the global economy) imposed sanctions on Russia[4] unprecedented in scope and severity[5]. Sanctions tried to pressure Russia to withdraw its forces from Ukraine and to deter future aggression. Russia adopted retaliatory measures against Western countries.

These Western sanctions were adopted in tranches.

(A) First group of sanctions

Initially, the United States, the European Union, and other Western countries introduced or expanded measures concerning Russian President Vladimir Putin, other government members, and prominent entrepreneurs[6], and in some cases, members of their families.

Other sanctions targeted the activities of Russian companies and individual sectors of the economy and imposed the closure of airspace and seaports. Some other sanctions focused on Russia's financial, energy, and military systems. For example, they banned certain Russian banks from using the SWIFT international payments system[7]. Sanctions included other large-scale restrictions on the Russian financial system (the Central Bank and other major banks)[8].

---

3 In February 2022, in retaliation for Russia's invasion of Ukraine, considered an unprovoked and unjustified military aggression, new sectoral sanctions of greater magnitude were implemented, particularly by the European Union, the United Kingdom, the United States, Canada, and Japan.

4 Certain Western sanctions were extended to Belarus and Belarusian individuals or organisations involved in recognizing the DPR and LPR's independence and the invasion of Russian troops in Ukraine in 2022.

5 By March 7, 2022, Russia became the world leader in the number of sanctions imposed, surpassing Iran.

6 Oligarchs and elites that enabled Putin's regime were sanctioned through multilateral fora like the REPO Task Force, which has frozen or blocked at least 58 billion dollars in ill-gotten assets.

7 These sanctions cut off Russian central banks from SWIFT, the global network for international payments. However, there was still (for a while) limited accessibility to ensure the payment for gas shipments.

8 Sanctions included asset freezes on the Russian Central Bank, which holds $630 billion in foreign-exchange reserves, to prevent it from overcoming the impact of

(B) Technological sanctions

The US and the Western coalition was the dominant producer of crucial components for modern warfare, such as the most advanced semiconductors, transistors, or software. As a result, the US instituted export controls, focused on restricting Russian access to high-tech components, both hardware, and software, made with any parts or intellectual property from the US. In addition, the sanctions required that any person or company that wanted to sell technology, semiconductors, encryption software, lasers, or sensors to Russia request a license, which by default was rejected. Finally, the enforcement mechanism concerned sanctions against the person or company, focusing on the shipbuilding, aerospace, and defence industries.

(C) Sanctions related to Russia's energy imports: The adoption of price-cap sanctions

The Western coalition was initially reluctant to eliminate all oil and gas imports. While the United States, Canada, and the UK on early March 2022 banned imports of Russian energy, Europe's dependence on such imports took much work to break[9]. Nevertheless, EU countries started refusing to buy Russian oil. The US crude exports have helped fill the gap[10]. A fleet of tankers carried more US crude oil to Germany, France, Italy, and Spain, which alone grew purchases by about 88 % over the period (2022 vs 2021). The pull of oil shipments from the US to Europe has made the continent a more important destination for US crude oil than Asia.

At this initial stage, the European Commission proposed[11] cutting Russian oil imports by two-thirds by the end of 2022. By June 2022,

---

sanctions. By March 1, 2022, the total amount of Russian assets frozen by sanctions amounted to $1 trillion.

9 Before the invasion, the continent imported about 40 % of its gas and a quarter of its oil from Russia.

10 https://www.reuters.com/article/us-usa-crude-exports-idUSKCN1TJ2AC.

11 Such a decision worried the US Administration since the US oil prices were spiking to $5 a gallon then (March–April 2022). Moreover, there were concerns that Europe would block too much Russian oil from the global market and inflate prices even more. So Treasury Secretary Janet L. Yellen went to European capitals to promote modifying the original measure by replacing it with price caps that would lower

the European Union (in the sanctions outlined by its sixth sanctions package) envisaged a measure banning most Russian oil imports from December 5, 2022, and prohibiting EU companies from insuring or financing Russian oil shipments to any buyer worldwide.

Russia answered at the beginning of September[12] to the announced measure by cutting out its gas supply to Europe and starting an "energy war". The EU's reaction was to accelerate its energy transition and complete long overdue projects or seek alternative supplies. With Russia's share of European gas imports dropping from 40 % to less than 10 % towards the end of 2022, European companies turned to global Liquefied Natural Gas (LNG) markets, sourcing 96.3 million tons in 2022, up from 56.3 million tons the year before.

On December 5, 2022, the Western block (mostly EU countries, G7 and Australia) added a price ceiling of $ 60/barrel to the oil ban. This price restriction was applied to crude oil, petroleum oils, and oils derived from bituminous minerals originating in or exported from Russia. If this ceiling was exceeded, exporters could not provide insurance for their transport by tanker, which European companies dominated[13]. Moreover, this embargo extended to oil by-products from February 5, 2023.

On December 19, 2022, after protracted discussions, the energy ministers of the EU countries decided to introduce a gas price ceiling under which the EU countries could conclude contracts. The mechanism entered into force on February 15, 2023, and will continue for a year.

Russia's revenue but prevent energy price spikes. Soon, a solution was reached: Europe would proceed with its import ban but allow companies to insure Russian oil shipments elsewhere so long as the buyers paid Russia no more than $60 a barrel. Cf https://www.nytimes.com/2022/07/14/business/yellen-russia-oil-cap.html

12 Sam Meredith, Russia has cut off gas supplies to Europe indefinitely, SEP 6 2022, 9:49 AM, CNBC, https://www.cnbc.com/2022/09/06/energy-crisis-why-has-russia-cut-off-gas-supplies-to-europe.html.

13 According to some estimates, during April-May 2022, 97 % of tankers were insured in only three countries: Great Britain, Norway, and Sweden. Cf https://english.nv.ua/opinion/seven-theses-on-how-sanctions-against-russia-work-50294083.html.

(D) Enforcement of adopted sanctions: The emerging secondary sanctions

On 24 February 2023, the anniversary of the invasion, the US started focusing on entities that helped Russia evade earlier rounds of sanctions. Top sanctions officials from the US Treasury Department made international trips in March 2023 to pressure firms and third countries still doing business with Russia to cut off financial ties because of the war on Ukraine: those working with Russia's government must decide if they continue to provide Moscow with material support or if they keep doing business with the Western alliance economy[14].

To prevent the evasion of sanctions, the EU has created a new function for applying sanctions (led by David O'Sullivan) and launched the Forum of Sanctions Coordinators in February 2023. Also, an upcoming 11th package of EU sanctions against Russia will aim to eliminate loopholes and prevent Russia and its military-industrial complex from finding a way to reach goods banned for them by previous sanctions. A recent report by the Financial Times underlines that the package could also include restrictions on seven Chinese companies for their supposed involvement in supplying Moscow with dual-use goods[15].

II. Effects of sanctions on Russia

1. *The immediate and uneven effects of the first round of sanctions on Russia*

Some of these first sanctions (immobilising Russia's central bank reserves, as well as sanctioning or de-SWIFT-ing some of Russia's largest banks) sent the rubble into a steep decline, creating a run on the Russian economy, as capital and foreign companies left the country as quickly as possible.

The Kremlin stopped the hurt with strict capital controls preventing money from leaving the country, providing capital from the Central

---

14 Fatima Hussein, US sanction officials plan missions to clamp down on Russia, April 8, 2023, AP NEWS.

15 https://www.ft.com/content/ca35ecf4-a5bd-4ff2-906e-10988a87a1ee.

Bank to sustain the financial sector, and using the remaining assets from Russia's sovereign wealth fund to support the economy.

Nevertheless, according to Russian estimations, the country's economy evolved better in 2022 than expected. Russia's current trade account balance and foreign currency reserves increased significantly due to decreased imports from Western countries. However, because of the enhanced military expenditure for the 2022 invasion of Ukraine, Russia posted a record budget deficit of USD 47.3 billion in 2022 (2.3 % of GDP).

Also, industrial production has declined. Russian car production fell 67 % from 2021 to 2022. Truck production decreased by 24 %. A particularly drastic fall occurred in May 2022 when car production dropped 97 % but rebounded after some adaptations. Nevertheless, car sales fell 63 %.

Some of the reduction in trade with Western Europe was compensated by a record trade balance with China of USD 190 billion in 2022. In addition, since Russia's primary source of revenues came from selling energy, the Kremlin's invasion of Ukraine inadvertently raised global prices for oil, hurting oil-importing countries and increasing Russia's oil gains. As a result, the Russian petroleum industry shifted its export market towards China, India, Saudi Arabia, Turkey, and Morocco.

International Monetary Fund, which has factored in Russia's economic projections in their analysis of the nation's economy, currently estimates Russia's GDP to grow by 0.7 % in 2023[16].

2. *Results of sanctions for the restrictions on the supply of high technologies*

According to The Economist, sanctions restrictions on the supply of high technologies, particularly processors and electronic components, have the most significant impact on Russia. According to the publication,

16 Jeffrey Sonnenfeld and Steven Tian, academics at the Yale Chief Executive Leadership Institute, contested Russia's economic forecasts. By some accounts, Russia's energy revenue has tanked amid the EU's Russian oil ban and $60 price cap, and other significant sectors of its economy have plunged 60–95 %, Cf Jennifer Sor, Russia's economic stats are "pure invention from Putin's imagination," and its economy is imploding, April 13, 2023, 1:18 AM GMT+9, Cf https://finance.yahoo.com/news/russias-economic-stats-pure-invention-001825789.html.

Russian weapons systems use electronic components manufactured by about 70 European and American companies. In addition, imported electronics and technologies are also needed in the civilian sectors of the Russian industry, in particular, in the mining and oil and gas industries and transport[17].

3. *Preliminary effects of price-cap sanctions*

As mentioned above, the Western Alliance imposed an oil price cap in late 2022 and early 2023. That directly limited Russia's oil revenues and gave negotiating leverage to those who bought Russian oil without using insurance services, further driving down prices. In addition, the system avoided a sharp spike in global oil prices by keeping Russian oil on the market. However, the effect of sanctions, especially the price caps on both crude oil and processed oil, resulted in an immediate fall in Russia's oil revenues, with the first quarter of 2023 recording income of just $19.61 billion, far below the 2023 budget of $35 billion per quarter and the 2022 results which averaged $42 billion per quarter. Some other economists predict Russia's budget deficit could reach 5 % of GDP this year, up from 2 % last year, because of the drop in energy exports and the rapidly falling tax revenue from the declining economy[18].

4. *Circumvention of sanctions by thirds is proving the impact of sanctions*

According to Eurostat, since February 2022, the export of goods from the EU to the Russian Federation has decreased by 47 %, but at the same time, it has grown by 48 % to the Commonwealth of Independent States (CIS)[19]. As a result, most of the goods from the European Union arriving in the CIS countries flow to Russia[20]. Many of the former Soviet states

---

17 Russia's economy can withstand a long war, but not a more intense one, https://www.economist.com/briefing/2023/04/23/russias-economy-can-withstand-a-long-war-but-not-a-more-intense-one.

18 https://www.washingtonpost.com/business/2023/02/15/russia-sanctions-impact-ukraine-war/

19 EU trade with Russia – latest developments – Statistics Explained, May 16, 2023, https://ec.europa.eu/eurostat/statistics-explained/index.php?title=EU_trade_with_Russia_-_latest_developments.

20 About 100 "sanction anomalies" were found to increase exports: supplies of used cars from Lithuania to Belarus, laptops and smartphones from the Czech Republic to

have substantial remittance inflows on the current account, and capital account, and significant errors and omissions inflows[21]. For example, the German authorities believe that countries within the CIS are allowing Russia to import German goods and bypass sanctions[22].

III. Forecasting the future of sanctions against Russia

We are in the face of a strategic map with many actors and moving parts. Moreover, many things will depend on how and when the war in Ukraine ends.

1. Russia will be able to finance its war (for a while)

Based on the recent leaks of classified documents, US intelligence believes that Russia can finance the war in Ukraine for at least another year, even under current harsh sanctions[23] while according to other opinions, the Kremlin will be able to continue funding its war machine for several more years but with an economical-structural price in the long term[24].

Kazakhstan, and kerosene for aircraft from Greece to Georgia. According to Zemlis-Balevichus, Greece, Cyprus, the Czech Republic, and Estonia, they have increased sales of sanctioned goods to the CIS countries by three to five times. The growth of similar exports from other countries grew at lower rates. The volume of supplies to the CIS has remained the same in Sweden and Malta. Cf. Anomalies found in trade between Uzbekistan and Russia, 2023-02-01 10:36:04, http://tashkenttimes.uz/national/10488-anomalies-found-in-trade-between-uzbekistan-and-russia.

21 Timothy Ash, War in Ukraine: Russia the Loser, the US a Winner, March 20, 2023. https://cepa.org/article/war-in-ukraine-energy-russia-the-loser-the-west-a-winner/.

22 German exports to Kazakhstan, Armenia, and Georgia doubled since the start of the full-scale invasion, and exports to Tajikistan increased by 150 %. German exports to Belarus increased by 77 % and to Kyrgyzstan by 994 %. German authorities reportedly believe Russia is using the Eurasian Economic Union to bypass sanctions.https://daryo.uz/en/2023/05/10/german-goods-to-reach-russia-through-cis-countries-bypassing-sanctions.

23 According to Washington Post 26 April, cf. https://www.washingtonpost.com/world/2023/04/26/russia-sanctions-impact-leaked-documents/.

24 The Russian authorities are cutting spending on non-military items such as road construction and education. The government has also raised money by issuing domestic debt and imposing taxes on energy companies, including Gazprom. Russia is also expected to use its National Wealth Fund to cover the deficit this year. However, economists consider that the fund could be depleted over the next two years." All

If we look into the future, the world has realised that Russia has lost the chance of re-emerging as a superpower. Russia is becoming a regional power, and its chances to be more assertive internationally are diminishing. Even a military victory (quite improbable) on Russian terms would be a Pyrrhic victory.

Furthermore, even if peace or an armistice in Ukraine is achieved soon, the economic, political, and demographical damage of sanctions (and of the war itself) will be felt by Russia for at least another generation. Conversely, Russia might remain under Western sanctions for long, absent a regime change or political direction turn. Whatever scenario materialises, Russia lost for the time being its most significant client for its gas and oil: Europe.

2. The future position of Europe: The high price of sanctions against Russia for Europe

The geopolitical atmosphere in Europe has completely changed after the military aggression carried out by Russia against Ukraine. As a result, the EU introduced ten sanctions packages against Russia. Also, the energy dependence on Russian hydrocarbons was reduced to a minimum. As a result, Europe is assured of sufficient energy supply well into 2024, at least providing enough time for cheaper alternative energy supplies to be accessed and operated within Europe.

Nevertheless, on average, LNG costs about triple of Russian gas price because of the costs of cooling, transport, and re-gasification. Also, the European change triggered energy problems worldwide, especially in countries like Japan, Korea, and Taiwan, which rely on LNG as their primary energy source. Unfortunately, this situation is here to stay.

It is a clear trade-off between security and the economy. Moreover, Europe has few choices. In the long run, everything depends on how the war ends. It would be one thing if a Ukrainian victory were to lead to the collapse of the Putin regime. It would be another if Russia were

---

of this together tells you the sanctions are a problem. But because the war is such a huge priority, it will not be the reason that makes Putin reconsider his Ukraine strategy. Yet." Cf. Jeanne Whalen and Catherine Belton, Sanctions haven't stopped Russia, but a new oil ban could cut deeper, The Washington Post, February 15, 2023, https://www.washingtonpost.com/business/2023/02/15/russia-sanctions-impact-ukraine-war/

to be defeated, but the regime as such was to survive. This energy policy will also be determined by the results of replacing Russian energy sources with supplies from other countries and the pace and scale of the green transition within the European Union.

3. Position of /and concerning third countries: the case of China

The People's Republic of China imposed no sanctions as such on Russia. From the perspective of contouring technological sanctions, China could not offer a solution to Russia. On one side, Beijing did not produce the advanced semiconductors needed by Russia. Furthermore, according to US sources, nearly 40 %of the less advanced microchips Russia received from China were defective[25]. Conversely, Chinese companies were attentive not to become the target of secondary Western sanctions[26] since the Russian market is significantly less important to them than the markets of the Western alliance[27].

China could not supply powerful weapons systems to Russia. It would be entering the trap that Russia finds itself in. China is more dependent on global trade than Russia, so any secondary sanctions added to the trade sanctions adopted already by the US could be devastating.

The Western alliance has identified China as their nearest and real competitor. In this respect, Western sanctions against Russia serve equally as an example and deterrent for the security posturing of China in the South China Sea and Taiwan.

Vice versa, the visible acceleration of economic-trade sanctions from the US and, lately, Europe against China provides a hint and signal of the resoluteness of the Western alliance regarding Russia.

We examine this last aspect by focusing on the position adopted by the US concerning China as a proxy for their future position regarding Russia.

---

25 See remarks by Deputy Secretary of the Treasury, Wally Adeyemo on International Sanctions Against Russia on February 21, 2023, seen on April 20 at https://home.treasury.gov/.

26 For example, Huawei relocated personnel from Russia to Kazakhstan and Uzbekistan to avoid possible secondary sanctions. Cf. Juan Pedro Tomás, Huawei moves Russian staff to central Asia: report, September 6, 2022, in https://www.rcrwireless.com/20220906/5g/huawei-moves-russian-staff-central-asia-report.

27 EU official warns of sanctions if China crosses "red line" and arms Russia, Reuters, March 4, 2023.

4. The future position of the US: continuity of Russian sanctions in the light of continuity of US trade sanctions against China

Besides different rhetoric, Biden Administration maintained former President Trump's general trade policies[28].

The Biden Administration has pursued and sometimes amplified, Trump-era sanctions against China. For example, in October 2022, the Biden administration imposed export controls (sanctions) to limit China's ability to access advanced chips, which can be used to make weapons, commit human rights abuses, and improve the speed and accuracy of its military logistics. In addition, in January 2023, the Dutch and the Japanese joined this American sanctions package against China for high-end semiconductors.

Shielded from the WTO settlement mechanism (still blocked), the Biden Administration embraced an "American First" industrial policy of subsidies to revive manufacturing[29]. US companies are rewarded for building factories or for sourcing components and critical minerals from the US or countries with which the US has a free trade agreement.

While an eventual future Republican Administration (or Congress) will be less focused on green energy subsidies, we believe that the frame and content of such industrial policy, including the regime of sanctions against China, will continue unabated or will even be expanded. That imposes a trade-off between economy vs. security because China is still an irrepressible part of the global and American value chains. Moreover,

---

28 While President Trump withdrew from the Trans-Pacific Partnership (TPP), President Biden showed no signs of rejoining it. The tariffs on Chinese imports under Section 301 of the 1974 Trade Act were also maintained. 2018 President Trump imposed tariffs on aluminum and steel imports from key allies, including the EU, the UK, Japan, and South Korea, claiming national security threats. Under the Biden Administration, some Trump-era tariffs become voluntary export restraints and quotas. However, others have remained in place. In December 2019, the Trump Administration blocked the multilateral dispute settlement by refusing to appoint WTO appellate judges. Silently, the Biden Administration has maintained the same position in respect of the trade court.

29 In 2022, the US passed two pieces of legislation to support its manufacturing sector. First, with bipartisan support, it passed the CHIPS and Science Act, which includes US$53 billion to expand domestic production of semiconductors and investments in research and development. Second, this time voted just by the Democrats, passed the Inflation Reduction Act (IRA) with US$370 billion in grants, loans, and tax credits to lower energy costs and accelerate private investment in clean energy solutions.

the US is able and willing to pay the cost of reducing the economic ties for better security.

*

Such a trade-off of economy vs. security does not exist in the US relation to Russia since the economic ties between the two are almost inexistent. In conclusion, any future US Administration that will likely follow a sanction policy against a global competitor as China will follow it more willingly against a revisionist power like Russia.

Customs protection of intellectual property rights within the framework of the Eurasian Economic Union and of the European Union

Zhuldyz SAIRAMBAEVA, Madina NURTAY
Kazakhstan

One most controversial current topics in international law is the link between international trade and ensuring intellectual property rights. Most intellectual property exporting countries point to the fact that the growth of trade in counterfeit goods disrupts markets, and also as a key factor misleading consumers into buying counterfeit, and sometimes even dangerous, products[1]. Deteriorating trends in cross-border counterfeiting and piracy among states have prompted international organisations to expand their legal framework to strengthen the protection of intellectual property rights within their borders[2]. Since the specific law enforcement role in the event of a border occurrence is assumed by the customs authority, it is called the customs protection of intellectual property. More precisely, the growing interest at the borders determines the need for a comprehensive study of regional regimes for ensuring compliance with intellectual property rights.

This chapter analyses the main aspects of the border regulation in the field of intellectual property within the framework of the Eurasian Economic Union (EAEU) and the European Union (EU). Effective methods of combating counterfeiting of the EU, as well as an effective mechanism for harmonising legislation in the field of intellectual

1 Henning Grosse Ruse-Khan, "A Trade Agreement Creating Barriers to International Trade?: ACTA Border Measures and Goods in Transit", *American University International Law Review*, V. 26, No. 3 (2011), pp. 645–726.

2 Min Li, "Improving Australian border enforcement of IPR by referring to the Chinese experience", *World Customs Journal*, 2014, 2, pp. 39–46.

property rights and unified customs protection are being considered. In addition, the EAEU has identified industries that can be significantly improved and strengthened by using the experience of the European partner. Interestingly, although many aspects of these unions comply with international standards, in some areas it has become clear that they even exceed international standards.

I. Legal regulation of customs protection of intellectual property rights in the EAEU and the EU

The legal basis for customs protection of rights in relation to intellectual property objects consists of acts of supranational (regional) law, primarily the Treaty on the EAEU[3] and the Customs Code of the EAEU[4] .

In accordance with the provisions of Article 89 of Section XXIII "Intellectual property" of the Treaty on the EAEU, the areas of interaction of the EAEU member states include ensuring effective customs protection of rights to intellectual property objects, including maintaining a single customs register of intellectual property objects of the member states[5].

From 1 January 2018, the Customs Code of the EAEU entered into force, which includes some conceptual and procedural innovations in the field of customs control, providing for the phased protection of exclusive rights for the EAEU countries. Chapter 52 of the Customs Code of the EAEU contains measures to protect the rights to intellectual property objects adopted by customs authorities[6]. Also, the Customs Code of the

---

3 Treaty on the Eurasian Economic Union, 2011. [online] Available at: https://www.wto.org/english/thewto_e/acc_e/kaz_e/wtacckaz85_leg_1.pdf (accessed:April 1, 2023).

4 « Таможенный кодекс Евразийского экономического союза» (ред. от 29.05.2019) (приложение N 1 к Договору о Таможенном кодексе Евразийского экономического союза) [Электрон. ресурс] Доступно: http://www.consultant.ru/document/cons_doc_LAW_215315/ [Дата обращения: 1 апреля, 2023].

5 Treaty on the Eurasian Economic Union, 2011. [online] Available at: https://www.wto.org/english/thewto_e/acc_e/kaz_e/wtacckaz85_leg_1.pdf (accessed: April 1, 2023).

6 « Таможенный кодекс Евразийского экономического союза» (ред. от 29.05.2019) (приложение N 1 к Договору о Таможенном кодексе Евразийского экономического союза) [Электрон. ресурс] Доступно: http://www.consultant.ru/document/cons_doc_LAW_215315/ [Дата обращения: 1 апреля, 2023].

EAEU is aimed at improving the transparency of customs operations and provides tools for the interaction of business and state bodies in order to ensure compliance with documents and direct contact with customs authorities. In addition, in some cases, the Customs Code of the EAEU contains the norms of reference of the EAEU member states to national legislation.

The initial legal basis for the European Union's counterfeit and anti-labour activities, mitigating measures and circumstances governing the activities of customs authorities in relation to goods suspected of infringing intellectual property rights, was the EU Council Regulation No. 1383/2003 of 22 July 2003[7].

After ten years of combating the counterfeiting of goods in the EU under the Regulation (EC) No. 1383/2003, a new Regulation No 608/2013 was adopted, which entered into force on 1 January 2014[8]. The new regulation should strengthen the protection of intellectual property rights by customs authorities and improve the effectiveness of legislation in the context of economic, commercial and legal changes.

The main innovations introduced by the new regulations are the following: (i) Customs protection applies to new rights and infringements; (ii) New special procedures for small consignments; (iii) Exchange of information with third countries about transit goods suspected of infringing intellectual property rights; (iv) Creation of a central electronic database in which all information related to applications requesting the customs authorities to take action for the enforcement of intellectual property rights is stored.

The Regulation (EC) No. 608/2013 establishes the conditions and procedures concerning the actions of customs authorities with respect to goods suspected of infringing intellectual property rights under their supervision or control. Within their procedural rights, customs authorities can only determine whether the goods are "Goods suspected of

---

7 Council Regulation (EC) №1383/2003 of 22 July 2003. Official Journal. L196. 2003, p. 7. [online] Available at: https://eur-lex.europa.eu/legal-content/EN/TXT/?uri=uriserv%3AOJ.L_.2003.196.01.0007.01.ENG&toc=OJ%3AL%3A2003%3A196%3ATOC (accessed: April 5, 2023).

8 Regulation (EU) No 952/2013 of the European Parliament and of the Council of 9 October 2013 laying down the Union Customs Code (recast). [online] Available at: https://eur-lex.europa.eu/legal-content/EN/TXT/PDF/?uri=CELEX:32013R0952&rid=1 (accessed: April 1, 2023).

infringing intellectual property rights". The Regulation (EC) No. 608/2013 does not establish any criteria to determine whether intellectual property rights infringements have occurred or not. The question of whether intellectual property rights have been infringed or not is decided by the substantive intellectual property law in accordance with the interpretation of the competent national courts and the Court of the EU[9]

When developing the system of intellectual property rights protection in the EAEU and the EU, much attention is paid to the provisions of the articles of the World Trade Organisation (WTO) Agreement on Trade-Related Aspects of Intellectual Property Rights (TRIPS), which was concluded following the Uruguay Round of multilateral negotiations with the participation of representative of the GATT in 1994[10]. It sets minimum standards for the protection of almost all categories of intellectual property rights that all WTO members must adopt. In this regard, it should be noted that both the EU regulations and the Customs Code of the EAEU are based on the provisions of the section "Border measures" of the WTO agreement on trips and the model of national legislation developed by the World Customs Organisation.

II. Customs mechanism for protecting rights to intellectual property objects within the EAEU

In accordance with the Customs Code of the EAEU, the customs authorities of the member State take measures to protect the rights to intellectual property objects included in the EAEU and the national customs register conducted by the customs authorities of the EAEU member State (clause 5, Article 384). To include an object in the unified customs register of intellectual property objects, it is necessary to coordinate with the customs authorities of all EAEU countries. Intellectual property objects that can be included in the unified customs register of intellectual

9 Commission notice on the customs enforcement of Intellectual Property Rights concerning goods brought into the Union's customs territory without being released for free circulation including goods in transit, (2016/C 244/03). https://eur-lex.europa.eu/legal-content/EN/TXT/PDF/?uri=CELEX:52016XC0705(02)&rid=4 (accessed: April 2, 2023).

10 Agreement on Trade-Related Aspects of Intellectual Property Rights, 1994. [Электрон. ресурс] Доступно: https://wipolex.wipo.int/en/text/379915 [Дата обращения: 1 апреля, 2023].

property objects of the member States include objects of copyright and related rights, trademarks, service marks and appellations of origin of goods (clause 3, Article 385). The term of protection of intellectual property rights by customs authorities is established when intellectual property objects are included in the unified customs register of intellectual property objects of the member states, taking into account the term specified by the right-holder in the application, as well as the validity of documents attached to the application, but may not exceed 2 years from the date of inclusion in such a register (clause 1, Article 387).

In accordance with Article 385 of the Customs Code of the EAEU, only intellectual property objects whose rights are registered in each country of the Union may be included in this register[11]. To include intellectual property objects in the unified customs register of intellectual property objects, it is necessary to provide an insurance policy equal to at least 10 000 €. This policy should be valid in all EAEU countries. If it is not possible to obtain a valid policy in all countries, it is necessary to obtain several policies used in all EAEU States in aggregate[12].

In accordance with Article 124 of the Customs Code of the EAEU, the legislation of the member states establishes that the customs authorities have the right to suspend the period of release of goods containing intellectual property objects that are not included in the unified customs register of the member states or the national register of intellectual property objects without the application of the right-holder. This means that, at the discretion of the EAEU member states, the right to use this procedure on the territory of their countries remains[13].

At the same time, measures to protect the rights to intellectual property objects are not accepted by customs authorities when placing under

---

11 « Таможенный кодекс Евразийского экономического союза» (ред. от 29.05.2019) (приложение N 1 к Договору о Таможенном кодексе Евразийского экономического союза) [Электронный ресурс] Доступно: http://www.consultant.ru/document/cons_doc_LAW_215315/ [Дата обращения: 1 апреля, 2023].

12 Сорокин А.М., Сорокин М.А. Актуальные направления развития института единого таможенного реестра объектов интеллектуальной собственности Евразийского экономического союза //Азимут научных исследований: экономика и управление. 2018. Том 7. № 4(25). С.291–294.

13 « Таможенный кодекс Евразийского экономического союза» (ред. от 29.05.2019) (приложение N 1 к Договору о Таможенном кодексе Евразийского экономического союза) [Электрон. ресурс] Доступно: http://www.consultant.ru/document/cons_doc_LAW_215315/ [Дата обращения: 1 апреля, 2023].

customs procedures goods intended for official use of diplomatic missions, consular offices, representations of states to international organisations, international organisations or their representations, other organisations or their representations located on the customs territory of the Union, transported across the customs border of the Union (clause 3, Article 384)[14].

An important role in the field of control over the movement of goods containing intellectual property objects is played by the powers (*ex-officio*) of customs authorities to suspend the release of goods containing intellectual property objects that are not included in customs registers, but have signs of counterfeiting. Currently, all customs authorities of member states, with the exception of Belarus, have *ex-officio* powers[15]. However, in this case, goods imported into the customs territory of the EAEU are further freely transported among member countries, since there are no customs borders between them. This significantly increases the risk of counterfeit products entering the territory of the EAEU.

III. Customs mechanism for protecting rights to intellectual property objects within the EU

EU legislation provides for a wide range of intellectual property objects, the rights of which are also subject to protection under customs procedures and are protected accordingly. The EU Customs Code establishes the main powers of customs authorities related to the movement of goods containing intellectual property objects across the EU customs border[16]. Regulation of the European Parliament and of the Council of 12 June 2013 No. 608/2013 "On the protection of intellectual property

---

14 « Таможенный кодекс Евразийского экономического союза» (ред. от 29.05.2019) (приложение N 1 к Договору о Таможенном кодексе Евразийского экономического союза) [Электрон. ресурс] Доступно: http://www.consultant.ru/document/cons_doc_LAW_215315/ [Дата обращения: 1 апреля, 2023].

15 Отчет о состоянии правоприменительной практики в сфере защиты прав на объекты интеллектуальной собственности в Евразийском экономическом союзе за 2020 год. [Электрон. ресурс] Доступно: //u.to/zD0OHA [Дата обращения: 7 апреля, 2023].

16 Regulation (EU) No 952/2013 of the European Parliament and of the Council of 9 October 2013 laying down the Union Customs Code (recast). [online] Available at: https://eur-lex.europa.eu/legal-content/EN/TXT/PDF/?uri=CELEX:32013R0952&rid=1 (accessed: April 1, 2023).

rights exercised by customs authorities" identifies intellectual property rights that may be infringed in Article 2. Among them are the rights to a trademark, industrial design, geographical indication, patent, utility model, plant varieties, copyright or related rights, among others[17]. At the same time, first of all, goods that infringe the rights to trademarks or geographical instructions, as well as packaging, emblems, labels, etc. are considered counterfeit. And pirated products infringe copyright or related rights, rights to industrial designs, as well as other intellectual property rights that are subject to protection at the level of the EU or individual countries[18].

The EU customs authorities have the right to detain goods at the border either on application of the right-holder, who believes that the goods infringe their intellectual property rights or *ex officio*, that is, on their own initiative, in case of suspected infringement. Unlike the EAEU, in the EU, in order to improve the quality of public services, a number of procedures are provided for the exchange of information between national customs authorities. At the same time, in order to ensure the processing of information, a central database is created in electronic form. The customs authorities of the EU member states and the European Commission will have access to the information contained in the central database. A right-holder may submit an application for the protection of their rights to the customs authority of a particular EU state, or a "Union application" may be filed for action in several EU countries, provided that there are special licenses valid throughout the territory of two or more EU member states. Thus, the issue of a single register is being resolved the right-holder does not need to apply to all national customs authorities, but at the same time he is not limited to the need for customs protection in all countries of the Union at once[19].

---

17 Regulation (EU) No 608/2013 of the European Parliament and of the Council of 12 June 2013 concerning customs enforcement of intellectual property rights and repealing Council Regulation (EC) No 1383/2003. [online] at: https://eur-lex.europa.eu/LexUriServ/LexUriServ.do?uri=OJ:L:2013:181:0015:0034:en:PDF (accessed: April 4, 2023).

18 Наку А.А., "Таможенно-правовая защита прав интеллектуальной собственности в Европейском Союзе", Таможенное дело, 2018, № 4, С. 31–34.

19 Сорокин А.М. Развитие государственных услуг в сфере таможенного контроля (на примере товаров, содержащих объекты интеллектуальной собственности): дисс. … канд. экон. наук. Москва, 2016. С. 209.

Customs authorities take measures to suspend the operation of goods that infringe the intellectual property rights of the right-holder, regardless of whether the intellectual property object is included in any customs register or not. Thus, any copyright-holder can apply for customs protection.

The period for which customs authorities can suspend goods at the EU customs border at the request of the right-holder is no more than 1 year (Article 11)[20]. According to the Customs Code of the EAEU, the term does not exceed two years. This period allows customs authorities to always have up-to-date information for more effective protection. It should also be noted that the right-holder, when submitting an application for the application of customs measures, undertakes to inform the authorised body of all changes related to intellectual property rights, updating information related to risk analysis.

Unlike the EAEU, neither insurance policies nor collateral are provided in the EU. In the event that the procedure is terminated due to the actions or omissions of the owner of the decision, or if it is determined that the goods do not infringe intellectual property rights, the right-holder must be liable to the owner of the goods or to the declarant who has suffered losses in this matter (point (a) of Article 24 (2))[21].

IV. Advantages of the customs mechanisms for the protection of intellectual property rights of the EU

Customs mechanisms for protecting rights to intellectual property objects of the EU offer established advantages.

Firstly, a distinctive feature of customs protection in the EU is the absence of mandatory material guarantees when applying to customs

---

20 Regulation (EU) No 608/2013 of the European Parliament and of the Council of 12 June 2013 concerning customs enforcement of intellectual property rights and repealing Council Regulation (EC) No 1383/2003. [online] Available at: https://eur-lex.europa.eu/LexUriServ/LexUriServ.do?uri=OJ:L:2013:181:0015:0034:en:PDF (accessed: April 4, 2023).

21 Regulation (EU) No 608/2013 of the European Parliament and of the Council of 12 June 2013 concerning customs enforcement of intellectual property rights and repealing Council Regulation (EC) No 1383/2003. [online] Available at: https://eur-lex.europa.eu/LexUriServ/LexUriServ.do?uri=OJ:L:2013:181:0015:0034:en:PDF (accessed: April 4, 2023).

authorities. This makes cross-border protection of rights to intellectual property objects more accessible and effective for rights holders. The right-holder, applying for customs protection, undertakes to compensate all expenses of the customs authority related to the suspension, storage and destruction of counterfeit goods (Article 24)[22].

Secondly, the EU regulation confirms the infringement of intellectual property rights in writing within ten working days or three working days in the presence of perishable goods from the moment that the customs authorities notify the owner of the decision to suspend the release or maintenance of goods (point (a) of Article 23(1))[23]. Nevertheless, the Customs Code of the EAEU does not contain such a norm that allows to regulate the suspension period depending on the period of damage to products.

Thirdly, a new special procedure for small consignments of counterfeit and pirated goods has been introduced to combat the sharp increase in postal or express courier consignment of counterfeit products as a result of online commerce and to reduce the administrative burden and costs. "Postal or express courier consignment" are defined as shipments consisting of three units or having a total weight of less than two kilograms (Article 2 (19)). Such goods may be destroyed without the explicit consent of the applicant. Customs notifies the declarant or the producer of the intention to destroy the goods without the consent or participation of the right-holder (Article 26)[24]. This special procedure was adopted on the condition that it would ensure the destruction of small batches of

---

22 М.А. Долгова, "Сравнительный анализ регулирования пограничных мер в отношении контрафактных товаров в Российской Федерации и Европейском союзе" [Электронный ресурс] Доступно: https://publications.hse.ru/en/chapters/73241333 [Дата обращения: 8 апреля, 2023].

23 Regulation (EU) No 608/2013 of the European Parliament and of the Council of 12 June 2013 concerning customs enforcement of intellectual property rights and repealing Council Regulation (EC) No 1383/2003. [online] Available at: https://eur-lex.europa.eu/LexUriServ/LexUriServ.do?uri=OJ:L:2013:181:0015:0034:en:PDF (accessed: April 4, 2023).

24 Regulation (EU) No 608/2013 of the European Parliament and of the Council of 12 June 2013 concerning customs enforcement of intellectual property rights and repealing Council Regulation (EC) No 1383/2003. [online] Available at: https://eur-lex.europa.eu/LexUriServ/LexUriServ.do?uri=OJ:L:2013:181:0015:0034:en:PDF (accessed: April 4, 2023).

counterfeit goods only on the customs initiative with minimal costs and at a reasonable price for the copyright-holder.

*

In conclusion, counterfeit products on the market of a certain territory, whether it is a separate state or an economic organisation, strongly affects the investment policy of this region as a whole. Experts attribute the widespread use of counterfeit goods to the rapid development of digital technologies and online commerce, on the one hand, and the lack of an effective set of mechanisms to counteract the turnover of counterfeit products, on the other. Nevertheless, the annual analysis shows that the procedure of suspension by the customs services of the clearance of goods at the request of the right-holder or in case of detection of signs of counterfeiting (*ex-officio* powers) at the discretion of customs officers remains the most effective measure to prevent the import of counterfeit goods.

As a result of this chapter analysing the activities of customs authorities for the protection of intellectual property rights in the EAEU, the following problems can be identified:

Firstly, there are differences in the application of the *ex officio* principle in the national legislations of the EAEU countries. Here, it is necessary to consolidate the unified powers of the customs authorities. In particular, to establish the application of the *ex officio* principle throughout the territory of the EAEU, which will allow initiating cases of administrative offenses and procedures for suspending the release of goods without including intellectual property objects in the customs register.

Secondly, it is necessary to develop methods at the regional level for classifying goods as counterfeit. In particular, it is advisable to extend customs protection to such intellectual property objects as patents, industrial designs, utility models, selection achievements and integrated circuit topologies.

Thirdly, the legislation of the EAEU establishes the obligation of the copyright-holder when submitting an application for the adoption by customs authorities of measures related to the suspension of the release. In addition to the obligation to compensate for damage, to make financial security for this obligation or to insure the liability of causing harm to the importer, if the counterfeiting of the goods suspended by customs is not proved. The amount of such guarantees is ten thousand euros.

Analysing the activities of the customs services of the EAEU, we conclude that effective methods of combating counterfeiting have been developed at the EU level and an effective customs protection mechanism has been created based on many years of experience in the harmonisation and unification of legislation in the field of intellectual property law.

Nevertheless, the customs legislation of the EU and the EAEU has many common features, both due to the existence of a common international legal framework, and in connection with the use of European experience in the preparation of acts of the customs legislation of the EAEU. And also, in order to improve the effectiveness of intellectual property rights protection, the EAEU and EU bodies closely cooperate with other countries within the WTO.

Dispute settlement in the WTO: International experience and prospects for Kazakhstan

Zulfiya BAIMAGAMBETOVA,
Assem AKHMETOVA
Kazakhstan

The World Trade Organisation (WTO) contributes to ensuring the stability of the development of global trade by defining common rules. These affect the growth of the world economy and makes it possible to predict its formation. At the same time, one of the key functions of this international organisation is the resolution of international trade disputes among its member through mechanisms. The WTO dispute settlement is an important aspect of its activities. In the modern world, more and more countries are oriented towards international trade, and this makes it necessary to have an effective dispute resolution mechanism.

This chapter reviews the experience of the international settlement of trade disputes in the WTO and determines its significance for Kazakhstan, as well as it proposes recommendations for improving Kazakhstan's participation in the WTO Dispute Settlement Mechanism (DSM). It draws on the analysis of scientific articles, WTO reports and other sources of information, as well as on the comparative analysis of the experience of other countries in participating in the WTO DSM. It reviews the WTO settlement mechanism, dispute classification and dispute statistics in the WTO.

I. Background information

The importance of the activities of the WTO lies in the regulation of world trade. As Herbert notes, the WTO, contributing to the economic globalisation of trade and maintaining economic stability, has established a mandatory mechanism for resolving disputes between the participating states of the organisation. However, the scientist recommends that the development of both free and fair trade should be carried out in that[1]. Moreover, some researchers believe that despite the fact that the WTO effectively influences the development of world trade, its distribution is uneven[2]. Thus, it can be recognised that the activities of WTO are aimed at developing the liberalisation of world trade, but that, at the same time, it requires the improvements of its mechanism.

At present, the DSM is one of the important components of the WTO system, the purpose of which is to settle trade disputes. The DSM ensures transparency, predictability and stability of international trade, which is an important factor for maintaining open markets and sustainable economic growth.

The DSM has the following objectives: i/ to resolve a trade dispute within the WTO in accordance with the Dispute Settlement Understanding (DSU); ii/ to ensure compliance by WTO participants with the obligations assumed within the WTO; iii/ to preserve the institutional stability and credibility of the dispute settlement mechanism.

The DSM carries out its activities on the basis of reciprocity of the parties to the dispute. However, if it is impossible to settle the dispute through consultation, the participants have the right to apply to the Panel and the WTO Appellate Body to resolve the dispute. In a situation where the parties refuse to accept the decision of the Appellate Body, the DSM settles the dispute by allowing the parties to take measures to bring their behaviour in line with WTO rules.

II. International experience of dispute settlement in the WTO

According to WTO data, for the period going from 1 January 1995 to 31 March 2023, 616 cases were registered in the DSM. These have been treated as follows.

---

1 Herbert, E. B. (2020). The role of World Trade Organisation in international trade and investment. Nnamdi Azikiwe University, *Journal of International Law and Jurisprudence*, 11(1), 47–55.

2 Subramanian, A., & Wei, S. J. (2007). The WTO promotes trade, strongly but unevenly. *Journal of international Economics*, 72(1), 151–175.

There are 182 cases of these are at the consultation stage; a Panel was established for 25 disputes, but the composition of the Panel has not been elected; 23 disputes are at the stage of a composed Panel; a Panel report was drawn up for 2 cases, but was neither accepted nor appealed; a report of the board of appeal would have been adopted for 22 disputes; 37 disputes were resolved by the adoption of reports, and accordingly, no further action is required; for 48 disputes, reports were adopted with recommendations to bring certain measures in accordance with WTO rules; for 95 disputes, the respondent State notified the DSM that it had implemented recommendations to bring its legislation in accordance with WTO rules; 23 disputed cases were resolved by concluding a mutual agreement on implementation; 9 disputes are under proceedings; 3 disputes were completed without establishing the fact of non-compliance with WTO rules; 6 disputed cases ended in non-compliance with WTO rules; 12 disputes were requested permission to take retaliatory measures; 9 disputes were settled by obtaining permits to take retaliatory measures; the Panel's powers lapsed for 18 disputes; 1 dispute is at the arbitration stage in accordance with article 25 of the DSU; 2 disputed cases were resolved by issuing a notification of acceptance with a recommendation to bring measures in accordance with WTO rules; 104 disputes were completed by a peaceful agreement of the parties, 2 disputes were withdrawn[3].

According to WTO official statistics, for the period from 1 January 1995 to 31 December 2021, 52 WTO members initiated at least one dispute, and 61 WTO participants were the respondent, respectively. At the same time, 90 States acted as third parties to the dispute. Thus, 111 WTO member States are active participants in trade disputes resolved within the organisation[4].

The main agreements under which disputes were initiated in the WTO are the General Agreement on Tariffs and Trade of 1994 (GATT 1994), the Agreement on implementation of Article VI of the General Agreement on Tariffs and Trade 1994 (Anti-dumping), the Agreement on Subsidies and Countervailing Measures (SCM Agreement), the Agreement on

3 See Current status of disputes, available at https://www.wto.org/english/tratop_e/dispu_e/dispu_current_status_e.htm (visited 14 April 2023).

4 See Dispute settlement activity – some figures, available at https://www.wto.org/english/tratop_e/dispu_e/dispustats_e.htm (visited 14 April 2023).

Agriculture, The Agreement on Safeguards (SG Agreement), The Technical Barriers to Trade (TBT) Agreement, the Agreement on Import Licensing Procedures, The Agreement on the Application of Sanitary and Phytosanitary Measures and others.

Thus, most trade disputes in the WTO involve issues of trade restrictions and subsidies.

Disputes within the WTO can be classified according to various criteria: by the subject of the dispute, by the type of trade measures, by the parties to the dispute, depending on the WTO Agreement, the norms of which were violated and others.

Thus, the following can be distinguished by the subject of the dispute: *(1) trade restrictions*: restrictions on the import of certain goods or services, including technical barriers and sanitary and phytosanitary measures. For example, the trade dispute between the US and the EU on the introduction of tariffs on steel and aluminium in 2018 (DS548: US – Steel and aluminium products (EU)). *(2) intellectual property*: protection of copyright and related rights, use of music in bars, regulation of trademarks. For example, a dispute between Indonesia and Australia on measures relating to trademarks, geographical indications and other plain packaging requirements applicable to tobacco products and packaging containers (DS467: Australia – Tobacco Plain Packaging (Indonesia)).

Depending on the type of trade measures applied: *(1) anti-dumping measures*: for example, the dispute between China and Australia on the introduction of anti-dumping measures on imports of Chinese wind towers, deep-drawn stainless-steel sinks and railway wheels (DS603: Australia – AD/CVD on Certain Products (China)). *(2) special protective measures*: for example, the dispute between Brazil and China over trade restrictions on sugar (DS568: China – Certain Measures Concerning Imports of Sugar); *(3) sanitary and phytosanitary measures*: for example, the dispute between South Africa and the European Union over trade restrictions on citrus fruits (DS613: EU – Citrus Fruit (South Africa)).

The classification of disputes within the WTO is not strict. Moreover, most disputes can be classified simultaneously on several grounds and sectors. The given examples illustrate that the DSM is actively used by the participating States to resolve trade disputes in various trade sectors.

III. Prospects for Kazakhstan

At present, Kazakhstan is the 162th state to be party to the WTO. The process the country's accession to the WTO began in 1996 and ended in 2015. During this time, Kazakhstan came a long way to fulfil all the necessary WTO requirements regarding economic reform, legal and regulatory changes.

During the accession negotiations, several important legislative acts were discussed and adopted, which reflect the principles of the WTO and establish the appropriate legal and regulatory framework. These include some amendments to legislation regulating customs issues, the agricultural sector, the protection of intellectual property rights and a number of other areas.

The accession procedure took 19 years, presumably due to the fact that it was difficult for Kazakhstan, as a former member of the Soviet Union, to switch abruptly to a market economy. Moreover, the accession process was complicated by the Russian crisis of 1998[5], as well as by Kazakhstan's entry into the Customs Union[6].

According to a group of Kazakh and Russian researchers, the process of Kazakhstan's accession to the WTO went through three main stages: (1) the introductory period (1996–2003), which was characterised by the procedure of information exchange between representatives of the WTO and Kazakhstan; (2) the negotiation stage (2003–2015), which included discussion of issues related to tariff obligations, subsidies, sanitary and phytosanitary measures and a number of other commitments between the Working Party of Kazakhstan, consisting of 35 states, and the WTO member States; (3) the final stage included signing required agreements and, accordingly, joining the WTO[7].

At the same time, Kazakhstani researchers note that WTO membership unconditionally contributes to Kazakhstan's unification under

5 Pomfret, R. (2007). Lessons from Kyrgyzstan's WTO experience for Kazakhstan, Tajikistan and Uzbekistan. *Asia-Pacific Trade and Investment Review*, 3(2), 27–46.

6 Aronov, A., & Otarbayeva, A. (2019). Critical analysis of the case of Kazakhstan's accession to the World Trade Organisation. *Bulletin of KazNU*. International relations and international law series, 85(1), 55–64.

7 Amirbekova, A., Madiyarova, D., &Andronova, I. (2017). What are the pros and cons for Kazakhstan of joining the WTO from an export potential point of view?. *Journal of Business and Retail Management Research*, 11(3).

a "single liberal economic roof[8]". Thus, after the final process of Kazakhstan's accession to the WTO, the country began to actively participate in the work of the international organisation, and take part in negotiations affecting the development of world trade.

WTO membership contributes to the strengthening of Kazakhstan's international trade relations and helps attract foreign investment. The WTO DSM also plays an important role for Kazakhstan in world trade, ensuring the protection of its economic interests and allowing it to participate in international trade on equal terms with other WTO members.

First, the DSM provides Kazakhstan with an opportunity to protect its economic interests at the international level if other WTO members violate the rules of world trade. This allows Kazakhstan to participate more freely in international trade and benefit from the export of its goods and services.

Second, the DSM contributes to the improvement of the investment climate in Kazakhstan and ensures the protection of investors' rights. Since joining the WTO, Kazakhstan has attracted a significant number of foreign investments, which have contributed to the development of the economy and the creation of new jobs.

Third, participation in the DSM helps Kazakhstan increase its export potential and expand markets for its products. The correct application of WTO rules and participation in the DSM ensures the protection of the interests of Kazakhstan's exporters on world markets and provides an opportunity to participate in international trade on equal terms.

However, despite the fact that the DSM is an important dispute resolution mechanism in international trade, there may be potential problems that Kazakhstan may face when applying it.

These include time and resource constraints, political pressure, problems with compliance with the implementation of the DSM decision within the WTO. For example, the DSM process can be lengthy and resource-intensive, and small economies such as Kazakhstan's may face difficulties in allocating the necessary time and resources to resolve a dispute. This may cause a disadvantage compared to larger and more powerful trading partners. In some cases, countries may face political pressure

---

8 Dyussembayeva, D., &Faizullayeva, A. (2019). Kazakhstan's membership in WTO and its impact on nation's economy. *Vestnik nauki*, 2(12 (21)), 102–106.

from their trading partners to end the dispute or accept an unfavourable outcome. This can be especially difficult for small economies such as Kazakhstan's, which may have less leverage in international negotiations. It may also be a potential problem that even if Kazakhstan succeeds in a trade dispute, there may be problems with the execution of the decision and ensuring that its trading partners fulfil their obligations. This can be especially difficult if the disputing party is a powerful country that does not want to comply with the decision.

The effective participation of Kazakhstan in the DSM requires highly qualified specialists in the field of international law and trade policy. Some researchers believe there is a shortage of specialists in Kazakhstan with high-quality knowledge of WTO law, which in the future may affect the increase in the number of trade disputes in which Kazakhstan is expected to become a violator or a losing party[9]. Moreover, the DSM is a complex mechanism that requires in-depth knowledge of the WTO legal framework, of DSM procedures and technical aspects of the application of WTO rules. Specialists should have experience in international trade issues and disputes, be able to analyse the situation and develop strategies, as well as represent the interests of Kazakhstan on international platforms.

IV. Learning from other countries: Lessons for Kazakhstan as a third party of the dispute

At present, from the moment of accession until 31 March 2023, Kazakhstan has been a party to one dispute as a defendant (DS530: Kazakhstan – Anti-dumping Measures on Steel Pipes) and has acted on 35 trade disputes within the WTO as a third party[10]. The trade dispute in which Kazakhstan participated as a defendant was initiated by Ukraine on 19 September 2017 over the introduction of anti-dumping measures against certain types of steel pipes imported into the territory

---

9 Baimagambetova, Z., & Gabdulina, A. (2019). Disputes in the WTO with participation of the member countries of the Eurasian economic union. *Bulletin of KazNU*. International relations and international law series, 84(4), 56–69.

10 Disputes by member, available at https://www.wto.org/english/tratop_e/dispu_e/dispu_by_country_e.htm (visited 14 April 2023).

of the Eurasian Economic Union (EAEU)[11]. This dispute was concluded at the consultation stage.

30 % of trade disputes in which Kazakhstan acted as a third party were initiated by the United States. In three disputes the plaintiffs were the European Union, Turkey, China, Canada and Korea. Leading respondent countries in disputes in which Kazakhstan acted as a third party are the United States and China, with quantitative data in 46 % and 17 % of disputes, respectively (table 1). The main subjects of the dispute were the issues of taxation, tariff duties and quotas, anti-dumping and countervailing duties and subsidies.

Kazakhstan's participation as a third party in trade disputes has a positive effect on improving its experience in resolving issues related to the dispute settlement procedure in the WTO DSM[12]. This is also true for other WTO members, such as Latin American countries, which, by participating as a third party in disputes, gain experience to initiate their own disputes in the future[13]. Moreover, States acting as third parties in disputes can influence not only decision-making in the WTO, but also the procedure for settling trade disputes[14].

Thus, studying the experience of other countries that have previously participated in disputes under the WTO DSM may be useful for Kazakhstan as a third party in future disputes.

Kazakhstan can learn from the experience of other countries is compliance with WTO rules: countries that comply with WTO rules usually have a higher level of trust among other participants, which can help in

11 Kazakhstan – anti-dumping measures on steel pipes, available at https://docs.wto.org/dol2fe/Pages/FE_Search/FE_S_S009-DP.aspx?language=E&CatalogueIdList=247994,239627,239537,239315,238874&CurrentCatalogueIdIndex=4&FullTextHash=&HasEnglishRecord=True&HasFrenchRecord=True&HasSpanishRecord=True (visited 14 April 2023).

12 Tleubekov, S. T, Aidarbaev, S. Z., & Moreno, G. P. (2022). Kazakhstan's participation in WTO disputes as a third party. (In Russ.) Bulletin of Institute of Legislation and Legal Information of the Republic of Kazakhstan, 3(70), 160–170.

13 Koval, A. G., Sutyrin, S. F., &Trofimenko, O. Y. (2019, November). Latin American experience in the WTO dispute settlement: recommendations for Russia and the EAEU states. In Third International Economic Symposium (IES 2018) (pp. 37–48). Atlantis Press.

14 Busch, M. L., & Reinhardt, E. (2006). Three's a crowd: third parties and WTO dispute settlement. *World Politics*, 58(3), 446–477.

Table 1. Disputes involving Kazakhstan as a third party, January 1995 – March 2023

Number of the dispute	Name of the dispute	Complainant	Respondent
DS493	Ukraine – Anti-Dumping Measures on Ammonium Nitrate	Russian Federation	Ukraine
DS502	Colombia – Measures Concerning Imported Spirits	European Union	Colombia
DS508	China – Export Duties on Certain Raw Materials	United States	China
DS509	China – Duties and other Measures concerning the Exportation of Certain Raw Materials	European Union	China
DS511	China – Domestic Support for Agricultural Producers	United States	China
DS513	Morocco – Anti-Dumping Measures on Certain Hot-Rolled Steel from Turkey	Turkey	Morocco
DS516	European Union – Measures Related to Price Comparison Methodologies	China	European Union
DS517	China – Tariff Rate Quotas for Certain Agricultural Products	United States	China
DS518	India – Certain Measures on Imports of Iron and Steel Products	Japan	India
DS523	United States – Countervailing Measures on Certain Pipe and Tube Products (Turkey)	Turkey	United States
DS526	United Arab Emirates – Measures Relating to Trade in Goods and Services, and Trade-Related Aspects of Intellectual Property Rights	Qatar	United Arab Emirates
DS533	United States – Countervailing Measures on Softwood Lumber from Canada	Canada	United States
DS534	United States – Anti-Dumping Measures Applying Differential Pricing Methodology to Softwood Lumber from Canada	Canada	United States
DS539	United States – Anti-Dumping and Countervailing Duties on Certain Products and the Use of Facts Available	Korea, Republic of	United States
DS541	India – Export Related Measures	United States	India

(*Continued*)

Table 1. Continued

Number of the dispute	Name of the dispute	Complainant	Respondent
DS542	China – Certain Measures Concerning the Protection of Intellectual Property Rights	United States	China
DS543	United States – Tariff Measures on Certain Goods from China	China	United States
DS544	United States – Certain Measures on Steel and Aluminium Products	China	United States
DS545	United States – Safeguard measure on imports of crystalline silicon photovoltaic products	Republic of Korea	United States
DS546	United States – Safeguard measure on imports of large residential washers	Republic of Korea	United States
DS547	United States – Certain Measures on Steel and Aluminium Products	India	United States
DS548	United States – Certain Measures on Steel and Aluminium Products	European Union	United States
DS550	United States – Certain Measures on Steel and Aluminium Products	Canada	United States
DS551	United States – Certain Measures on Steel and Aluminium Products	Mexico	United States
DS552	United States – Certain Measures on Steel and Aluminium Products	Norway	United States
DS553	Korea – Sunset Review of Anti-Dumping Duties on Stainless Steel Bars	Japan	Korea, Republic of
DS554	United States – Certain Measures on Steel and Aluminium Products	Russian Federation	United States
DS556	United States – Certain Measures on Steel and Aluminium Products	Switzerland	United States
DS557	Canada – Additional Duties on Certain Products from the United States	United States	Canada
DS558	China – Additional Duties on Certain Products from the United States	United States	China
DS559	European Union – Additional Duties on Certain Products from the United States	United States	European Union
DS560	Mexico – Additional Duties on Certain Products from the United States	United States	Mexico
DS561	Turkey – Additional Duties on Certain Products from the United States	United States	Turkey

Table 1. Continued

Number of the dispute	Name of the dispute	Complainant	Respondent
DS564	United States – Certain Measures on Steel and Aluminium Products	Turkey	United States
DS566	Russian Federation – Additional Duties on Certain Products from the United States	United States	Russian Federation

Source: the World Trade Organisation

resolving disputes in a more constructive atmosphere. This will also allow diversify the field of experts' interests: the use of experts with different specialisations and cultural backgrounds can help to provide a more balanced and objective solution to the dispute.

Applying the experience of other countries will be associated with the implementation of consultations with the parties: closer interaction with the parties and consultations on various aspects of the dispute. This can help reduce tensions and achieve a more satisfactory solution. It will also lead to compliance with the principle of "fast and effective procedure": countries that resolve disputes quickly and effectively usually have a higher reputation among other participants and can better protect their interests in the future.

In addition, applying the experience of other countries will create a proactive approach to conflicts: countries that adopt a proactive approach to conflict resolution often have fewer problems in the future, as they seek to prevent disputes from arising.

*

In conclusion, the DSM plays an important role in ensuring the development of efficient and fair international trade. Moreover, the WTO continues to improve this mechanism. This chapter gives examples of successful settlement of disputes of various countries with the help of the WTO DSM, including disputes in which Kazakhstan participated as a third party. It justifies the need for highly qualified specialists in the field of international law and trade policy for Kazakhstan's effective participation in the WTO DSM, as well as the experience of other countries, which could be a lesson for Kazakhstan as a third party in a dispute. As a result, it provides an overview of the WTO DSM, analyses the problems, which Kazakhstan may face when using the WTO DSM and offers recommendations for improving Kazakhstan's participation in the WTO dispute settlement mechanism.

Kazakhstan may face problems associated with high costs for legal experts and consultants. Thus, it is recommended that Kazakhstan should actively use cooperation with countries that already have experience in the field of dispute settlement within the WTO DSM, as well as strengthen its expert resources. The availability of qualified specialists in the field of international law and trade policy in Kazakhstan will help the country to participate more actively in the international arena and protect its trade interests. It will enable Kazakhstan to use WTO instruments, including the DSM, more effectively to settle disputes and protect its rights in international trade. In this regard, Kazakhstan has created special educational programs in higher educational institutions aimed at training specialists in the field of international law and trade policy. In addition, Astana supports the holding of trainings and seminars to improve the skills of experts in this field.

Each trade dispute is unique and may require its own approach, but studying the experience of other countries can help Kazakhstan better understand how to participate in the WTO DSM and effectively protect its economic interests. Despite the problems, the DSM remains an important dispute resolution mechanism in international trade, and Kazakhstan has already used it to protect its interests. By continuing to interact with the WTO and participating in the DSM process, Kazakhstan can help promote a rules-based global trading system that is fair to all countries.

Normalisation of Korea-Japan relations: The "comfort women" agreement and the judicial decision on compensation for forced labour

Sung-Kee HONG
Korea

Paragraph 4 of the 「U.S.-Japan Joint Statement」 signed by Japanese Prime Minister Eisaku Sato and U.S. President Richard Nixon in 1969 is the so-called Korean clause. The United States and Japan "highly appreciated the efforts made by the United Nations to maintain peace on the Korean Peninsula" and declared that "Korea's security is essential to Japan's own security." Korea-Japan relations, which were the cornerstone for peace in Northeast Asia, have changed significantly in half a century. While South Korea's interest was focused on relations with North Korea and it assumed itself as a mediator in North Korea-U.S. negotiations, relations with Japan became uncomfortable. The Abe administration's distrust of the Moon Jae-in government peaked during the 2018 PyeongChang Winter Olympics. Direct negotiations between North Korea and the United States were pursued, and such relations continued as the leaders of South Korea, North Korea, and the United States met at Panmunjom, the military demarcation line on the Korean Peninsula, on 30 June 2019, right after the G20 summit was held in Osaka.[1]

Relations between Korea and Japan have changed dramatically due to an issue that has nothing to do with North Korea relations. The Moon Jae-in administration's handling of the 2015 comfort women agreement, which resulted in significant concessions from Japan, and the Moon Jae-in administration's immature attitude after the 2018 ruling on compensation for forced labour were very inconsistent with the status of the

---

1 Kang Sang-joong, translated by Roh Su-gyeong, 『The Future of the Korean Peninsula and Japan』, Four Seasons, 2021, p. 122

Republic of Korea in the international community. Regarding these issues directly related to former Japanese Prime Minister Shinzo Abe, there are many claims calling for "sophisticated and meticulous responses" now that he has left.[2]

As the Korean government has led the discord, the Korean government has to come up with a solution first, and it would be better if the solution was as simple as possible. Below, I address the history of the 2015 comfort women agreement and the 2018 Supreme Court ruling on compensation for forced labour, and propose earnest measures to improve relations between Korea and Japan.

I. The 2015 Comfort Women Agreement

(A) Scope of the 1965 Property and Claims Settlement Agreement

In 2005, the Roh Moo-hyun administration disclosed diplomatic documents related to Korea-Japan diplomatic negotiations. After the Seoul Administrative Court's ruling on document disclosure, the government pre-emptively decided to disclose documents before the high court's decision. Around that time, a "Public-Private Joint Committee on Measures to Disclose Documents from the Korea-Japan Talks" was organised. Attorney Lee Yong-hoon, who later became Chief Justice, and Prime Minister Lee Hae-chan chaired the public-private joint committee. Moon Jae-in, senior secretary for civil affairs to the President, was also included. On 26 August 2005, the Public-Private Joint Committee announced the issue of the scope of effect of the 1965 Korea-Japan Property and Claims Settlement Agreement. It argued that the comfort women issue "cannot be seen as resolved by the Property and Claims Settlement Agreement, and the Japanese government remains legally responsible."

In the second Korea-Japan talks held from April 1953, the South Korean side demanded compensation for forced labour for the conclusion of the Korea-Japan Basic Relations Treaty, and also demanded the solution

---

2 Chosun Ilbo, 2022. 7. 16. Kang Cheon-seok column "It can be more difficult to deal with Japan without Abe", Seoul Shinmun, July 13, 2022, Kimiya Tadashi "The death of former Prime Minister Abe and Korea-Japan relations", Segye Ilbo, 2022 July 13, 2013, Choi Eun-mi, "Where will Korea-Japan relations go after Abe's death?"

of the "comfort women" issue from the viewpoint of "receivables". Such a fact was omitted from the minutes of the meeting on the Korean side, but it exists in the records on the Japanese side. In other words, Jang Ki-young, representative of the Korean side, told at the "Claims Committee" on May 19, 1953, "there were cases where Korean women went to the South East Asian countries such as Singapore under the jurisdiction of the Navy as 'comfort women' during the war and returned home leaving money or property behind" that asked for a refund. Jang Ki-young said, "comfort women are asking us to do something while presenting receipts issued by the military."[3]

The mobilisation of comfort women during the Japanese colonial era was a known fact. Among the soldiers at the time, including Koreans, there was not a small amount of experience surrounding comfort women. Since the comfort women were an underprivileged class, the discussion may not have been focused in earnest, and since it was an uncomfortable topic to discuss, it may have been implicitly understood and passed on. Regardless of the circumstances, I do not agree with the conclusion of the public-private joint committee that the comfort women issue cannot be seen as resolved by the Property and Claims Settlement Agreement. Since the Property and Claims Agreement is a lump-sum agreement, it should be understood that the comfort women issue has been resolved by the provision "completely and finally settled"[4] in relation to "all claims of one State Party and its nationals against the other State party and its nationals".[5]

Meanwhile, regardless of whether or not the Property and Claims Settlement Agreement includes the comfort women issue, that issue appears to be a typical sovereign immunity case. On 8 January 2021, the Seoul Central District Court recognised damages of 100 million won each for claims made by former comfort women for the Japanese military against Japan,[6] on 21 April 2021, however, a decision was made to dismiss the claims of other comfort women on the grounds of state immunity.[7] Even if sovereign immunity is excluded and a decision is made in

3 Lee Dong-Jun, An Uncomfortable Retrospective on 70 Years of Korea-Japan Relations from Diplomatic Historical Records, Samin, 2016, pp. 79~80

4 Article 2, paragraph 3

5 Article 2, Paragraph 1

6 Seoul Central District Court 2021. January 8 Decision 2016 Gahap 506092

7 Seoul Central District Court 2021. April 21. Decision 2016 Gahap 580239

favour of a plaintiff against a defendant state it is virtually impossible to enforce,[8] so there is no need for the judiciary to trigger discord with neighbouring countries with an unnecessary judgment.

(B) Process of the Agreement

1. Background

The "Comfort Women Agreement" in December 2015 was a difficult achievement. The comfort women activists cantered on the "Jeongdaehyeop" persistently demanded Japan's state responsibility, that is, compensation for damages by the state, which Japan accepted. The Japanese government, which has consistently maintained that the issue had already been settled by the 1965 Korea-Japan Claims Settlement Agreement, made a difficult decision. The comfort women agreement was a result of the Korean government's tenacity, Japanese Prime Minister Shinzo Abe's political power, the Obama administration's persuasion, and even Xi Jinping's rear support. The two governments agreed that the issue had been "finally and irreversibly" resolved. Japanese Prime Minister Shinzo Abe announced, "I offer my heartfelt apology and remorse to all those who experienced countless suffering as comfort women and suffered incurable physical and mental wounds."

However, NGO and activists in South Korea criticised this as a "hashed agreement against the will of the victim," and the media agreed with this claim. President Park Geun-hye was impeached and the government has changed. On 9 January 2018, Foreign Minister Kang Kyung-wha of the Moon Jae-in government announced that the Korean government would ignore the fund from the Japanese government, and would finance the equivalent of 1 billion yen from the Korean government's budget by the statement of "government's position on the direction of handling the comfort women agreement". On 21 January 2019, the Ministry of Gender Equality and Family revoked the permission to establish the "Reconciliation and Healing Foundation," an executive

---

8 Vienna Convention on Diplomatic Relations
Article 22.
3. The premises of the mission, their furnishings and other property thereon and the means of transport of the mission shall be immune from search, requisition, attachment or execution.

body for the "2015 Korea-Japan comfort women agreement." President Moon Jae-in, who had made "renegotiation of the comfort women agreement" a presidential campaign promise, disbanded the "Reconciliation and Healing Foundation."[9]

However, at a New Year's press conference on 18 January 2021, President Moon Jae-in suddenly changed his position and confirmed that the 2015 agreement on comfort women between the governments of Korea and Japan was "an official agreement between the two governments." On 22 January 2021, Kang Chang-il, the new ambassador to Japan, made an excuse at Narita Airport that the dissolution of the Reconciliation and Healing Foundation was caused by the resignation of the chairman and directors and not because of government pressure.[10]

2. Progress

In December 2012, the Liberal Democratic Party won a landslide victory in the general election, and the second Abe administration was launched. In February 2013, President Park Geun-hye was inaugurated, and conservative governments took power consecutively. President Park Geun-hye was adamant that she would not hold a meeting with Prime Minister Abe unless the comfort women issue was resolved. After taking office, President Park Geun-hye broke the custom of visiting the United States and Japan in that order, and visited China first. In 2015, despite opposition from the United States, President Park Geun-hye, who took part in China's "70th anniversary parade of the military victory over Japan, stood side by side with Xi Jinping and Vladimir Putin to give Japan a blow. She suggested President Xi Jinping that a three-country summit be held in Seoul.[11] Professor Emeritus of Tokyo University Haruki Wada evaluates that she tried to pressure Prime Minister Abe with the support of the US and China by holding a Korea-Japan summit along with a trilateral summit. A trilateral summit was held on 1 November 2015, and President Xi Jinping also stressed the importance of historical issues and put pressure on Prime Minister Abe.[12]

---

9 Kang Sang-jung(translated by No Su-kyung), Korean Peninsula and Japan's Future, Four Seasons, 2021, pp. 111~112.

10 Donga Ilbo 2021.01.22.; Chosun Ilbo 2021.01.23.

11 Ibid., p. 110.

12 Haruki Wada (translated by Jung Jae-jung), For the Settlement of the Comfort Women Issues by Japanese Soldiers, History Space, 2016, pp. 238～243.

The contents of the comfort women agreement between the governments of Korea and Japan on 28 December 2015 acknowledged the Japanese military's involvement in the recruitment of comfort women according to the Kono Statement, supplemented the deficiencies of the Asian Women's Peace Fund in 1995, and through the foundation established by the Korean government, the comfort women's honour and dignity were restored and their wounds were healed. On the premise that these measures are steadily being taken, it is confirmed that the comfort women issue has been "finally and irreversibly resolved" and that the two countries refrain from accusing each other regarding the comfort women issue. Afterwards, the Japanese government remitted 1 billion yen to the foundation, and the foundation paid 100 million won each to 35 out of 47 surviving comfort women and 20 million won each to 64 families of 199 deceased comfort women.

3. *Victim-Cantered Approach*

The 2015 comfort women agreement was criticised for being contrary to "Victim-Cantered Approach." On November 29, 1985, the UN General Assembly adopted the Declaration of Basic Principles of Justice for Victims of Crime and Abuse of Power.[13] Since then, the "Principle of Protection of Victims' Rights" has been developed into principles of international human rights law, and on 16 December 2005, Basic Principles and Guidelines on the Right to a Remedy and Reparation for Victims of Gross Violations of International Human Rights Law and Serious Violations of International Humanitarian Law was adopted as major principle in the UN.[14] After the Ministry of Foreign Affairs decided to initiate director-general-level consultations for the comfort women agreement, it met with victims' groups and private experts across the country, and it is said that it contacted victims and related groups more than 15 times in 2015 alone.[15] This was confirmed on 26 May

---

13 <https://www.un.org/en/ga/search/view_doc.asp?symbol=A/RES/40/34> (2021. 8. 20. visited)

14 Basic Principles and Guidelines on the Right to a Remedy and Reparation for Victims of Gross Violations of International Human Rights Law and Serious Violations of International Humanitarian Law <https://undocs.org/A/RES/60/147> (2021. 8. 20. 접속).

15 Shim Gyu-sun, Comfort Women Movement, from Sanctuary to Plaza, Nanam, 2021, p. 297.

2022 as a result of a lawsuit filed against the Ministry of Foreign Affairs by the Lawyers for Human Rights and Peace on the Korean Peninsula.

On 17 October 1990, in the early days of the comfort women movement, six conditions were presented to Japanese Prime Minister Toshiki Kaifu and President Roh Tae-woo including "acknowledgment of the fact of forced mobilisation", "official apology", "apology to survivors and bereaved families", and "compensation for damage" etc. by eight women groups. These six protests were unilaterally organised by women activists without any discussion with the victims.[16] In particular, there are complaints from comfort women that the publication and sale of the "Comfort Women's Testimonies" were carried out arbitrarily by the activists without considering the position of comfort women.

Even after the establishment of the "Reconciliation and Healing Foundation", the foundation sent an official letter of cooperation to meet the comfort women living together in the "House of Sharing", but was rejected. The House of Sharing sent an official letter saying, "the comfort women are against the Agreement and Reconciliation Healing Foundation and cannot cooperate because they do not want to meet the officials."[17] If so, the Ministry of Foreign Affairs has adhered to the principle of Victim-Centred Approach, and there is no ground for activists to criticise the "2015 comfort women agreement" under the guise of Victim-Cantered Approach.

4. *Retrospection of Haruki Wada*

On 13 June 1995, on the 50th anniversary of the end of the war, Japan announced the launch of the Asian Peace and Friendship Fund for Women (hereinafter referred to as the Asian Women's Fund). The contents of the project were to raise funds for national atonement from the private sector, and to provide medical welfare and other projects with government funds. The government intended to express its candid remorse and apology to the comfort women and organise historical materials on the comfort women to serve as a lesson in history. In a joint statement on June 14, the following day, 22 Korean activist groups,

---

16 Shim Gyu-sun, Comfort Women Movement, from Sanctuary to Plaza, Nanam, 2021, p. 297.

17 Shim Gyu-sun, Comfort Women Movement, from Sanctuary to Plaza, Nanam, 2021, p. 307.

demanded that "the Asian Women's Fund plan be abandoned, and the victims receive an apology and legal compensation through a resolution of the National Diet."

On 11 January 1997, the Japanese government launched a project with a plan to provide an apology letter from the Prime Minister, 2 million yen in compensation and 3 million yen in medical welfare subsidy to each of the 7 comfort women who expressed their intention to receive funds in Korea despite the opposition of Jeongdaehyeop. Jeongdaehyeop, which demanded recognition of Japan's state responsibility and state compensation, accused the Japanese government of bribe operation through private funds. Yoon Mi-hyang said, "If you receive the money from the Japanese who does not admit guilt, that means you admit you were a 'volunteer public prostitute' as Japanese politicians and right-wingers have said so far."[18] Haruki Wada recorded that Jungok Yoon also made the same remarks, and expressed his thoughts, saying, "My respect for Jungok Yoon has not changed then and now, but I think this was something she shouldn't have said."[19] Comfort woman Seok Bok-soon (pseudonym) also testified that Jeongdaehyeop "only made harsh noises in her ears," saying that she was a "horror bitch when she received the money."

The "Civic Solidarity" of Korean activists independently raised funds and paid consolation money, excluding 7 people who received the "Asian Women's Fund" The new government of President Kim Dae-jung, who was elected in the December 1997 election, like the position of the Kim Young-sam government, proclaimed that it would no longer make any demands to the Japanese government on the comfort women issue. The government decided to pay 35 million won uniformly to the comfort women who chose not to receive the Asian Women's Fund.[20] In October 1998, President Kim Dae-jung visited Japan and announced the "Joint Declaration of New Korea-Japan Partnership in the 21st Century" with Prime Minister Obuchi. The Asian Women's Fund project ended in 2002, and the number of Korean recipients who received the consolation money from the Asian Women's Fund was 61.[21]

---

18 "Process and Prospects of the Resolution Movement", Sharing *Newsletter*, 1998.3.

19 Haruki Wada (translated by Jung Jae-jung), For the Settlement of the Comfort Women Issues by Japanese Soldiers, History Space, 2016, p. 167.

20 Chung Eui-yeon's Position on the Press Conference of Lee Yong-soo, 2020.5.8.

21 Haruki Wada (translated by Jung Jae-jung), For the Settlement of the Comfort Women Issues by Japanese Soldiers, History Space, 2016, p. 191.

II. Judicial decision on compensation for forced labour

(A) Claims of forced labour

The claims of forced labour are clearly included in the Property and Claims Settlement Agreement. Item 5 of the "Eight Guidelines for Korea's Claims to Japan" revealed in the Agreed Minutes (1) of the Property and Claims Settlement Agreement stipulates "reimbursement of uncollected money, compensation, and other claims by the Korean forced labours." However, the Supreme Court judged that the eight guidelines presented by the South Korean side were basically about the financial and civil debt relationship between Korea and Japan, and that there was no content premised on the illegality of Japanese colonial rule anywhere else in the eight guidelines. Paragraph 5 also does not presuppose an illegal act on the part of Japan, and therefore, it is difficult to see that the claim for compensation for forced labour is included in the "claim for reimbursement of uncollected money, compensation and other claims of the Korean forced labours".[22]

This is because the Park Chung-hee government recognises the funds for claims as the "price of the blood of our nation", and the principle of use of funds and management of funds is to warn descendants not to repeat the shame of the past and to create large-scale projects that will remain with the nation. It is a judgment contrary to the historical fact that the idea of "national blood tax" was frequently injected for the sake of the people.[23]

(B) Background

On 30 October 2018, the Supreme Court rejected Nippon Steel's reappeal.[24] This was a ruling that directly contradicted Japan's position that the scope of the 1965 Property and Claims Settlement Agreement

---

22 Supreme Court 2018. 10. 30. Decision 2013da61381.

23 Jung Jae-jung, 『The History of Korea-Japan Relations in the 20th Century Reading by Topics and Issues』, History and Criticism, 2014, pp. 224~225.

24 Supreme Court 2018. 10. 30. Decision 2013 da61381. The original judgment was made by the Seoul High Court on July 10, 2013. Sentence 2012 Na44947 judgment. Nippon Steel merged with Sumitomo Metals in October 2012 and changed its name to Nippon Steel & Sumitomo Metal.

included individual claims. With the number of victims of forced labour recognised by the Korean government reaching 220,000 and more than 70 cases of forced labour lawsuits filed against Japanese companies, the ruling has emerged as the biggest issue between Korea and Japan. The Supreme Court's ruling in 2018 is based on the Supreme Court's reversal of two High Court rulings in May 2012 that dismissed the claims of forced labourers, saying, "High court's rulings presupposes the recognition that colonial rule is legal, and therefore runs counter to the values of the Constitution."[25] Regarding the Supreme Court ruling in May 2012, it should be noted that most of the post-war responsibility after World War II was handled as a lump sum compensation agreement concluded through state-to-state negotiations and individual rights extinguished through it. According to the Supreme Court's judgment, even after a diplomatic agreement between countries, individuals who are not satisfied with the result can still file a lawsuit, so there was criticism that the other country may not respond to diplomatic negotiations itself.[26]

Later, the remanded High Court recognised damages, and Nippon Steel re-appealed to the Supreme Court. The Japanese government protested that it would bring the case before the International Court of Justice (ICJ) if the Korean judiciary acknowledged responsibility for damages.

On 30 October 2018, the entire Supreme Court dismissed Nippon Steel's re-appeal, and the relationship between Korea and Japan turned to the worst.

(C) Separation of powers and International Law

Right after the Supreme Court ruling in 2018, President Moon Jae-in put forward the separation of powers as an excuse for not trying to do any actions to cope with the impasse between two countries. On the other hand, since the Japanese government held that the Korean government should resolve individual claims according to the Property and Claims Settlement Agreement, a dispute arose between Korea and Japan over the interpretation of the Agreement. From the Japanese point of view, the Supreme Court ruling that colonial rule was illegal under the

---

25 Supreme Court 2012. 5. 24. Decision 2009 da68620.

26 Jung In-sup, International Law, Pagyoungsa, 2018, p. 454.

Korean constitution would be an unacceptable logic as it went beyond the Property and Claims Settlement Agreement and ignored the Treaty on Basic Relations between Korea and Japan of 1965.[27] In January 2019, the Japanese government requested diplomatic negotiations pursuant to Article 3, Paragraph 1 of the Property and Claims Settlement Agreement, followed by an arbitration committee pursuant to Article 3, Paragraphs 2 and 3 of the Agreement by setting a deadline for response on 20 May 2019. However, the Korean government did not respond at all.[28]

The "separation of powers", the constitutional principle of national governance, cannot be presented as a justification for a domestic judgment that violates international law. The preamble to the Vienna Convention on the Law of Treaties, which reflects customary international law, provides that states should not violate their treaty obligations under the guise of their own constitutions.[29] Article 27 of the Treaty stipulates that a Party may not invoke the provisions of its national law as its justification of its failure to perform a treaty. Japan's protest would not be a request for the Korean government to ignore the separation of powers and intervene in the final judgment, but rather a request for appropriate measures to prevent the judgment from affecting Japanese companies.

(D) Lower Court's attitude after 2018s ruling

On 7 June 2021, the Seoul Central District Court dismissed a claim for damages against 16 Japanese companies, including Nippon Steel, Nissan Chemical, and Mitsubishi Heavy Industries, by 85 conscripted workers and bereaved families. The court issued a ruling in conclusion consistent with the minority opinion of the Supreme Court decision in 2018, stating that "the individual right of a Korean citizen to make a claim against Japan or Japanese nationals cannot be said to have been extinguished or waived by the Korea-Japan Property and Claims Settlement Agreement, but that right cannot be exercised through a lawsuit."

---

27 Treaty on Basic Relations between Korea and Japan.

28 Kim Chnag-jun, "The Nature and Solution of the Controversy over the Korea-Japan Claims Settlement Agreement", Law Times 2019.10.14.

29 Recognizing the ever-increasing importance of treaties as a source of international law and as a means of developing peaceful co-operation among nations, whatever their constitutional and social systems,

Noting that the principles of free consent and of good faith and the pacta sunt servanda rule are universally recognised, ...

III. Illegal occupation

(A) Interpretation of "Already Null and Void"

Article 2 of the 1965 「Treaty on Basic Relations between the Republic of Korea and Japan」 (Korea-Japan Basic Relations Treaty) states, "it is confirmed that all treaties or agreements concluded between the Empire of Korea and the Empire of Japan on or before August 22, 1910 are already null and void". The "already null and void" part of this regulation corresponds to an "agree to disagree" that South Korea and Japan are expected to interpret differently. Korea interpreted it as null and void at the time of signing the Annexation Treaty in 1910, while Japan thought it was valid until August 15, 1945, and interpreted it as "already invalid" at the time of signing the Basic Relations Treaty in 1965. In other words, it is a provision that is expected to be understood domestically in the way each country wants, assuming that both Korea and Japan have completely different positions on the illegality of colonial rule.

(B) Illegality of colonial rule

Since the 19th century, imperialism has emerged as a universal phenomenon. At the time Western imperialism divided the world into colonies, it is said that Thailand, Nepal, Afghanistan, and Ethiopia were all countries that did not suffer from colonial rule due to geopolitical factors. Among them, Thailand is the least stable, while others are impoverished or at war.[30] The illegality of colonial rule must be judged according to the international law of the time of imperialism. Current domestic norms should not be used as a tool for interpreting colonial illegality.

The imperialist powers, including China and Russia, which were competing with Japan, did not pay attention to the Korean Empire's claim that the 1905 Eulsa Protectorate Treaty and the 1910 Annexation Treaty were invalid. The United States, Britain, France, etc., which signed treaties with Joseon, did not raise objections to Japan's measures to suspend the validity of each treaty. After the Eulsa Protectorate Treaty in 1905, Russia received the consul general's credentials from the Japanese government, blocked the Korean Empire's access to the Hague Peace Conference at Japan's request, and handled the Korean Empire-related affairs through

30 Hae-dong Yun, *Colonial State and Symmetrical State*, Somyung Publishing, 2022, p. 4.

the Japanese Residency-General.[31] The background of the Allied Powers discussing Korea's independence at the Cairo Declaration in November 1943 and the Potsdam Conference in July 1945 was only to separate part of the territory in order to hold Japan accountable for the defeat, but it was not based on the premise of the illegality of colonial rule. In the 1951 San Francisco Peace Treaty, even former colonies of the Allied Powers, such as the Philippines, Laos, and Vietnam, received war reparations as members of the Allied Powers, but the reason why Korea was unable to participate in the Peace Treaty was probably because the Korean Empire was deemed to have disappeared with the 1910 Annexation Treaty.[32]

On the other hand, the fact that Japan gave up considerable property located on the Korean Peninsula after defeat in the Pacific War and separated Korea should also be considered. As of August 1945, 5.25 billion dollars (24 % of the total amount) of Japan's total foreign assets of 21.88 billion dollars were located in Korea. The Allied Forces Supreme Command (GHQ) estimated that Japanese assets in South Korea were $2.28 billion and Japanese assets in North Korea were $3 billion.[33] The U.S. Military Authorities, which had jurisdiction over South Korea, reverted Japanese property in Korea to the U.S. Military Government, regardless of state or private ownership, according to the Military Government Ordinance No. 33 promulgated on December 6, 1945. It was transferred to the Government of the Republic of Korea according to the 「Initial Agreement on Finance and Property between the Government of the Republic of Korea and the Government of the United States」 that took effect on 20 September 1945. The Korea-Japan Basic Relations Treaty and the Property and Claims settlement Agreement were established in this context.

*

[31] Choi Deok-kyu, "Russia's policy toward Korea and Japan's annexation of Korea(1905–1901)", Siberian and Far East Research Vol. 5, 2009, pp. 119–121.

[32] Joo Jin-yeol, "A Study on International Law Issues in the 1965 Korea-Japan Claims Settlement Agreement and the Individual Claims Case – Focusing on the Supreme Court's 2013 Da 61381 Decision on October 30, 2018", *Seoul International Law Review*, 25(2), December 2018, p. 189.

[33] Jung Jae-jung, 『The History of Korea-Japan Relations in the 20th Century Reading by Topics and Issues』, *History and Criticism*, 2014, p. 67

In conclusion, Article 38(1) of the Statute of the International Court of Justice recognises "the general principles of law recognised by civilised nations" as the source of international law. The principle of "a contract must be kept" (*pacta sunt servanda*) corresponds to the "principle of law recognised by civilised nations". If a problem arises between Korea and Japan due to a misunderstanding of international norms by the judiciary, the problem should first be resolved in accordance with the dispute resolution procedure of diplomatic consultation and arbitration stipulated in the Property and Claims Settlement Agreement. If there was a special reason not to go through such a procedure, Korea should have asked Japan for understanding and pledged to take measures to ensure that Japanese companies would not be affected by the execution of the ruling.

The deterioration of bilateral relations between Korea and Japan was mostly attributable to the fact that the Korean government avoided taking appropriate measures. Korea, a party to the Property and Claims Settlement Agreement, should not unilaterally interpret or change the treaty, excluding Japan, the other party. Nonetheless, the Korean courts used the preamble of the Korean constitution in defying the Property and Claims Settlement Agreement. Given the nature of the Property and Claims Settlement Agreement, which is a lump sum compensation treaty, it is appropriate to interpret that "all claims related to colonial rule" fall within its scope.

Therefore, necessary measures must be taken so that the ruling on compensation for forced labour does not adversely affect Japanese companies. This is a measure that the Moon Jae-in administration should have taken right after the Supreme Court ruling in 2018. The government proposed a plan to reimburse the plaintiffs through a government-affiliated foundation. If it is a subrogation method, I understand that direct payment from the national treasury is more desirable.

The government need to express regret over the Moon Jae-in administration's crippled attitude toward the "2015 comfort women agreement" and restores the Reconciliation and Healing Foundation to implement the comfort women agreement. It is appropriate to relocate the statue of comfort women in front of the Japanese embassy. The Vienna Convention on Diplomatic Relations obliges the receiving State to take all appropriate measures to protect the security of the foreign mission (Article 22, paragraph 2).

The Singapore Convention on Mediation: An opportunity for Korea

Guillermo PALAO
Spain

The context of the Singapore Convention is one whereby Eurasia constitutes a vast territory where trade relations between its component countries multiply, making it a fertile area for cross-border commercial disputes. However, its legal fragmentation and the absence of common international Conventions make the legal management of this type of disputes problematic, generating a high level of uncertainty and costs for the parties. This situation is evident with respect to the recourse to Courts, as there are no Conventions binding Eurasian countries. Nor have even to two recent Conventions drawn up by the Hague Conference on Private International Law been broadly ratified by Eurasian countries[1]. This can increase legal certainty and overcome the challenges posed for traders.

In this context, Alternative Dispute Resolution (ADR) mechanisms offer valuable incentives to ensure predictability and legal certainty for traders in Eurasia. A landscape which, until recently, was dominated by International Commercial Arbitration, thanks to the texts of the United Nations Commission on International Trade Law (UNCITRAL): the 1958 New York Convention on the Recognition and Enforcement of Foreign Arbitral Awards[2], and the 1985 Model Law on International Commercial Arbitration -amended in 2006-[3].

---

1 *Convention of 30.6.2005 on Choice of Court Agreements and* Convention of 2.7.2019 on the Recognition and Enforcement of Foreign Judgments in Civil or Commercial Matters, at: https://www.hcch.net/

2 *Treaty Series*, vol. 330, nº 4739.

3 A/40/17, Annex I, Supplement nº 17 and A/61/17, Supplement nº 17. See BINDER, P., *International Commercial Arbitration and Mediation in UNCITRAL Model Law jurisdictions*, Alphen aan den Rijn, Kluwer, 2019 (4ª ed.), pp. 5–548.

This this legal landscape has changed significantly with the adoption of the United Nations Convention on International Settlement Agreements Resulting from Mediation (the Singapore Convention) of 2018[4]. An international instrument applicable from 2020, for 13 of the 53 countries that signed the Convention[5], complemented by the UNCITRAL Model Law on International Commercial Mediation and International Settlement Agreements Resulting from Mediation of 2018 (amending the UNCITRAL Model Law on International Commercial Conciliation of 2002)[6]. Two instruments which, due to the growing popularity of mediation[7], provide a remarkable opportunity for the resolution of cross-border commercial disputes in the Euro-Asian context.

Before the adoption of the Singapore Convention, international mediation lacked a Convention that favoured its promotion in relation to conflicts of a private and cross-border character. The Singapore Convention is thus expected to play a decisive role in favouring the promotion of mediation in an area in which party autonomy prevails, and has resulted in an appropriate breeding ground for the development of self-regulatory initiatives[8], as well as the practice developed by Mediation and Arbitration Centres and the elaboration of "Codes of Conduct" to guide the performance of mediators[9]. Besides, the UNCITRAL Conciliation Rules of 1980[10], followed by the UNCITRAL Model

---

4 A/RES/73/198.

5 Belarus, Ecuador, Fiji, Honduras, Georgia, Kazakhstan, Republic of Korea, Philippines, Qatar, Saudi Arabia Singapore, Turkey and Uruguay.

6 BINDER, P., *cit.*, pp. 549–667.

7 ESPLUGUES, C., "Mediation", in *Encyclopaedia of Private International Law*, 2, Cheltenham, Edward Elgar, 2017, pp. 1246–1255, p. 1246; STRONG, S.I., "Beyond International Commercial Arbitration? The Promise of International Commercial Mediation", *Washington University Journal of Law & Policy*, 2014, 45, pp. 1–39, p. 12.

8 ANDERSON, D.Q., "Supporting party autonomy in the enforcement of cross-border mediated settlement agreements: A brave new world or unchartered territory", in *Max Planck Institute Luxembourg Summer School-International Association of Procedural Law Summer School 2018: Privatizing Dispute Resolution and Its Limits* (Nomos, 3rd edition), Singapore Management University School of Law Research Paper No. 41/2019, pp. 1–27.

9 BÜHRING-UHLE, CH., *Arbitration and Mediation in International Business*, La Haya, Kluwer Law International, 2006, pp. 224–228.

10 AG 35/52.

Law on International Commercial Conciliation of 2002[11], stand out. Although, despite their positive effect[12], not only they were criticised[13], but also their non-binding nature does not favour a relevant impetus for cross-border commercial mediation.

However, Arbitration relied on a successful regulatory framework with the 1958 New York Convention, as a too significant precedent to be ignored by the promoters of the Singapore Convention[14].

After the 2014 proposal[15], the negotiation of the Convention was not easy until 2017[16], thanks to a "compromise package" concluded at UNCITRAL Working Group II[17], agreeing on: (a) the legal effect of mediated agreements; (b) their relationship with those concluded in the framework of judicial proceedings or arbitration; (c) the possibility that Parties could declare the need for disputants to opt in to the regime established by the Convention; (d) the impact of the procedure and the

---

11 At: https://uncitral.un.org/sites/uncitral.un.org/files/media-documents/uncitral/en/03-90953_ebook.pdf. ALEXANDER, N., *International and Comparative Mediation. Legal Perspectives*, Alphen aan den Rijn, Kluwer, 2009, pp. 385–440.

12 HOPT, K.J./ STEFFEK, F., "Mediation: Comparison of Laws, Regulatory Models, Fundamental issues", in *Mediation. Principles and Regulation in Comparative Perspective*, Oxford, OUP, 2013, pp. 3–130, pp. 107–108.

13 ALEXANDER, N., *cit.*, pp. 346–350.

14 WOLSKI, B., "Enforcing mediated settlement agreements (MSAs): critical questions and directions for future research", *Contemporary Asia Arbitration Journal*, 2014, 7, pp. 87–118; LO, CH., "Desirability of a New International legal framework for cross-border enforcement of certain mediated settlement agreements", *Contemporary Asia Arbitration Journal*, 2014, 7, pp. 119–138; SUSSMAN, E., "The Singapore Convention. Promoting the Enforcement and Recognition of International Mediated Settlement Agreements", *ICC Dispute Resolution Bulletin*, 2018, 3, pp, 42–54, pp. 44–45.

15 A/CN.9/WGI.I/WP.188 A/CN.9/822.

16 ABRAMSON, H., "The New Singapore Mediation Convention: The Process and key Choices", *Cardozo Journal of Conflict Resolution*, 2019, 20, pp. 1037–1062; CHUA, E., "The future of international mediated settlement agreements: Of conventions, challenges and choices", *Tan Pan Online: A Chinese-English Journal on Negotiation*, 2015, pp. 1–11; McCORMICK, K./ ONG, S.S.M., "Through the looking glass: an insider's perspective into the making of the Singapore Convention on mediation", *Singapore Academy of Law Journal*, 2019, 31, pp. 520–546; MORRIS-SHARMA, N.Y., "Constructing the Convention on Mediation. The Chairperson's Perspective", *Singapore Academy of Law Journal*, 2019, 31, pp. 487–519.

17 SCHNABEL, T., "The Singapore Convention on Mediation: A framework for Cross-Border recognition and Enforcement of Mediated Settlements", *Pepperdine Dispute Resolution Law Journal*, 2019, 19, pp, 1–60, pp. 6–7, 55–58.

conduct of mediators on enforcement; and (e) the form of the instrument as a Convention.

I. Main elements of the Singapore Convention

The Singapore Convention is a concise, highly flexible and functional text of 16 articles[18], which not only builds on precedents and models such as the New York Convention, but also offers innovative responses and an advanced circulation model for mediation settlement agreements[19].

(A) Objectives and scope of application

The Singapore Convention tackles one of the main obstacles for the promotion of international commercial mediation: the cross-border circulation of international settlement agreements resulting from mediation[20]. An aim to be achieved by overcoming the merely contractual consideration of settlement agreements and by developing a delocalised title with a direct enforceability in the required Party[21].

The Convention is fully applicable as of 12 September 2020, for those mediation settlement agreements concluded after its entry into force (Art. 9[22]), and it is exclusively applicable *inter partes.*

---

18 DEVAUX, C., "Entrée en vigueur de la Convention de Singapour: de noveaux horizons pour la mediation commerciale internationale", *Journal du Droit International,* 2020, 4, pp. 875–896, p. 878.

19 CLAXTON, J., "The Singapore Convention for Mediation: From Promotion to Workable Standards by Way of New York" (2020), at: https://ssrn.com/abstract=3612380.

20 SÁNCHEZ LÓPEZ, B., "La eficacia transfronteriza de los acuerdos de mediación y la Convención de Singapur: ¿Grandes esperanzas?", *CDT,* 2020, 12, pp. 1406–1445, p. 1428; STRONG, S.I., "Realizing Rationality: An Empirical Assessment of International Commercial Mediation", *Washington and Lee Law Review*, 2016, 73, pp. 1973–2085, pp. 2064–2067.

21 ESPLUGUES, C., "La Convención de Singapur de 2018 sobre mediación y la creación de un título deslocalizado dotado de fuerza ejecutiva: una apuesta novedosa, y un mal relato", *Revista Española de Derecho Internacional,* 2020, 72, pp. 53–80, pp. 61–66.

22 ALEXANDER. N./ CHONG, S., *The Singapore Convection on Mediation. A Commentary*, Alphen aan den Rijn, Kluwer, 2019, p. 167.

Its material scope of application is covered by Arts. 1 and 2. Art. 1 provides that the Convention applies to settlement agreements resulting from mediation in writing, solving disputes in commercial matters of an international character[23]. Thus, four essential elements delimit its scope.

(a) According to Art. 1(1), it must be an agreement resulting from mediation. From a positive perspective, Art. 2(3) defines "mediation" in a very extensive way[24], regardless of its possible denomination, by referring to any procedure whereby the parties attempt to reach an amicable settlement of their dispute with the assistance of one or more third parties (the mediator) who has no authority to impose a solution on them. From a negative dimension, it applies to agreements reached only as a result of a mediation procedure, in order to avoid overlapping with those of another nature. Thus, its Art. 1(3) excludes agreements that took place as a result of a judicial procedure or when they could be enforced as a judgement or an arbitration award[25].

(b) Art. 1(1) also provides that the agreement must be concluded "in writing", together with the requirements of Arts. 4 and 5: not only the need for the agreement to be in writing, but also for the signature of the parties, as well as evidence of the existence of the mediation[26], including electronic communications[27].

(c) The Convention covers disputes of a "commercial" character, which is delimited in a negative way in Art. 1(2), excluding mediation procedures in matters where party autonomy is limited (i.e., consumer, family, inheritance or employment disputes)[28].

---

23 DEASON, E. E., "What´s in a Name? The terms "Commercial" and "Mediation" in the Singapore Convention on Mediation", *Cardozo Journal of Conflict Resolution*, 2019, 20, pp. 1149–1172.

24 DEVAUX, D., cit., p. 879; SCHNABEL, T., "The Singapore", cit., pp. 15–17.

25 ZELLER, B./ TRAKMAN, L., "Mediation and Arbitration: the process of enforcement", *Uniform Law Review*, 2019, pp. 1–18, p. 8; ROSNER, N., "The Singapore Convention: reflections on articles 1.3 on scope, 8.1(b) on reservations, and 12 on Regional Economic Integration Organisations", *Cardozo Journal of Conflict Resolution*, 2019, 20, pp. 1259–1263, pp. 1260–1263.

26 SCHNABEL, T., "The Singapore", cit., pp. 27–34.

27 DEVAUX, C., cit., p. 887.

28 TASENDE ITURVIDE, I.J., "Reflexiones sobre la nueva Convención de las Naciones Unidas sobre los acuerdos de transacción internacional resultantes de mediación ("Convención de Singapur")", *Revista de Derecho de la Universidad de Montevideo*, 2020, 37, pp. 71–91, p. 79.

However, from a positive point of view, it covers disputes in which a State is involved and even those that might arise in relation to foreign investment[29].

(d) Art. 1(1) provides that the settlement agreement must have an "international" character at the time it was concluded (but also it could serve as a model for domestic situations)[30]. Such character is defined in paragraphs (a) and (b), based on: (a) whether the parties have their "place of business" in different countries or, if they have more than one "place of business", the one which is most closely connected with another country – i.e., a substantial part of the it is to be performed-; and (b), in their absence, where they have their habitual residence. However, the place where the mediation procedure took place is irrelevant, as the Convention designs a "delocalised" title in which the "seat" of the mediation procedure is no relevant[31].

(B) Principles and requirements for the enforcement

The Singapore Convention creates a title which may circulate practically freely and directly among the Parties to it. In this sense, it avoids conflicting terms such as "recognition"[32], mentioning in different provisions expressions such as "enforcement", "invoke", "enforce" or "grant measures"[33].

The important Art. 3[34] stresses the dual function that a mediation settlement agreement may play in practice (positive and negative)[35].

---

29 SCHNABEL, T., "The Singapore", cit., pp. 22–23.

30 Ibid., p. 20.

31 SILVESTRI, E., "The Singapore Convention on mediated settlement agreements: a new string to the bow of international mediation", *Revista Eletrônica de Direito Processual,* 2019, 20, pp. 189–200, p. 193.

32 Ibid., p. 35.

33 ESPLUGUES, C., "La Convención", cit., pp. 67–69.

34 PALAO, G., "Article 3. General principles", in *The Singapore Convention on Mediation. A Commentary on the United Nations Convention on International Settlement Agreements Resulting from Mediation*, Cheltenham, Edward Elgar, 2022, pp. 107–129; SCHNABEL, T., "Recognition by Any Other Name: Article 3 of the Singapore Convention on Mediation", *Cardozo Journal of Conflict Resolution*, 2019, 20, pp. 1181–1196.

35 SCHNABEL, T., "The Singapore", cit., pp. 35–36 y 39–40.

Art. 3(1) assigns to it a function of a "sword", authorising to call its execution in broad terms, as well as to the requested authority to order its enforcement. While Art. 3(2) reflects its "shield" effect, as a party may invoke it as an exception, in order to prove that the conflict has already been solved. A double effect to be guaranteed in accordance with the conditions established by the Convention and on those set out in the procedural rules of the requested Party; apart from the clarifications regarding the formal requirements of the agreement (Art. 4), and the grounds to refuse to grant measures to it (in Art. 5). Consequently, the Singapore Convention even grants this agreement a more favourable position than arbitration awards covered by the New York Convention[36].

Art. 4 of the Convention sets out the formal requirements to be fulfilled by settlement agreement[37]. Art. 4(1) provides that the party should submit to the authority of the requested Party: both the agreement signed by the parties – although not requiring the signature of the mediator- as well as to "evidence" that it was reached as a result of a mediation procedure; such as: the signature of the mediator on it or a separate document referring to it, as well as a certificate issued by the institution where it was concluded, or any other evidence that could be provided to prove it. Art. 4(2) establishes that the signature requirement may also be satisfied by electronic means. Art. 4(3) states that the authority may request a translation of the agreement into its, while Art. 4(4) determines that the requested State authority may request such documentation as it needs to verify compliance with the conditions of the Convention. Art. 4(5) underlines that the authority must always operate "expeditiously" when examining the request for the measures in question.

(C) Refusal to grant relief

The model of cross-border circulation of settlement agreements of the Singapore Convention enables a direct enforcement, when they fulfil the

36 CHUA, E., "The Singapore convention on mediation. A brighter future for Asian dispute resolution", *Asian Journal of International Law*, 2019, pp. 1–11, p. 11, PALAO, G., "Las relaciones entre las Convenciones de Singapur sobre mediación y de Nueva York sobre arbitraje de 1958; entre el mito y la realidad," in *Meditaciones sobre mediación (MED+)*, Valencia, Tirant lo Blanch, 2022, pp. 201–230.

37 SITT, A.J., "The Singapore Convention: When has a Mediation Taken Place (Article 4)?", *Cardozo Journal of Conflict Resolution*, 2019, 20, pp. 1173–1180.

requirements laid down in the Convention and the procedural rules of the requested Party. Among these conditions, Art. 5 plays a key role[38] and it is modelled on Art. V of the 1958 New York Convention[39]. However, the grounds for refusal (*numerus clausus*[40]) do not mention either the governing law of the mediation or the law of the country of origin of the settlement, with an autonomous delimitation in the absence of a "seat" of the mediation procedure for the purposes of its supervision.

The grounds for refusal to enforce a foreign settlement agreement are found in Art. 5(1) of the Convention, and requires the party against whom measures are requested to prove one of the five grounds in paragraphs (a) to (f).

The first ground refers to the incapacity of the parties, for their personal circumstances or the subjective lack of "mediability" of the conflict. Secondly, others relate to the settlement agreement: to the circumstances affecting it, whether due to its invalidity, its ineffectiveness, the impossibility of its fulfilment or of its being binding, its non-definitive status or its subsequent modification. Similarly, some grounds relate to the obligations contained in it, either because they have already been fulfilled or because they are not clear or comprehensible. In addition, the cases in which measures could not be granted due to the contradiction of their execution with the terms of the agreement itself. Besides, some grounds relate to the mediator and conduct during the procedure[41], being one of the few references made by the Convention to the minimum quality standards the procedure must meet to guarantee the rights of the parties. A positive mention, but also worthy of criticism[42], with a restrictive interpretation, that refer to breach of the rules applicable to the mediator or to the procedure – i.e., those established in a Code of Conduct -, provided that this has led to the adoption of the agreement; or that the mediator failed to disclose circumstances affecting his lack of impartiality or independence.

---

38 SCHNABEL, T., "The Singapore", cit., pp. 41–47.

39 *Cfr.* ESPLUGUES, C., "La Convención", cit., pp. 57–58.

40 Ibid., pp. 57–58 y 69–77.

41 JALLIPETIS, M., "Singapore Convention Defences Based On Mediator's Misconduct: Articles 5.1 (e) (f)", *Cardozo Journal of Conflict Resolution*, 2019, 20, pp. 1197–1208.

42 DEVAUX, C., cit., pp. 888–893.

This ground should be interpreted restrictively, when the agreements were not concluded if those elements were disclosed at the appropriate time.

With regard to the grounds to reject enforcement *ex officio* (Art. 5(2)), two are mentioned in paragraphs (a) and (b). First, the traditional ground related to the contradiction with the public order of the law of the requested Party. The second ground relates to the lack of objective "mediability" of the conflict, which has to be delimited with regard to the provisions of the law of the requested Party. Once again, since there is no law on the "seat" of the mediation procedure.

II. The Singapore Convention as an opportunity for Eurasia

The Singapore Convention plays a significant role in promoting mediation both internationally and in relation to the regions and countries that constitute Eurasia. It offers a mechanism for the resolution of private international disputes to trades in this vast territory and fills a significant gap, as the first multilateral instrument in this field, favouring the cross-border circulation of mediation settlement agreements, with a symbolic effect for the promotion of mediation in Eurasian[43].

In this respect, its elaboration within the framework of the UNCITRAL (Art. 10), or its parallelism with the New York Convention, are decisive elements to be taken into consideration by Eurasian countries when considering its ratification (Art. 11), just like the publication of a Model Law.

Anyway, this Convention may relate to other Conventions present in the Eurasian context. In its regard, Art. 7 establishes the principle of "maximum effectiveness" when overlapping with other instruments[44], so the application of the Convention shall not deprive the right to invoke a settlement agreement when provided by the Law or Treaties of the Party to the Convention in which such an agreement is sought to be enforced. In addition, Art. 1(3) includes a series of exclusions to its scope

---

[43] MORRIS-SHARMA, N.Y., "The Singapore Convention is Live, and Multilateralism, Alive¡", *Cardozo Journal of Conflict Resolution,* 2019, 20, pp. 1009–1021, pp. 1020–1021.

[44] SÁNCHEZ LÓPEZ, B., cit., p. 1427.

of application that affect its implementation when it derives from a judicial or arbitral decision[45]. However, this limitation does not avoid their interference and the need to coordinate mediation and Courts[46]. Art. 6 refer to "parallel" requests or claims before a judicial or arbitral authority[47], providing that the requested State authority may not only delay its decision (as mentioned in Art. 4), but also require the other State authority to guarantee that effect[48].

The implications of the Convention for the Regional Economic Integration Organisations (REIO) that coexist in Eurasia must also be considered, bearing in mind Arts. 8 and 12[49].

Art. 8 (1) contains the available reservations[50]. While subparagraph (a) provides that a Party may exclude its application to agreements involving a State agency or a person acting on its behalf, subparagraph (b) determines that signatory countries may do so on the basis of an opt-in model, so that the Convention applies only if the Parties had so provided.

Art. 12 provides for the possibility for REIOs to become Parties to the Convention[51]. According to paragraph 1, REIOs may enjoy the same rights and obligations of any other Party. This refers to how they must formalise its membership, declare its competence and any reservations (paragraph 2), and equivalence in relation to the different terms used in the Convention to refer to a Party (paragraph 3). This provision also states that a REIO can give precedence to its own rules in respect of cases occurring within the Organisation if they conflict with those of

45 SCHNABEL, T., "The Singapore", cit., p. 26.

46 ANDERSON, D.Q., "The Singapore Convention on Mediation: Supplying the missing piece of the puzzle for dispute resolution", *Journal of the Malaysian Judiciary*, 2020, pp. 194–220, pp. 198–199.

47 ALEXANDER. N./ CHONG, S., cit., pp. 149–153.

48 TASENDE ITURVIDE, I.J., cit., p. 89.

49 *Cf.* ESPLUGUES, C./ IGLESIAS, J.L., "Mediation and private international law: improving free circulation of mediation agreements across the EU", in *The Implementation of the Mediation Directive. Compilation of In-depth Analyses*, Brussels, EPPO (PE 571.395), 2016, pp. 70–94, pp. 87–92.

50 APTER, I./ HENIG MUCHNIK, C., "Reservations in the Singapore Convention – Helping to Make the "New York Dream" Come True", *Cardozo Journal of Conflict Resolution*, 2019, 20, pp. 1267 ff.

51 ROSNER, N., cit., p. 1265. *Cr.* SCHNABEL, T., "The Singapore", cit., p. 59.

the Convention and if a substantial part of the agreement is not to be performed in a third country (paragraph 4).

*

In conclusion, the entry into force of the Singapore Convention offers an opportunity in a Eurasian context lacking common uniform international rules devoted to the resolution of international commercial disputes. In this regard, the effort of compromise underlying the Convention, the fact that it is supported by a renewed Model Law, its drafting within the UN and its inspiration in the New York Convention of 1958, are positive elements to be taken into consideration for its promotion in Eurasia.

Part III

Legal and political impact on security institutions (SCO, CSTO …): Expansion, re-"centration" or deconstruction of great ensembles?

Introduction

Pierre CHABAL
France

Bringing in the political and legal dimensions of the dynamics of Eurasian systems in the contemporary scene, part III of the book brings in focus the regional turmoil, the impact on institutions into the evolution of regional organisations. Its premisses are that it is through such regional organisations that the new Eurasian region is being built, despite ups and downs affecting their credibility and efficiency. To take but one example, the Shanghai Cooperation Organisation is indeed pursuing its track, despite events in 2022 (both the CSTO intervention into Kazakhstan and the Russian special military operation in Ukraine), with a 2023 SCO Summit that confirms the full membership of Iran and prepares for that of Belarus.

Its various chapters address an array of such organisations, of issues pertaining to their areas of work as well as stumbling and stepping stones regarding their evolution.

As a rapidly developing issue, migrations (Klara Makasheva, Leila Delovarova) play the greatest role at regional level, among neighbour countries. This "region-ness" also applies to the management and solution-seeking to problems and tensions, also among neighbours, due to migration flows. As to Central Asia and the Eurasian post-soviet space, solutions are both specifically regional and with a global impact. Yet, in Central Asia and more broadly in the Eurasian post-soviet space, there is still no single mechanism for coordinating migration processes. Existing Eurasian and Central Asian organisations do not have supranational powers, even if the Eurasian Economic Union (EAEU) has a coordinating role including for migrations.

The regional dimension of the Caspian (Zhulduz Baizakova) is enhanced by the centrality of the Collective Security Treaty Organisation (CSTO) in the defence and security architecture of post-soviet partners. With the activation of the CSTO in the 2000s and the eruption of conflicts (Azerbaijan, Armenia, Ukraine, Russia …), the Caspian region has attracted the attention and interest of the West. Conflicts in the region are no longer limited and risk destabilising parts of Eurasia. Territorial as well as cultural identities carry the resolve of lasting tensions, especially Armenia-Azerbaijan, with no certainty that the CSTO alone in the Caspian region can offer viable umbrellas. The key seems now how Russia and Iran will build new relations with the new Central Asia, especially if Armenia leaves the CSTO.

To put it simply, almost aphoristically, if the Organisation for Security and Cooperation in Europe (Philippe Lagrange) symbolises a Eurasia with peace in the making, and if the OSCE undergoes excessive criticism – as over the Russia-Ukraine war –, then it is the political integrity of Eurasia and her chance to maintain "security and cooperation" that is threatened. If not from Vancouver to Vladivostok, certainly from Brest (in France) to Vladivostok. In this sense, Ukraine is today the OSCE's test and as J. Monnet put it (as to the European communities), "Europe [Eurasia] will be built through its capacities to overcome crises". So, it is of particular relevance today for Eurasia how it manages present crises (Russia, Ukraine, Armenia, Azerbaijan, …) concretely, not just as an institutional buildup.

Shifting from the CSCE Eurasia (Lagrange) to the Eurasia proper (Gulmira Mashimbayeva) with the Collective Security Treaty Organisation (CSTO) and the Conference for Interaction and Confidence-building in Asia (CICA) as its core, it is clear that security has but a regional meaning. Central Asia as a region must lower its dependence on external security-providers (the USA, NATO, the EU) and devise its own security-architecture. Common political interests exist in that direction, all five Central Asian countries are members of the Central Asian Forum, established in November 2017, whereas they are not all members of the other existing organisations (CICA, CSTO, SCO …). This fact alone bears testimony to the other (simple) fact that, without a security structure that fully associates the whole of Central Asia, the new Asia cannot be "complete" in the middle and long term.

Characterised as other world regions by a clear conflict-potential, Eurasia (Leila Delovarova, Alibek Yermekov), is in principle stabilised and securitised by the Shanghai Cooperation Organisation. The Organisation was gradually but solidly built between the 1996 "process" and the 2004 "additions" of Observers, then further consolidated from 2017 with additional Members (India, Pakistan). In 2022, the SCO

Summit then qualified Central Asia as "the core of the SCO" dynamic, suggesting its enhanced role in Eurasia, somewhat easing out the China-Russia-(India) grip on the SCO Eurasia. The latter is being "activated" as a geopolitical entity by its gradual capacity to contain bilateral tensions among some of its SCO members, making it more able to meeting the challenge of the Indo-Pacific, with India's pivotal role vis-à-vis the West.

A Eurasian space *par excellence*, the Caspian region (Bakhyt Uderbaeva) connects both Europe's southeast and Asia's west, as a long-lasting geo-political stake of intercontinental trade. Having of late become a military back-base for open conflicts, notably the Russia-Ukraine war, the Caspian space has also become the object of new legal agreements, especially since the 2010s agreements signed by all five Caspian states. The sub-region has designed itself as sole guarantor of its own security, fending off both the OSCE (Lagrange) and the CICA (Mashimbayeva) in this role. Yet, for all their recent political determination to cast off dependence on Russia, other Caspian states acknowledge that recent international texts adopted do not provide a legal basis for stopping missile-launch by Russia from the Caspian Sea.

While it would be epistemologically satisfying to solve the conundrum of which came first: the egg (human) or the hen (institutions, especially regional) – Pierre Chabal –, the matter must, still, be addressed pragmatically. Four angles are proposed: parallel, consequential, diachronic and concomitant, to qualify relations and links between institutions and human deeds. Thus better put in perspectives, modern regions as illustrations of institution-building, are relevant to studying anew the way in which, to paraphrase J. Monnet, "institutions serve human actions but it is humans who give a meaning to institutional constructs". Eurasia and the new (Shanghai) Asia illustrate this rather well.

This institutional and organisational overview (part III of the book) does rather enlighten the topic of the "dynamics" of Eurasia, that is its "completion" – or not.

Migration management issues and regional organisations

Klara MAKASHEVA, Leila DELOVAROVA
Kazakhstan

Migration is a global phenomenon that affects not only the lives of millions of people in the world, but also the transformation of the modern system of international relations. It is a strong driver of sustainable development both in countries of origin and in countries of transit and of destination. Along with this, migration dynamics affect the processes of formation of cultural identity, security, and cooperation among countries and even regions of the world. According to the 2022 Report of the International Office for Migrations (IOM), the number of international migrants is 281 million. Most of international migrants are labour migrants (about 170 million), and the volume of their remittances exceeds $700 billion, despite decrease due to the pandemic[1].

Along with the quantitative increase of international migrants, the number of challenges and risks also multiplies both for the migrants themselves, who face violations of their rights, and for the countries of origin and of reception of migrants. In this regard, the connection of migration with international politics, development, trade, health, environment, security, integration, and most importantly with the human rights of migrants, is increasingly being traced. Migration is a transformer of social, scientific, and technological innovations to the countries of origin from the host countries of migrants.

Migration processes play the greatest role at the regional level. At the present stage, almost all regions of the world are covered by migration processes. Along with traditional migration hubs in North America,

---

1 World Migration Report 2022. International Organisation for Migration (IOM), Geneva, 2021. https://publications.iom.int/books/world-migration-report-2022.

Western Europe, the Asia-Pacific region there are some relatively new zones such as Africa and the post-Soviet space[2].

This chapter covers Central Asia, and the wider Eurasia as a migration space which was formed in the end of the 20th century. Central Asia, and more broadly in the post-Soviet space, it formed its own migration system and trends, certain patterns with a hub, first in Russia, and then in Kazakhstan. At present, due to geopolitical and geo-economic changes, the role of Central Asia and Kazakhstan as a centre and transit of migration is increasing.

The reasons for active migration processes at the regional level are related to the balance of interests of developed and developing countries. In developed countries, migrants fill empty niches in sectors of both low-prestige, unskilled, low-paid labour, and highly skilled and high-tech labour. Remittances from migrants are becoming an indispensable source of income for a certain number of households, helping to solve the economic problems of poor countries.

However, migrations can have negative consequences, such as the loss of a highly skilled workforce in the countries of origin, or a growing xenophobia that leads to poor social integration, discrimination, and various abuses against migrant workers in countries of destination. However, if properly managed, migration can reduce poverty and improve well-being in both donor and recipient countries. Migration cannot be controlled by closed and one-sided national politics.

In an era of increased mobility and economic integration, a thoughtful, pragmatic migration policy contributes to building a secure and sustainable state and system of relations. In addition to a migration policy, international cooperation is very important not only among states, but also within the framework of international and regional organisations. Central Asia is developing its own system for coordinating migration processes. Coordination and regulation of migration processes, minimisation of negative effects is the sphere of UN agencies (ILO, IOM, UNHCR), and others (CIS, EEU, Almaty Process, SCO, CICA).

---

2 Makogon, Y. International Economics / Y. Makogon, V. Mironov, N. Budarina. Donetsk: DonNU, 2006. 340 p. In RUSSIAN (Макогон, Ю. Международная экономика / Ю. Макогон, В. Миронов, Н. Бударина. Донецк: ДонНУ, 2006. 340 с.).

This chapter shows that the coverage of migration processes at the regional level is different but similar trends influencing migration processes are observed almost everywhere. In its "Strategic Forecast of Migration Policy by 2035", the OECD indicates three interrelated megatrends that will influence migration and integration in the next 10–15 years[3]: (i) changes in the environment and extreme climatic conditions will displace millions of people from their regions of residence; (ii) geopolitical instability and conflicts are initiate forced forms of migration; (iii) demographic shifts due to the global trend of population ageing.

These trends are relevant for each region, but they have their own dynamics and implication. It is necessary to develop appropriate approaches and solutions both at the global and regional level.

The number of international migrants in the regions of the world varies. This affects the development of the migration processes themselves and their consequences. At the regional level, Europe hosts the largest number of international migrants (82 million), followed by North America (59 million) and North Africa and Western Asia (49 million). Thus, about half of all international migrants live in just 10 countries of the world, with the United States of America hosting the largest number of international migrants (51 million – about 19 % of the world's total). Germany and Saudi Arabia are in second and third place in terms of the number of migrants (13 million), followed by Russia (12 million), Great Britain (10 million), the United Arab Emirates (9 million), France, Canada, and Australia (about 8 million each) and Italy (6 million)[4].

All these countries face challenges and have their own migration management systems, but a more unified and integrated approach is needed in changing realities. The data on the number of migrants presented above are quite impressive figures that require attention and appropriate coordination with the participation of global and regional organisations.

The volume of migration processes in Central Asia with the participation of Russia is estimated at about 5 million people[5]. In Central Asia

---

3 OECD Making Migration and Integration Policies Future Ready. 2020 [Электронный ресурс]. https: // www.oecd.org/migration/mig/migration-strategic-foresight.pdf.

4 United Nations. Department of Economic and Social Affairs. https://www.un.org/development/desa/en/news/population/ international-migrant-stock-2019.html.

5 World Migration Report 2022. International Organisation for Migration (IOM), Geneva, 2021. https://publications.iom.int/books/world-migration-report-2022.

and more broadly, in the post-Soviet space, there is no single mechanism for coordinating migration processes. The regulation of migration there is carried out with the involvement of both global organisations and inter-regional ones.

I. International regulation of migration processes within UN agencies: A brief overview and experience of international organisations for migration

The problems of migration are in the focus of attention of international organisations. This includes UN agencies which have mandates on different aspects on migration management. Specialised UN institutions on migration include the International Labour Organisation (ILO), the World Bank (WB), the Office of the High Commissioner for Refugees (UNHCR).

This chapter underlines the role of the International Organisation for Migration (IOM). The IOM is the leading international organisation dealing with migration issues, working with governmental, intergovernmental, and non-governmental bodies. Established in 1951, it became part of the UN in 2016[6]. The IOM is the UN's specialised agency for migration and works with all 175 participating countries at the government level, establishing links with the relevant authorities, with the non-governmental sector and the migrants themselves. The organisation is working on the implementation of the 17 UN Sustainable Development Goals[7] as to migration and the Global Compact for Safe, Orderly and Regular Migration[8], recognising the integral role of managed migration in all regions of the world and the key contribution of migrants to sustainable development.

The work of the IOM is also carried out at the regional level through the development of special strategies. The IOM is actively working in the countries of Central Asian governments, NGOs and migrants and implementing various projects, in particular on labour migration[9]. Thus, at the global level there is sufficient capacity to coordinate migration processes,

6 IOM general information folder. https://www.iom.int/who-we-are.

7 Sustainable Development. https://sdgs.un.org/.

8 GLOBAL COMPACT FOR MIGRATION. https://www.iom.int/global-compact-migration.

9 IOM Launches Regional Project "IOM Labour Migration Programme – Central Asia", Phase I.

in particular the International Organisation for Migration, which is active at all levels and effective at the regional and country levels.

II. Migration coordination through the prism of regional and interregional organisations in Eurasia

Considering the dynamics of migration processes in the region and beyond, it is noteworthy that there is no single migration agreement or structure for coordinating migration processes among the countries of Central Asia and, more widely, in this Eurasian post-soviet space, despite the need to assess the potential of existing organisations and platforms operating both at the regional and interregional levels with the participation of the countries themselves. Similar studies were previously initiated based on the IOM research projects, and it is important to continue them[10]. To this end, it seems necessary to consider such organisations and structures as the Commonwealth of Independent States (CIS), the Eurasian Economic Union (EAEU), the Shanghai Cooperation Organisation (SCO) and the Almaty process (AP), and even the potential of the Conference on Interaction and Confidence Building Buildings in Asia (CICA).

III. Migration coordination within the Commonwealth of Independent States (CIS)

The foundations of cooperation at the international and regional levels were laid within the framework of the CIS activities from the moment the countries of the Central Asian region gained independence in 1991.

The Commonwealth of Independent States (CIS) is a cooperation organisation of post-Soviet states that began its work in 1993. The CIS does not have supranational powers: the member states cooperate in the social, legal and economic spheres, and also have visa-free agreements.

---

https://kazakhstan.iom.int/news/iom-launches-regional-project-iom-labour-migration-programme-central-asia-phase-i.

10 Delovarova, L. F. Multilateral migration cooperation in Central Asia through the prism of international extra-regional structures: brief overview. *Farabi Journal of Social Sciences*, Vol. 8, No. 2 (2022), pp. 34–38. https://doi.org/10.26577/FJSS.2022.v8.i2.01

The CIS includes Azerbaijan, Armenia, Belarus, Kazakhstan, Kyrgyzstan, Moldova, Russia, Tajikistan, Turkmenistan, Uzbekistan and Ukraine[11].

The Council of Heads of Migration Authorities of the CIS Member States was formed to coordinate interaction and resolve issues in the field of migration policy. The priority areas of cooperation between the heads of migration authorities in the field of migration are the following: i/ formation of conditions for the implementation of a coordinated migration policy; ii/ regulation of labour migration on the basis of achieving compliance of the volumes, directions and structure of migration flows with the interests of migrants, taking into account the legislation of the host state; iii/ formation of a common labour market, creation of legal, economic and organisational conditions for the transition to the free movement of labour; iv/ ensuring the integration of immigrants into society and the formation among citizens of the CIS member states of a respectful attitude towards the legislation, language and culture of the host country; v/ continued counteraction to illegal migration; vi/ increasing the degree of protection and reliability of passport and visa documents (including the use of biometric data); vii/ conclusion of readmission agreements.

Beyond this overview of the CIS legal frames on migration, the following acts have been developed and are functioning: the 1992 Agreement on issues related to the restoration of the rights of deported persons, national minorities and peoples; the 2002 Agreement on cooperation of the CIS member states in matters of the return of minors to their states of permanent residence; the 2007 Declaration on the coordinated migration policy of the CIS member states; the 2003 Agreement on Cooperation between the Member States of the Commonwealth of Independent States in the fight against illegal migration[12].

Important and sensitive migration aspects within the CIS relate to the issues of forced migration and regulation of the status of refugees and internally displaced persons.

Moreover, within the framework of the organisation, optimisation of the legal regulation of labour migration and counteraction to

---

11 CIS official website: https://e-cis.info/.

12 Delovarova, L. F. Multilateral migration cooperation in Central Asia through the prism of international extra-regional structures: brief overview. *Farabi Journal of Social Sciences*, Vol. 8, No. 2 (2022), pp. 34–38. https://doi.org/10.26577/FJSS.2022.v8.i2.01

illegal migration is being considered. The current relevant agreement, ratified by Kazakhstan, is the Agreement on cooperation in the field of promoting employment of the population of the member states of the Commonwealth of Independent States.

The CIS plays an important role in terms of coverage of participants, experience of countries in the development and regulation of migration processes from the prospects of historical, socio-cultural, economic, legal and political aspects. It seems that this is an international platform in the context of migration cooperation, covering the Central Asian states and defining key relevant aspects of migration in space.

IV. Migration coordination within the Eurasian Economic Union (EAEU)

The Eurasian Economic Union (EEU) is an integration association of post-Soviet states that began work on 1 January 2015. It is an international organisation that ensures the free movement of goods, services, capital and labour coordination of economic and social policy management. The EEU includes Russia Federation, Belarus, Kazakhstan, Kyrgyzstan and Armenia.

Migration within the EEU space is not the exclusive responsibility of the national authorities. Labour migration is under the jurisdiction of the Eurasian Economic Commission (EEC). The issues of movement of labour resources fall within the competence of the Department of Labour Migration and Social Protection of the EEC as part of the Economics and Financial Policy area. The Department of Labour Migration and Social Protection consists of departments of labour resources, migration and social protection proper. The Department monitors and controls the implementation of Member States' obligations in the field of labour migration[13]. The Union is the only mechanism in the Eurasian space that regulates in detail the processes of labour migration.

The following documents are in force within the framework of the union: Protocol on the provision of medical assistance to workers of the Member States and family members (Appendix No. 30 to the Treaty on the Eurasian Economic Union), Agreement on cooperation in combating

---

13 Labour Migration Department. https://eec.eaeunion.org/en/commission/department/migration/

illegal labour migration from third countries, Agreement on pensions for workers in states – members of the Eurasian Economic Union dated 20 December 2019, Acts of the Eurasian Economic Commission.

Section 26 of the Treaty on the Eurasian Economic Union "Labour Migration" defines the general principles for regulating labour migration issues in the space of the EEU member countries. The section consists of 3 articles – Art. 96, 97 and 98[14].

The specified articles of the Treaty determine the procedure and forms of cooperation of the Member States in the field of labour migration, the procedure for conducting labour activities by workers of the EEU Member State, and also approves the principle of free access to the labour market in relation to migrant workers from the EEU member countries, and also provides guarantees for family members of migrant workers to stay on the basis of an employment contract, the rights and obligations of labour migrants.

The Eurasian Economic Union is so far the only platform that contains specific rules and regulations for labour migrants for member countries and is a good model for managing labour migration.

V. Migration coordination in non-economic interregional organisations and platforms: TheAlmaty Process (AP)

The Almaty Process (AP) on Refugee Protection and International Migration is a regional consultative and advisory body established to protect refugees and migrants in Central Asia at the initiative of the Government of Kazakhstan, the UN High Commissioner for Refugees (UNHCR) and the International Organisation for Migration (IOM). The AP was conceived in 2010 and launched on 5 June 2013. The members of the platform are Afghanistan, Azerbaijan, Kazakhstan, Kyrgyzstan, Tajikistan, Turkey, Turkmenistan. Observer States – Iran, Pakistan and Uzbekistan is an invited party[15].

---

14 Treaty on the Eurasian Economic Union (2014). Consolidated version.2022 http: // pravo.eaeunion.org/SESSION/PILOT/main.htm.

15 UNHCR (2021). About the Almaty Process. https://www.unhcr.org/centralasia/about-almaty-process.

This platform aims to address the multifaceted aspects of migration, which are determined by the complex dynamics of mobility and enhance regional and international cooperation and management on migration and refugee issues.

VI. Regulation of migration within the framework of the Shanghai Cooperation Organisation (SCO)

The SCO is a permanent regional international organisation founded in June 2001. Initially, it included Kazakhstan, China, Kyrgyzstan, Russia, Tajikistan, and Uzbekistan, with now in addition India, Pakistan and Iran as members. Four countries – Belarus, Iran, Mongolia and Afghanistan – have observer status in the organisation, and six – Armenia, Azerbaijan, Cambodia, Nepal, Turkey, Sri Lanka – dialogue partners[16]. The SCO is not a specialised organisation for migration, but migration issues within the framework of this organisation are considered through the prism of the fight against separatism, terrorism, trafficking in arms, drugs and people.

In this regard, the SCO has not adopted a separate document regulating migration issues. Migration processes for the SCO are perceived in the context of economic, social and political security. The SCO Declaration of 2001, as well as the 2002 St. Petersburg SCO Charter and 2005 Astana declarations mention migration processes in the context of the fight against terrorism, separatism and extremism[17].

Nowadays, one of the important aspects within the SCO in terms of migration is a regulation of migration processes to create a system of safe and efficient movement in accordance with the main goals of the organisation. The main focus is on addressing issues of human trafficking and illegal migration. This is important in the new geopolitical realities.

---

16 SCO Official web site (2022). What is SCO. http://eng.sectsco.org/docs/about/faq.html

17 Delovarova, L. F. Multilateral migration cooperation in Central Asia through the prism of international extra-regional structures: brief overview. *Farabi Journal of Social Sciences*, Vol. 8, No. 2 (2022), pp. 34–38. https://doi.org/10.26577/FJSS.2022.v8.i2.01.

VII. Issues of migration within the framework of the CICA

The Conference on Interaction and Confidence Building Buildings in Asia (CICA) is an intergovernmental forum aimed at promoting peace, security and stability in Asia. The CICA focuses on promoting dialogue, building confidence and developing cooperation among its member states in various fields, including politics, security, economics and culture. The CICA covers 27 member-states from several regions[18].

In 2008, a Memorandum of Understanding was signed between the CICA and the IOM, which indicates the need for bilateral cooperation on migration issues and coordination of efforts on migration issues. An agreement was reached between the parties on the exchange of open information and documentation[19].

Even though migration is not within the scope of CICA activities, migration issues are important in the context of the meetings, as they are important in the context of security issues, the economics of humanitarian cooperation.

*

In conclusion, migration is a multifaceted phenomenon, covering all regions of the world. Migration volumes keep on increasing and the trends accompanying migration processes require constant attention. Central Asia and the entire Eurasian space at the present stage are seen as a zone of active and diversified migration. Multilateral cooperation in the field of migration at the regional level and more broadly is seen as a key link in the creation of coordinated migration. Multilevel cooperation at the present stage has great potential. This is necessary for more coordinated migration processes at the regional and interregional levels.

Analysing the activities of the IOM, agreements concluded on the basis of the CIS, we can conclude that this is the base that served to further improve and develop migration legislation in the Central Asian region and beyond. The most advanced structure in the field of labour

---

18 Member states // https://www.s-cica.org/index.php?view=page&t=member_states.

19 Memorandum of Understanding was signed between CICA and IOM https://www.s-cica.org/russian_pdf/(MOI)rus.pdf.

migration is the EEU, but not all countries of the region are involved. The Almaty process has great potential. Of note are the efforts of the SCO to counter illegal migration and human trafficking. The CICA has great potential for coordinating migration over a wide area. Based on the results of the analysis of the activities of international regional and interregional organisations involved in migration issues in Central Asia and Eurasia, to varying degrees, it can be concluded that there is sufficient potential for effective cooperation in this area.

The CSTO as an unlikely partner for sustaining the Caspian security architecture

Zhulduz BAIZAKOVA[1]
Kazakhstan

The Caspian region is widely considered today as a geopolitical battleground among major powers and their national interests in a regional security environment that is rather complex and heavily calibrated. Geopolitical turmoil, currently reverberating across Eurasia, cannot help but impact the region in, broadly, unpredictable ways. Moreover, the understanding of the role that military and security alliances should play in the region is slowly being reconfigured.[2]

At the same time, regional security alliances continue playing an increasingly valuable role in maintaining peace and stability as well as in helping to advance the foreign policies of its member states.

The Collective Security Treaty Organisation (CSTO) is widely perceived as a military-political alliance. Many Western experts have been regarding the CSTO as a continuation of the post-Soviet version of the former Warsaw pact that attempts to bind Moscow's allies together in a similar fashion. In turn, these allies perceived the organisation as an organic part of the newly emerging post-Soviet space.

---

1 This paper is written as part of implementing the research project Nr.BR18574168, commissioned by the Ministry of Education and Science of the Republic of Kazakhstan.

2 Olexandr Honcharenko, Caspian-Black Sea Security Challenges and the Regional Security Structures // Astana: Digital Library of Kazakhstan (BIBLIO.KZ). 08.12.2021. URL: https://biblio.kz/m/articles/view/caspian-black-sea-security-challenges-and-the-regional-security-structures.

This chapter considers whether the CSTO is in any way contributing to the regional security architecture in the Caspian Sea and which important factors are involved into it.

I. The CSTO: Bases and aims

The Collective Security Treaty Organisation (CSTO) dates back to 1992, when the Collective Security Treaty was signed between Russia, Kazakhstan, Armenia, Kyrgyzstan, Uzbekistan and Tajikistan. Since 2002, the Organisation was established on the basis of the Collective Security Treaty, which later received an observer status at the UN.[3]

During the 1990s, the CSTO's existence remained relatively inert. Throughout the 2000s, the organisation has gone through its own transformation. Confidence-building measures among CSTO member states occur within the framework of regular cooperation in both the military-political and the military-technical areas. In particular, military-technical cooperation involves the supply of military products by Russia on a preferential basis, that is significant discounts for its partners. This particular benefit is highlighted when listing the advantages of CSTO membership.

The Charter of CSTO determines the goals of the organisation as "strengthening the world, international and regional security and stability, protecting independence, territorial integrity and sovereignty of member states on a collective basis".[4] Article 7 of the Charter specifies that member states should take joint measures to achieve an efficient collective security system in case of a threat to security, stability, territorial integrity and sovereignty and exercise the right to collective defence. It also includes the establishment of joint collective forces, and regional contingents of peacekeeping forces.[5]

For the most part of its existence, the CSTO had been experiencing heavy criticism due to its inefficiency and practical inability to solve crises among its member states, as well as for failing to deliver its key

---

3 Javaid, Faisal. "Collective Security Treaty Organisation (CSTO) and Central Asian Region: Opportunities and Challenges." *European Academic Research* 4(12) (2017), 10614–10633.

4 Charter of the CSTO. https://odkb-csto.org/documents/documents/ustav_organizatsii_dogovora_o_kollektivnoy_bezopasnosti_/#loaded.

5 Ibid.

principle: collective security when it comes to Armenia. So far, the only major privilege left is the opportunity to purchase discount-priced Russian weapons and other military equipment. There are also regular military trainings and exercises held in various locations, but that was compromised twice with Armenia and Kyrgyzstan pulled out at the last minute.[6]

However, one should keep in mind that CSTO members sometimes prefer solving their issues bilaterally, particularly when dealing with conflict situations. When border skirmishes erupted between Kyrgyzstan and Tajikistan in 2022, both countries addressed their concerns to Moscow directly.

II. The January 2022 events in Kazakhstan

In January 2022, the CSTO proved its effectiveness for the first time. During its existence, the organisation had been criticised mostly for its lack of practical, battlefield experience in the fight against the declared threats and challenges.[7]

At the request of the Kazakhstan's President Tokayev, as well as by the decision of the CSTO Collective Security Council, peacekeeping contingents of the CSTO member countries began to arrive in the country from 6 February 2022. The peacekeeping contingents of Russia, Armenia, Belarus, Tajikistan and Kyrgyzstan, were deployed in the country until 19 January 2022.[8] Their goals included the normalisation and stabilisation of the situation through the defence and protection of various important facilities in the country, in particular those located in Almaty.

When CSTO peacekeeping forces were deployed in Kazakhstan, it happened according to the Article 4 of the treaty which determines the

---

6 Kyrgyzstan cancels Russian-led military drill on its land, 9.10.2022, AP, https://apnews.com/article/russia-ukraine-asia-kazakhstan-central-tajikistan-8bd4550ca3831c25990165685a92cac6, Armenia cancels military drills of Russian-led alliance, 10.10.2023, Aljazeera, https://www.aljazeera.com/news/2023/1/10/armenia-cancels-russian-led-military-drills-amid-conflict.

7 Евген Цыбуленко, Причина недееспособности ОДКБ в слабости России Международный центр обороны и безопасности (ICDS), 2 сентября, 2022, https://icds.ee.

8 Cooley, Alexander A. "What is the CSTO? Kazakhstan Called for Assistance. Why Did Russia Dispatch Troops so Quickly?." (2022).

terms and conditions of the potential deployment. They include a relevant response by other members to an armed attack threatening security, stability, sovereignty and territorial integrity of any of the member states.

When CSTO forces deployed to Kazakhstan, many questions emerged on the part of the international community, such as the duration of the deployment, the exact mandate of the peacekeeping forces, their precise tasks, etc. Similar concerns had been present in Kazakhstani society too. The most surprising element was about the terms and conditions of the deployment: Kazakhstan, as this was the first time that Article 4 was tested.[9]

Kazakhstan had evolved as one of the most peaceful and stable societies in the post-Soviet space, having never experienced the horrors of the civil war like Tajikistan or of interstate war, like Armenia and Azerbaijan; it was even exempt from the external incursion from the Islamic radicals as happened with Kyrgyzstan and Uzbekistan in late 1990s.[10] No regional observer ever believed that Kazakhstan might ever require CSTO assistance in the manner and framework it received it in January 2022.

Interpretations as to why Astana was granted institutionalised help varied greatly, with some suggesting that Kazakhstan matters too much to risk the slightest destabilisation. Anyhow, the January 2022 events provided the CSTO with a much needed excuse to finally prove itself as an efficient structure capable of defending the safety of its member states.

III. The Caspian dimension of the CSTO

This should highlight another significant point. The Collective Security Treaty Organisation encompass two Caspian littoral states: Kazakhstan and Russia.

Before the fall of Soviet Union, Iran and the URSS shared the Caspian Sea, managing to establish some sort of regional balance of power. The emergence after 1991 of Azerbaijan, Kazakhstan and Turkmenistan as independent actors shattered that balance and forced the involved participants to start shaping a new security architecture. This proved even

---

[9] Ibid.

[10] Bayramov, Agha. (2020). Conflict, cooperation or competition in the Caspian Sea region: A critical review of the New Great Game paradigm. Caucasus Survey. 9. 1–21. 10.1080/23761199.2020.1774856.

harder to do so with natural resources, oil and gas deposits discovered around the territorial waters of the three newly independent republics. The quest for a fair and just division of the Caspian Sea took nearly three decades, with a Convention on the legal status of the Caspian Sea signed on 12 August 2018 in Kazakhstan.[11]

The Caspian Sea is shared by the five countries belonging to four different regions: Central Asia (Kazakhstan, Turkmenistan), Middle East (Iran), South Caucasus (Azerbaijan) and Europe (Russia). Moreover, these countries carry distinctive ethno-cultural, religious and linguistic backgrounds. With countries representing four particular regions, the Caspian Sea area has always presented a diverse patchwork of intertwined interests, opportunities, intentions and commitments to the point that one cannot talk about shaping a single security architecture. Caspian states have different values, goals and ideological foundations. In other words, regional complex geopolitics is closely tied to the political and economic development of the littoral states.

Initially both the US and the EU assessed the Caspian Sea area as rather insignificant in terms of posing any serious threat to regional or international peace.[12] However, that changed when a first war broke out between neighbouring Armenia and Azerbaijan.

Yet, as early as 1992–1997, Washington provided as much as $1.9 billion under the Freedom Support Act, with the view to promote democratisation, and social-economic reforms in the region. Moreover, there were joint military exercises held with the US 82nd Airborne Division paratroopers. NATO offered its Partnership for Peace programme (PFP) to strengthen practical military cooperation.[13] However, both Iran and Russia felt strongly resentful about a Western interference into the region and tried to curtail such an involvement as much as possible, particularly in the area of defence and security.

---

11 Karataeva, Elena. "The Convention on the Legal Status of the Caspian Sea: The final answer or an interim solution to the Caspian question?." *The International Journal of Marine and Coastal Law,* 35(2) (2020), 232–263.

12 Ali Akbar Jafari; Dayyan Jaanbaaz. "Ontological Security: An Instrument for Western Geostrategic Intervention in the Caspian Sea (Emphasizing the Energy Issue)". *Central Eurasia Studies,* 11(1), 2018, 39–58. doi: 10.22059/jcep. 2018.113444.449554.

13 Bahgat, Gawdat. American oil diplomacy in the Persian Gulf and the Caspian Sea / Gawdat Bahgat University Press of Florida Gainesville 2003.

Nowadays, with the war between Russia and Ukraine in its second year, the interest from the West towards the Caspian region have taken a more notable and conspicuous shape.

High level visits from Western officials have become a regular routine for Central Asian states since the beginning of the crisis around Ukraine. These were followed by an array of various political, diplomatic and financial proposals to the leadership of Caspian states leaders with the view to distance them from Moscow. Bearing in mind that no CA republic joined anti-Russian sanctions, attempts to find new leverages were made to influence the decision-making process in the region. Similarly, the US and the EU were closely monitoring the Caspian Sea region, which remains to be viewed as zone of strategic interests due to its abundance of natural resources.

The fact that Iran and Russia, as two key adversaries of the West, share the Sea, facilitates further involvement with the other three littoral states (Kazakhstan, Turkmenistan, Azerbaijan). Washington has been uneasy about the rising power of China in the region as well.[14] Iran's attempts to advance bilateral ties with Central Asian republics is another cause of concern.

IV. The CSTO-Caspian convergence

The key convergence point between the CSTO and the Caspian region in terms of security is the state of affairs between Armenia, a member of CSTO, and Azerbaijan, a Caspian littoral state. There are experts who claim that the South Caucasus is sometimes perceived as a gateway to Central Asia and vice-versa.

Azerbaijan's interests lie in the economic field, including boosting the bilateral trade, constructing and operating transit and transport land corridors via its territory in Western, Southern and Northern directions. As a fellow oil producing country, Baku understands and shares some grievances in this field with Astana and Ashgabat. Sharing one Turkic

---

14 Mamuka Tsereteli, Turkey and the Evolving Black Sea-Caspian Region; Potential for a New Positive Agenda, Nisan 24, 2020, https://www.uikpanorama.com/blog/2020/04/24/turkey-and-the-evolving-black-sea-caspian-region-potential-for-a-new-positive-agenda/

origin, all three countries find political divisions challenging to deal with, especially when it comes to the interstate conflict.

During the short-term war between Armenia and Azerbaijan in September-November 2020, the CSTO limited its involvement by issuing a few declaratory statements on the occasion of various events.

After failing to conclude legal document with Armenia's territorial concessions, Azerbaijan is busy to gather round allies, and to pressure Erevan to give up Karabakh. Long-term political and diplomatic efforts of Baku are clearly aimed at Central Asian republics to persuade them to take its side.

During none of the three attacks by Azerbaijan could Erevan rely upon the assistance from the CSTO organisation. Indeed, this fact should make Moscow realise that there are situations when hard choices should be made.

Armenia had recently been discussing the idea of withdrawing from the organisation altogether. Recently, the Secretary of the Security Council of Armenia, Armen Grigoryan, claimed that it's almost impossible to find a case of the CSTO helping Armenia since 2020.[15]

Erevan perfectly comprehends the fact that Moscow would never deploy troops against Baku to protect Armenia. There are certain reasons for this. One includes keeping the balance of power in the South Caucasus, since Russia already has a history with Georgia dating back to 2008 and today it cannot afford to get involved into another major war in its periphery. The other reason lies in the value of the bilateral ties with Baku itself: by antagonising Azerbaijan, Russia might lose vital transport corridors, chiefly the International North-South Transport Corridor (INSTC) land route crossing three countries, Russia, Azerbaijan and Iran.

Moscow would be cut off from the southern route that also leads to India.

Still, Russia has several tools to manipulate its CSTO allies: military weapons and equipment sold at discounted prices; thousands of Central Asian legal and illegal migrants, whose remittances constitute massive share of GDP of Kyrgyzstan and Tajikistan; security guarantees in general.

---

15 Секретарь Совбеза не находит примера содействия ОДКБ Армении, 05.06.23, https://inbusiness.kz/ru/last/sekretar-sovbeza-ne-nahodit-primera-sodejstviya-odkb-armenii

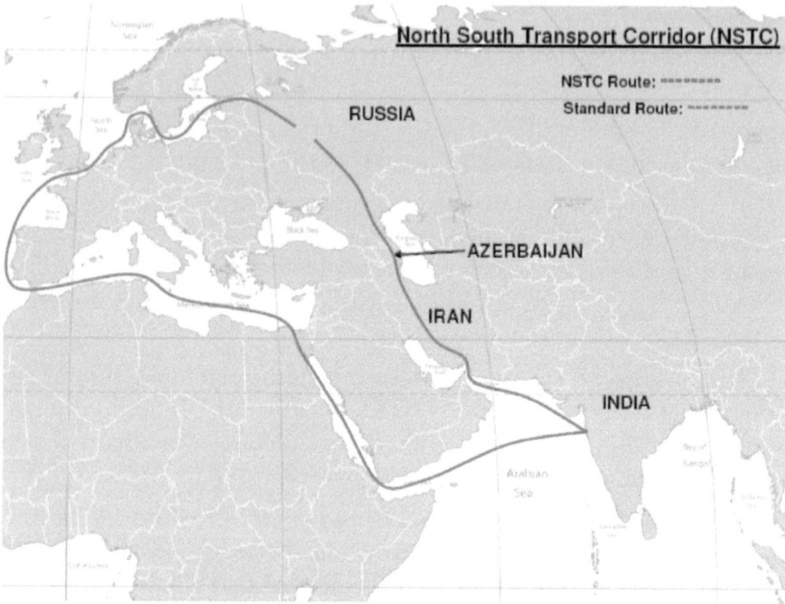

Source : Wikipedia, consulted 29 June 2023: https://en.wikipedia.org/wiki/International_North%E2%80%93South_Transport_Corridor

V. Azerbaijan's Caspian significance

Azerbaijan's close cooperation with Turkey, a NATO member, cannot help but cause certain concerns in both Moscow and Tehran.[16] Baku might be an unpredictable partner today, as it owes so much to Ankara for its assistance during the 2020 Karabakh war. Today, Turkey continues to further encroach into both the South Caucasus and Central Asia politically, economically and culturally. Turkish "soft power" and its idea to unite Turkic nations under Ankara's umbrella serve as an exclusive instrument to advance the country's foreign policy ambitions in the post-Soviet space. Moscow has been aware of the fact since the early 1990s.

16 Aslan Doukaev, Azerbaijan Is Drifting Away From Russia, and Moscow Has Only Itself to Blame, 30.05.2023, *Eurasia Daily Monitor*, Vol. 20, No. 86. https://jamestown.org/program/azerbaijan-is-drifting-away-from-russia-and-moscow-has-only-itself-to-blame/

There were tensions when, in 2021, Azerbaijani and Turkish special forces held joint military exercises which was interpreted as illegal military presence by the third party in the Caspian Sea, the Iranian authorities.[17] According to the 2018 Convention on the Legal Status of the Caspian Sea, no external actor, apart from the five coastal states, can have their forces deployed there. However, Baku claimed those exercises took place within Azerbaijan's territorial waters and never posed any risk or threat for others. In this regard, the Convention on the Legal Status of the Caspian Sea clearly states that "non-use of force or the threat of force" and "non-presence of armed forces" of the third parties is allowed.[18]

No legal document on the Caspian Sea includes provisions that prohibit participants from arming and enhancing both offensive and defensive capabilities. The Convention allows "developing military capabilities within the limits of reasonable sufficiency with due regard to the interests of all the Parties"[19], which in other words predisposes the countries to militarise as they see fit.

Moscow had been modernising its Caspian Fleet and even changed the location in 2017, from Astrakhan to Kaspyisk in Dagestan, where new naval infrastructure was built, including civilian housing objects for the personnel.[20]

When Russia launched missile attacks against ISIL fighters in Syria in 2015, no littoral state filed a protest, as Moscow claimed it was done as part of anti-terrorist operation.[21] Moreover, the missiles flew across Iranian territory having been approved by Tehran at the highest level of command.[22] Moscow and Tehran were in close contact during the

17 Javid Agha, Iran refers to "illegality" of Turkish presence in Caspian Sea military drills, September 14, 2021, https://www.intellinews.com/iran-refers-to-illegality-of-turkish-presence-in-caspian-sea-military-drills-220699/.

18 Конвенция о правовом статусе Каспийского моря, https://adilet.zan.kz/rus/docs/Z1900000222.

19 Ibid.

20 Igor Delanoe, Russia's Black Sea Fleet: Toward a Multiregional Force, June 2019, CNA Occasional Paper.

21 Путин связал удары из Каспия с поиском виновных в атаке на A321, 23.11.2015, https://www.rbc.ru/politics/23/11/2015/565336d99a794754c5bcbb72.

22 A New Military Order in the Caspian Sea?, Stratfor, November 24, 2015, https://www.realcleardefense.com/articles/2015/11/25/a_new_military_order_in_the_caspian_sea_108724.html.

Syrian civil war coordinating their policies and actions with each other and ensuring that both advanced their respective goals.

At the same time, neither of them regard the Caspian Sea as extremely vital in terms of the national security; Iran stationed the bulk of its fleet in the Persian Gulf, the Red Sea and the Ormuz strait, while Russia focused on beefing up its Black Sea fleet.[23]

No Caspian country so far can be considered as hegemon, yet all of them carry certain grievances. The interests of the Caspian Five is so much intertwined and interdependent, that it sometimes presents a complex task to determine their discernible claims and aspirations. For example, Moscow cannot afford to deteriorate relations with either Tehran, Baku or Astana, as they hold the access to the Southern and Eastern export and import routes, towards India and China. Similarly, Iran requires steady and stable a Central Asian region to promote its own geopolitical ambitions, and to connect with China and India.[24]

At the same time, Moscow and Tehran continue to closely monitor the military expenditure of other coastal states; every military training, event and exercise held jointly between each other, or with other third parties is being heavily scrutinised and analysed.

Early in September 2022, Russia hosted a large-scale military drill called "Vostok-2022" with over 50,000 military personnel participating from affiliates of both the Collective Security Treaty Organisation (CSTO) and the Shanghai Cooperation Organisation (SCO), including Azerbaijan, Algeria, India, Laos, Mongolia, Myanmar, Nicaragua, Syria, and others.[25] These exercises demonstrated that Russia, together with China, is capable of arranging multi-faceted and inclusive interactions among various actors, among whom were Armenia with Azerbaijan. The role of the mediator between these two countries is currently being challenged by Ankara, and possibly Beijing with European countries

23 Igor Delanoe, Russia's Black Sea Fleet: Toward a Multiregional Force, June 2019, CNA Occasional Paper.

24 Dante Schulz, China's Growing Involvement in the Caspian Region, 26.01.2022, Caspian Policy Center, https://www.caspianpolicy.org/research/security-and-politics-program-spp/chinas-growing-involvement-in-the-caspian-region.

25 Emily Ferris and Veerle Nouwens, Russia's Vostok 2022 Military Drills: Not Size or Tanks, but Context, 15 September 2022, Royal United Services Institute, https://rusi.org/explore-our-research/publications/commentary/russias-vostok-2022-military-drills-not-size-or-tanks-context.

attempting to find the middle ground to operate inside this complex region.

If and when Erevan determines to finally leave the CSTO would prove a serious game-changer for both the CSTO and Central Asia countries.

*

In conclusion, numerous factors contribute to disrupting the regional stability in terms of the long-term development. Lately, things have become rather difficult for the CSTO in terms of organisational cohesion, integrity and operational unity. Moscow has been exploiting the organisation as a tool to project its military power within the post-Soviet space and by luring Central Asian states in terms of ensuring their safety and stability. Today, that role might be changing due to the ongoing crisis in Ukraine.

Few experts have been talking about Russia's diminishing influence in both the Caspian region and Central Asia as a result of Chinese industrious activities.

The CSTO as a regional institution had been established to provide and guarantee stability and security within the post-Soviet space. At the same time, the dynamics of the CSTO evolving into a truly functional, efficient and trust worthy organisation is yet to be seen.

Since the Armenia-Azerbaijan conflict erupted in the 1990s, external observers could tell that the way the CSTO has been developing may not necessarily bring it to function in terms of interfering into the conflict on behalf of Erevan.

This fact alone renders the principle of collective security in the Caspian region unattainable. In other words, the CSTO would remain on the side-line of the Caspian and Central Asian geopolitics, while Moscow continues focusing its activities elsewhere.

The OSCE and the Ukraine crisis: What future for global and cooperative security?

Philippe LAGRANGE
France

The war in Ukraine and its follow-up have plunged the European continent back into a recent past that it thought was well behind it: two ideologically opposed camps with capability to launch a major armed conflict that could lead to the very destruction of humanity.

This crisis requires us to requestion the very origins of the Organisation for Security and Cooperation in Europe (OSCE), an organisation that was specifically designed to avert such a calamity by creating pan-European security cooperation through conferences on security and cooperation in Europe (CSCE) initiated by the "Helsinki process" in the 1970s.[1]

This process saw NATO and Warsaw Pact states shift from an attitude of distrust and hostility to a more positive, more cooperative position. The process gradually spread, enduring throughout the cold war and, after the fall of communism in Europe, morphing into a veritable international organisation, the Organisation for Security and Cooperation in Europe, aimed at building a new form of inter-state relations based on the principle of cooperative security.

Now counting 57 participating states,[2] including all western and many eastern European countries, Eurasia, the United States, Canada and the

---

1 The process was ultimately formally established on 1 August 1975 with the adoption of the Final Act of the Helsinki Conference on security and cooperation in Europe.

2 Albania, Andorra, Armenia, Austria, Azerbaijan, Belarus, Belgium, Bosnia and Herzegovina, Bulgaria, Canada, Croatia, Cyprus, Czech Republic, Denmark, Estonia, Finland, France, Georgia, Germany, Greece, Holy See, Hungary, Iceland, Ireland, Italy, Kazakhstan, Kyrgyzstan, Latvia, Liechtenstein, Lithuania, Luxembourg, Malta, Moldova, Monaco, Mongolia, Montenegro, Netherlands, North Macedonia, Norway, Poland, Portugal, Romania, Russian Federation, San Marino, Serbia,

Russian Federation, the OSCE also has eleven "partners for cooperation", including South Korea,[3] and seeks to ensure peaceful co-existence for more than one billion people.

This makes it a key organisation for Eurasian cooperation and a major security actor on the continent.

Based on the fundamental principles of international law as restated in the Helsinki Decalogue, which include sovereign equality, refraining from the threat or use of force, and the inviolability of frontiers, the OSCE is a security organisation that is both conventional and innovative.

It is conventional because its absolute affirmation of the underlying principles of sovereignty and non-interference encourages recourse to consensus and reduces its scope of action in that it prohibits any intervention in internal crises without the agreement of the states territorially concerned.

It is innovative in that the OSCE has managed, despite these limitations, to develop a unique approach to security that is both global and cooperative. Its approach is global in that it deals with the three dimensions of security – politico-military, economic and environmental and human. It is cooperative in that all states participating in the bodies and activities of the OSCE have equal status.

With two of the OSCE's participating states engaged in high-intensity armed conflict, the crisis in Ukraine calls into question the usefulness of this type of organisation.

Contrary to what one might think and despite increasingly strained relations with the Russian Federation, the OSCE has played and continues to play an important role in resolving the crisis in Ukraine. Present in Ukraine since 1 June 1999, the organisation continued its activities with the project co-ordinator in Ukraine (PCU) after the annexation of Crimea, deploying two long-term missions in March 2014: the special monitoring mission to Ukraine (SMM) and the OSCE border observer mission (BOM) deployed at the two border posts in Donetsk and Gukovo. It also acted as mediator with the trilateral contact group,

---

Slovakia, Slovenia, Spain, Sweden, Switzerland, Tajikistan, Turkey, Turkmenistan, Ukraine, United Kingdom, United States, Uzbekistan.

3 Afghanistan, Algeria, Australia, Egypt, Israel, Japan, Jordan, Morocco, the Republic of Korea, Thailand, Tunisia.

comprising representatives from Ukraine, Russia and the OSCE and which led to the Minsk agreements.

Since launching its "special military operation" on 24 February 2022, the Russian Federation has done everything it could to limit the action of the OSCE, refusing to extend various mission mandates and turning down all proposals for negotiation from the organisation.

These actions have called into question the very relevance of the organisation – at least as it is currently structured. While it may be appropriate to review the functioning of the OSCE and some elements of its politico-military approach to security (I), its economic, environmental and human dimensions remain as relevant as ever and merit further development, as does the global security rationale (II).

I. Rationalising the OSCE's politico-military dimension

Under the objectives laid down when the CSCE was established, the OSCE's main competence covers in issues relating to security in the military sense of the term – the politico-military dimension. Thus, when the CSCE process was launched, the OSCE hosted conferences on arms control and confidence-building measures. The organisation has played a key role in conflict-prevention by setting up and operating early-warning systems within the OSCE space to identify potential flashpoints, as well as plan operations to deal with these. All these are essential long-term missions (A) but today the organisation and its decision-making processes appear somewhat ill-adapted to deal with the crisis in Ukraine (B).

(A) Essential role and missions

In 1975, the main objective of the CSCE, at least for westerners, was to re-establish confidence between the two blocs to avoid a situation where a military confrontation between them, even if confined to the European continent, could result in "mutually assured destruction". This objective was reached in the early conferences. Diplomats, military advisers and civilian experts met to discuss the balance of forces between the two blocs but also technical cooperation and human rights. The CSCE process thus enabled a dialogue between East and West to take form, become established, bedded down and expand. Initially just between the Americans and the Soviets, dialogue expanded multi-laterally as the

Europeans became involved. Regular CSCE meetings also helped defuse tension, ushering in an element of routine and an environment where no subject was taboo. Dialogue bedded down, its recurring nature providing constancy and stability that stood in contrast with the early days of the cold war.

It became essential to maintain a forum for negotiations, with regular meetings involving all states interested in European security. Confidence-building and disarmament measures were undoubtedly the greatest achievement of the CSCE politico-military dimension. Recommended in the Helsinki Final Act, these measures helped lead to several agreements on arms control, such as the Treaty on Conventional Armed Forces in Europe (CFE) of 19 November 1900 and the Treaty on Open Skies of 24 March 1992.

The OSCE also introduced confidence- and security-building measures (CSBM), which provide for information sharing and various forms of military cooperation to reduce the risks of conflict and boost confidence among participating states while encouraging increased openness and transparency in military planning and activities. Based on the Vienna Document on confidence- and security-building measures of 30 November 2011,[4] these measures were guaranteed and developed by the Forum for Security Cooperation, the main decision-making body today in the OSCE as regards security in its politico-military aspects. Associated with the Conflict Prevention Centre managed by the OSCE secretariat in Vienna, the forum handles monitoring and political and military coordination for the other main aspect of the OSCE's politico-military dimension: long-term missions.

In its Charter for European Security, adopted in Istanbul in November 1999, the OSCE reaffirmed its role as a "regional arrangement in the sense of Chapter VIII of the Charter of the United Nations".[5] This enabled it to intervene under the auspices of the UN and in cooperation with the North Atlantic Treaty Organisation (NATO) in various operations conducted on European soil, particularly in former Yugoslavia, where the two organisations worked well together.

4 FSC.DOC/1/11 30 November 2011.

5 Charter for European Security (Istanbul Document), adopted in Istanbul at the summit meeting of the Organisation for Security and Cooperation in Europe, 18–19 November 1999, section 7.

On its own initiative, the OSCE has deployed and continues to deploy field operations – also known as long-term missions – in over ten central and eastern European countries. Some of these are mediation missions where there are serious tensions between a government and part of the population. One example of this was when Baltic states denied citizenship to Russian-speaking minorities, who were on the brink of insurgency as a result. Some, such as the long-standing mission in Nagorno-Karabakh, are ceasefire monitoring missions. Others are election observation missions, regularly deployed at the request of countries in transition happy to accept the presence of the OSCE even though not required to do so under international law. Examples include Bosnia and Herzegovina under the Dayton Agreement, Kosovo with Resolution 1244 (1999) of the UN Security Council and Ukraine after the Orange Revolution in 2004.

All of the above incorporate both the human and the politico-military dimensions of global and cooperative security but long-term missions are generally specifically designed to include both the economic and environmental and the human dimensions. In the case of Ukraine, the project coordinator in Ukraine (PCU) had a wide variety of tasks, ranging from providing assistance and expertise to both authorities and civil society on constitutional reform and justice, human rights, using dialogue as a crisis management and reform implementation tool, the psychological and social recovery of persons affected by conflict, combating cybercrime and human trafficking. They also included action on mines, democratic oversight of the security sector, environmental protection, border security, media freedom, elections, governance and gender equality, etc.

On the other hand, the duties of the special monitoring mission to Ukraine had a mainly military focus. It was tasked with monitoring the ceasefire, verifying the withdrawal of heavy weapons and impartially reporting on the country's security situation. It produced several reports condemning the Russian forces before being dissolved.[6] Russian Federation objected to the extension of its mandate, as it was permitted

---

[6] See in particular, OSCE Office for Democratic institutions and Human Rights, *Report on Violations of International Humanitarian Law and Human Rights Law, War Crimes and Crimes Against Humanity committed in Ukraine since 24 February 2022*, ODIHR.GAL/26/ 22/Rev.1, 13 April 2022, pp. 34–35: https://www.osce.org/files/f/documents/f/a/515868.pdf.

to do under the OSCE operating rules, which proved a little outdated on this aspect.

(B) Inadequate structure

The CSCE was above all an informal diplomatic process – no formal institution was set up. Although the USSR had argued for one early on, NATO countries turned the idea down, preferring periodic meetings to setting up an international organisation that Moscow might use to control or monitor European affairs. The Helsinki meeting was followed by other conferences, at a steady rate. At the Budapest summit on 5 and 6 December 1994, following on from the proposals contained in the Charter of Paris for a New Europe, signed on 21 November 1990 at the end of the Paris Conference,[7] the Conference on security and cooperation in Europe, an informal diplomatic forum with no legal personality, was transformed into the Organisation for Security and Cooperation in Europe, a truly intergovernmental organisation.

From an institutional point of view, the OSCE is a highly conventional organisation. Its main body is the ministerial council, comprising foreign ministers of OSCE states, which meets at least once a year. The ministerial council is assisted by a permanent council made up of representatives of participating states and is responsible for day-to-day operations. Assistance is provided by the secretary general, who is appointed for three years by the ministerial council and runs the secretariat, based in Vienna. The OSCE is chaired for one year on a rotating basis by the foreign minister of each participating state.

Finally, the parliamentary assembly, comprising three hundred and twenty-three national parliamentarians, meets in a different city in Autumn and Summer every year and in Vienna every February to evaluate the implementation of OSCE objectives and discuss subjects addressed during meetings of the ministerial council.

This day-to-day management structure is supplemented by other bodies, whose interventions may be less regular but are just as decisive. These include summit meetings of heads of state and government, which

[7] The Charter proposed formalising the CSCE into an organisation, establishing a mechanism for regular political consultation and instituting a secretariat based in Prague.

set the main political priorities and can be convened by any participating state. Five summits were subsequently held in Helsinki, each one resulting in declarations and documents that marked important stages in the organisation's history: Paris in 1992, Budapest in 1994, Lisbon in 1996, Istanbul in 1999 and Astana in 2010.

The structure of the OSCE was not designed to enable a quick and effective response to major crises, and is even less suitable when two participating states are on opposing sides and one of them is diplomatically isolated.

The OSCE is a forum for consultation and dialogue, it is not designed for action. Consensus, the decision-making procedure retained, illustrates this perfectly: because one single state can stand against all the other states. Consensus means that all decisions require the agreement of all fifty-seven states, considerably limiting the OSCE's scope of action. Adopted to preserve and guarantee the absolute affirmation of principles of sovereignty and non-interference and barring the OSCE from intervening in internal crises without the consent of the states involved, this decision-making technique necessarily limits any intervention in a conflict between states if one of the protagonists objects. Thus, Russia was able to prevent any real action by the OSCE in Chechnya, while in the former Yugoslavia, the OSCE had to temporarily exclude the Federal Republic of Yugoslavia, which objected to any operation on its former territory.

As well as limiting the response to internal crises, limitations on managing international armed conflicts also appeared. For example, the Russian Federation objected to the OSCE acting as mediator in Georgia in August 2008, despite being invited to do so by Georgia. In Ukraine, Russia refused to extend the mandate of the project coordinator in Ukraine (PCU), which was forced to discontinue operations on 30 June 2022. The Russian Federation also refused to agree to extend the special monitoring mission to Ukraine (SMM), whose activities were first suspended and then definitively shut down on 31 March 2022. It also blocked the extension of the OSCE border observer mission (BOM) at the two border posts of Donetsk and Gukovo, which were forced to close on 30 September 2021.

Ultimately, the means of pressure available to OSCE institutions are quite limited and, in the absence of any legal mechanism, they in fact amount to little more than the power to suspend participating states.

Thus, Poland refused entry to the Russian delegation, including Minister Sergey Lavrov, for a ministerial council meeting in December 2022 which was to have been chaired by Lavrov. Represented only by its permanent representative, the Russian Federation, which denounced the decision as provocative, was unanimously criticised for its action in Ukraine. Representatives of the Russian Duma and Senate were also excluded from sessions of the parliamentary assembly in 2022 in Birmingham and Warsaw because as they were denied a visa. However, Russian representatives were able to go to Vienna in February 2023 because Austria considered that as host-state it was obliged to issue a visa to all participating state representatives, including those from the Russian Federation.

Countering obstructionist policies can also involve circumvention strategies, such as that put in place since 1 November 2022 by the secretary general with the support programme for Ukraine (SPU). The Russian Federation were not able to object to this extra-budgetary programme, which has taken on most of the projects and activities of the former PCU and is funded by a group of donor states.

But it would be better to develop a system whereby states directly concerned by the decision-making process could be formally excluded. Of course, this would run the risk of measures being decided that would be objectively impossible to implement on the ground or would entail losses or obstruction that could potentially lead to dangerous excesses. A similar system, known as the "Moscow mechanism", is already in place for the human dimension, indicating that the OSCE has far greater potential for development in terms of both the economic and environmental dimension and the human dimension than for the politico-military component.

II. Developing the OSCE's economic, environmental and human dimension

The politico-military dimension remains the most important facet of global and cooperative security as designed and developed by the OSCE, despite the equal importance formally awarded to the economic and environmental dimension (A) and the human dimension (B). However, with the difficulties caused by Russia's obstructionist policy in the politico-military arena, these two latter dimensions need to be further developed to ward off potential new conflicts and encourage Eurasian states to focus on cooperation and development.

(A) Developing partnership for cooperation within the framework of the economic and environmental dimensions

Because security is closely linked to economic and social disparities, the absence of rule of law, weak governance, corruption, endemic poverty, high unemployment and increasing environmental damage, the OSCE has developed a set of mechanisms to reinforce cooperation on economic and environmental questions. The office of the co-ordinator of OSCE economic and environmental activities (OCEEA) is active in most of the organisation's field operations, helping plan and implement projects in these areas. The same body organises an economic and environmental forum every year to assess implementation by participating states of economic and environmental commitments and to define priorities for future activities. The office works in close collaboration with the chairmanship of the organisation and under the guidance of the economic and environmental committee, a subsidiary body of the permanent council. Since 2003, the OSCE has partnered closely with other international organisations within the environment and security initiative (ENVSEC), which provides a framework for cooperation on environment and security issues within and across borders. Through ENVSEC, the OSCE works to promote peace and stability through environmental cooperation and sustainable development in south-eastern Europe, eastern Europe, the south Caucasus and central Asia. The OSCE also addresses environment and security challenges in its activity with the OSCE Mediterranean and Asian partners for cooperation.

The economic and environmental dimension remains very small and could be seen as the poor relation to global and cooperative security. Given the stakes it entails and the interest it generates in states neighbouring the OSCE, this dimension should be further expanded, to ensure even closer collaboration between the eleven Asian and Mediterranean partners for cooperation to better address shared security challenges. With support from the secretariat, events with these partners, including annual Asian and Mediterranean conferences, are regularly planned and organised. Although encompassing the full range of the organisation's activities, each group of partners engages on specific issues of common interest.

The Mediterranean partners are particularly focused on combating terrorism, border security, water management, challenges to environmental safety, migration management, inter-cultural and inter-religious dialogue, tolerance and non-discrimination.

The Asian partners look to the OSCE's comprehensive approach to security and to confidence- and security-building measures as potential sources of inspiration for their own region. They also have shared experiences in responding to transnational threats, managing borders, addressing transport issues, combating trafficking in human beings, building democratic institutions and administering elections.

All these areas involve the human dimension of security.

(B) Establishing the human dimension over the long term

As we know, human rights make up one of the three main baskets negotiated at the Helsinki Conference and their acceptance by the eastern bloc led ultimately to the latter's demise. Human rights also enabled the CSCE to support and manage the exit from totalitarianism of countries in central and eastern Europe, organising a peaceful transition from communism to liberal democracy through a crisis prevention mechanism and focusing on the human dimension of security.

Stalin, Khrushchev and Tito all applied the principle of divide and rule when drawing up internal administrative boundaries, knowingly mixing ethnically different populations and splitting up areas with close historical and cultural ties in their respective states to prevent secessionism. Under this system, if the people in any given republic claimed the right to self-determination within the confines of existing administrative divisions, a minority in that territory would be sure to assert its independence or to claim allegiance to a neighbouring republic. This scenario effectively played out in former Yugoslavia with dissident Serbs in Croatia and in Bosnia and Herzegovina, and then in the former USSR – in Azerbaijan (Nagorno-Karabakh), Chechnya, Georgia, the Baltic states and, more recently, Ukraine.

Due to the risk of conflict in these former communist states, the CSCE decided to set up a conflict-prevention centre and develop mechanisms to facilitate the states' transition from communist authoritarianism to democratic regimes that uphold fundamental human rights. This "human rights mechanism" was formally laid down in the concluding document of the 1989 Vienna conference and it allows participating states to share information on human rights. It also establishes a mechanism for investigating human rights violations.

The content of this human dimension was further clarified in meetings in Paris in 1989, Copenhagen in 1990 and Moscow in 1991. In addition to respect for human rights and fundamental freedoms, the human dimension now included liberal democracy. The human dimension was also extended to include respect for the rule of law. The human dimension understood in a wider sense was the essential value promoted by the CSCE in the Charter for a new Europe adopted in Paris on 21 November 1990. That instrument introduced two new topics for cooperation, namely reinforcing democratic institutions and protecting national minorities.

This dimension should be further developed and it would be highly regrettable if the crisis in Ukraine were to lead to a scaling down of OSCE activities in the area of fundamental rights because of obstruction by some participating states egged on by Russia. From this point of view, the Moscow mechanism could provide a real opportunity to get beyond the inherent limitations of the organisation's structure and provide a minimum guarantee of human rights on the Eurasian landmass by maintaining the ability to denounce key violations.

Born out of different contexts, the concluding document of the Moscow conference (1991) and that of the Vienna conference (1989) form the basis of the OSCE human dimension mechanisms – the Vienna and Moscow mechanisms. The Moscow mechanism, which allows missions of experts to be set up to look at questions relating to the human dimension on the territory of a participating state, has only ever been used on an exceptional basis.[8] While a mission in theory must be accepted by the states territorially concerned, the mechanism also allows "a participating state [which] considers that a particularly serious threat to the fulfilment of the provisions of the CSCE human dimension has arisen in another participating state" to seek to have a mission of experts constituted without the consent of the state concerned, provided it has "the support of at least nine other participating States".[9] This mechanism

8 See Emmanuel Decaux, "Mort et résurrection du mécanisme de Moscou", *Annuaire français de Relations internationales*, Vol. VIII, 2007, pp. 233–248.

9 Moscow Document, par. 12. Moscow Mechanism, 1991, as amended by Rome 1993 (Chapter IV, par. 5), available at https://www.osce.org/files/f/documents/5/e/20066.pdf par. 5 and 8.

has already been invoked twice in support of Ukraine against Russia.[10] The first time was on 23 March 2023, when thirty-eight OSCE participating states invoked it to have Belarus investigated for human rights violations[11] and on 30 March 2023, when forty-five of them invoked it in response to the deportation to the Russian territory of children from Ukrainian territory under its control.[12]

*

In conclusion, with several highly critical reports already submitted by experts and assuredly more to come, these are strong signals to Belarus and to its powerful protector, Russia, sent out by a majority of OSCE states, flagging their determination not to compromise on the human dimension and on respect for the most fundamental rights on the Eurasian landmass.

If over one billion individuals are to coexist peacefully, they must have a bedrock of shared values and it is essential from this perspective that the OSCE system be maintained if only to avoid ostracising a state and its population because of the atrocities committed by some of their leaders.

---

10 Statement by the delegation of Canada (also on behalf of 44 other states) at the 1360th plenary meeting of the permanent council of the OSCE, 3 March 2022, available at https://www.osce.org/files/f/documents/d/7/514480.pdf, Annex 22; Permanent Representation of France to the OSCE, "Statement by France on the invocation of the Moscow Mechanism to address the human rights and humanitarian impacts of Russia's invasion and acts of war against Ukraine", to the 1376th meeting of the permanent council, 2 June 2022, available at https://osce.delegfrance.org/STATEMENT-BY-FRANCE-ON-THE-INVOCATION-OF-THE-MOSCOW-MECHANISM-TO-ADDRESS-THE-1788.

11 https://by.ambafrance.org/OSCE-Invocation-du-mecanisme-de-Moscou-sur-les-violations-graves-des-droits-de.

12 https://jp.ambafrance.org/OSCE-Invocation-du-mecanisme-de-Moscou-sur-les-deportations-d-enfants-ukrainiens-par-la-Russie-dans-le-cadre-de-la-guerre-d-agression-russe-en-Ukraine.

Ensuring Security in Central Asia: Legal aspects of the activities of the CSTO and of the CICA

Gulmira MASHIMBAYEVA
Kazakhstan

In the current situation of global geopolitical instability and the rapid deformation of the international security system, the vulnerability of the Central Asian region to external challenges is increasing. The growth of confrontation between the West, on the one hand, and Russia and China, on the other, creates additional risks for the region. The most serious challenges for the region are the military-political situation in Eurasia (the Russian-Ukrainian armed conflict), the need for the countries of the region to adapt to the conditions of the new reality under the sanctions against Russia, and the continued uncertainty factor in the Afghan direction.

Under such conditions, there is a growing need to study the effectiveness of existing institutional and other international formations, particularly the Collective Security Treaty Organisation (CSTO) and the Conference on Interaction and Confidence Building Measures in Asia (CICA). To what extent can these ensure peace and stability in the region?

This chapter considers the issues of legal regulation of the CSTO and CICA activities from the point of view of their ability to ensure the security of the Central Asian region.

The history of the creation of the CSTO and the CICA, their goals and objectives, and the problems of membership and cooperation of the participating states have been studied, and a comparative legal analysis of the statutory international documents of the CSTO and NATO has been made. The issues of the numerical composition of the CSTO joint forces, the contribution of participants to the budget, and their role in the organisation are considered. In addition, the prospects for the further institutionalisation of the CICA – its transformation from a forum into an international organisation are analysed.

I. Formation of Central Asia and the threats to security today

Central Asia was formed as an independent region in 1992 to gain international legal personality of the Asian republics of the former USSR: Kazakhstan, Kyrgyzstan, Uzbekistan, Tajikistan and Turkmenistan. They share a common history, and ethnic, cultural, linguistic, and socio-economic ties. At the same time, these countries had different political and economic conditions for further development after the collapse of the Soviet Union, which served as a barrier to the creation of economic integration communities and effective security structures on the territory of this region.

In the 1990s, many foreign experts predicted the worst scenarios for the development of the situation in Central Asia[1] due to internal problems and unresolved contradictions among the countries themselves. However, subsequent historical events have shown that severe security threats came from the territory of adjacent regions, where intrastate conflicts existed for an extended period. In particular, one of the leading causes of the civil war in Tajikistan, as well as the emergence of the problem of drug-trafficking, was the withdrawal of Soviet troops from Afghanistan, the armed confrontation of political forces in Afghanistan for many years, and its transformation into a centre of international terrorism[2].

The latter circumstance predetermined the implementation of repeated incursions by international terrorist groups in the territories of Tajikistan, Uzbekistan, and Kyrgyzstan.

To this day, Afghanistan continues to be a severe source of instability, not only for the Central Asian region but also for the entire world community. The next round of destabilisation in the region began with the withdrawal of the American military contingent from this country in the fall of 2021; the situation escalated even more and led to the capture of the Afghan border districts with Central Asian countries by the Taliban[3].

---

1 Makkambaev, P. A. (2021). The current state of the emerging system of regional security in Central Asia. *Economics of Central Asia*. Vol. 5, No. 3. 273–296.

2 Umnov, A. Yu. (2009). Afghan crisis. *The World Economy and International Relations.* No. 3. 49–57.

3 Khrolenko, A. How neighbours react to the successes of the Taliban. Sputnik Uzbekistan. [Electronic resource]. URL: https://uz.sputniknews.ru/20210712/kak-sosedi-reagiruyut-na-uspexi-talibov-19652055.html.

In addition to the Afghan factor, Central Asia has enough of its problems, both domestic and international: these are issues of demarcation of state borders, legal regulation of transboundary water resources in the region, problems of intra-elite struggle in the states of the area, problems of ensuring human rights, etc.

Analysing this situation, it seems that players like the USA, NATO, and the EU will not take responsibility for maintaining stability in the Central Asian region (too expensive, too far, even though their interests are undoubtedly present in the region). Moreover, some experts believe that destabilisation of the region is even beneficial for these players since it will weaken and distract Russia from the situation in Eastern Europe and China from the Pacific region.[4]

Therefore, the countries of Central Asia should themselves look for ways to ensure security and build an effective system in the region, based on economic interests, historical ties, and balancing between Russia, China, the US and the EU. In particular, Kazakhstan remains committed to the multi-vector principle when building a dialogue with neighbours and regional partners.

Despite criticism of the multi-vector foreign policy of partners in integration associations, Kazakhstan intends to implement initiatives to promote the policy of peace and dialogue, which is confirmed by the VII Congress of Leaders of World and Traditional Religions held in the fall of 2022, as well as the CICA summit.

II. The Collective Security Treaty Organisation: Goals, tasks and prospects

The Collective Security Treaty Organisation originates from the conclusion of the Collective Security Treaty, which was signed in Tashkent (Uzbekistan) on 15 May 1992, by the heads of Armenia, Kazakhstan, Kyrgyzstan, Russia, Tajikistan, and Uzbekistan. Azerbaijan, Belarus (Georgia joined it in 1993). The Collective Security Treaty was concluded for a period of five years with the possibility of subsequent extension. In 1999, Armenia, Belarus, Kazakhstan, Kyrgyzstan, Russia, and Tajikistan signed the Protocol on the extension of the Collective Security Treaty.

---

4 Tamer, J. Security of Central Asia: threats and opportunities. https://www.ankasam.org/ security-central-Asia-threats//?lang=ru.

Azerbaijan, Georgia, and Uzbekistan have now ceased their membership in the Treaty.

On 14 May 2002, the Collective Security Council adopted a decision to give the Collective Security Treaty the status of an international regional organisation in Moscow. On 7 October 2002, the Presidents of Armenia, Belarus, Kazakhstan, Kyrgyzstan, Russia, and Tajikistan approved the CSTO Charter at the CIS summit in Kishinev. In December 2003, the CSTO Charter was registered with the UN Secretariat. In 2004, the Organisation received the observer status in the UN General Assembly.

Thus, in 2002, the main organisational procedures were carried out related to the legal registration of the current status of the CSTO as an international, regional organisation that unites independent states with common interests in the field of ensuring collective security. As a result, today, the members of the Organisation are Armenia, Belarus, Kazakhstan, Kyrgyzstan, Russia and Tajikistan.

The goals of the Organisation are to strengthen peace, international and regional security, and stability and to protect on a collective basis the independence, territorial integrity, and sovereignty of the Member States by Article 3 of the Charter.[5] The Organisation cooperates with non-member states of the Organisation and maintains relations with international intergovernmental organisations operating in security by Article 4.[6] The Organisation contributes to forming a just, democratic world order based on the generally recognised principles of international law. The document defines the following directions by which the Organisation is guided in its activities: the priority of political means over the military, strict respect of independence, voluntary participation, equality of rights and obligations of Member States, and non-interference in matters of the Member States falling under the national jurisdiction.[7] Thus, the Collective Security Treaty Organisation (CSTO) operates on the principles of the UN Charter. The same provision is enshrined in Article 1

---

5 Charter of the Collective Security Treaty Organisation of October 7, 2002, art. 3. http://www.odkb.gov.ru/b/azg.html.

6 Charter of the Collective Security Treaty Organisation of October 7, 2002, art. 4. http://www.odkb.gov.ru/b/azg.html.

7 Charter of the Collective Security Treaty Organisation of October 7, 2002, art. 5. http://www.odkb.gov.ru/b/azg.html.

of the NATO Charter: The Contracting Parties undertake to settle all international disputes peacefully in which they may become parties by the Charter of the United Nations, without endangering international peace, security, and justice, and to abstain from any use of force or the threat of its use in their international relations, if this is contrary to the purposes of the UN.[8]

By its legal nature, the CSTO is a classic international organisation established based on an international treaty, pursuing clearly defined goals, having a system of permanent bodies, and being called upon to coordinate the actions of member states on an ongoing basis by the powers granted to it. Thus, the CSTO was undoubtedly endowed with international legal personality and can express its will. At the same time, the CSTO Charter clearly defines that the provisions of the Collective Security Treaty and the international treaties and decisions adopted in its development are binding both for the Organisation's member states and for the Organisation itself. Therefore, any state in the region that shares the goals and principles of the CSTO and is ready to assume the obligations contained in international treaties and decisions operating within the framework of the CSTO can become a member of the CSTO.

On 10 December 2010, the CSTO member states signed the Agreement on the status of formations of forces and means of the CSTO collective security system. According to this Agreement, the armed forces of one of the Member States may be sent to the territory of the host country by the official request of the latter to exercise the right to collective defence in the event of a threat and/or commission of an armed attack (aggression) against one or more Parties, countering other challenges and threats to collective security, liquidation of emergencies, as well as for joint command-staff and military exercises.[9]

It can be assumed that over the years of the existence of the CSTO, a solid legal framework has been created that regulates the organisation's activities in all major areas of security. To date, international treaties have been signed and ratified on the most fundamental issues of interstate

---

8 North Atlantic Treaty Washington, DC, April 4, (1949). https://www.nato.int/cps/ru/natohq/official_texts_17120.htm.

9 "On the main results of the CSTO activities for 2002–2012. and Priority Directions for the Development of the Organisation" http://www.odkb-csto.org/news/detail.php?ELEMENT_ID=360.

cooperation in the field of collective security.[10] Practical cooperation with other international organisations is being increased. Working contacts were established with the UN, and meetings with officials of the SCO, the CIS, and the EAEU became regular, which makes it possible to optimise the distribution of functions between regional organisations whose responsibility is to ensure security in Eurasia.

The supply of weapons and military equipment to the CSTO allies at subsidised, domestic prices have been organised. Cooperation is being developed at the level of the military-industrial complexes of the CSTO member states. An essential element of collaboration has become the joint personnel training for the member state's armed forces, law enforcement agencies, and special services. Thus, today the CSTO is an established multifunctional regional collective security organisation.

The future of the CSTO undoubtedly depends on the further development of its member states, and above all, Russia, on their ability to form competitive economies, successfully implement plans for economic integration, build an economic union, and, on its basis, constantly improve their military-political interaction.

It should be noted that in the modern period, due to the complicated international situation, much criticism is being addressed to the CSTO.

The CSTO is accused of being ineffective and inactive. In addition, the problem of contradictions among members of the organisation still needs to be solved. In particular, this refers to the situation between Tajikistan and Kyrgyzstan, which has become systemic and has led to numerous casualties, including among the civilian population. The CSTO chose in 2010 the strategy of "inaction" during violent inter-ethnic clashes in the south of Kyrgyzstan. For the first time, Bishkek asked for help and was denied. Russia explained that the criterion for the involvement of the CSTO peacekeeping forces is the violation of the borders of an ally state by another state, and the weakness and unwillingness of the former government to "deal with the needs of the people" are to blame for the internal problems of the Kyrgyz people.[11]

---

10 Organisation of the Collective Security Treaty (2023, April 13). http://www.odkb-csto.org/structure.

11 "The CSTO forces will not be used to stabilize the situation in Kyrgyzstan yet – Medvedev." (2011, November 6). http://today.kz/news/mir/2010-06-11/61874-medvedev-3/.

The CSTO did not interfere either in the crisis during the third revolution in Kyrgyzstan in October 2020, considering the ongoing events to be the internal affairs of Kyrgyzstan.

During the escalation of the conflict in Nagorno-Karabakh, the CSTO and the Russian Foreign Ministry told the Armenian government that the organisation's defensive potential could not be used to protect an ally because the war did not unfold on its territory. This decision is explained by Article 5 of the CSTO Charter[12], which states that the organisation adheres to the principle of non-interference in members' internal affairs and is obliged to protect allies only in case of threats from third countries or actors.

Unfortunately, neither the crisis of 2010 in Kyrgyzstan nor the war over Nagorno-Karabakh fell into this category.

In principle, such provisions of the Collective Security Treaty are consistent with the NATO Charter of 1949. In particular, under Article 5 of the Charter, the Contracting Parties agree that an armed attack against one or more of them in Europe or North America will be considered an attack against them as a whole and, therefore, agree that in case of such an armed attack, each of them, in the exercise of the right of individual or collective self-defence recognised by Article 51 of the Charter of the United Nations, will assist the Contracting Party or Contracting Parties that have been subjected to such attack by immediately taking an individual or collective action, as it deems necessary, including the use of armed force to restore and subsequently maintain the security of the North Atlantic region.[13]

The inefficiency of the CSTO is also associated with the uneven distribution of financial injections into the organisation's budget, 50 % of which is the Russian contribution.

At the same time, the allocation of the budget in NATO is more diversified[14], the US mandate is only 16 %, and Germany pays the same

12 "Charter of the Collective Security Treaty Organisation". (2002, July 9), https://odkb-csto.org/documents/documents/ustav_organizatsii_dogovora_o_kollektivnoy_bezopasnosti_/.

13 North Atlantic Treaty Washington, DC. (1949, April 4) https://www.nato.int/cps/ru/natohq/official_texts_17120.html.

14 "NATO common-funded budgets and programs cost share arrangements valid from 1 January 2021 to 31 December 2024", NATO. (2020). https://nato.int/nato_static_fl2014/assets/pdf/2020/5/pdf/200505-cost-shares-cb-mb-is-20-24.pdf.

amount. Of 30 countries participating in the military bloc, four countries together cover more than 50 % of the budget: the USA, Great Britain, France, and Germany. As can be seen, the distribution of financial obligations in NATO is more proportional than the CSTO.

In addition, experts note the unproportional size of the military contingent of the CSTO joint forces, 80 % of whom are Russian military personnel. The number of armies of the CSTO member states is 1 million and 256 thousand soldiers. In the NATO army, the number of soldiers is 3 million and 462 thousand people, of which only 40 % are American military personnel. Here you can consider the dependence of organisations on significant players, the participating countries in NATO depend on the United States two times less than the CSTO participating countries on Russia, which makes the collective and organisational capabilities of the CSTO weaker than NATO[15].

The only case of use of the joint forces of the CSTO was their participation in stabilising the crisis in Kazakhstan in January 2022, when the president of the country turned to the CSTO with a request for military assistance.

No matter how experts and politicians evaluate the activities of the CSTO today, the relevance and necessity of organisations such as the CSTO remain in times of old conflicts escalate along the perimeter of the borders of Central Asia and the CIS, and new local hotbeds of tension arise.

III. The role of CICA in ensuring security in Asia

The Conference on Interaction and Confidence Building Buildings in Asia (CICA) is an international forum to strengthen cooperation to ensure peace, security, and stability in Asia.

The CICA was initiated by Kazakhstan at the 47th session of the UN General Assembly on 5 October 1992. At the heart of the idea of president, Nazarbayev, was "the desire to create an effective and acceptable structure for all to ensure peace and security in Asia."

---

15 Karimov, N. The effectiveness of the CSTO in the context of the changing regional security system. https://cabar.asia/ru/effektivnost-odkb-v-kontekste-menyayushhej sya-sistemy-regionalnoj-bezopasnosti.

CICA has 28 member states, including Kazakhstan, Russia, Azerbaijan, Bangladesh, Bahrain, Vietnam, Egypt, Israel, India, Iraq, Iran, China, Palestine, Turkey, South Korea, etc. The geography of participation is vast. It is important to note that to become a CICA member, a state must have a part of its territory in Asia.

The following documents are the legal basis for the activities of the forum: Declaration of Principles – adopted on September 14, 1999, at the first meeting of CICA foreign ministers; The Almaty Act and the Charter of the CICA – were adopted at the first summit on 4 June 2002.

According to the Declaration of Principles governing relations between the CICA member states, the participants must comply with the following: Sovereign equality, respect for the rights inherent in sovereignty; The non-use of force or threat of force; Territorial integrity of the Member States; Peaceful settlement of disputes; Non-intervention in internal affairs; Disarmament and arms control; Economic, social, and cultural cooperation; Human rights and fundamental freedoms.

The forum operates in the form of Summits. The highest decision-making body of the CICA is the meeting of heads of state or governments of the CICA. The summits are held every four years, and the meetings of the foreign ministers of the participating countries every two years. The CICA Secretariat is located in Astana. The sixth CICA summit was held in October 2022 in Kazakhstan, as in 2020, the republic was elected as the chairman state.

Today, the CICA is an authoritative multilateral structure. Efforts are needed to improve the efficiency and international competitiveness of the forum. This requires its step-by-step, gradual transformation into a full-fledged regional organisation. All the necessary conditions have been created for the institutional development of the CICA, a legal framework has been developed, and its permanent structures are working.

What will it give? Undoubtedly, when there is a structure that enables states to interact systematically, this gives a much more significant effect than spontaneous events that do not have any conceptual severe basis. The work of the Member States under the auspices of the international organisation will allow for a more structured dialogue and a systematic and coordinated approach in the main areas of activity. The CICA aims to create a synergy between the efforts of countries that today stretch from the Pacific to the Mediterranean, from the Urals to the Indian Ocean. This is a vast geography with colossal cultural diversity and various economic and political systems, and finding in all this a thread that would bind us is a great art. This is what the states of the conference are striving for today.

At the same time, while emphasising the diplomatic, dialogue nature of this association, it is worth noting the ineffective advisory nature of its activities from a practical point of view. All this does not ensure stability and security in Central Asia.

The CICA is a diplomatic platform for communication so that the participating countries can demonstrate harmony and friendship. There is an element of solemnity, emotionality, and pomposity in holding the Summits. This is important in international relations.

However, the practical content of the adopted declarations is very often limited. Unfortunately, from year to year, the forum participants repeat the same slogans and declarative statements about adherence to the principles of the UN, international law, rejection of the unipolar world, and so on.

This shows that CICA today is more of a diplomatic forum than a practical and functional structure for implementing specific projects – large geography of participation and a wide range of issues discussed.

Unfortunately, the same can be said about the SCO, which has achieved a lot in the fight against terrorism and extremism; practical steps have been taken in matters of SCO economic cooperation. But also, it is optional today to consider the SCO as an effective mechanism for ensuring the security of Central Asia as well as the CICA.[16]

According to an Uzbek expert, the participation of Central Asian countries in CICA cannot bring tangible benefits, either in economic problems or in security issues. This is explained by the fact that the CICA still needs to be clearly structured and therefore is more inert in implementing any important interstate decisions[17].

*

16 Izimov, R. How can security be ensured in Eurasia? https://www.caa-network.org/archives/24224/kak-mozhno-obespechit-bezopasnost-v-evrazii.

17 Makkambaev, P. A. (2021). The current state of the emerging system of regional security in Central Asia. *Economics of Central Asia*. Vol. 5, No. 3. 273–296.

In conclusion, the existing associations in Central Asia do not guarantee the region's security. First, it failed to ensure the participation of all states of the area in the CSTO (Uzbekistan withdrew, and Turkmenistan is not a member of the organisation). Second, the existing contradictions among members, internal political issues related to the struggle of elites, clans, and the lack of influential democratic societies do not allow maximum use of the CSTO mechanisms. Third, the recent events of the Russian-Ukrainian confrontation have undermined the organisation's credibility in the West and within the member states. Finally, the refusal of the Armenian side to assist in the Karabakh confrontation in 2022 also led to a crisis within the CSTO when Armenia sabotaged some of the steps of the Organisation and even raised the issue of withdrawal.

All this confirms the need to revise some of the conceptual approaches in the organisation's activities. In addition, preventive and consultative mechanisms should be used to prevent conflict. To solve this problem, it is necessary to strengthen cooperation in the scientific field and begin the practice of annual regional analysis and drawing up methods and recommendations to prevent new threats to the security system of Central Asia, Belarus, and Armenia.

Central Asian countries should start discussing their own regional formats or regional security architecture in some way. The Central Asian countries have sufficient potential to create their regional security system. This does not mean that the region's countries should move away from cooperation with Russia. It is necessary to create our cooperation formats on security issues along with the CSTO.

This could be a bilateral format of consultations between the heads of state of the region. Creating a new security organisation does not make sense. It is expensive, and there are already enough associations. Many multilateral structures in which Kazakhstan participates often duplicate functions. These are the SCO and the CSTO; we have the EAEU and the Belt and Road.

There is almost no organisations representing the region without "patrons". Central Asia must try to take the region's fate into her hands.

There has been an attempt by the Central Asian states to create an effective mechanism of regional security that would allow them to adequately respond to external challenges and threats. So, in December 1995, the military departments of Kazakhstan, Kyrgyzstan, and Uzbekistan, under the auspices of the Central Command of the US Armed Forces, formed a joint peacekeeping unit, "Centrazbat".[18] The project lasted only a short time. At the same time, completing this battalion, maintaining its combat capability, and keeping it permanent became the first joint experience of cooperation of military efforts aimed at maintaining peace in the region for the three states of Central Asia.

According to Kushkumbaev S., Central Asian subjectivity is a current and prospective agenda; all countries of the region are equal regardless of economic potential, population size, and GDP level; they have a common similar history; therefore, similar issues are on the agenda. Of course, there are also differences, but it is necessary to focus on what unites.

> [editor's note: since November 2017 (Samarkand meeting) there exists a Central Asia Forum with all five Central Asian countries, even if it remains to be seen to what direct extent this Forum will contribute to set up effective sub-regional security mechanisms that will not be perceived as challenging other regional or pan-continental ones (SCO, SCTO, CICA, etc).]

---

18 Kosmarsky, A. Why does Central Asia need its peacekeepers? https://fergana.news/articles/104572/?country

The transformation of the SCO in the new conditions of a multipolar world: Prospects for enlargement and positional changes

Leila DELOVAROVA, Alibek YERMEKOV
Kazakhstan

The Shanghai Cooperation Organisation is a unique diplomatic platform, that has today entered a serious stage of transformation. This process is driven both by the expansion of its membership and by the changing realities within and around the Organisation. In modern conditions, the transformation of the SCO indicates the emergence of a new model of cooperation. Such a new model will be based on the principles of a multipolar world and will enable participants to cooperate in novel conditions, to form an alternative architecture for security, trade, and economic cooperation.

The modern system of international relations is undergoing constant transformation against the background of changing realities, political and socio-economic turbulence. Under these conditions, an important role is played by international regional and interregional organisations and platforms that have the potential for a timely and comprehensive response to security challenges and threats.

At present, world regions are subject to global challenges in the field of economy, ecology, energy, and security due to the increase in conflict potential and the impact of adverse effects of innovative international processes. Eurasia is one of the spaces that has a greater conflict potential and is faced with many various challenges and threats of mixed genesis. Under these conditions, an ever-greater role and potential for strengthening multilateral international cooperation and maintaining sustainable stability is seen in the activities and development of the Shanghai Cooperation Organisation (SCO).

The SCO was initiated as a multilateral association to ensure security and maintain stability in the vast Eurasian space, to unite efforts to counter emerging challenges and threats, and to strengthen trade, cultural and humanitarian cooperation

I. Key stages of the SCO formation and transformation

Today the SCO space extends from the from the Mediterranean to the Pacific Ocean and from the Arctic to the Indian Ocean. In the ranks of the Organisation there are two permanent members of the UN Security Council (Russia, China), four states with nuclear potential (Russia, China, India, Pakistan), two countries with the largest population on the planet (China, India) and the two largest consumers of energy in the world (China, India), as well as three of the five BRICS countries[1] (Russia, China, India). Of note is also the demographic and economic potential of the Organisation, which are important indicators of the processes of its transformation and development.

The SCO represents 40 % of the world's population and a third of its GDP, albeit due to China and India[2]. Such coverage of the Organisation shows the colossal potential and opportunities and, accordingly, the role in modern international processes.

The SCO consists of nine member states – China, India, Iran, Kazakhstan, Kyrgyzstan, Pakistan, Russia, Tajikistan, and Uzbekistan. Along with this, three countries have the status of an observer state in the SCO – Afghanistan, Belarus, and Mongolia. In 2022, at the Samarkand SCO Summit, the process of raising the status of the Republic of Belarus within the Organisation to the level of a member state was launched. And, it should be noted that 14 countries are partners in the SCO dialogue[3] (Belarus, Sri Lanka, Turkey, Cambodia, Azerbaijan, Nepal, Armenia,

---

1 20 years of Shanghai Cooperation Organisation: a View from Kazakhstan. By Yerlik Ali. URL: https://astanatimes.com/2021/06/20-years-of-shanghai-cooperation-organisation-a-view-from-kazakhstan/.

2 New Delhi is carving out a lonely furrow in SCO. The SCO represents 40 % of the world's population and a third of its GDP, albeit due to China and India. By Srikanth Kondapalli. URL: https://www.deccanherald.com/opinion/new-delhi-is-carving-out-a-lonely-furrow-in-sco-1235239.html.

3 SCO official website. General information. URL: http://eng.sectsco.org/cooperation/20170110/192193.html.

Egypt, Qatar, Saudi Arabia, Kuwait, Maldives, Myanmar, United Arab Emirates).

The formation of the SCO as an international organisation was preceded by a number of interstate agreements signed by China, Russia, Kazakhstan, Kyrgyzstan and Tajikistan in 1996–1997. Tensions in interstate relations, in general, and in border issues, in particular, during the confrontation between the former USSR and the PRC was one of the main destabilising factors in this space of the world.

After the 1991 disintegration of the USSR, a special commission was formed in the format of "Joint Delegation – PRC" to resolve these issues, which determined the lines of the state border between the two countries on the basis of topographic maps. After that, there was carried out a demarcation work and installation of boundary-markers in the agreed areas[4]. From this point on, the foundations for the creation of the SCO can be considered to have been launched. There were several stages of this process, and until 2017 there were usually three periods.

The first period is defined as the initial or preparatory period for the activities of the "Shanghai Five". This period is defined as the foundation of the SCO, from 1992 to 1996, when the necessary conditions for its functioning were created. During this period, the PRC and the four states of Kazakhstan, Kyrgyzstan, Russia and Tajikistan held talks in the "Joint Delegation – PRC" format to resolve border issues and ensure mutual confidence building measures in the border areas[5].

The second stage covered 1996–2001. At that time, there was a gradual transition from a limited to an expanded format of relations, which included both the settlement of border issues and the counteraction to new security threats and the tasks of economic cooperation.

The third stage covered June 2001–2004. The fundamental difference between the new stage and the previous ones is that the Shanghai Cooperation Organisation concentrated its efforts primarily on

---

4 Omarov, A. N. Evolution and priorities of the Shanghai Cooperation Organisation through the prism of the national interests of the Kyrgyz Republic. A.N.Omarov // Problems of the Far East, (IFES RAS RF). 2005. No. 2. pp. 28–31. In Russian (Омаров А. Н. Эволюция и приоритеты деятельности Шанхайской Организации Сотрудничества через призму национальных интересов Кыргызской Республики. А.Н.Омаров // Проблемы Дальнего Востока, (ИДВ РАН РФ). 2005. № 2. pp. 28–31).

5 Ibid.

countering new threats to security and enhancing the economic vector of its activities.

Between 2001 and 2004, the "Shanghai Spirit" was introduced, characterised by "mutual trust, mutual benefit, equality, consultation, respect for cultural diversity and the pursuit of common development."[6] To establish the rules and legal framework, the SCO member states agreed on the SCO charter in June 2002, determined that they would counteract the three forces of evil (terrorism, separatism, extremism) and approved the multilateral trade scheme. By 2004, two permanent institutions had been established: a secretariat in Beijing and a regional anti-terrorist structure in Tashkent.

The next step may be considered since 2005 till 2017. This is a period of strengthening the institutional foundations of the Organisation, improving relations within the Organisation itself and the external vector of cooperation.

This period is marked by the external cooperation: the SCO established cooperation and concluded Memorandums of Understanding (MoU) with international and regional organisations since 2005[7]: with the Executive Committee of the Commonwealth of Independent States (CIS, Beijing, 12 April 2005), with the Secretariat of the Association of Southeast Asian Nations (ASEAN, Jakarta, 21 April 2005), with the Collective Security Treaty Organisation (CSTO, Dushanbe, 5 October 2007), with the Secretariat of the Economic Cooperation Organisation (ECO, Ashgabat, 11 December 2007), a Joint Declaration on Cooperation with the United Nations Organisation (UN, Tashkent, 5 April 2010), an MoU with the UN Office on Drugs and Crime (Astana, 14 June 2011), an MoU with the Secretariat of the UN Economic and Social Commission for Asia and the Pacific (Zhengzhou, 15 December 2015), with the Secretariat of the Conference on Interaction and Confidence-Building Measures in Asia (CICA, Shanghai, 20 May 2014), with the International Committee of the Red Cross (ICRC) (Astana, 9 June 2017).

Since the early 2010s, there has been a strengthening of cooperation within the framework of the SCO through the reinforcement of ties among the countries of Central Asia and China. In 2011, China-Russia

---

6 Charter of the Shanghai Cooperation Organisation. URL: http://eng.sectsco.org.

7 SCO official website. External cooperation. URL: http://eng.sectsco.org/cooperation/20170110/192193.html.

relations were upgraded to a "comprehensive strategic partnership of coordination" and in 2019 to a "comprehensive strategic partnership of coordination of a new era."[8] Modernisation of relations among member states gives an impetus to the development of the SCO. Due to the China-Kazakhstan Comprehensive Strategic Partnership established in 2011 and subsequently made permanent, and the China-Uzbekistan Strategic Partnership in 2012, all SCO member states in Central Asia are China's strategic partners. The Sino-Uzbek, Sino-Tajik and Sino-Kyrgyz partnerships are now comprehensive strategic partnerships. China's relations with the SCO member states in Central Asia have steadily improved during those years, and Tajikistan and Kyrgyzstan formed a strategic partnership with China in 2013[9]. Strengthening relationships within the Organisation enabled it to strengthen its institutional framework, trust, and set long-term goals.

Expanding of international cooperation led to broadening not only the potential of the Organisation, but also to expand the opportunities for partners. This period also coincided with China's unprecedented economic growth in the early 2000th and the launch of its mega Belt and Road project in 2014. Despite the ambiguous perception and possible ambiguous consequences of this process, in general, this gave impetus to the development of the Organisation.

The next stage of the transformation of the SCO can be noted from 2017. The Astana SCO summit opened a new chapter in the Organisation's development. For the first time in the history of the SCO, the number of its members expanded due to the admission of new member states – India and Pakistan. The participation of UN Secretary-General António Guterres in the SCO summit was a clear confirmation of the growing authority of the Organisation and the strengthening of its influence at the global level[10]. With the completion of the institutional formation of the SCO, new mechanisms of international cooperation emerged, which are characterised by a novel type of relations that takes into account the

---

8 20 Years of the SCO: Development, Experience and Future Direction. By Deng Hao. URL: https://www.ciis.org.cn/english/ESEARCHPROJECTS/Articles/202112/t20211203_8276.html.

9 Ibid.

10 20 years of Shanghai Cooperation Organisation: a View from Kazakhstan. By Yerlik Ali. URL: https://astanatimes.com/2021/06/20-years-of-shanghai-cooperation-organisation-a-view-from-kazakhstan/.

opinion of each member state. The most valuable aspect in the activities of the Organisation is the establishment of decision-making by consensus, to resolve all issues through dialogue.

There are two more important steps to be noted. One of them is the Samarkand Summit which took place on 15–16 September 2022 and the New Delhi Summit which took place in 2023.

At the summit in Samarkand, the SCO countries signed the Samarkand Declaration[11] and the largest number of documents, the total number of which was forty-four. It is necessary to note several of them[12]:

- On the Comprehensive Action Plan for the Implementation of the Provisions of the Agreement on Long-term Good Neighbourliness, Friendship and Cooperation of the SCO Member States for 2023–2027;
- On the concept of the SCO member states on the development of interdependence and the creation of efficient transport corridors;
- On the "road map" of a gradual increase in the share of national currencies in the mutual settlements of the SCO member states;
- On the signing of a memorandum on Iran's obligations to obtain the status of a SCO member state;
- On the beginning of the process of admission of the Republic of Belarus to the members of the SCO;
- On granting the status of SCO dialogue partner to the Republic of Maldives, Bahrain, the United Arab Emirates, the Republic of the Union of Myanmar and the State of Kuwait.

All these documents are aimed at both strengthening the Organisation and reflecting the new global challenges facing it, including the environmental and digital fields, food security, agriculture, and supply chain expansion in the new geoeconomic realities. Key points to mention were launching Iran's joining the SCO, and the status of Belarus in the SCO. One more important point which makes the SCO unique is the proclamation of the SCO as an organisation not directed against third countries[13]. Non-direction against third countries is a important aspect in the

---

11 SCO official web site. The Samarkand Declaration of the Heads of State Council of the Shanghai Cooperation Organisation. URL: eng.sectsco.org.

12 Documents of the SCO summit, 2022. URL: https://sco-summit2022.uz/ru/documents.

13 SCO becoming more attractive to other countries for non-bloc status principle, mutual benefit: former Uzbek deputy PM. Joint prosperity path. By Xie Wenting and Lin Xiaoyi. URL: https://www.globaltimes.cn/page/202209/1275922.shtml.

new geopolitical realities, which shows the readiness of the Organisation for further dialogue and strengthening its status as a negotiating platform.

In 2023, the 23rd SCO Summit held in New Delhi, India on 4 July, is also of note. During the Summit chaired by India, Iran officially became a full member of the SCO. The summit resulted in the adoption of the New Delhi Declaration[14], which proposed five joint statements on various issues such as combating terrorism, de-radicalisation, sustainable living to combat climate change, millet production and digital transformation.

India has again refused to support China's Belt and Road Initiative (BRI), which aims to connect China with Asia, Europe, and other countries through major infrastructure projects. India remains the only SCO member that does not support the project.

The summit showed that so far, the SCO has not been able to reach a full consensus. Thus, India also did not take part in the joint statement on the SCO's Economic Development Strategy until 2030. Within the framework of the summit India proposed strengthening the democratic foundations in the SCO countries through the strengthening of civil society.

It's interesting to note that in the final declaration it was announced that Central Asia is the "the core of SCO", perhaps replicating its "ASEAN centrality" approach in the Indo-Pacific in this Eurasian grouping[15]. This could mean that Central Asia is to increase its role in Eurasia in the difficult realities and weaken the economic interdependence from Russia and China and realise necessary potential.

Also, the SCO countries called for a peaceful settlement of differences among states through dialogue. The declaration once again confirms the non-direction of the Organisation's activities against other countries and international organisations.

---

14 NEW DELHI DECLARATION OF THE COUNCIL OF HEADS OF STATE OF SHANGHAI COOPERATION ORGANIZATION. URL: http://eng.sectsco.org/documents/.

15 New Delhi is carving out a lonely furrow in SCO. The SCO represents 40 % of the world's population and a third of its GDP, albeit due to China and India. By Srikanth Kondapalli. URL: https://www.deccanherald.com/opinion/new-delhi-is-carving-out-a-lonely-furrow-in-sco-1235239.html.

II. The geopolitical role of the SCO and positioning changes

In the period from the late 2000s to the first half of the 2010s, there were reduced confrontational tendencies in the international system. The SCO was not active, but acted as an institution to support the Russian-Chinese balance in Eurasia. The situation has changed since the 2020s, when China's geopolitical rise, its institution-building, the strategic shift influenced by the Russian-Ukrainian conflict, the intensification of confrontational tendencies in Russian-American and Chinese-American relations, and the admission of Iran to the SCO in this context, all this led to some diplomatic "activation" of this Organisation. Therefore, the SCO primarily acts as a diplomatic platform.

It is necessary to note the geopolitical role of the SCO, since the factor of global interdependence and economic globalisation plays a central role in shaping the strategic narratives of the leading states.

Several aspects should be singled out that characterise the SCO in a geopolitical context. First, within the SCO, along with multiple coincidences of interests in the field of security, economy and logistics, there are obvious and potential contradictions between the participants. The conflict between India and Pakistan and that between China and India, which in general constitute the strategic triangle of Pakistan-India-China. Another aspect is the situation in Central Asia, where there are integration intentions and close cooperation, but there are also border disputes, including very serious ones, for example, between Kyrgyzstan and Tajikistan. It is also necessary to consider the factor of China's geopolitical rise, which can reformat Central Asia, which may be important for Russia, which is now not in the most advantageous position due to the conflict with Ukraine and sanctions imposed against Russia. Along with this, China is seen as an important partner of Russia in this situation.

By "geopolitical rise", we mean the global institutional-hegemonic construction by China, as well as the formation of a system of alliances in East Asia, which was already reflected in the formation of the Indo-Pacific Security Cluster during the Trump presidency[16].

16 Elbridge, C., & Wess, M. (January/February 2020). The Age of Great-Power Competition. How the Trump Administration Refashioned American Strategy, Council on Foreign Relations, Foreign Affairs, p. 121.

It is also obvious that one of the leading SCO member countries, India, is actively involved in American projects, or security institutions such as QUAD, which, of course, will not contribute to the active promotion of Chinese initiatives within the SCO. It is also necessary to consider the factor of global economic interdependence. The interdependence between the participants of the Organisation and outside it determines the need for coexistence and constant search for compromises.

The structure of the balance of power within the SCO consists of two dimensions, the first is within Central Asia, and the second is the macro-regional Eurasian dimension. Within the framework of Central Asia, the SCO contributes to maintaining the Russian-Chinese balance, where the traditional tandem Russia-security, China-economy has been formed. Today, such a balance is no longer entirely relevant and new approaches are needed. Within the macro-regional dimension of Eurasia, there is a balance of power between Russia-India on the one hand, and China-Pakistan on the other. This status quo no longer fully reflects the structure of the world, and with the intensification of trends in the "multi-polarisation" of the system of international relations, the balance of power began to change. In this context, it is important to assess Iran's entry into the SCO and the further expansion of the Organisation.

The main mechanism of the balance of power within the SCO can be called the Russia-China-India-Pakistan quadrangle. The intensification of the West's confrontation with Russia has led to the strengthening of Russian-Chinese ties, while Russian-Indian ties have weakened. Also, India, which has traditionally been considered a Russian-oriented country, since the Modi period, has turned towards cooperation with the United States, where India has become a full member of QUAD. In the case of Pakistan, during the reign of Imran Khan, on the contrary, cooperation or direction towards China and Russia increased.

Another aspect of the balance of power within the SCO is the balance of influence between Russia and China. This influence concerns the Far East and Central Asia. The Sino-Indian strategic aspect also underlies the mechanism of the balance of power within the SCO. Sino-Indian rivalry includes not only territorial issues in Tibet and the Indian Ocean, but also logistics and economic aspects. It also seems that China sees the SCO during last decade as one of the tools of its institutional building in Eurasia as part of building the sphere of influence of the Belt and Road.

This aspect also needs to be considered in the process of analysing the activities of the Organisation and the implementation or limitation of the interests of the participants. An important role within the framework of the SCO is played by the countries of Central Asia both individually and as a region for Russia, China, and India in a strategic perspective. It is important for the Central Asian countries themselves to find a balance in the SCO system and use the potential of the Organisation to promote it and to realise their own national interests. Such an arrangement within the SCO will not be able to lead to the formation of institutions or mechanisms of collective security.

Within the framework of the balance of power, the SCO will be able to perform the functions of a negotiating mechanism, but within the framework of the institutional provision of collective security, this is unlikely. This prevents the SCO from turning into a bloc directed against third parties. Therefore, it remains a priority for the parties to preserve the SCO as a diplomatic platform, or a platform for containing the escalation of nuclear confrontation.

*

In conclusion, the SCO as a structure functioning as a macro-regional organisation acting as a diplomatic platform, the purpose of which is to solve a regional problem and reflect global challenges. Given the size of the SCO, it seems that this organisation has a broad military-political potential as a military alliance, but geopolitical and strategic realities bring to the fore other conditions and determine the need to organise a negotiating platform.

The Organisation has undergone a serious transformation both internally and externally – from a structure that was aimed at resolving border disputes to a macro-regional organisation that brings together actors and has the potential to determine a new emerging system of international relations.

The activities of the SCO make it possible to strengthen the territorial integrity of the countries involved, playing the role of a stabilising factor in the Eurasian space, acting as a buffer against threats from South Asia and the Middle East. Moreover, the SCO is a convenient negotiating platform, it does not oblige the participants, but at the same time responds to the request of countries to expand cooperation, reduce multiple risks, and prevent the impact of certain challenges and threats.

In modern conditions, it seems important to prevent a geopolitical split and strengthen trust within the Organisation to further increase its integration potential. The main mission of the SCO in modern conditions is seen as strengthening mutually beneficial cooperation, preventing confrontation and conflicts, maintaining equal and indivisible security, building a fair polycentric world order that meets the interests of each state, considering their mutual interests.

Legal aspects of the security of the Caspian region in light of the Russia-Ukraine conflict

Bakhyt UDERBAYEVA
Kazakhstan

The Caspian region is an invariable subject of interest of major international actors, due to its favourable geostrategic location at the junction of Europe and Asia and the crossroads of transit and transport corridors between the North, South, East and West, close proximity to the key subjects of modern geopolitics (the Black Sea region, the states of the Middle and Near East, China, India), as well as the presence of large explored reserves of hydrocarbon resources.[1] The proximity of the Caspian Sea to the zones of geopolitical instability (Afghanistan, Iraq, Syria) makes the issues of ensuring regional security even more relevant.[2]

Therefore, the news that on April 28, 2022, Russia fired missiles at Ukraine from the Caspian Sea met with a wary attitude from the Caspian states and world powers. According to Ukrainian media, a total of 23 cruise missiles were fired from the Caspian Sea on the territory of Ukraine, 21 of which were shot down. 11 missiles were shot down over Kyiv. In the city of Uman, as a result of a missile attack, at least 9 people were killed, another 17 were injured – such data were reported by the Minister of Internal Affairs of Ukraine I. Klymenko.[3]

---

1 Zhil'tsov, S. S. Politics of Russia in the Caspian Region. Moscow: Aspekt Press Publ., 2016. 240 p. (In Russ.).

2 Rozhkov, I. S. In the Face of the Strategic Choice: New Imperatives of World Policy. Post-Soviet Issues. 2017. № 4 (3). pp. 210–220. p. 218. (In Russ.).

3 Russia fired missiles at Ukraine from the Caspian Sea (April 28, 2023). https://forbes.kz/actual/worldwide/rossiya_obstrelyala_ukrainu_raketami_iz_kaspiyskogo_morya/ (In Russ.).

The opposition newspaper of Kazakhstan "Azattyk", reported that on May 3, Tu-95 strategic bombers launched high-precision missiles from the Caspian Sea at the infrastructure of Lviv, Dnepropetrovsk, Kirovograd, Vinnitsa, Kiev and Zakarpattia regions. In the west and in the centre of the country there were explosions on the railways, trains stopped. In a number of regions, electricity generating facilities failed and residents were left without electricity. On June 26, Russia fired six X-101 high-precision missiles from Tu-95 and Tu-160 rocket launchers in the direction of Kyiv from the Caspian Sea. The Ukrainian air defence system shot down several missiles, but one hit a residential building in Kyiv, the led to the death of one person and injury of five others.

In July, August and September, Russia continued to launch missiles from the Caspian Sea. In October and November, the Russian army even stepped up its missile strikes after retreating in southern and eastern Ukraine after setbacks at the front. Missiles launched by Moscow (Russia launched missiles from missile-carrying aircraft in the Caspian Sea, ships in the Black Sea and the Rostov region) disabled energy and water facilities in the regions of Ukraine, leaving millions of people without water and electricity.[4]

All these facts, confirming the use of the Caspian Sea for military purposes, put on the agenda the question of whether the legal status of the Caspian Sea as a zone of peace is respected.

I. The situation with the use of the Caspian Sea for rocket attacks

The first question that arises on the facts of rocket attacks on the territory of Ukraine from the Caspian Sea is how expedient it is, given the long distance (several hundred kilometres) that separates the Caspian from Ukraine.

Answering this question, on April 30, 2023, a representative of the command of the Air Force of Ukraine stated that a rocket fired from an aircraft does not always start and fly to its target. Sometimes it just falls. It's easier when it falls into the Caspian Sea than somewhere in Russia, on people's heads. This has already happened when rockets fell directly on

4 Alimova E. Russia uses the Caspian Sea for war. Why are the Caspian countries silent? (December 1, 2022). https://rus.azattyq.org/a/32145041.html (In Russ.).

houses. Therefore, Russian troops are launching missiles towards Ukraine from the Caspian Sea region in order to reduce the likelihood that they will fall on Russian settlements.[5] This means that the probability of further continuation of rocket attacks on Ukraine from the Caspian Sea is very high.

Rocket attacks on Ukraine from the Caspian are not the first case of military use of the sea. Previously, similar shelling took place against Syria.

In October 7th, 2015, the BBC Russian Service reported that the Caspian ships attacked Syria, using sea-based long-range cruise missiles in a combat situation for the first time in Russian history. According to the Russian Ministry of Defence, 26 long-range missiles were fired from Dagestan missile ship flotilla and 3 small missile ships at 11 targets at a distance of over 1,500 kilometres. To reach Syria, the missiles flew at an altitude of about 50 meters, over the terrain of the sparsely populated regions of Iran and Iraq. Permission from the authorities of these countries was previously obtained. Almost the entire Arabian Peninsula turned out to be in the radius of destruction of launched 3M14 missiles (according to published data, 2600 km), which are an analogue of the American Tomahawk sea-based cruise missile.[6]

According to the American expert, it was an advertising campaign and a demonstration of the ability to accurately attack from a long distance – to show that there is parity with the United States. There was no military need to launch expensive missiles at a distance of 1,500 kilometres, especially since Russia had already tested these missiles on the Caspian flotilla.[7]

As you can see, the assessments of American and Russian military experts regarding the missile attacks on Syria from the Caspian waters match up.

Thus, since 2015, the Caspian Sea has been constantly used for military purposes. Under these conditions, the issue of those international

---

5 The Air Force explained why Russia launches missiles from the Caspian Sea region (April 30, 2023). https://zn.ua/war/v-vozdushnykh-silakh-objasnili-pochemu-rossija-zapuskaet-rakety-iz-rajona-kaspijskoho-morja. html (In Russ.).

6 Caspian “Caliber” in Syria: why was it necessary? (BBC, Moscow, October 8, 2015). https://www.bbc.com/russian/russia/2015/10/151008_russia_syria_cruise_missiles_analysis (In Russ.).

7 Ibidem.

legal documents that are designed to ensure the security of the Caspian region is being updated. And the review, in our opinion, should begin with the Baku summit in 2010, at which for the first time security issues were considered as a separate item on the agenda.

II. Baku summit of the heads of the Caspian states in 2010 and its results

The Baku summit was held on November 18, 2010 in the capital of Azerbaijan, and following the results of the summit, the heads of the Caspian states made a statement. Point 12 of the Statement draws attention, according to which the Parties consider conflicts in the Caspian Sea region as a threat to security, peace and stability. They consider the main condition for sustainable peace to be the resolution of these conflicts in accordance with the UN Charter on the basis of respect for sovereignty, respect for territorial integrity and inviolability of state borders.

According to paragraph 13, the Parties consider any violent manifestations of extremism, especially aggressive separatism, as challenges to global and regional security. According to the Russian scientist I.S. Rozhkov, The III Caspian Summit was the first high-level meeting in which an agreement was signed on one of the most promising areas of cooperation – security.[8]

In the result of the Baku Summit, the role of this Agreement was emphasised. In paragraph 11, the Parties expressed their conviction that the signed Agreement on cooperation in the field of security in the Caspian Sea will contribute to strengthening cooperation to ensure regional security. We believe that for a more complete coverage of the problem, it is necessary to consider the features of the Agreement.

8 Rozhkov, I. S. In the Face of the Strategic Choice: New Imperatives of World Policy. Post-Soviet Issues. 2017. № 4(3). pp. 210–220. p. 216. (In Russ.).

III. The 2010 Caspian Sea Security Cooperation Agreement: General description and legal features

Agreement on Security Cooperation in the Caspian Sea (Baku, November 18, 2010)[9] is a small compact document consisting of 15 articles. Articles 10–15 are of a technical nature.

To resolve any possible disputes under the Agreement, a mechanism of consultations and direct negotiations is provided (Article 12). The Agreement does not affect the rights and obligations of the Parties arising from other agreements in which they participate (Article 11).

All changes or additions to the Agreement are possible only by mutual agreement of the Parties (Article 13). Azerbaijan is recognised as the depositary of the Agreement (Article 14).

The Agreement is subject to ratification and shall enter into force on the thirtieth day from the date of receipt by the Depositary of the last instrument of ratification. Withdrawal from the Agreement is possible by notifying the Depositary 12 months prior to withdrawal (Article 15).

All these provisions give a general description of the Agreement, but do not affect its specific features. According to A.A. Salimgerey and R.F. Mammadov, the essence of this Agreement was the statement of the leaders of the Caspian states that security in this region is exclusively their prerogative.[10] This idea is enshrined in Article 1 of the Agreement, which consists of just one sentence, which reads: "Ensuring security in the Caspian Sea is the prerogative of the Caspian states."

It should be assumed that this wording, in accordance with the understanding of Russia and Iran – as the main beneficiaries of the Agreement – is designed to exclude the Caspian Sea from the zone of action of organisations such as the Organisation for Security and Cooperation in Europe or the Conference on Interaction and Confidence Building Measures in Asia. In addition, it also limits the ability of other world powers (USA, China) or their associations (EU) to carry out any activity to ensure security in the Caspian Sea. Another feature of the Agreement is the fact

---

9 Agreement on Security Cooperation in the Caspian Sea (Baku, November 18, 2010). https://adilet.zan.kz/rus/docs/Z1400000221. (In Russ.).

10 Mamedov, R. F., & Salimgerei, A. A. Constitution of the Caspian Sea: Convention on the legal status of the Caspian Sea: on the way from an idea to its implementation. Almaty, 2022. p. 96. (In Russ.)

that two provisions of the preamble at once loudly declare the peaceful intentions of its participants: (1) the norm on the readiness of the Parties to contribute to the development and strengthening of cooperation in the use of the Caspian Sea for exclusively peaceful purposes; (2) a norm that declares the Caspian Sea a sea of peace, stability, friendship and good neighbourliness.

The third legal feature of the Agreement is its subject matter, which covers any aspects of security in any areas, "with the exception of military aspects of security" (paragraph 2 of Article 2).

To fill the subject of the Agreement with a solid meaning, paragraph 1 of Article 2 directly lists the areas in which the Parties cooperate. These are: (1) the fight against terrorism; (2) fight against organised crime; (3) combating illegal circulation of weapons of any kind and ammunition, explosives and poisonous substances, military equipment; (4) combating illicit trafficking in narcotic drugs, psychotropic substances and their precursors; (5) combating money laundering, including money obtained by criminal means; (6) fight against smuggling; (7) combating human trafficking and illegal migration; (8) fight against illegal extraction of biological resources (poaching); (9) ensuring the safety of maritime navigation and combating piracy; (10) ensuring the safety of navigation; (11) any other areas corresponding to the subject of the Agreement and of mutual interest of the Parties.

The listed 10 main areas of cooperation could be conditionally divided into two large groups: (1) cooperation in the fight against international crimes of a criminal nature (points 1–8 of the list); (2) cooperation in the field of ensuring the safety of navigation and maritime navigation (paragraphs 9–10 of the list).

When carrying out the classification, it can be understood that without military aspects, the concept of international security is deprived of its main component and is reduced to a very narrow area, covered by interstate cooperation in the field of fighting felony of an international nature.

The fourth specific feature of the document is the guarantee rule, according to which nothing in the Agreement should be considered as predetermining the legal status of the Caspian Sea (paragraph 3 of Article 2).

IV. Implementation mechanism of the 2010 Caspian Sea Security Cooperation Agreement

The mechanism for implementing the Agreement is enshrined in Articles 3–9 and its essence lies in the exchange of information. There are two formats of interaction – bilateral and multilateral – and the following forms, as well: (1) exchange of information; (2) meetings and consultations; (3) exchange of experience; (4) carrying out agreed activities in the envisaged areas; (5) other agreed forms. For the implementation of interaction, protocols on cooperation between the central competent authorities are concluded, the list of which is enshrined in Art. 3 (point 1). Basically, these are law enforcement, economic, transport and environmental authorities. The Parties also appoint an authorised body that is responsible for coordinating cooperation under the Agreement.

The exchange of information is carried out on the basis of written requests. At the same time, there might be some cases of complete or partial refusal to provide information (for example, if the execution of a request may harm national interests or contradict the law or international obligations of the state).

The information provided is considered confidential and is subject to protection. A mechanism is provided for annual meetings and consultations to address current issues.

This is, in general terms, the mechanism for implementing the Agreement. It was ratified by all the Caspian states, including Russia on November 30, 2011[11] and Kazakhstan on June 30, 2014.[12] The agreement entered into force on September 27, 2014.

The general conclusion on the Agreement is that the subject of its regulation does not fully correspond to its name, since it does not cover the military aspects of ensuring security in the Caspian Sea.

---

11 Federal Law "On Ratification of the Agreement on Cooperation in the Sphere of Security in the Caspian Sea" dated November 30, 2011 N 367-FZ (last edition). http://www.consultant.ru/document/cons_doc_LAW_ 122352/ (In Russ.).

12 On the ratification of the Agreement on cooperation in the field of security in the Caspian Sea. Law of the Republic of Kazakhstan dated June 30, 2014 No. 221-V ZRK. https://adilet.zan.kz/rus/docs/Z1400000221 (In Russ.).

V. Aktau Summit of the Heads of the Caspian States in 2018 and its results

On August 12, 2018, the Fifth Caspian Summit was held in Aktau (Kazakhstan). The main event of the summit was the signing of the Convention on the Legal Status of the Caspian Sea. As was noted in the Summit Communiqué, this fundamental document creates a new legal regime of the Caspian Sea that meets modern requirements and is aimed at further intensifying the comprehensive interaction of the coastal countries. In addition, in order to ensure the interests of the coastal states in the field of security, the Presidents confirmed the need to develop and adopt coordinated confidence-building measures in the Caspian Sea in the field of military activities at sea.[13]

If the main document adopted at the summit was the Convention on the Legal Status of the Caspian Sea, then the second most important document adopted can be recognised as the Agreement on the Prevention of Incidents in the Caspian Sea.

The Convention on the Legal Status of the Caspian Sea of August 12, 2018 is the result of a 22-year negotiation process of five states.[14] It is a small document consisting of 24 articles, among which there is not a single article that would be devoted to the military aspects of the security of the Caspian Sea.

From the entire text, there are several assumptions that are directly related to our topic. First of all, this is paragraph 8 of the preamble, which says about the conviction of the Parties that "the Convention will … promote the use of the Caspian Sea for peaceful purposes."

Secondly, this is Article 3 of the Convention, which establishes the principles of the activities of the Parties in the Caspian Sea. From the 17 principles listed in this article, only principles 1–5 are relevant to security issues. First of all, these are the basic principles of international law – respect for sovereignty, territorial integrity, independence, sovereign equality of states, non-use of force or threat of force, mutual respect,

---

[13] Communique of the Fifth Caspian Summit (Aktau, August 12, 2018). https://www.akorda.kz/ru/events/astana_kazakhstan/astana_other_events/kommyunike-pyatogo-kaspiiskogo-sammita (In Russ.).

[14] Convention on the Legal Status of the Caspian Sea (Aktau, August 12, 2018). https://adilet.zan.kz/rus/docs/Z1900000222 (In Russ.).

cooperation, non-interference in each other's internal affairs. Further, under paragraphs 2–5 of Article 3, the following principles follow:

(2) the use of the Caspian Sea for peaceful purposes, its transformation into a zone of peace, the solution of all issues related to the Caspian Sea by peaceful means;
(3) ensuring security and stability in the Caspian region;
(4) ensuring a stable balance of armaments of the Parties in the Caspian Sea, not damaging each other's security;
(5) observance of the agreed trust-building measures in the military sphere in accordance with the common efforts to strengthen regional security and stability, as well as, in accordance with the international treaties concluded between all Parties.

With regard to non-military aspects of security, Article 17 can be noted, which states that the Parties will cooperate in order to counter international terrorism, illegal trafficking in weapons, narcotic drugs, psychotropic substances and their precursors, poaching, preventing and suppressing the smuggling of migrants by sea, as well as other crimes in the Caspian Sea.

Thus, based on the results of the review of the norms of the Convention, it can be concluded that the military aspects of security in the text were reflected only in the form of two principles of a general nature, as well as the intentions of the Parties to use the sea for peaceful purposes.

The next important document of the Fifth Caspian Summit was the Agreement on the Prevention of Incidents in the Caspian Sea.[15] Its purpose, stated in the preamble, is to ensure the safety of navigation of warships and flights of aircraft of the armed forces of the states of the Parties in the Caspian Sea.

The Agreement applies to warships and aircraft of the Parties operating at sea, outside the territorial waters and airspace above them. The Agreement is based on the 1972 International Regulations for Preventing Collisions at Sea, which must be strictly observed by all warships. The agreement establishes the rules for manoeuvring ships (Article 4) and aircraft (Article 5), establishing and implementing radio communications between them (Article 6), and precautions when sailing warships (Article

15 Agreement on the Prevention of Incidents in the Caspian Sea (Aktau, August 12, 2018). https://adilet.zan.kz/rus/docs/Z1900000256 (In Russ.).

7). In Art. 8 fixes the terms for notification of the establishment of areas for the operations of ships and aircraft that pose a danger to navigation or air navigation.

The Parties agreed to timely exchange information through diplomatic channels on cases of incidents resulting in material damage and other incidents at sea between warships and aircraft of the Parties or cases that could lead to them (Article 9).

Articles 10–13 of the Agreement are devoted to technical issues (consultations and negotiations as the main method of resolving disputes; rules for amending the Agreement; etc.).

A review of the Agreement allows us to conclude that the document does not contain rules governing missile launches from ships in the Caspian Sea.

On June 29, 2022, the Sixth Caspian Summit was held in Ashgabat, the capital of Turkmenistan, at which the Heads of Five States reaffirmed their commitment to the principles and norms of the UN Charter and international law, as well as those principles of the activities of coastal states in the Caspian Sea, which were enshrined in Article 3 of the Convention on legal status of the Caspian Sea in 2018.

The Presidents noted the importance of cooperation in the military sphere in the Caspian Sea and spoke in favour of advancing the negotiation process to agree on a draft Agreement on trust-building measures in the field of military activities in the Caspian Sea, which will serve to ensure security and stability, establish norms and rules for cooperation between the Caspian states in the military sphere in accordance with the principles of the Convention on the Legal Status of the Caspian Sea.[16] Thus, the question of the military aspects of the security of the Caspian Sea and the region remained open.

VI. Legal aspects of the military use of the Caspian Sea

On June 30, 2022, Ukrainian Foreign Minister Dmytro Kuleba stated that “Russia’s use of the Caspian Sea for rocket attacks on Ukraine violates the 2018 Convention on the Status of the Caspian Sea, which

---

16 Communiqué of the Sixth Caspian Summit (Ashgabat, June 29, 2022). https://www.akorda.kz/ru/kommyunike-shestogo-kaspiyskogo-sammita-2952030 (In Russ.).

defined it as a zone of peace. The use of the Caspian Sea for acts of aggression is disrespectful to other countries in the region and undermines regional security." The Ministry of Foreign Affairs of Ukraine noted that paragraph 2 of Art. 3 of the Convention provides for "the use of the Caspian Sea for peaceful purposes, turning it into a zone of peace, good neighbourliness and cooperation, the solution of all issues related to the Caspian Sea by peaceful means." In this regard, Ukraine called on the states of the Caspian region to make every effort to force Russia to adhere to its international legal obligations, including under the Convention on the Status of the Caspian Sea. Here are the words from the text of the official statement of the Ukrainian Foreign Ministry: "We call on the countries participating in the convention to encourage Russia to stop using the Caspian Sea to continue armed aggression against Ukraine, and also to make it impossible to further militarise the region and involve it in an armed conflict".[17]

E. Alimova notes that Azattyk, an opposition publication, sent a request to the Ministry of Foreign Affairs of Kazakhstan and asked why Kazakhstan did not respond to the violation of the Caspian Convention by Russia, that sent missiles to Ukraine from the Caspian Sea. The ministry stated that "all the provisions of the Convention, including paragraph 2 of Article 3 (use of the Caspian Sea for peaceful purposes, turning it into a zone of peace, resolving all issues related to the Caspian Sea, by peaceful means), apply only to the Caspian littoral states and are focused on relations between them and do not regulate the sphere of interaction with third countries". In addition, the Ministry said that the Convention had not entered into force, so "Kazakhstan has no legal grounds to require Russia to comply with the provisions of the convention." Indeed, Iran refused to ratify the Convention, since the issue of determining the baselines dividing the sovereign territory of the state in sea waters was not resolved.[18] According to experts, the Convention is really aimed only at regulating relations between the participating parties. One of these experts, professor of law from Poland M. Petkevich, draws attention to the fact that the Convention is only a regional document, a closed system

---

17 Russia's use of the Caspian Sea for strikes against Ukraine violates the Convention on its Status – Kuleba (June 30, 2022). https://ru.krymr.com/a/news-ukraina-rossiya-kaspiyskoye-more-udary-narusheniye-konventsii/31923474.html (In Russ.).

18 Alimova, E. Russia uses the Caspian Sea for war. Why are the Caspian countries silent? (December 1, 2022). https://rus.azattyq.org/a/32145041.html (In Russ.).

for coastal countries. Therefore, according to him, Russia did not violate the provisions of the convention in relation to the Caspian states.[19]

To this it must be added that the fact that the Convention has no legal effect, does not belittle the importance, since there are many other rules of international law on the basis of which the question of liability can be raised. Apparently, the true reason for the silence of these states, after all, lies in their dependence on Russia. For example, Russia's share in Kazakhstan's imports is 38 %. The export of Kazakh oil to Europe passes through Russia. Since the beginning of the year, Russia has partially or completely stopped the operation of a pipeline exporting Kazakh oil through its territory four times. Experts attributed this to the fact that Kazakhstan did not support Russia in the war with Ukraine.[20] The situation is the same in Turkmenistan and Azerbaijan, and Iran, like Russia, is a state under the regime of international sanctions.

Thus, the current documents regulating the legal status and mode of use of the Caspian Sea do not contain norms prohibiting missile launches from the sea. All documents that relate to the security of this region do not apply to the military aspects of the security regime of the Caspian Sea.

*

In conclusion, the silence of the Caspian littoral states regarding Russian missile strikes launched from the Caspian Sea on the territory of Ukraine may turn into problems for these states themselves. We are talking about the possibility of a return flight to the Caspian Sea of any missiles that can cause damage to the property or interests of Kazakhstan or other Caspian states. Hypothetically, such a situation is not excluded. Therefore, the Caspian countries should speed up the adoption of special regulations on military activities at sea. Secondly, the Caspian countries should call on Russia to respect the peaceful status of the Caspian Sea and stop rocket attacks from its waters.

19 Ibidem.

20 Ibidem.

Are institutions, especially regional, still called to last or to become mere transient constructs ?

Pierre CHABAL
France

From Bentley's sociological analysis of political dynamics, in particular his emphasis on transient pressure groups that form and reform in various configurations in order to contain "pressures" in society[1], to the institutionalist trend that seems almost to suggest that structures "precede" construed actions in the polity, whether local, national or international, what are we to make of modern **regions** emerging in the wake of post-war dynamics?

Such post-war dynamics apply in general, not just for post-cold war dynamics in particular. These dynamics as contexts of innovative modes of management of, notably, international tensions, seem nowadays to be caught up in the **world-regions**, one resolute step "above" the national (State) level and one "forceful" step in competition with the world governance illusion of united nations. Yet, however much the modern **regions** impose themselves as frameworks, they are also open to challenges and floundering.

Four types of relations seem to exist between formalising institutional constructs and pragmatic, human endeavours. These are parallel dynamics (1), consequential dynamics (2), diachronic dynamics (3) and chronological dynamics (4).

---

1 In *The Process of Government, a Study of Social Pressure*, The Belknap Press, 1908.

I. Parallel dynamics: Institutions as independent from human dimensions

Classically, this is the case when absolutism reigns and the affairs of the State have little or nothing to do with the interests of the People in the Nation. The absolute monarch "is" the State, in divine right, and even the origin of his power is extra-societal. This is the *degré zero* (Barthes) of the absence of link between social "groups" (Bentley) and the regulating framework within kingdoms. Here the two worlds, royal and social, the two bodies politic, hardly interact.

What the English revolution culminating in the 17th century announced is that this "independence" of institutions cannot eternally survive social pressures, and that the rigid institutional mould breaks up sooner or later. Yet, until that happens, rulers are not humans in the sense that they rely on purely traditional legitimacy (Weber) and are not accountable to governing logics that necessarily, sooner or later, include the *vox populi* in its own right. For as long as this lasts, this means logically, at the **regional** level, that ententes and alliances may be formed but that they never merge the rights and powers of individual rulers and that, as to the "people", these alliances are often formed to its detriment, e.g., the Holy Alliance of 1815.

It even took centuries before institutions began to (pretend to) represent the people, at least in name and principle. There was indeed a long evolution, known as the evolutions of Parliaments that shifted from being courts of justice to becoming debating and voting chambers with increasing legislative and budgetary powers. That evolution paved the way to national transformations, in many ways democratic, but did not do much – yet – for the global taking into account national destinies as the destinies of all.

This explains that for centuries, human constructs were hardly able to go from competing empires to mutually-challenging kingdoms, with little capacity to build alliances that lasted. These were narrow, short-lived or even to some degree insincere alliances. Furthermore, alliances among neighbours – géographie oblige! – quite unable to form "regions" in the modern sense. And this also explains that modern regions, that can today be considered as common-sense solutions to conflicts among neighbours, did not see light for long centuries.

The "delaying" of the modern regions is almost logical: they could not emerge so long as the excesses of State sovereignty were not exposed for what they are, potentially so "war-monging" that they beget an actual risk of mutually assured destruction. Even from the 1648 European peace (that did not work), 160 wars in Europe (Lacoste) proved that such excesses had to curtailed and that took three more centuries through the 1815 peace system, WWI and WII, after which the Europeans invented a totally new system of peace in the hope that it would "work": the integration under supra-sovereign coercion.

II. Consequential dynamics: Institutions derive from perennialisation of human activities

Following the idea, dear to French law-scholar L. Duguit and others, according to which "law follows (proceeds from) society", that is to say, legal constructs are essentially codifications of human practices, it is possible to view institutions this time not as detached from human realities but as deriving from the latter. Here, law "echoes" society; humans come first, institutions second.

In this vein, indeed, it is only after the people begin to have a say, a "voice" (Hirschman), even before that voice is democratically expressed by a vote, that institutions give the impression to take that voice into consideration. Roughly after WWI and the atrocities of mass-massacres of soldiers, often very young men, and for the first time the decimation of whole populations, an awareness came about: humanity "matters", not just leaders and their personal (or royal family) ambitions. Even if the lesson will not be properly learnt until after the atrocities of WWII, it is clear that Wilson's doctrine, the attempts at a League of nations (in French a "society" of nations), and later the angelism of "united" nations all through a new light on the inclusion of populations into the political 1 process, became one of the strong and lasting motos of international relations.

Even if at the early stages, decisions are leaders' decisions, it is clear that for instance R. Schuman's concept of the "small steps" in the European process seems an anticipation on the later inter-German process of reconciliation where persons and families "matter": *rapprochement* not just of two countries but also, within the divided nation, of individual families allowed to interact, communicate, meet and renew – a process that is precisely lacking in the inter-Korean case, hence the essentially artificial and manipulated dynamic of "families' meetings" in that case.

That the Helsinki process, the transformation eventually of the CSCE into a fully-fledged OSCE, and in the meantime the *Ostpolitik* and inter-German relations became habitual dynamics that paved the way for historic turn, the end of the cold war and the unification of Germany, is logical. Easing out structural rigidity is a precondition to human success.

The historic turn here is that ideas and projects come first and are at a later stage comforted by institutional embodiments that enable them to last longer. Thus, the "idea of Europe" over a thousand year from Carlus Magnus, or the "idea of Asia" – all under the sun or all under Tangri's blue sky – are at least centuries-old even if regional and sub-regional constructions in Eurasia are essentially realities of the lst century, ever since the Baltic and the Balkanic *ententes* of the 1920s.

In short, there is a pre-institutional institutionalism, a dynamic that is a "thick" process (Geertz) of the emergence of foundations (structuring ideas) that later are codified and registered through their "administrativisation" or "legalisation" (Schemeil). Once this has come about, the "end-institutionalisation" can take place through treaties (Europe), charters (Shanghai Asia), declaration (ASEAN), etc.

III. Diachronic dynamics: Both institutional and human constructs "happen" as "facts"

Whether institutions and humans thrive in parallel or in sequence, they also tend to "happen" or occur a little randomly or even chaotically, unlike in a celestial harmony. Prehistory tells us that humans appeared and disappeared as species, often as a result of an unpredictable change in climate, vegetation or animal migrations; that societal orders came about and crumbled. And history shows us that even well-ordered empires, nay civilisations, collapsed and did not survive their scientific, political, organisational advancement, however precisely they were advanced, including scientifically.

Institutions and humans can exist and develop, it seems, in parallel to one another, not without links but these very links are uncertain or unclear, certainly not organic. The reason is that before institutions can be relied upon by humans, the latter need to trust the former and begin by learning to trust that constructs that are "above and beyond" human capacities are both possible and necessary. Law and its "essence" are essentially this. The essence of law is to remedy the original absence of trust. Law was invented because people did not trust each other, but law (the ten Commandments, the Hammurabi code) was invented after politics.

There can be progress in both human and institutional constructs, but separately, not necessarily in echo to each other, and at different moments in time, thus diachronically. Again, Bentley suggests that humans, individuals, what he calls "groups" undergo a dynamic of their own, and that in his view, what is the essence of politics is that these fluctuant and transient groups are "part" of the institutions and even "are" the institutions, that what we call institutions in the narrow, formal, legalistic sense, do not exist. Conversely, Weber and neo-institutionalists suggest that unless there is some codification – and in international relations – some formalisation with positive law and treaties, charters or constitutions, there are no institutions.

Yet, more than a contradiction, one may venture that what is at stake, whether humans or institutions are rather like the two faces of a coin, only at different levels and different moments. Humans invent structures and need structures to support organised life beyond chaos and violence, but institutions make no sense without the humans who give them life and activation. In this sense they both "happen" sooner or later, *hic et nunc*, and cannot be differentiated other than for the convenience of the sequential analysis. As Monnet put it "Only men can transform and enrich things, that the institutions then pass on to successive generations.[2]"

"Institutions as a means, and human deeds as ends" is a useful but simplistic summary. Yet, if compelled to synthesis our thinking, it seems a fact that humans pre-exist institutions. What nuances this simplism is that precisely as Bentley demonstrates, what we call institutions are not detached from humans but two aspects of the same. Collective and social life is exactly this: not the juxtaposition of individuals but, decidedly, the organising of togetherness.

2 "Seuls les hommes peuvent transformer et enrichir les choses, que les institutions transmettent ensuite aux générations successives." (Jean Monnet).

IV. Chronological dynamics: Institutions and humans follow each other

But not necessarily in a consequential sequence, and rather as both the "result of a third phenomenon" (Durkheim). If humans and institutions know of combined dynamics, and even of dynamics that complement each other, they are not in a simple or single relation of concomitance. This is the whole contextual question, that may also be called a systemic question. Durkheim put its rather clearly in his own terminology:

"Concomitance may be due not to the fact that one of the phenomena is the cause of the other, but to the fact that they are both the effects of the same cause, or even to the fact that there exists between them a third phenomenon, intercalated but unperceived, which is the effect of the first and the cause of the second.[3] *"*

Some link exists, at least in appearance, between human actions and institutions, as they both evolve, but to what degree of linkage are we referring to? What we infer from Durkheim is that the regional dynamic that we are looking at is much more complex than one whereby the will of some humans (cause) would lead to region-building (consequence) or one whereby the need for inter-neighbour cooperation (cause) would convince certain humans, leaders, decision-makers to create a modern region (consequence).

Rather it is the context or the system (as "third phenomenon") that creates a dynamic affecting both humans in a region and institutions to go supra-sovereign (or juxta-sovereign – Chabal 2019). Such a context can be referred as being a "post-war" context, whether post-independence war, post-cold war, post-world war, etc. These are particular moments, that one could call "superstructural" moments (Gramsci) where all existing frameworks and value and beliefs and determinants have to be "re-thought".

Wanting to define a region, after having identified and characterised it, completes our analysis. The search was causality is uneasy, even if

---

[3] E. Durkheim, Les règles de la méthode sociologique, Alcan, 1919, p. 161 : « La concomitance peut être due non à ce qu'un des phénomènes est la cause de l'autre, mais à ce qu'ils sont tous deux des effets d'une même cause, ou bien encore à ce qu'il existe entre eux un troisième phénomène, intercalé mais inaperçu, qui est l'effet du premier et la cause du second. »

determinism, nuanced by the notion of concomitance. Does a (regional) phenomenon occur because another phenomenon (crisis) occurs, in causal relation to this one? Or is a phenomenon (multi-regionalisation) occurring as a new context arises, where old imperatives (of conflict regulation) fit into new mechanisms (inter-sovereign)? Insertion as much in another space as in another region of the world, without a causal (determining) relationship with any particular region. This question of specificity connects methodology of analysis and epistemology of explanation, by the search for a context of determination.

Generalising from regional cases sheds light on the modern regional fact not as specific but common, avoiding the trap of *sui generis*. This phenomenon is defined by its openness in its composition, its sectors and above all its relationship to time; by its coherent contribution to regulation, beyond its factual existence; through its functional impact by which it puts institutions at the service of mobility, beyond borders; by its ambivalent nature, both a source of tension (obligation to negotiate) and provider of regulatory frameworks (common procedures); in short, by a dynamic of "partnership" favouring a hard core or axis between certain neighbouring actors.

*

In conclusion, one should not contend with the "chicken" and "egg" conundrum: which came first is of less interest than which takes precedence and which shall rule in the long history – *l'histoire longue*. Clearly, institutionalisation especially in the regional case, that is regionalisation in the modern sense of post WWII in Europe and post-cold war in the major world-regions, is both a novel dynamic that turns neighbours into partners and an ancient phenomenon by which neighbours precisely sought a way out of their aggressive neighbourliness.

Modern regions are founded around this very concept of good neighbourliness, that has in the case of the new (Shanghai) Asia become an official moto. Partnership has come to replace the notion of alliances (most of them failed in the past) and alliances are narrowing down to military arrangements (NATO, CSTO, …) whereas regional economic arrangements (EU, EAEU, …) are labelled "unions" or "communities", characterised by their openness in time, membership and scope. The trend is towards their capacity to last, beyond tests: after Brexit, a "Kazakhexit"?

Part IV

Artificial Intelligence and Big data

Introduction

Amandine CAYOL
France

One of today's major challenges is the transition to the digital age. All sectors of activity are affected by digitalisation: health, labour, artistic creation, security, insurance, etc. The development of increasingly powerful and autonomous artificial intelligence (IA) and algorithmic data processing, while promising progress in many fields (early detection of disease, for example), also raises major legal and ethical issues (data protection, risk of a surveillance society, discriminations, etc.). How can these new digital tools be reconciled with fundamental rights and freedoms? Are current legal rules adapted to these technological developments, or is the revolution so great that new rules need to be invented? These are the questions addressed in Part 4 of this book.

The first chapter (Louis-Philippe Gratton) deals with China's regulation of algorithms and its implications for regional and international trade. The Chinese regulations, which came into force on 1 March 2022 and 10 January 2023 respectively, are considered to be the world's first comprehensive rules on the subject at the national level. This chapter examines the compatibility of these national measures regulating algorithms and artificial intelligence with international commercial treaties. The chapter begins by defining the scope of the Chinese legislation and exploring how it may advance China's national interests. It then considers the international implications of these regulatory texts.

The second chapter (Bing Chen) discusses the effort to regulate the digital platform economy through antitrust law. Since the end of 2020, China has promoted and guaranteed the stable and healthy development of the platform economy by optimising antitrust law and maintaining strong regulation. On 24 June 2022, the 35th Session of the 13th National People's Congress Standing Committee passed the Revised Anti-Monopoly Law ("the RAML"), which provides a legal basis for the effective supervision of the platform economy.

The third chapter (Young-Soon Kim) questions the possibility of a tax imposed on artificial-intelligence robots. The rise of AI, robotics, and automation have the potential to replace human decision-making and cognitive tasks. As a result, the government's tax revenue may be reduced since its tax base rests on labour income. To address these concerns, many scholars propose a "robot tax," which aims to tax companies that use robots or automated technologies to replace human workers. This chapter examines such a robot tax, including how it could be drafted and implemented.

The fourth chapter (Amandine Cayol) is about insurance in the face of the increase of cyber risks in the wake of regional instability. The cyber risk has been accentuated by regional instability in Ukraine, that has contributed to an increase in cyber-attacks. The development of cyber risk insurance is part of desire to fight against cybercrime. Indeed, to be fully effective, a cyber-risk management strategy must include three aspects: prevention, crisis management and insurance, in order to cover the damage caused by cyber-attacks. The insurance of cyber risk raises many questions: to what extent is cyber risk insurable? How should it be insured? France has just adopted specific rules in this area with the law of 24 January 2023, trying to reconcile the need to protect the interests of companies that are victims of cyber-attacks and the need to ensure better visibility of cyber risk.

The fifth chapter (Soo-Mee Lee) analysis artificial intelligence generated works and Korean patent law. It tends to demonstrate that Korean patent law reforms needed to accommodate the growth of artificial generated inventions. Advancements in artificial intelligence, big data, and semiconductors have resulted in software systems that are automating the creation of new works. As the traditional patent and copyright laws were never designed to work with AIs that create and manufacture, the laws struggle with the growth in the number and the scale of AI created works. This chapter explores the issues of invention, authorship and the requirements of traditional patent and copyright laws when dealing with AI-generated works. It aims to propose reforms to take account of these changes.

The last chapter (Hyun-Jin Kim) looks at generative IA and bias in legal perspective. Generative Artificial Intelligence systems, such as ChatGPT, create new content based on input data, relying on deep-learning. If pre-trained on biased, incomplete, or unrepresentative data, generative AI models may produce misleading or false outputs. This chapter presents several milestone cases, discusses the problems arising from these biases, and proposes solutions to mitigate their negative consequences.

Artificial intelligence and algorithms regulations in China: Implications for regional and international commerce

Louis-Philippe GRATTON
Belarus/Canada

Algorithms and artificial intelligence have become keys in the digital age and permeate the daily lives of millions of people. They recommend books, films or music on entertainment platforms, sort information on social media, filter results on search engines, promote products on e-commerce sites, rank *curriculum vitæ* for human resources departments, convert spoken words to text through speech-recognition, predict consumer behaviour for online retailers, suggest new partners on dating applications, assist healthcare professionals in making diagnoses, recognise faces in video surveillance-systems, assess credit risk and detect fraud in financial institutions, generate content (code, images, or text), or determine social scores (e.g., Chinese Social Credit System).[1]

These technologies impact society as a whole. They have multiple implications and offer potentially immense benefits, but carry risks and may have unintended consequences.[2] They can increase efficiency, positively influence decision-making, improve health outcomes, broaden artistic and intellectual horizons, or automate routine tasks, yet they also

---

1 Aurélien Géron, *Hands-On Machine Learning with Scikit-Learn, Keras, & TensorFlow – Concepts, tools, and techniques to build intelligent systems*, 2nd ed., Sebastopol, O'Reilly, 2019, pp. 5–7; Jaemin Lee, *Artificial Intelligence and International Law*, Singapore, Springer, 2022, pp. 15–35; Rex Martinez, "Artificial intelligence: Distinguishing between types & definitions", (2019) 19 *Nev. LJ* 1015, pp. 1018–1022; Nils J. Nilsson, *The Quest for Artificial Intelligence – A history of ideas and achievements*, New York, Cambridge University Press, 2009, pp. 615–621; and Jacob Turner, *Robot Rules – Regulating artificial intelligence*, Cham, Palgrave Macmillan, 2019, pp. 22–28.

2 J. Lee, *Artificial Intelligence and International Law*, *ibid.*, pp. 51–61.

raise ethical, legal, philosophical, and technological questions.[3] They make decisions in complete opacity, as most people are not even aware of their intervention, and no one really knows the basis on which their decisions are made.[4] Hence a growing interest in regulating them; with many countries introducing new legislation to address these concerns.

China has already implemented specific provisions governing algorithms[5] and deep synthesis[6]. The Chinese regulations, which came into force on 1 March 2022 and 10 January 2023 respectively, are considered to be the world's first comprehensive rules on the subject at the national level. They are supplemented by detailed rules on generative artificial intelligence[7] that entered into force on 10 July 2023. Other countries, such as Canada,[8] are considering general legislation on artificial intelligence, while countries like the United-Kingdom[9] and the United States[10] favour a principle-based approach.

In order to gain a better understanding of the national measures and the vocabulary borrowed from computer science, it is necessary to clarify the meaning of the main technical terms used. '*Artificial intelligence*' (AI) refers to the ability of machines to perform tasks commonly associated

---

3 *Ibid.*, pp. 63–79.

4 Jenna Burrell, "How the machine 'thinks': Understanding opacity in machine learning algorithms", (2016) 3:1 *Big Data & Soc.* 1; and Frank Pasquale, *The Black Box Society – The secret algorithms that control money and information*, Cambridge/London, Harvard University Press, 2015, pp. 6–7 and 160–165.

5 *Regulations on the Management of Algorithmic Recommendations for Internet Information Services*, 31 December 2021 (entry into force: 1st March 2022); hereinafter *Regulations on Algorithmic Recommendations.* NB: Chinese translations are based on automated translation and translations provided by the China Law Translate (chinalawtranslate.com) and DigiChina (digichina.stanford.edu) projects.

6 *Regulations on the Management of Deep Synthesis for Internet Information Services*, 25 November 2022 (entry into force: 10 January 2023); hereinafter *Regulations on Deep Synthesis.*

7 *Interim Measures for the Management of Generative Artificial Intelligence Services*, 11 April 2023 (entry into force: 10 July 2023); hereinafter *Interim Measures on Generative Artificial Intelligence.*

8 Canada, 44th Parliament, 1st sess., *Bill C-27 – Digital Charter Implementation Act*, House of Commons, 2nd reading, 24 April 2023.

9 UK, Department for Science, Innovation and Technology, Office for Artificial Intelligence, *A Pro-Innovation Approach to AI Regulation* (2023), pp. 17–19.

10 USA, White House, Office of Science and Technology Policy, *Blueprint for an AI Bill of Rights – Making automated systems work for the American people* (2022), p. 4.

with human-like intelligence, such as learning, reasoning, solving problems, or making decisions.[11] The process of "*feeding*" machines large amounts of data to be able to accomplish these tasks is called "*machine learning*" (ML).[12] The machine analyses the data, automatically uncovers patterns in them, and then makes decisions or predictions based on these uncovered patterns.[13] An "*algorithm*" is a set of rules or instructions used to perform a specific task or solve a defined problem, such as searching or sorting data according to specified criteria.[14]

The boundary between these concepts is not always clear, as algorithms are essential to machine learning, and machine learning is a subset of artificial intelligence. Moreover, they do not exhaust the subject, as other concepts are regularly evoked, such as "*deep learning*"[15] (DL) and "*large language model*"[16] (LLM) – also referred to as "*language model*"

11 See Andrew Butterfield and Gerard Ekembe Ngondi (eds.), *A Dictionary of Computer Science*, 7th ed., Oxford, Oxford University Press, 2016, p. 26; B. Jack Copeland, "Artificial intelligence", *Encyclopædia Britannica*, Chicago, 2023, [britannica.com]; Les Goldschlager and Andrew Lister, *Computer Science – A modern introduction*, 2nd ed., Englewood Cliffs, Prentice Hall, 1988, p. 246; and Peter Norvig and Stuart Russell, *Artificial Intelligence – A Modern Approach*, 3rd ed., Upper Saddle River, Pearson, 2009, pp. 1–5.

12 See Andriy Burkov, *The Hundred-Page Machine Learning Book*, Québec, A. Burkov, 2019, pp. 1–3; A. Butterfield and G. Ekembe Ngondi (eds.), *A Dictionary of Computer Science*, *ibid.*, p. 324; A. Géron, *Hands-On Machine Learning*, *op. cit.*, pp. 1–2; John D. Kelleher, *Deep Learning*, Cambridge/London, MIT Press, 2019, pp. 11–16; and N. J. Nilsson, *The Quest for Artificial Intelligence*, *op. cit.*, p. 495.

13 Kevin P. Murphy, *Machine Learning – A probabilistic perspective*, Cambridge/London, MIT Press, 2012, p. 1.

14 See A. Butterfield and G. Ekembe Ngondi (eds.), *A Dictionary of Computer Science*, *op. cit.*, p. 16; Thomas H. Cormen *et al.*, *Introduction to Algorithms*, 3rd ed., Cambridge/London, MIT Press, 2001, p. 5; Andrew Goffrey, "Algorithm", *in* Matthew Fuller (ed.), *Software Studies – A lexicon*, Cambridge, MIT Press, 2008, pp. 15–20; L. Goldschlager and A. Lister, *Computer Science – A modern introduction*, *op. cit.*, pp. 1–13; and Steven S. Skiena, *The Algorithm Design Manual*, 2nd ed., London, Springer, 2009, p. 3.

15 See Kate Crawford, *Atlas of AI – Power, politics, and the planetary costs of artificial intelligence*, London/New Haven, Yale University Press, 2021, p. 7; and J. D. Kelleher, *Deep Learning*, *op. cit.*, pp. 1–10.

16 See Borja Balle *et al.*, "Taxonomy of risks posed by Language Models", *in ACM Conference on Fairness, Accountability, and Transparency*, New York, Association for Computing Machinery, 2022, p. 214, 215; and P. Norvig and S. Russell, *Artificial Intelligence*, *op. cit.*, pp. 860–865.

(LM) or "*natural language processing*"[17] (NLP) – both subfields of machine learning. Based on "*neural networks*",[18] an analogy to the structure of the human brain, they offer substantial advantages when the data available is complex and very large.[19] They have proved essential in the development of "*generative artificial intelligence*", a type of artificial intelligence capable of generating text or images in response to a prompt,[20] such as ChatGPT, DALL-E, or Midjourney.

There have been several attempts to define artificial intelligence from a legal perspective,[21] but here we seek to understand the particular meaning of the relevant terms under the Chinese law. The *Regulations on Algorithmic Recommendations* apply to the provision of information to the public using, *inter alia*, generative and synthesis technologies, personalised recommendation technologies, ranking technologies, filtering technologies, and decision-making technologies.[22] The scope of application of the *Regulations on Deep Synthesis* is limited to the use of technologies such as deep learning, virtual reality, and other synthesis algorithms to create text, images, audio, video, virtual scenes, or other information.[23] The material scope of the *Interim Measures on Generative Artificial Intelligence* is very similar, as it covers technologies that generate text, images, sound, video, and other similar content.[24]

---

17 See Christopher D. Manning, "Human language understanding & reasoning", (2022) 151:2 *Dædalus* 127, 128–132; and N. J. Nilsson, *The Quest for Artificial Intelligence*, *op. cit.*, pp. 141–146.

18 See A. Burkov, *The Hundred-Page Machine Learning Book*, *op. cit.*, pp. 61–65; J. D. Kelleher, *Deep Learning*, *op. cit.*, pp. 65–70; N. J. Nilsson, *The Quest for Artificial Intelligence*, *ibid.*, p. 423–424; and P. Norvig and S. Russell, *Artificial Intelligence*, *op. cit.*, pp. 727–737.

19 C. D. Manning, "Human language understanding & reasoning", *op. cit.*, p. 127; and J. D. Kelleher, *Deep Learning*, ibid., p. 1 and pp. 65–67.

20 C. D. Manning, "Human language understanding & reasoning", *ibid.*, pp. 131–132.

21 Miriam C. Buiten, "Towards intelligent regulation of artificial intelligence", (2019) 10 *European Journal of Risk Regulation*, 41, 43–45; Bryan Casey and Mark A. Lemley, "You might be a robot", (2020) 105 *Cornell L. Rev.* 28; R. Martinez, "Artificial intelligence", *op. cit.*, pp. 1029–1039; Jonas Schuett, "Defining the scope of AI regulations", (2023) 15 *Law, Innovation and Technology* 60; and J. Turner, *Robot Rules*, *op. cit.*, pp. 7–22.

22 *Regulations on Algorithmic Recommendations*, *op. cit.*, art. 2.

23 *Regulations on Deep Synthesis*, *op. cit.*, art. 23.

24 *Interim Measures on Generative Artificial Intelligence*, *op. cit.*, art. 2.

These regulations adopted at the national level may further local interests and businesses to the detriment of foreign ones. The Chinese regulations may potentially pursue that goal and affect trade relations between Eurasian countries. It may infringe on China's international commercial commitments – in particular the *Regional Comprehensive Economic Partnership*[25] (RCEP) – and curb the free exchange of goods, services, and ideas. This chapter examines the compatibility of these national measures regulating algorithms and artificial intelligence with international commercial treaties. It begins by defining the scope of the Chinese legislation and exploring how it may advance China's national interests (I). It then considers the international implications of these regulatory texts (II).

I. Advancing national interests through regulation

The State Council unveiled a detailed strategy, in 2017, aiming to establish China as the world leader in artificial intelligence by 2030.[26] On 18 October 2021, Xi Jinping reiterated the goals set by the State Council and stressed the importance of regulating the development of the digital economy.[27] Two months later, the *Regulations on Algorithmic Recommendations* were adopted, followed by the adoption of the *Regulations on Deep Synthesis* and the *Interim Measures on Generative Artificial Intelligence*. These three legal texts share the common objective of promoting the "Core Socialist Values" through the regulation of algorithmic recommendations, artificial intelligence, and deep synthesis.[28]

---

25 *Regional Comprehensive Economic Partnership*, 15 November 2020 (entry into force: 1st January 2022); hereinafter Partnership or RCEP.

26 China, State Council, *New Generation Artificial Intelligence Development Plan* (2017). See Josh Cowls *et al.*, "The Chinese approach to artificial intelligence: An analysis of policy, ethics, and regulation", (2021) 36:1 *AI & Soc.* 59; J. Lee, *Artificial Intelligence and International Law*, *op. cit.*, pp. 25–27; and J. Turner, *Robot Rules*, *op. cit.*, pp. 232–235.

27 Xi Jinping, *Continue to Grow Our Country's Digital Economy Stronger, Better, and Bigger*, speech delivered at the 34th collective study session of the 19th Political Bureau of the Central Committee of the Communist Party of China, in Beijing, on 18 October 2021.

28 *Regulations on Algorithmic Recommendations*, *op. cit.*, art. 1; *Regulations on Deep Synthesis*, *op. cit.*, art. 1; and *Draft Measures on Generative Artificial Intelligence*, *op. cit.*, art. 4(1).

The legislation potentially introduces a *legal bias* into the technology used (B), a technology that itself already harbours intrinsic biases (A).

(A) Biases in the technology architecture

Algorithms and artificial intelligence thrive on data – "the more data, the better".[29] They require massive amounts and continuous flows of data,[30] consuming any information that can be turned into raw data.[31] The data sets used to train an algorithm are selected by computer engineers and data scientists, as are the goals assigned to the algorithm, the appropriate method, and the parameters of the system. None of these choices can be entirely neutral or objective, as they are determined by human beings living in a particular environment. Human biases and values are present – intentionally or unintentionally – in every single decision made.[32] Algorithms and artificial intelligence thus embed the cultural, linguistic, social, or political biases and values of their designers.[33] The biases embedded in the *code*,[34] in the architecture[35] of the

---

29 N. J. Nilsson, *The Quest for Artificial Intelligence*, *op. cit.*, p. 495.

30 K. Crawford, *Atlas of AI*, *op. cit.*, pp. 111–115; and Jathan Sadowski, "When data is capital: Datafication, accumulation, and extraction", (2019) 6:1 *Big Data & Soc.* 1, 1–3.

31 Datafication refers to the rendering into data of previously unquantifiable aspects of life in society, such as a person's location or social interactions: Kenneth Cukier and Viktor Mayer-Schoenberger, "The rise of big data – How it's changing the way we think about the world", *Foreign Affairs*, May/June 2013, pp. 28, 29, 34–35; and Jose van Dijck, "Datafication, dataism and dataveillance: Big Data between scientific paradigm and ideology", (2014) 12:2 *Surveillance & Society.* 197, 197–201.

32 Kate Crawford, "The hidden biases in big data", *Harvard Business Review*, 1st April 2013, [hbr.org]; and F. Pasquale, *The Black Box Society*, *op. cit.*, p. 35.

33 Batya Friedman and Helen Nissenbaum, "Bias in computer systems", (1996) 4:3 *ACM Transactions on Information Systems*, 330, 333–335; M. C. Buiten, "Towards intelligent regulation of artificial intelligence", *op. cit.*, pp. 51–52; K. Crawford, *Atlas of AI*, *op. cit.*, pp. 8–9 and 135–136; and A. Goffrey, "Algorithm", *op. cit.*, pp. 15–16.

34 Lawrence Lessig, *Code – And other laws of cyberspace*, New York, Basic Books, 1999, p. 6; and L. Lessig, *Code – Version 2.0*, New York, Basic Books, 2006, p. 6.

35 The '*architecture*' includes the technical specifications of the system, the programming instructions, the software, the hardware, the user interface, etc.: A. Butterfield and G. Ekembe Ngondi (eds.), *A Dictionary of Computer Science*, *op. cit.*, pp. 22–23.

technology employed[36], may also reveal the national or geographical origins of the system's architects.[37] (*Cf. infra* Hyun-Jin Kim)

Biases may be the result of the personal selection of data made by the designers – and their implicit or explicit, and conscious or unconscious biases.[38] They can be called pre-existing biases, i.e., biases rooted in existing social institutions, practices, and attitudes.[39] They exist independently of the algorithm being developed because they reflect either the personal biases of the developers or the biases of the society, institutions, or organisations to which they belong.

Another type of bias arises from the technical aspects of the project.[40] They may come from the limitations associated with the tools used, the algorithm itself, the availability, quality, source, or selection of the data, or the difficulties of converting reality into data. Data drawn exclusively from Chinese/other sources and in the Chinese/other language, for example, can lead to biased outputs. Finally, emergent biases materialise during the use of the designed system.[41] This may be the case when the system is used in a new context, different from the one that led to its development, or if the society in which it was initially implanted changes, evolves, or faces new challenges.

These biases pose risks that frequently justify the intervention of the legislative or executive branches of government. They may mirror harmful language present in the training data, such as profanities, insults, threats, or incitement to violence; disseminate false or misleading information; compromise privacy by revealing personal or sensitive information; lead to gender or racial discrimination; perpetuate unfair representation of marginalised groups; exclude minority languages; or

---

36 Joel R. Reidenberg, "Lex informatica: The formulation of information policy rules through technology", (1997) 76 *Texas Law Review.* 553, 554–555 and 570.

37 K. Crawford, "The hidden biases in big data", *op. cit.*

38 B. Friedman and H. Nissenbaum, "Bias in computer systems", *op. cit.*, p. 333; and J. Turner, *Robot Rules*, *op. cit.*, pp. 337–342.

39 B. Friedman and H. Nissenbaum, "Bias in computer systems", ibid., pp. 333–335.

40 Ibid., pp. 334–336.

41 Ibid., po. 335–336.

perpetuate stereotypes.[42] The regulation of algorithms and artificial intelligence contemplated by some states may lead to the introduction of new biases – *legal biases*.

(B) How legislation may introduce biases

Biases may be the deliberate consequence of decisions made by public authorities. A government may be inclined, for example, to promote certain values, favour national content, encourage a particular language, or advantage search results for local products[43] – an attitude that may be seen as a new form of data nationalism or data protectionism.[44] If regulated at the national level, algorithms and artificial intelligence could therefore potentially favour domestic interests and businesses over foreign ones. Consequently, regulations may reinforce biases by the very terms of the law.

This is the path China has taken, as the afore-mentioned regulations bear the requirement to promote the "Core Socialist Values". This expression refers to a set of principles and ideals outlined on 8 November 2012 by the General Secretary of the Central Committee of the Communist Party, Hu Jintao, in his report to the 18th National Congress of the Party. They comprise twelve ideals divided into three groups of values: (i) national values: prosperity, democracy, civility, and harmony; (ii) social values: freedom, equality, justice, and the rule of law; and (iii) individual values: patriotism, professionalism, integrity, and friendliness.[45]

---

42 B. Balle *et al.*, "Taxonomy of risks posed by Language Models", *op. cit.*, pp. 216–222; and K. Crawford, *Atlas of AI*, *op. cit.*, pp. 128–131.

43 "We can build, or architect, or code cyberspace to protect values that we believe are fundamental, or we can build, or architect, or code cyberspace to allow those values to disappear." (L. Lessig, *Code*, *op. cit.*, p. 6.)

44 Anupam Chander and Uyên P. Lê, "Data nationalism", (2015) 64 *Emory LJ* 677, 679–681; and Martina F. Ferracane, "The costs of data protectionism", *in* Mira Burri (dir.), *Big Data and Global Trade Law*, Cambridge, Cambridge University Press, 2021, pp. 63–65.

45 Michael Gow, "The Core Socialist Values of the Chinese Dream: Towards a Chinese integral state", (2017) 49:1 *Crit. Asian Stud.* 92, 99; Xi Jinping, *How to Deepen Reform Comprehensively*, Beijing, Foreign Languages Press, 2014, p. 115; Tong Lam, "The people's algorithms: Social credits and the rise of China's Big (Br)other", *in* Andrea Mennicken and Robert Salais (eds.), *The New Politics of Numbers – Utopia, evidence and democracy*, Cham, Palgrave Macmillan, 2019, p. 71; Ying Miao, "Romanticising the past: Core Socialist Values and the China Dream as legitimisation strategy", (2021) 49:2 *Journal of Current Chinese Affairs*, 162, 166–167; and Elizabeth J. Perry,

The Core Socialist Values reflect Chinese characteristics, traditional Chinese culture, and China's national identity.[46] They are intended to forge a sense of unity and belonging among the population. These values serve as a code of conduct for the daily life of individuals, guiding their behaviour, influencing their ways of thinking, and encouraging good habits. They pursue the goal of fostering social cohesion by imposing moral standards in the country. Xi Jinping called for these values to be transformed "into binding laws" and for the law to be used "to promote their development."[47] Guaranteed by institutions and legal mechanisms, they shape Chinese society by emphasising the importance of their underlying ideals.

If the *Regulations on Algorithmic Recommendations* and the *Regulations on Deep Synthesis* simply state that these "regulations are formulated in order to promote Socialist Core Values",[48] the *Interim Measures on Generative Artificial Intelligence* are more explicit. They require that the content created through the use of generative artificial intelligence reflect these values[49]. This is confirmed by the words of Xi Jinping himself, who links the importance of these values to the development of the cultural sector and cultural productions.[50] Moreover, the Core Socialist Values are specific to Chinese society, at least the interpretation given to principles such as freedom, democracy, and the rule of law.[51] It is therefore unclear whether the requirement to promote these values contravenes China's international trade commitments.

"The populist dream of Chinese democracy", (2015) 74:4 *Journal of Asian Studies*, 903, 905.

46 X. Jinping, *How to Deepen Reform Comprehensively*, ibid., pp. 118–123; and E. J. Perry, "The populist dream of Chinese democracy", ibid., p. 909–910.

47 X. Jinping, *How to Deepen Reform Comprehensively, ibid*, p. 123. "The State […] promotes the dissemination of Core Socialist Values", stipulates the *Cybersecurity Law of the People's Republic of China* (7 November 2016, entry into force: 1st June 2017).

48 *Regulations on Algorithmic Recommendations, op. cit.*, art. 1; and *Regulations on Deep Learning, op. cit.*, art. 1.

49 *Interim Measures on Generative Artificial Intelligence, op. cit.*, art. 4(1).

50 X. Jinping, *How to Deepen Reform Comprehensively, op. cit.*, p. 117 and 123.

51 See M. Gow, "The Core Socialist Values of the Chinese Dream", *op. cit.*, pp. 99–104; Y. Miao, "Romanticising the past", *op. cit.*, p. 168; E. J. Perry, "The populist dream of Chinese democracy", *op. cit.*, pp. 905–909; and Frank N. Pieke, *Knowing China – A Twenty-First-Century Guide*, Cambridge, Cambridge University Press, 2016, pp. 41–43 and 84–120.

II. Barriers to data flow in Eurasian commerce

The *Regional Comprehensive Economic Partnership*, a free trade agreement between 15 East Asian and Pacific countries, including China, entered into force on 1 January 2022.[52] The economies of the world's largest trading bloc represent about 30 % of global gross domestic product (GDP) and a market of 2.3 billion people.[53] The agreement covers trade in goods and services, as well as investment, intellectual property, and electronic commerce. At the heart of the agreement, as with all modern trade agreements, are the Most Favoured Nation (MFN) and National Treatment (NT) clauses. The latter is of particular interest because it could be invoked by China's trading partners to denounce its national regulatory measures on algorithms, artificial intelligence, and deep synthesis (A), unless an exception can preserve them (B).

(A) The national treatment clause

1. Advantaging national goods through biased legislation

The RCEP's national treatment clause with respect to the imposition of internal taxation and regulation on goods[54] incorporates *mutatis mutandis* Article III of the *General Agreement on Tariffs and Trade* (GATT).[55] It is therefore legitimate to refer to the work of the World Trade Organisation (WTO) panels and Appellate Body in interpreting the provisions of the Partnership. Generally speaking, national treatment implies equal treatment of imported and domestic products that cannot

---

[52] Norainie Ahmad, Muhammad Anshari and Mahani Hamdan, "An overview of Regional Comprehensive Economic Partnership (RCEP)", *in* N. Ahmad, M. Anshari and M. Hamdan (eds.), *Regional Comprehensive Economic Partnership*, Singapore, Bentham Science Publishers, 2023, pp. 1, 2–4; and Asian Development Bank, *The Regional Comprehensive Economic Partnership Agreement – A New Paradigm in Asian Regional Cooperation?* (2022), p. 2.

[53] UNCTAD, *A New Centre of Gravity – The Regional Comprehensive Economic Partnership and its trade effects* (2021), pp. 5–7.

[54] RCEP, *op. cit.*, art. 2.3.

[55] The *General Agreement on Tariffs and Trade 1994* (15 April 1994, 1867 UNTS 192 (entry into force: 1st January 1995), art. 1(a)) includes the *General Agreement on Tariffs and Trade Commerce* (30 October 1947, 55 UNTS 194 (entry into force: 1st January 1948)) "as rectified, amended, or modified". GATT refers hereinafter to the latter in its consolidated version.

be distinguished on the basis of their origin.[56] The principle comes into play as soon as a product is imported into the territory of a Party.

Internal taxes and other internal charges, as well as laws, regulations and requirements affecting a product, shall not be applied as to afford protection to domestic production.[57] This general principle, set out in article III:1 GATT, is supplemented by specific obligations contained in the following paragraphs of the provision:[58] internal taxes and other internal charges imposed on imported products shall not exceed those imposed on like domestic products;[59] nor shall imported products be subject to treatment less favourable than that accorded to like products of national origin.[60] The main purpose of article III GATT – and by extension of article 2.3 RCEP – is to avoid the adoption of protectionist measures when a domestic product is in competition with an imported one[61] and to ensure equal competitive conditions between the two products.[62]

How could regulatory measures on algorithms, artificial intelligence, or deep synthesis conflict with a Party's commitments on trade in goods? The *Regulations on Algorithmic Recommendations* deserve special attention here as they apply to personalised recommendations, ranking, and filtering. It is difficult to predict how the Chinese authorities will interpret the requirement to promote Core Socialist Values as the concept is deliberately vague and abstract,[63] but it could be implemented as strictly as other requirements pertaining to the digital economy.[64] It could compel,

---

56 GATT, Panel for Conciliation, *United Kingdom Complaint on Italian Discrimination Against Imported Agricultural Machinery*, 15 July 1958, doc. L/833 (adopted), par. 11.

57 GATT, *op. cit.*, art. III:1.

58 WTO, Appellate Body, *Japan – Alcoholic Beverages II*, 4 October 1996, doc. WT/DS8/AB/R, WT/DS10/AB/R and WT/DS11/AB/R, pp. 17–18.

59 GATT, *op. cit.*, art. III:2.

60 *Ibid.*, art. III:4.

61 *Japan – Alcoholic Beverages II*, *op. cit.*, p. 16–17; and WTO, Appellate Body, *Korea – Alcoholic Beverages*, 18 January 1999, doc. WT/DS75/AB/R and WT/DS84/AB/R, par. 120.

62 GATT, Panel, *United States – Taxes on Petroleum and Certain Imported Substances*, 5 June 1987, doc. L/6175 (adopted), par. 5.1.9; and WTO, Appellate Body, *Canada – Periodicals*, 30 June 1997, doc. WT/DS31/AB/R, p. 18.

63 Y. Miao, "Romanticising the past", *op. cit.*, pp. 168–169.

64 Xi Jinping has asserted the need to "ensure that the internet can be supervised and controlled": X. Jinping, *How to Deepen Reform Comprehensively*, *op. cit.*, pp. 115–116. See Henry S. Gao, "Data regulation with Chinese characteristics", *in* Mira

for example, e-commerce sites to develop algorithms that favour Chinese products under the guise of protecting local values and ideals. While the national measure would not namely exclude imported products, it would have *the effect of* excluding them from the market. Since imported products would not promote or embed Core Socialist Values, the market would be left *de facto* to goods produced in China by Chinese companies. A similar reasoning applies to trade in services.

2. Advantaging national services through biased legislation

Before addressing the issue of international commerce of services, a distinction must be made between national treatment and the concept of market access. The former implies that a Party shall accord to services and service suppliers of any other Party treatment no less favourable than that it accords to its own like services and service suppliers.[65] This requirement is met by granting to services and service suppliers of another Party either formally identical treatment or formally different treatment to that which a Party accords to its own like-services and service-suppliers.[66] Treatment is considered less favourable if it favours the services or service suppliers of the Party by altering the conditions of competition in the market to the detriment of foreign services or service suppliers.[67]

The concept of market access refers to the conditions under which foreign services will obtain the right to enter the market of a Party.[68] A Party shall accord to the services and service-suppliers of any other Party a treatment no less favourable than that provided for under the agreed terms, limitations, and conditions.[69] It is prohibited to adopt or maintain restrictions on the number of service suppliers, on the total value of service transactions, on the total number of service operations,

---

Burri (ed.), *Big Data and Global Trade Law*, Cambridge, Cambridge University Press, 2021, pp. 245, 247–260.

65 RCEP, *op. cit.*, art. 8.4:1.

66 Ibid., art. 8.4:3. This formulation takes into account the practice of the GATT, as there are situations where a foreign service supplier enjoys *de jure* equality with a domestic service supplier, but *de facto* inequality. See Mary E. Footer, "The international regulation of trade in services following competition of the Uruguay Round", (1995) 29 *International Law,* 453, 473–474.

67 RCEP, ibid., art. 8.4:4.

68 M. E. Footer, "The international regulation of trade in services following competition of the Uruguay Round", *op. cit.*, p. 472.

69 RCEP, *op. cit.*, art. 8.5:1.

on the total number of natural persons who may be employed in a given service sector, or on the participation of foreign capital, as well as measures requiring certain types of legal entities to provide the service.[70]

The rules on national treatment and market access are binding only for service sectors and subsectors that a Party has opened up to competition. The RCEP negotiators have adopted a hybrid approach to services liberalisation: Parties have to make commitments either through Schedules of Specific Commitments or Schedules of Non-Conforming Measures.[71] Eight countries made commitments through a positive list approach, i.e., that only services on a Party's list are liberalised.[72] The other seven Parties committed themselves to a negative list approach at the time of entry into force of the Partnership, i.e., that all their services are liberalised unless they are included in a list of reservations.[73]

Artificial intelligence is not mentioned *per se* in the latest version of the *Central Product Classification*, which was used to schedule Parties' commitments,[74] but many positions echo how artificial intelligence can actually be used.[75] China's Schedule of Specific Commitments liberalises,[76]

---

70 Ibid., art. 8.5:2.

71 Ibid., art. 8.3:1. See Asian Development Bank, *Liberalising Services Trade in the Regional Comprehensive Economic Partnership: Status and Ways Forward* (2022), p. 2.

72 Ibid., art. 8.7. The eight Parties are Cambodia, China, Laos, Myanmar, New Zealand, the Philippines, Thailand, and Viet Nam.

73 Ibid., art. 8.8. The seven Parties are Australia, Brunei Darussalam, Indonesia, Japan, Korea, Malaysia, and Singapore.

74 UN, Department of Economic and Social Affairs, Statistics Division, *Central Product Classification (CPC) – Version 2.1*, doc. ST/ESA/STAT/SER.M/77/Ver.2.1 (2015). The CPC needs to be updated to reflect new technological realities: UN, Intersecretariat Working Group on National Accounts, Advisory Expert Group on National Accounts, Digitalisation Task Team, *Improving the Visibility of Artificial Intelligence in the National Accounts*, doc. SNA/M3.22/6 (2022), par. 20–24. See Martin Roy and Lee Tuthill, "GATS classification issues for information and communication technology services", *in* Mira Burri and Thomas Cottier (eds.), *Trade Governance in the Digital Age – World Trade Forum*, New York, Cambridge University Press, 2012, p. 157.

75 See Mira Burri and Rolf H. Weber, *Classification of Services in the Digital Economy*, Berlin/Heidelberg, Springer, 2013, pp. 17–21; and Anupam Chander, "Artificial intelligence and trade", *in* Mira Burri (ed.), *Big Data and Global Trade Law*, Cambridge, Cambridge University Press, 2021, p. 115, 122–125.

76 China has scheduled its commitments according to the 1991 *Provisional Central Product Classification*: UN, Department of International Economic and Social Affairs, Statistical Office, *Provisional Central Product Classification*, doc. ST/ESA/

among other services, translation and interpretation services, data processing services, online information, database retrieval, electronic data interchange, computer reservation system services, and video and sound recording distribution services, but it excludes "the economic activity consisting of the provision of content services which require computer and related services as a means of supply".[77] It leaves a strong incertitude whether services associated with algorithmic recommendations, artificial intelligence, and deep synthesis are open to competition in China.

The provisions of the RCEP apply to any liberalised service in any sector,[78] including services delivered electronically,[79] but the agreement does not define the term "service" itself. The concept of service, in the absence of a legal definition, is more easily understood by using the concept of "supply of a service".[80] It is defined by the obligation of one party ("service supplier"[81]) to provide a service to another ("service consumer"[82]). The supply of a service includes the production, distribution, marketing, sale, and delivery of a service by a natural[83] or juridical[84] person by any of four modes of supply.[85]

The first mode of supply concerns *cross-border services*. These are services originating from the territory of one Party to the territory of another. The second covers *services offered to a foreign consumer*. It therefore involves the movement of that consumer, a tourist, for example, to the territory of another Party. The third refers to the supply of a *service to consumers in the territory of a Party through the "commercial presence" of a foreign supplier*. It may, for example, maintain a branch or a subsidiary within the territory of the Party. Finally, the fourth mode involves the

---

STAT/SER.M/77 (1991). See Li Xiaofu and Cao Xiaorui, "Opening of China's service industry in the 14th Five-Year Plan – Taking RCEP and CPTPP as references", (2022) 12:3 *J. WTO & China* 55, 71–73.

77 RCEP, *op. cit.*, Annex II – Schedule of Specific Commitments for Services – China.

78 Ibid., art. 8.1(l).

79 Ibid., art. 12.3:5.

80 Ibid., art. 8.1(q).

81 Ibid., art. 8.1(p).

82 Ibid., art. 8.1(m).

83 Ibid., art. 8.1(i).

84 Ibid., art. 8.1(d and e).

85 Ibid., art. 8.1(r).

temporary movement of a foreign natural person to the territory of a Party to provide a service to local consumers.

The supply of cross-border services or services through the commercial presence of a foreign supplier is definitely impacted by the Chinese regulations on algorithms, artificial intelligence, and deep synthesis. How would a foreign supplier generate content that embed the Core Socialist Values? Would it mean that foreign services like video-on-demand, music streaming, or artificial intelligence generative tools would be disadvantaged? Their content may be pushed back to the bottom by the algorithm in the first two cases, it may simply be considered illegal in the third case. The arbitrary application of a requirement that is *prima facie* discriminatory will inevitably lead to a breach of the rules on national treatment or market access. Thus, the Chinese measures can only be saved by an appropriate exception.

(B) The public morals exception

An exception, in international economic law, precludes the application of a regional or multilateral rule in order to maintain a national measure that is *a priori* incompatible with that rule.[86] It is a derogation aimed at protecting specific national interests – health, national treasures, or public order, for example – that takes into account the requirements of international trade. The national measure is examined on the basis of a series of criteria to determine its compatibility with international commerce law. It can only be saved if it strictly meets these criteria.

Article XX GATT, which contains numerous exceptions to the general rules of liberalisation for goods, is incorporated into the RCEP.[87] As for trade in services, it is article XIV GATS and its exceptions that are incorporated into the regional trade treaty.[88] The only enumerated exception in both provisions that could save the Chinese measures is the necessity to protect "*public morals*".[89] The protection of public morals, a

86 WTO, Panel, *US – Tariff Measures*, 15 September 2020, doc. WT/DS543/R, par. 7.104.

87 RCEP, *op. cit.*, art. 17.12:1.

88 Ibid., art. 17.12:2.

89 GATT, *op. cit.*, art. XX(a); and *General Agreement on Trade in Services*, 15 April 1994, 1869 UNTS 219 (entry into force: 1st January 1995), art. XIV(a); hereinafter GATS. See Henry Gao, "Googling for the trade-human rights nexus in China: Can the

WTO panel recalled, "ranks among the most important values or interests pursued by Members as a matter of public policy".[90] It amounts to "standards of right and wrong conduct maintained by or on behalf of a community or nation".[91]

The applicability of the "public morals" exception is determined by a three-step analysis:[92] i/ examine whether the national measure falls within the scope of the public morals exception; ii/ verify whether the measure is conceived to protect that public morals objective; iii/ involve a process of "weighing and balancing" a number of factors to determine whether the measure is "*necessary*" within the meaning of articles XX GATT and XIV GATS. The WTO Panels and the Appellate Body make an overall assessment of the measure through a holistic approach and reach a final conclusion without giving definitive answers to all intermediate questions.[93]

China has previously invoked the public morals exception to support measures regulating the content of certain publications and audiovisual products.[94] It was not disputed in that case that the purpose of the Chinese measures was to protect public morals.[95] Indeed, WTO Panels and the Appellate Body leave it to Members to define the concept of public morals according to their scale of values and to determine the appropriate level of protection to be afforded to those values.[96] The Core Socialist Values reflect a system in which moral values are the basis of

---

WTO help?", *in* Mira Burri and Thomas Cottier (eds.), *Trade Governance in the Digital Age – World Trade Forum*, New York, Cambridge University Press, 2012, p. 247, 268–270.

90 WTO, Panel, *China – Publications and Audiovisual Products*, 12 August 2009, doc. WT/DS363/R, par. 7.817.

91 WTO, Panel, *US – Gambling*, 10 November 2004, doc. WT/DS285/R, par. 6.465. See *US – Tariff Measures, op. cit.*, par. 7.115; Panagiotis Delimatsis, "The puzzling interaction of trade and public morals in the digital era", *in* Mira Burri and Thomas Cottier (eds.), *Trade Governance in the Digital Age – World Trade Forum*, New York, Cambridge University Press, 2012, p. 276, 277–282; and Jeremy C. Marwell, "Trade and morality: The WTO public morals exception after gambling", (2006) 81 *New York University Law Review*, 802, 807–811.

92 *US – Tariff Measures*, ibid., par. 7.112.

93 Ibid., par. 7.111.

94 *China – Publications and Audiovisual Products* (Panel), *op. cit.*, par. 7.754, 7.755 and 7.762.

95 Ibid., par. 7.762 and 7.763.

96 *US – Gambling* (Panel), *op. cit.*, par. 6.461; *China – Publications and Audiovisual Products* (Panel), *op. cit.*, par. 7.819; and *US – Tariff Measures, op. cit.*, par. 7.131.

China's very existence as a society, according to Xi Jinping.[97] The regulations on algorithmic recommendations, artificial intelligence, and deep synthesis that aim to promote them could therefore be seen as genuinely protecting public morals.

Is the Chinese measure conceived to protect public morals? Is the connection between the measure and the objective of protecting public morals demonstrated?[98] It is difficult to assess whether the measure in question is designed to protect public morals in the light of the criteria set out in WTO case law.[99] Neither the Panel nor the Appellate Body clearly addressed this issue in the *China – Publications and Audio-visual Products* case, which involved a defence based on the "public morals" exception. The requirement of the Chinese regulations under study is to "*promote*" the Core Socialist Values or to generate content that embeds these values. It is a positive obligation that does not seek to "*protect*" public morals *per se*. The connection between the measure and its objective is consequently difficult to establish.

The final step of the analysis also has three parts.[100] First, it is necessary to evaluate the importance of the interests or values at stake. The importance of the public policy objective should be assessed in relation to the responding Member and not *in abstracto*.[101] The objective that China might invoke if its domestic measures were to be challenged definitely reflects societal interests that its leaders describe as highly important in the official documents cited in this paper.[102]

Second, it is required to examine whether the measure contributes to the realisation of the objective pursued. There is no pre-determined or minimum threshold of contribution that the measure must meet.[103] The Panel in the *China – Publications and Audio-visual Products* case found that the Chinese measures under consideration did not appear to

---

97 X. Jinping, *How to Deepen Reform Comprehensively*, *op. cit.*, pp. 120–121.

98 WTO, Appellate Body, *US – Gambling*, 7 April 2005, doc. WT/DS285/AB/R, par. 292; and WTO, Appellate Body, *EC – Seal Products*, 22 May 2014, doc. WT/DS400/AB/R and WT/DS401/AB/R, par. 5.169.

99 *US – Tariff Measures*, *op. cit.*, par. 7.151.

100 Ibid., par. 7.159. See H. Gao, "Googling for the trade-human rights nexus in China", *op. cit.*, p. 270–272.

101 *US – Tariff Measures*, ibid., par. 7.168.

102 See *China – Publications and Audiovisual Products* (Panel), *op. cit.*, par. 7.848.

103 *US – Tariff Measures*, *op. cit.*, par. 7.174.

contribute directly to protection of public morals in China.[104] The conclusion may be different with respect to the regulations on algorithmic recommendations, artificial intelligence, and deep synthesis. They appear *prima facie* to contribute to the stated objective.

Third, the restrictive impact of the domestic measure on international trade must be considered. The Panel in the *China – Publications and Audio-visual Products* case concluded that the Chinese measures had a restrictive effect on trade,[105] a conclusion that can also be reached with respect to a requirement that cannot be met by any foreign entity aspiring to compete in the Chinese domestic market. The requirement to promote Core Socialist Values would directly collide with the general objective of eliminating "discriminatory treatment in international trade relations" in the preamble to the *Marrakesh Agreement Establishing the World Trade Organisation.*[106]

It is therefore not necessary to continue the analysis and consider reasonably available less trade-restrictive alternatives[107] or to study the measures against the "*chapeau*" of articles XX GATT and XIV GATS.[108] It can be concluded that the Chinese measures would not be saved by the public morals exception if it were to be challenged under the RCEP.

*

In conclusion, the regulation of algorithms and artificial intelligence addresses national concerns about the use of these technologies, but it also brings forth a new potential consequence: the introduction of legal biases into the architecture of the technology itself. Governments possess the legitimate authority to intervene in order to advance certain values, regulate content, favour a particular language, or enhance the visibility

---

104 *China – Publications and Audiovisual Products* (Panel), *op. cit.*, par. 7.848–7.849. Affirmed: WTO, Appellate Body, *China – Publications and Audiovisual Products*, 21 December 2009, doc. WT/DS363/AB/R, par. 337.

105 *China – Publications and Audiovisual Products* (Panel), ibid., par. 7.848–7.849.

106 *Marrakesh Agreement Establishing the World Trade Organisation*, 15 April 1994, 1867 UNTS 165 (entry into force: 1st January 1995). See *US – Tariff Measures*, *op. cit.*, par. 7.160.

107 *US – Tariff Measures*, ibid., par. 7.159 and 7.232.

108 *China – Publications and Audiovisual Products* (Panel), *op. cit.*, par. 7.912; and *US – Tariff Measures*, ibid., par. 7.241.

of local products and services. China, for instance, has employed this approach to promote the Core Socialist Values through laws and regulations. While such intervention may serve legitimate interests, it can also give rise to international trade disputes.[109]

Domestic regulations that do not respect the principle of national treatment and create barriers to market access can hinder the free flow of data and information. This is particularly relevant in today's era of "global digital interdependence"[110], where national legislation can impede international trade by imposing restrictions on cross-border data movements. However, if the local intervention can be saved by an exception to the rules of international commerce, legitimate local concerns can be protected while still adhering to the principles of liberalisation of goods and services. Otherwise, it could become a barrier to international trade.

---

[109] Joris van Hoboken and Svetlana Yakovleva, "The algorithmic learning deficit – Artificial intelligence, data protection and trade", *in* Mira Burri (ed.), *Big Data and Global Trade Law*, Cambridge, Cambridge University Press, 2021, p. 212, 215–224; and Neha Mishra and Andrew D. Mitchell, "WTO law and cross-border data flows: An unfinished agenda", *in* Mira Burri (ed.), *Big Data and Global Trade Law*, Cambridge, Cambridge University Press, 2021, pp. 83–86.

[110] Edward D. Mansfield and Nita Rudra, "Embedded liberalism in the digital era", (2021) 75 *International Organization*, 558, 559 and 562–563.

The transformation of the antitrust regulation: China's Digital Platforms' development at a new phase

Bing CHEN
China

The digital economy is rapidly growing across the world. While it has greatly freed up and optimised the allocation of resources and stimulated the innovative development of new forms of business and technologies, the digital economy is observing a large number of disputes. In particular, problems in the platform economy such as compulsory "either-or" choice, self-preferencing, data-monopolisation, algorithm-discrimination, and algorithm-abuse have emerged from the rise and innovative application of digital platforms. For this reason, the effort to regulate the digital platform economy through antitrust law has taken over the world, which also gives rise to concepts such as the New Brandeis movement in the United States, the gatekeeper platform's obligations in the European Union, and the notion of cross-market impacts in the platform sector in Germany, calling for new ways of approaching the matter by the legislative, enforcement, and judicial branches.

As one of the world's leaders in the development of the digital economy, China's massive user-base provides a strong and continuous market demand for digital applications, which has led China to become the world's second-largest digital economy in 2020 and the first in overall growth rate. Along with the rapid growth in the platform economy, cases of restrictions, exclusion of competition, unfair competition, and unfair trading have also increased.

Since the end of 2020, China has promoted and guaranteed the stable and healthy development of the platform economy by optimising antitrust law and maintaining strong regulation. For example, on 7 February 2021, the Anti-Monopoly Commission of the State Council issued the *Antitrust Guidelines on Platform Economy*, the world's first government-issued normative document specifically governing competition in the digital platform economy. In April and October 2021, Alibaba and Meituan were slapped with administrative penalties for compulsory "either-or choice" practices. These measures produced substantial results for the implementation of the explicit requirements of the CPC Central Committee and the State Council to strengthen antitrust enforcement and prevent the disorderly expansion of capital, and laid a solid foundation for fostering new development pattern and smoothing the dual circulation economy.

The CPC Central Committee and the State Council jointly released a guideline on accelerating the establishment of a unified domestic market on 10 April 2022. This document seeks to "cultivate new advantages in international competition and cooperation. Make better use of global factors and market resources to better connect the domestic market with the international market, supported by the major domestic circulation and unified market" and to "[c]ultivate a group of digital platform enterprises with global influence." China should pay attention to the standardisation, specialisation. and improvement of rule of law in China's governance in the digital platform economy. China should keep up with international standards, summarise our own experience, refine our own experience and voice our viewpoints in the international arena.

On 24 June 2022, the 35th Session of the 13th National People's Congress Standing Committee passed the Revised Ani-Monopoly Law ("the RAML") on the premise that opinions were fully coordinated and the conditions were ripe. The RAML was officially implemented on 1 August 2022. Anti-monopoly regulation over key elements of the platform economy has attracted widespread attention, and responded to general concerns over all sectors of the society in a timely and effective manner. At the same time, the RAML also provides a legal basis for the next steps in refining and delivering an effective supervision of the platform economy.

The RAML not only directly responds to the demand for regulation of digital platforms – it also focuses on refining the fundamental aims, [economic and legal] principles, and key next-steps for Chinese anti-monopoly law in the long term. Particularly, the RAML pays much attention to the characteristics and justification for competition practices. RAML is in an effort to incorporate these policies into the legislature to reduce uncertainty.

For example, Article 9 of the RAML reads: "[o]perators shall not use data, algorithms, technologies, capital advantages and platform rules to engage in monopoly activities prohibited by this Law." This article has been seen as a direct response to the prevalence of these issues in the digital platform economy. We can say that antitrust regulation in the digital economy has focused on the specific, rather than general, elements of digital platform activities. From which can be found that the digital platform of antitrust regulation of the economy has been focused on the specific elements, the precise type legislation rather than in general about the digital platform of antitrust regulation of the economy, fully embodies the legislature, the national antitrust law enforcement agencies and other relevant departments on the digital platform economy antitrust legislation and law enforcement to strengthen professional next. Only by linking the specific behaviours with effects can the authorities adapt to the characteristics and needs of competition regulation in the digital economy.

I. The basic context of China's Platform Antitrust Regulation

China's antitrust policies and laws for platform enterprises are also formulated and improved intensively and rapidly. The implementation of the Anti-Monopoly Law has been sustained and normalised, while precise regulatory concepts, principles, methods, and technologies are constantly adjusted and improved.

Since November 2020, a series of political meetings, including that of the Political Bureau of the CPC Central Committee, the Central Economic Work Conference, and the 9th Meeting of the Central Financial and Economic Committee, have clearly demonstrated the attitude and determination of the Chinese authorities to strengthen antitrust regulation and prevent the disorderly expansion of capital. The 21st Meeting of the Commission for Deepening Overall Reform of the CPC Central Committee, held in August 2021, deliberated and approved the *Opinions on Strengthening Anti-Monopoly and Furthering the Implementation of the Policy of Fair Competition*, stressing that they "attach equal importance to both regulatory norms and development promotion." The Central Economic Work Conference held in December 2021 proposed the goal "to boost the confidence of market entities, further promote the implementation of fair competition policy, strengthen antitrust and anti-unfair competition, and ensure fair competition with fair regulation", further confirming a push for the implementation of normalised and standardised antitrust oversight.

On 19 January 2022, the National Development and Reform Commission and nine other departments jointly issued the document entitled *Several Opinions on Promoting the Standardised, Sound and Sustainable Development of Platform Economy.* In view of the current focal issues in the platform economy, building on the new advantages of this sector and promoting its high-quality development is required. In March 2022, Premier Li Keqiang also mentioned in his government work report that in 2022, China would "further promote the implementation of fair competition policies, fight against monopoly and unfair competition, and maintain a fair and orderly market environment." Li also called for the "timely improvement of regulatory rules in key areas, emerging areas and foreign-related areas, innovation of regulatory methods, and improvement of regulatory accuracy and effectiveness."

In the formulation of relevant supporting regulations such as the *Antitrust Guidelines on the Platform Economy* were released in February 2021. Those supporting regulations are comprehensive responses to the highly controversial "either-or choice" and "big data-based price discrimination" practices in the platform economy that mounted, covering hot issues including the relevant market definition, the determination of antitrust violation through most-favoured-nation clauses, and emerging innovative corporate takeovers. Those supporting regulations were significant efforts in strengthening antitrust regulation for the platform economy, as well as a helpful guide for operators in the platform economy to act in accordance with the law and promote orderly innovation and the healthy development of the platform economy.

On20 August 2021, the 30th Session of the Standing Committee of the 13th National People's Congress voted to pass the Personal Information Protection Law, which also put forward special requirements on data processing for large platforms, stipulated the system of information disclosure, external audit, and regulation of the platform subject, increased their responsibilities, and reduced their monopoly risks. These supporting rules have further strengthened the standardisation and rigor of digital governance.

As said above, on 24 June 2022, the 35th Session of the 13th National People's Congress Standing Committee passed the RAML. The RAML further refined the applicable rules and provided stronger institutional support for the next steps of platform regulation. For example, Article 9 and Article 22 of the RAML include special provisions on platform antitrust. Article 22 of the RAML states that "[o]perators with a dominant market position [that] use data, algorithms, technologies and platform rules to set up barriers and impose unreasonable restrictions on other operators" will violate the law by their abuse of dominant market position.

In addition, the State Administration for Market Regulation ("SAMR") published *Guidelines for the Classification and Hierarchy of Internet Platforms (Exposure Draft)* and *Guidelines for the Implementation of Main Responsibilities of Internet Platforms (Exposure Draft)* on 29 October 2021. The guidelines provide that the operation, behaviour, and responsibility of various types of platforms should be regulated "comprehensively, multi-dimensionally, and hierarchically."

It can be inferred from the policy positioning of the CPC Central Committee that revising the antitrust policy and the implementation thereof in the digital and platform economy has become a top priority for competition regulation in the Chinese market.

II. Under the guidance of antitrust regulatory policies and laws, China continues to carry out Antitrust Regulation of Digital Platform Enterprises

On 14 December 2020, the SAMR announced its decision to impose the maximum administrative penalty available on three illegal business concentration cases, including Alibaba's investment in acquiring equity in Yintai Commercial, Yuewen's acquisition of Xinli Media, and Fengchao's acquisition of Zhongyouzhidi. This is the first time that China's antitrust authority imposed an administrative fine over the concentration of operators in the digital economy.

In addition, according to the Antitrust Working Conference of the National Market Regulation System on 17 March 2022, 176 monopoly cases were investigated and resolved nationwide in 2021, and the total amount of fines was of 23.586 billion yuan (roughly 3.4 billion US$).

The court system reviewed 727 business concentration cases, conditionally approved four cases and enjoined one. The Chinese antitrust regulators achieved remarkable results, along with significant law enforcement breakthroughs, especially new developments in the field of digital and platform economy.

Of particular note is that 10 April 2021, the SAMR issued an administrative penalty decision on Alibaba's monopolistic behaviour of compulsory "either-or choice". On 10 July 2021, the SAMR issued an antitrust review decision on the concentration of operators in the merger of Huya and Douyu declared by Tencent, forbidding the concentration and rejecting Tencent's promise of additional restrictive conditions. This is the first case of Internet platform merger and acquisition prohibition in China, effectively strengthening the antitrust regulation of the digital and platform economy.

On 24 July 2021, the SAMR issued an administrative penalty for illegal concentration in the case of Tencent Holdings' acquisition of China Music Corporation, ordering Tencent and its affiliates to take measures to reinstate competitive order in the relevant market, notify the authority of any concentration in accordance with the law, and pay a fine of 500,000 yuan. This is the first case involving an illegal merger that has been ordered to restore competition in the market in over thirteen years since the implementation of the Anti-Monopoly Law and marks a significant step toward maintaining fair competition and promoting innovation and growth in the industry.

The SAMR has also held several administrative guidance meetings with industry-specific regulators in the digital economy to present specific guidelines and requirements for *ex ante* regulation. On the eve of "Double 11" in the past two years, a digital sale day in China like the Amazon Prime Day, SAMR co-hosted with other agencies the Administrative Guidance Symposium on Regulating Online Business Activities and Administrative Guidance Conference on Regulating Online Economic Order which was also attended by major digital platform enterprises. It attaches great importance to the supervision of centralised network promotion activities. In the meeting, for the false discount misleading consumers, false publicity and illegal advertising, unfair format terms, "brush single fried letter", restrictions on the choice of commercial platform and other issues were explained. It hopes that the major digital platform enterprises will carefully examine the above issues, respond to consumer demand, and earnestly fulfil their responsibilities in terms of platform governance, information disclosure, fair competition and consumer rights protection.

The agencies in charge of regulating various industries have also put forward relevant work requirements for strengthening antitrust law enforcement and standardising the healthy development of new business models in the industry. On 30 July 2021, the Joint Inter-Ministerial Meeting on Transportation and Coordinated Regulation of New Forms set out "to strengthen antitrust regulation and oversight over unfair competition, investigate and punish online car-hailing and freight transportation platforms for monopolising, excluding and restricting competition . . . to further strengthen network and data security regulation, [and] to protect consumers' personal information." Local market regulatory departments have also organised administrative guidance meetings for digital platform enterprises to help them operate within the parameters set by law. At present, a comprehensive, multi-level and multi-dimensional digital platform governance system and implementation mechanism are shaped into existence by local and central governments.

III. The main characteristics and development trend of Chinese Platform Antitrust Regulation

Although China's attitude towards digital platform governance is similar to that of other major nations, there are differences with regard to regulatory concepts, methods, and specific measures. In practice, China usually pays more attention to policy guidance and multilateral governance, stressing the importance of maintaining "stability" while making progress. In line with the general direction of policies, China pursues coordinated governance at a multi-level, multi-faceted and multi-field approach in an orderly fashion and under the rule of law. This is achieved through the scientific and prudent diversification of accurate and effective measures, where enforcement is characterised by consistency, science, and transparency.

Both the current legislation and agencies have fully implemented the central government's directions in strengthening antitrust regulation and enforcement against unfair competition, promoting fair competition, setting useful guideposts for market entities, and introducing systematic, holistic and scientific decision-making. The interpretation of specific laws and regulations and the implementation of regulatory measures should be more objective and based on scientific principles. Focusing on "regulations" aims to prevent the disorderly expansion of capital, promote fair market competition and help in the healthy development of China's digital economy.

In other words, the regulation of digital platform enterprises should focus on scientific, accurate, and effective regulation strategies and methods, stimulate the innovation in the market, and enhance the sustainable growth in the digital and platform economy. Meanwhile, it is necessary to balance the relationship between short-term policy goals and long-term, high-quality development requirements, avoid the excessive pursuit of short-term regulatory benefits, form a long-term sustainable model that assigns equal weight to development and regulation so as to build a fair and orderly digital market.

Recently, the safeguarding of free, fair, and orderly competition and the standardised development of the digital market have become the indispensable requirement of China's "14th Five-Year plan" and its guiding mission, which is to promote the sustainable and high-quality development of the digital economy and to create new advantages in international competition. Faced with increasingly fierce competition in the regulation game, China should take the initiative and adapt to the new trend of competition and regulation in the global digital economy. On the basis of improving and strengthening the rule of law and its own regulation strategy, China should clarify the key direction for adjusting the concept, subject matter, and methodology of its digital antitrust regulation.

In terms of regulatory philosophy, China should implement the concept of science-based and prudent supervision subsidised by the rule of law, attach equal importance to development and regulation, and seek a dynamic equilibrium among cracking down on monopolistic behaviours, containing the risks of unfair competition, and encouraging the innovation and development of digital platform enterprises. China should also strive to provide clear demarcation of liability and regulatory boundaries to facilitate transparent antitrust enforcement and avoid overlapping liabilities or enforcement crossover between regulators. Tailoring to the characteristics and principles of the digital market and preventing market harms caused by stringent or improper enforcement through multi-disciplinary regulatory cooperation that improves the efficacy and efficiency of digital oversight would also befit the Chinese regulators and the Chinese society as a whole.

It can be said that China's current legislation and law enforcement have fully implemented the central government's decision to "strengthen antitrust" deployment. However, our understanding of "strengthening antitrust" should not go to extremes. **"Strengthening antitrust" cannot be simply equivalent to "strengthening platform antitrust", nor can it just strengthen antitrust law enforcement with regard to platforms.** As the 26th Meeting of the Commission for Deepening Overall Reform of the CPC Central Committee stressed on 22 June 2022:

> [t]o strengthen the regulation of platform enterprises against monopoly and unfair competition, strengthen the regulation of platform enterprises over sediment data, and regulate the big data-based price discrimination and algorithm discrimination, China needs to consolidate the regulatory responsibilities of all relevant departments, improve the coordinated regulatory framework between the central and local governments, strengthen functional, **penetrating, and sustained oversight, strengthen regulatory coordination and joint law enforcement, and maintain consistency between online and offline oversight**.

On 24 June 2022, the 35th Session of the 13th National People's Congress Standing Committee passed the RAML. Compared with Article 10 of the first draft, article 11 of the RAML adds the goal of "strengthening anti-monopoly law enforcement and judiciary, hearing monopoly cases fairly and efficiently in accordance with the law, and improving administrative law enforcement and judicial connection mechanisms." Specifically in the field of platform regulation, it is clear that antitrust is a part of platform regulation, but platform regulation cannot be equated with platform antitrust. At the same time, platform antitrust should not be understood as merely involving antitrust law enforcement, but should also include platform antitrust justice, as well as platform enterprises and other participants' compliance with the anti-monopoly law, such as platform enterprises' compliance and supervision of other participants.

The interpretation of specific laws and the implementation of regulatory measures should be objective and scientific. The purpose of focusing on "regulations" is to prevent the disorderly expansion of capital, promote fair market competition, and encourage the healthy development of the digital economy. In other words, China should pay attention to scientific, accurate, and effective regulation strategies and methods for digital platform enterprises, adhere to both development and regulation as guiding principles, stimulate innovation among market entities, and enhance the driving force and sustainability of growth within digital platform enterprises.

At the same time, it is necessary to balance the relationship between phased policy goals and long-term high-quality development requirements, avoid excessive pursuit of short-term regulatory benefits, form a long-term sustainable development model that pays equal attention to development and regulation, and build a unified, fair and orderly digital market.

In terms of regulation subjects, taking market operation as the starting point and respecting the basic laws of market operation, an all-round, multi-level and multi-dimensional regulation system led and regulated by the General Administration of Market Regulation and coordinated with other actors and local regulation departments should be established to improve regulation efficiency.

The SAMR was set up through the institutional reform of 2018, integrating anti-monopoly law enforcement powers originally scattered across three departments, thus offering a partial solution to the problem of overlapping functions and a more efficient antitrust regulation. At the same time, it should be noted that compared with traditional physical platforms, digital economy platforms are more convenient for expansion. Hidden monopolies, complex competition mechanisms, and a diversified operation with cross market competition are more serious issues. Therefore, all industries and market entities are required to participate in the multi-faceted regulation. This approach links market entities with industry-specific authorities, forms a complete set of regulatory chains, establishes regulatory coordination in the finance, manufacturing, information technology, Internet, and other industries, and encourages the sharing of information, joint enforcement, and regulatory cooperation. China will open channels for market entities to report, attach importance to supervision by public opinion, improve correspondence procedures, and emphasise the disclosure of results. Under the overall management of the SAMR, the regulatory subjects in all fields and on different regulatory levels should play active roles in improving regulatory efficiency.

In terms of regulatory methods, China's authorities could improve the anti-monopoly review mechanism to form a chain of supervision and control over consolidations *ex ante* and *ex post*. To achieve this goal, it is necessary not only to clarify the rules regulating business conduct in the platform market and strengthen structural control and other obligations through legal norms, but also to introduce scientific and technological tools to link regulatory authorities and platform operators to establish a real-time, digital, intelligent and full-cycle regulation mechanism as well as to respond to the digital economy in the whole cycle, the whole airspace, the whole scene, the whole chain, the whole value of the new competition paradigm and the new requirements of antitrust regulation.

In terms of regulatory logic and procedures, China should promote scientific and prudent *ex ante* regulation, encourage and support platform entities to actively participate in compliance governance, and take accurate measurements to ensure effective prevention and control while fully respecting the independent operation of platform entities. China can make comprehensive use of administrative guidance, interview, investigation and other administrative methods to link industry regulation departments and market regulation departments, increase input in science and technology regulation, and enhance capacity for prior regulation. Concrete measures including but not limited to scientifically issued relevant policy documents in time, strengthen communication between enterprises and government authorities, provide policy explanations and consultation for all platform entities, provide scientific and timely behavioural guidance, advocate for guidance first, encourage platform subjects to combine self-compliance with external regulations so as to improve efficiency in advance. Regarding *ex post* regulation, this should be strictly in accordance with the law, setting up a list of positive and negative scientific management systems. Policy makers should also clarify and publicise start-up procedures, investigation procedures, hearing procedures, and result disclosure procedures, which would enhance the authority's position in its enforcement to deliver open, fair, and equitable regulation.

In terms of regulatory content, China should pay attention to the balance of diverse interests in the dynamic process of data collection, use and management to effectively deter and regulate data monopolisation, blockade, and abuse by players in the platform economy. At the same time, it should standardise and provide guidance for the lawful operation of cross market digital platform enterprises, incentivise their innovation, creativity and competitiveness on a global scale, and seize the vantage point of international competition in the digital economy. In accordance with the *Guidelines for Overseas Antitrust Compliance* issued by SAMR in November 2021, Chinese digital platform enterprises should raise their awareness of overseas regulation compliance by establishing and improving international antitrust compliance solutions, as well as accurately identifying and assessing the potential risks in the international arena including antitrust risks and the associated risks relating to data security, financing, and IP infringement.

*

In conclusion due to the highly dynamic, cross-industrial, and transnational activities of competitions among digital platform enterprises, the effective antitrust regulation of the digital economy in an international context depends on countries and regions to continuously deepen bilateral, multilateral, and regional cooperation in antitrust enforcement. On the basis of safeguarding the sovereignty, national security and economic interests of all countries in the digital field, it is necessary that authorities promote the establishment of practical international governance rules for competition in the digital economy that will reflect the interests and demands of all countries, so as to build a new regime for global competition in the digital economy featuring joint construction, joint governance, and shared benefits. These subjects need to be considered and further explored in the future research and practice.

Is it possible to impose a tax on Artificial-Intelligence robots?

Young-Soon KIM
Korea

The "Fourth Industrial Revolution" is transforming not just industries but also society and the economic structure. While previous industrial revolutions occurred in the past, this one may be different due to the rise of AI, robotics, and automation, which have the potential to replace human decision-making and cognitive tasks.

The labour market is one area where this transformation is having a significant impact. This industrial revolution could bring a massive displacement. As a result, the government's tax revenue may be reduced since its tax base rests on labour income. Additionally, the government may require more funding to retrain and educate laid-off workers. To address these concerns, many scholars propose a "robot tax," which aims to tax companies that use robots or automated technologies to replace human workers. While the term "robot tax" has commonly been used, proposals have also included AI, robotics, and smart automation.

However, there are many legal hurdles to implementing such a tax, despite its potential policy benefits. This chapter examines the aspects of a robot tax, including how it could be drafted and implemented. It discusses the correlation between the robot industry and the labour market (1), weighs the pros and cons of various robot tax proposals (2), looks at statutory examples of a robot tax (3), analyses several potential problems associated with implementing a robot tax (4) and delves into the specifics of a robot tax (5), before in concludes.

I. Correlation between robots and labour

From the International Federation of Robotics (IFR), South Korea has held the title of second highest robot density in the world – a record 868 robots per 10,000 employees in the manufacturing industry in 2019.[1] Historically, one of the causes of the robot development has been the replacement or reduction of human labour. However, the robot development has unexpectedly resulted in the fear of losing one's job.

There are two groups: the optimists and the pessimists. First of all, experts are predicting that automation will increase productivity and also create new jobs. As a result, AI, robots and automation may increase employment, especially skilled workers. This new technology is likely to result in job shifts, not to take away jobs. According to the McKinsey Global Institute, 60 % of occupations consist of jobs that can be automated to up at least 30 %, but less than 5 % can be fully automated. On the other hand, other experts predict that robots will seriously disrupt the labour market. Frey and Osborne said that about 47 % of all jobs belong to a high-risk group with a 70 % or higher chance of being replaced by automated robots. In analysing the labour market in South Korea using the research method of Frey and Osborne, about 63 % of Korean jobs are in the high-risk group.[2]

Although there is a long-term disagreement, in the view of short-term they both agree about automation's effects on job-losses and significant disruption. And this time may be different. As AI and robots continue to advance, they will likely replace human thought and decision-making in various fields. In fact, robots are already being used as doctors, lawyers, artists, and writers.[3] Many experts are predicting that future technological advances are different from the past.[4]

---

1 IFR, executive summary world robotics 2019.

2 Seokwon Kim, "Changes in future jobs", 2016 SPRI Spring Conference, Software Policy Institute, 2016. 3. 8.

3 Ryan Abbott, Bret Bogeenschneider, "Should Robots Pay Taxes?", tax policy in the age of automation, 12 *Harvard Law & Policy Review*, 145, 2018. pp. 159.

4 Cousins Stevens, "Is A Robot Tax Really An Innovation Penalty", (techcrunch.com), 2017. 4. ("This time there may be some distinctions requiring widespread and perhaps novel solutions, unlike other periods in history.").

II. Controversy over a robot tax

(A) Proponents of a robot tax

The proponent view predicts that technological innovation will lead to unemployment. Labour income is the base of tax system. Across the member states of the Organisation for Co-operation and Development (OECD), approximately 50 % of all tax revenues in 2015 came from either individual income taxes or social insurance taxes.[5] On the other hand, corporate taxation is trending downwards in nearly all nations. Therefore, if the massive displacement happened, tax revenue would be reduced.

Robots a sort of capital of a company. Income obtained using robots often benefits from numerous and generous tax deductions, including accelerated depreciation and R&D tax preferences.[6] These preferences reduce the effective tax rate on income of companies. Many companies are investing in automation only because the tax code is urging them to do so. It is necessary to impose a robot tax for achieving tax neutrality.

(B) Opponents of a robot tax

In history, there is no evidence that automation brought the massive lay-off. On the contrary, automation created new jobs and increased employment. If a robot tax is imposed, a company will not invest in the robotics industry, as a result technological innovation will be stifled. The opponents suggest that it will be need for groups with high unemployment rates to introduce subsidies beside wage, massive investments in infrastructure and public recruitment programs.[7]

---

5 Amir El-Sibaie, Sources of Government Revenue in the OECD, 2018, TAX FOUNDATION (https://files.taxfoundation.org/20180322141501/Tax-Foundation-FF581.pdf.)

6 Tax depreciation is the one kind of the deduction. An accelerated tax deduction is a deduction which may be claimed earlier than its actual economic depreciation. By this means, the company can reduce the amount of tax which is payable when they want to do.

7 Lawrence Summers, "Robots are wealth creators and taxing them is illogical", *Financial Times*, March 6, 2017.

To impose a robot tax, the first step is to define what is a robot. How far has the mechanisation progressed? The definition of a robot is very various from a mere automated machine to artificial intelligent robot. There is no consensus reached.[8] Jumping over the obstacle of definition of a robot, the problem of calculation of tax base is expected. Does it only disallow the deduction or credit of investment in a robot? Or even actively impose a tax on a robot? How can it divide the portion of income created by a robot displaced human workers? In all of this view, a robot tax is impossible to put into practice. Moreover, multinational companies might be expected to prefer to minimise taxes levied on capital including robots and migrate into jurisdictions with low or no taxes on robots.[9]

III. A so-called "robot tax" in South Korea

While there are many scholastic proposals for a robot tax, actual legislative proposals are few. There is no jurisdiction to legislate a robot tax.

It has been said that South Korea introduced what has been called the first robot tax in August 2017 by limiting tax incentives for automated machines.[10]

Article 24 of the Restriction of Special Taxation Act ("RTSA") provides a tax credit for investment in "productivity increase facilities." It is a system that provides a tax credit for the investment to actively encourage the introduction of robot automation systems. The automation tax credit has been extended many times since its initial enactment in 1998. The credit is allowed to be invested in automation equipment from their corporate taxes, depending on the size of the operation. For instance, large enterprises account for 3 %, medium-sized enterprises 5 %, and small-sized enterprises 7 %. However, in 2017, the rate of tax credit was reduced by up to two percentage points (large enterprises for 1 %,

---

8 Bret N. Bogenschneider, "Will robots agree to pay taxes? further tax implications of advanced AI", *North Carolina Journal of Law & Technology*, 2020, p. 22.

9 Robert D. Atkinson, The Case Against Taxing Robots, May 29, 2019. p. 17. (stating that some prominent economists, including Lawrence Summers, have further described robot tax proposals as "illogical").

10 Ryan Abbott, Bret Bogeenschneider, Ibid, p. 145.; Cara McGoogan, South Korea Introduces World's First "Robot Tax", TELEGRAPH: TECH, Aug.9, 2017. Orly Mazur evaluated that it was not technically a robot tax, but seek to achieve similar policy goals.

medium-sized enterprises 3 %, and small-sized enterprises 7 %), and the sunset date extended until 31 December 2019. Press reports indicated that the proposal was motivated by a desire to slow the implementation of automation in Korea's high-tech manufacturing sector. Regarding this government policy, a high-ranking official of the Ministry of Strategy and Finance even evaluated that it was the first step in the Korean robot tax.[11] According to a report by the National Assembly Budget Office, total tax expenditure is estimated at 243.7 billion won (about 18.7 million $).

However, this introduction in not as such a robot tax, because it can only be as a process of reducing excessive tax preferences for large enterprises and mid-sized enterprises. There is no specific plan to use the reduced tax expenditure for workers who have lost their jobs due to automation. In the 2022 revision, the rate of tax credit for medium-sized enterprises is raised up to two percentage points (5 %). Moreover, the new tax credit revised in 2021 for the investment in facilities for new growth and R&D of original technologies is added-namely, large enterprises for 3 %, medium-sized enterprises 5 %, and small-sized enterprises 12 %. Robot technology is included among the new growth and original technologies, and listed in the enforcement ordinance of the Ministry of Strategy and Finance.

In conclusion, the policy of South Korea is to allow tax credit for the investment of robots, automation in promoting private investment in AI robot business. A robot tax is far from South Korea.

IV. Challenges of implementing a robot tax

As professor Mazur has put it, "these proposals involve substantial elements of arbitrariness and complexity in implementation, likely increasing compliance and administrative burdens on companies and tax authorities."[12]. There are many significant hurdles are as discussed below.

---

11 Sisa Journal, "Is the 'Korean-style robot tax introduction' real?", 2017. 8. 11. (https://www.sisajournal.com/news/articleView.html?idxno=170862)

12 Orly Mazur, Taxing the Robots, 46 PEPP. L. REV. 2019. p. 27.; Xavier Oberson, Taxing Robots? From the Emergence of an Electronic Ability to Pay to a Tax on Robots or the Use of Robots, 1 World Tax Journal, 2017. p. 247.

(A) What is a taxable robot?

This is a fundamental problem: What is a taxable robot? There are many usages of a robot. A "robot" refers to any mere machine reducing labour, or automatic machine in a factory, or something more complex (say AI robots). What degree of automation should be? Does it include an intangible algorithm embedded in code, or must it have a physical form?

In the European Union's 2017 Report to the Commission on Civil Law Rules on Robot, a uniform definition of smart autonomous robots included the following features: (1) autonomy through sensors and/or exchanging data with its environment (inter-connectivity); (2) self-learning (optional criterion); (3) has a physical support; and (4) adapts its behaviours and actions to its environment.[13] Despite this attempt, the EU recognised that "defining robots is no easy task in the absence of any real consensus within the global scientific community."

Although there are various technical definitions, there is no commonly-accepted legal definition. The common thread is that they tend to focus on the autonomy based in AI, self-learning and decision-making process. To solve this problem, a "white list" is also possible like South Korea. It would be to implement a narrowly-targeted tax on specific type of AI, robotics, or automation.[14] But as the technological innovation became faster, the white list might be quickly obsolete and impractical. The purpose of a robot tax is to impose taxes on robots that pose a significant risk of causing mass unemployment. To achieve this tax purpose, a robot would be defined as a smart machine imbedded in self-learning, artificial intelligent and interact with the external environment. However, in legal terms, the definition provisions should have clarity and predictability. We can define each specific type and more broadly similar types in tax purpose.

---

[13] Comm. on Legal Affairs, European Civil Law Rules in Robotics: Study, E.U. DOC. PE 571.379, 2016, p. 8.

[14] Robert Kovacev, "A TAXING DILEMMA: robot taxes and the challenges of effective taxation of AI, automation and robotics in the fourth industrial revolution, *The OHIO State Technology Law Journal*, Vol. 16.1, 2020. p. 215.

(B) Is a robot tax a punitive or sin tax?

The effect of robotisation is displacement of human workers, economic inequality and reducing tax revenues from labour-based taxes. It is regarded as the same character as negative externalities, like pollution, cigarettes, alcohol or sugary drinks to deter consumption. In this meaning, the opponents urge that a robot tax is the "punitive tax", "sin tax" or "Pigouvian tax". It is the kind of "fear-based law-making".[15] However, it is uncertain whether or not a robot reduces jobs.

And so, tax policy for innovation should honour both economic progress and social welfare.[16] Tax incentives should enhance social welfare by stimulating industry research towards advancements. However, innovation brings only economic progress currently. Wealth accumulates for the person who owns the robot and the technology. However, whether automation will cause the displacement of human workers is still a matter of controversy. To be honest, a robot tax is a tax based on fear.

However, by the time the fear becomes a reality, it may already be too late. It is rational for a nation to establish tax policies while preparing for the worst.

(C) The problem of the legal personality

To consider a robot as a taxpayer, it would need to first be recognised as having legal personality. This means that the robot would be considered a subject of rights and be legally obligated to fulfil certain obligations. In most countries, legal personality is recognised for individuals, corporations and organisations. However, it is not out of the realm of possibility to recognise robots as legal persons. In the past, corporations were not initially recognised as legal persons. However, to separate shareholder liability in case of default, the legal personality of corporations was eventually recognised.

The decision to grant legal personality to robots is simply a matter of policy. Once robots are granted the legal personality, they would be assigned legal rights and duties separate from those of their creators.

---

15 Kathryn Kisska-Schulze & Rodney P. Mock, "The robotic revolution: a tax policy collision course", 93 *Temple Law Review* 301, 2021, p. 327.

16 Kathryn Kisska-Schulz & Karie Davis-Nozemack, humans vs. robots: rethinking tax policy for a more sustainable future, 79 *Maryland Law Review*, p. 1039.

(D) Who actually pays a tax?

The scholars suggest the diverse forms of robot tax systems. As a result, the taxpayer is different from each proposal. A robot acts and collects money on behalf of the owner. It must legally do so as human agent. This means that a robot tax is only a tax on humans (or entities formed by humans) who won, used, or benefited from use of robots.[17]

On the other hand, it has been proposed that robots be regarded as having a legal personality. If it is approved in the law, robots will then be entitled to property ownership, enter into contracts in their own name and manage bank accounts on their own behalf, and legal protections. At the same time, robots would also assume legal obligations and be required to compensate injured parties, and become legally responsible for paying taxes. There are objections to this. According to this view, if either legal or electronic personality is bestowed, robots themselves have no actual or practical ability to pay any tax liabilities.[18] If a robot has the financial capacity, there is room for acknowledgment of the tax burden. Financial capacity refers to the ability to manage one's money and financial affairs and make related decisions while bearing in mind all possible financial and legal consequences of one's actions. AI robots are able to have this financial capacity. And it is also needed to prevent tax avoidance. When an owner reserves income for a robot and does not distribute it, they can potentially avoid paying income tax by deferring the income to the robot. This could be a reason to consider recognising robots as dependent taxpayers.

(E) The problem of tax base

If the consensus on imposing a robot tax were reached, other questions arise. What is the tax base for a robot tax and how would it be measured? The popular proposal is that a tax be imposed on the forgone taxes of displaced employee. Such a tax could be levied on the "hypothetical salary" that robots should receive from equivalent work done by humans. On the other hand, there are many opinions that point out problems with this view. It is necessary the allocate income between robot sourced and non-robot-sourced, but it is very complex and disputable.[19]

---

17 Robert Kovacev, Ibid., p. 196.

18 Kathryn Kisska-Schulze & Rodney P. Mock, Ibid., p. 317.

19 Robert Kovacev, Ibid., p. 198.

It is not easy to measure the profits or value created by the robot or automation program. However, in terms of tax policy, it may not be necessary to strictly classify income through book-keeping. Instead of calculating real income, it may be possible to tax using a formula. Factors such as the degree of automation in a company, statistics on displacement, and average wages of workers etc. could be taken into account to calculate a tax base.

(F) International tax avoidance and competition

If one nation imposes a robot tax on a company, the income of the company would be reduced due to the robot tax. In the view of international market, the company would not invest robot innovation technologies or move to the no- or low-tax jurisdiction. If the capital is easy to move, the company would be relocated to the other country that does not impose a robot tax. A company in the countries that impose a robot tax will lose international competitiveness. Moreover, if the definition and tax base of a robot tax are different from each country that introduces a robot tax, significant tax avoidance would be occurred.[20]

In order to avoid these situations, a global multilateral solution would ultimately have to found.[21] The recent "digital tax" debate provides a useful guidance of this problem. This is a structure that aims to distribute the income of multinational corporations among the countries where they operate. Such an agreement should be concluded as a multilateral treaty. While reaching a consensus may not be easy, international cooperation is necessary in the long term to establish a fair and effective system for taxing multinational corporations

V. A proposal to implement a robot tax

The form of a robot tax can be changed as technological innovation advances. Ray Kurzweil divides the stages of robotic technology into three stages.[22] According to this view, forms of a robot tax are as below.

---

20 Kathryn Kisska-Schulze & Rodney P. Mock, Ibid., p. 333.

21 Robert Kovacev, Ibid., p. 201.

22 Ray Kurzweil, 「The Singularity Is Near: When Humans Transcend Biology, 2005.

(A) A stage before passing the Turing Test

The first turning point is when it passes the Turing Test. Kurzweil estimates this to be around 2029. This is the point of leaping from weak artificial intelligence to strong artificial intelligence.

As of today, robots are a type of mechanical equipment used to improve productivity. Robots at this stage are not limited to AI robots, but extended to automatic machines. A major policy issue is how to adjust the tax system to be neutral as between robot and human workers. An option is to disallow of the corporate income tax deductions or tax credits for capital investments in automated machines.[23] Of course, this would hinder a corporation to invest in automation, robots. However, as long as the profit of tax preferences is contributed only to the owners, it is rational to reduce tax preferences. In the category of the depreciation system, there are measures such as different depreciation methods for each machine, different depreciation rates based on the automation level of each company, or lower depreciation rates as a whole.[24] On the other hand, on can create incentives for companies that employ human workers, or provide tax preferences for retraining and re-education of the workforce.

Another option is to levy an incremental automation tax to the extent that workers are laid off or replaced by machines.[25] It is similar system to unemployment compensation. It would be calculated as a substitute for what employment taxes would have been on human workers. The gross amount of the automation tax could match the wage taxes and social security.[26] It is better to design tax policies based on salaries rather than on profits, as taxation of income could result in double taxation.

---

23 Cara McGoogan, South Korea Introduces World's First "Robot Tax", TELEGRAPH: TECH, (Aug. 9, 2017).

24 Kim Joo-Seong, "A Study on Robot Taxes – From the Tax Neutrality Perspective of Human and Machine Labour." *Law & Technology*, Vol. 16, No. 5, Center for Technology and Law, Seoul National University, 2020, p. 90.

25 Michael Kraich, The Chilling Realities of the Telecommuting Tax: Adapting Twentieth Century Policies for Twenty-First Century Technologies, 15 *The Pittsburgh Journal of Technology Law and Policy,* 224, 2015.(providing a comprehensive discussion of a "telecommuting tax").

26 William Meisel, The Software Society: Cultural and Economic Impact 226, 2013. p. 220.

Although it may be perceived as a punitive tax in the short term, it can be offset by new employment opportunities in the long term.

(B) A stage after passing the Turing Test

Robots that pass the Turing Test would have the same intelligence in making decisions and passing judgments as humans. It will be discussed seriously whether a robot can be granted legal personality and whether a robot can be regarded as taxpayers or not. It depends on a policy decision to grant legal personality. If robots are capable of independent decision-making like humans, then granting them legal personality would allow them to hold legal rights and obligations separate from their owners.

The next step is to discuss about whether a robot can be a taxpayer or not. Robots can bear taxes independently of their owners. However, if the income generated by robots is subject to taxation, it may result in double taxation. It is reasonable to tax based on the salaries of the workers who are no longer needed due to the use of robots. Value-added tax can also be imposed on the value added by robots.

*

In conclusion, it is uncertain how technological innovation will affect the labour market. However, the current wave of innovation differs from previous industrial revolutions in terms of its speed and scope of improvements.

If the technological innovation leads to significant displacement of human workers and widens the wealth gap, it is necessary to reconsider tax preferences for such innovation. Tax policies should be designed to promote both innovation and social welfare. In this context, it may be necessary to impose a tax on companies or individuals using robots and automation instead of human workers. The revenue generated from this tax could be used to fund retraining or re-education programmes for the workers who have been displaced.

Insurance in the face of the increase of cyber risks in the wake of regional instability

Amandine CAYOL
France

Born in the maritime field in the 16th century, insurance has gradually developed and diversified in order to accompany economic and social developments and to cope with the emergence of new risks. One of the main challenges facing the European Union today is the increase in cyber risk, which could be systemic in nature due to the interconnection between information systems. Sectors providing essential services (transport, energy, health) are now all dependent on digital technologies. Such digitalisation of the economy increases exposure to cyber risks. Thus, in 2021, 54 % of French companies were subject to cyber-attacks[1]. For the fifth year in a row, cyber-attacks are the number one risk according to France Assureur (a union representing most French insurers)[2].

The cyber risk has been accentuated by the Covid-19 pandemic, which has increased the use of digital technology in all sectors of activity (notably with the development of teleworking and e-commerce). Since February 2022, it is the regional instability in Ukraine that has contributed to an increase in cyber-attacks[3]. It is indeed a hybrid conflict that also takes place in cyber space[4]. In the third trimester of 2022, there is

1 Directorate General of the Treasury (France), « *Le développement de l'assurance du risque cyber*, 2022, p. 9.

2 France Assureurs, *Cartographie Prospective de l'assurance 2022.*

3 "With the war in Ukraine, cyber-attacks in Europe jumped by 140 % last year", according to Thierry Breton, interviewed by L. Marchand et D. Barroux, *Les Echos* April 5, 2023: https://www.lesechos.fr/tech-medias/hightech/nous-allons-doter-leurope-dun-bouclier-cyber-annonce-thierry-breton-1922112

4 S. Caulier, « La guerre en Ukraine fait basculer le monde dans l'ère des cyberattaques », *Le Monde* February 12, 2023: https://www.lemonde.fr/economie/article/2023/02/12/la-guerre-en-ukraine-fait-basculer-le-monde-dans-l-ere-des-cyberattaques_6161549_3234.html

a clear shift from cyber warfare centred on Ukraine and Russia to cyber warfare across Europe (particularly in Poland, the Baltic States and the Nordic countries)[5].

This context has strengthened the European Union's determination to develop a cyber-security strategy, which began in the early 2000s with the creation, in 2004, of the European Union Agency for Cybersecurity (ENISA), whose powers were reinforced in 2019[6]. The EU Cybersecurity Act also introduced a uniform EU-wide certification scheme in 2019 to ensure high cybersecurity standards.

As early as 2016, a directive on the security of networks and information systems (NIS) was adopted in order to organise cooperation between the countries of the European Union on cybersecurity[7]. In particular, it imposed obligations on operators providing essential services in sectors deemed critical (such as energy, transport and health). This directive was revised in December 2022[8] with the aim of consolidating cooperation between Member States. In parallel, in December 2022, a directive aimed at strengthening the resilience of critical entities was adopted[9]. IT security for the financial sector is also being sought with the adoption of

---

5 Thales, *Threat Landscape Report – Second Semester 2022*, 2023: « EU member states have seen a dramatic increase in the number of conflict-related incidents over the last 6 months, from 9.8 % to 46.5 % of global attacks. […] The beginning of 2023 confirms this trend with the overwhelming majority of incidents concentrated in European countries (80.9 %) » : https://www.thalesgroup.com/fr/monde/securite/press_release/lukraine-leurope-entiere-tournant-cyberguerre

6 Regulation (EU) 2019/881 of the European Parliament and of the Council of 17 April 2019 on ENISA (the European Union Agency for Cybersecurity) and on information and communications technology cybersecurity certification and repealing Regulation (EU) No 526/2013 (Cybersecurity Act).

7 Directive (EU) 2016/1148 of the European Parliament and of the Council of 6 July 2016 concerning measures for a high common level of security of network and information systems across the Union.

8 Directive (EU) 2022/2555 of the European Parliament and of the Council of 14 December 2022 on measures for a high common level of cybersecurity across the Union, amending Regulation (EU) No 910/2014 and Directive (EU) 2018/1972, and repealing Directive (EU) 2016/1148 (NIS 2 Directive).

9 Directive (EU) 2022/2557 of the European Parliament and of the Council of 14 December 2022 on the resilience of critical entities and repealing Council Directive 2008/114/EC.

the Digital Operational Resilience Act (DORA) on 28 November 2022 to prevent and mitigate cyber threats[10].

Other texts are planned in the short term to further strengthen cyber security in the European Union. The Cyber Resilient Act, presented by the European Commission on 15 September 2022, aims to strengthen the security of connected objects by creating new obligations for their producers. The European Commission also presented, on 18 April 2023, the draft Cyber Solidarity Act. This project was initiated in March 2022 as a reaction to the regional instability in Ukraine presenting an increased threat of a major cyber-attack in Europe. It provides for the establishment of a European cyber shield, consisting of national and cross-border security operations centres located throughout the European Union. In order to strengthen the response capacity in case of a cyber-attack, it is also proposed to create an EU "cyber security reserve"[11].

The development of cyber risk insurance is part of this desire to fight against cybercrime. Indeed, to be fully effective, a cyber-risk management strategy must include three aspects: prevention, crisis management and insurance, in order to cover the damage caused by cyber-attacks[12]. Insurance "has a key role to play in addressing this risk[13]", by helping to build business resilience. Although the first cyber risk insurance policies appeared in the United States in the 2000s[14], their development is still weak in Europe[15].

---

10 Regulation (EU) 2022/2554 of the European Parliament and of the Council of 14 December 2022 on digital operational resilience for the financial sector and amending Regulations (EC) No 1060/2009, (EU) No 648/2012, (EU) No 600/2014, (EU) No 909/2014 and (EU) 2016/1011.

11 The vast majority of Member States are, however, currently hostile to such a proposal due to concerns about retaining power at national level over the certification and deployment of such a reserve.

12 S. Meurant et R. Cardon, *Rapport relatif à la cybersécurité des entreprises*, Rapport Sénat n° 678, 2021, p. 132 et pp. 141–143.

13 Directorate General of the Treasury (France), « *Le développement de l'assurance du risque cyber*, 2022, p. 11.

14 B. Spitz et V. Lafarge-Sarkozy (dir.), *Assurer le risque cyber*, Rapport du Club des juristes, 2018, pp. 44–46.

15 "In 2018, the global cyber insurance market was estimated at between 3 and 3.5 billion dollars, with the American market accounting for 85–90 % of these premiums. Europe still accounts for only 5–9 % of this market", Senate Report No. 678, cited above.

The insurance of cyber risk raises many questions: to what extent is cyber risk insurable? How should it be insured? France has just adopted specific rules in this area with the law of 24 January 2023[16], trying to reconcile the need to protect the interests of companies that are victims of cyber-attacks and the need to ensure better visibility of cyber risk. This example illustrates the challenges linked to the development of insurance against cyber risk. After recalling the difficulties raised by this type of insurance (1), it is appropriate to study the methods adopted by the French legislator (2).

I. The difficulties raised by cyber risk insurance

Cyber risk is still poorly identified by both companies and insurers (a). Moreover, its insurability has been questioned, particularly with regard to administrative fines and ransoms (b).

(A) The still insufficient identification of cyber risk

The cyber risk insurance market is currently underdeveloped[17]. This is due, first of all, to the fact that companies tend to underestimate this risk[18], especially small and medium-sized enterprises. However, the latter are particularly concerned in practice[19]. "Less armed than large companies in the face of this threat, they are prime targets for malicious actors[20]". An effort to raise awareness of the cyber risk among companies is therefore essential.

Secondly, insurers lack reliable data to successfully establish a pricing model and propose an adapted insurance offer[21]. Most insurance and

16 Loi n° 2023–22 du 24 janvier 2023 d'orientation et de programmation du ministère de l'intérieur, *JO* 25 janvier 2023.

17 "Only 8 % of mid-sized companies have taken out cyber insurance": AMRAE, *Lumière sur la cyberassurance*, 2021.

18 Directorate General of the Treasury (France), « *Le développement de l'assurance du risque cyber*, 2022, p. 13.

19 According to a Eurobarometer, 28 % of European small and medium-sized enterprises experienced a cyber-attack in 2021: https://europa.eu/eurobarometer/surveys/detail/2280

20 CNIL, *Rapport annuel* 2021.

21 Ibid., p. 19 ; Institut Montaigne, *Cybermenace : avis de tempête*, 2018, pp. 55–56.

reinsurance organisations in Europe do not sufficiently measure their exposure to cyber risk[22]. This could disrupt the financial stability of the insurance sector. The European Insurance and Occupational Pensions Authority (EIOPA) thus recommended several supervisory measures to the competent national supervisory authorities at the end of 2022. In France, a decree of 13 December 2022[23] created new categories in the accounting of insurers concerning cyber risk[24]. The objective is to allow better statistical recognition of this risk.

The assumption of cyber risk could also result from the use of innovative solutions. Some companies are considering self-insurance with the creation of reinsurance captives. The development of parametric insurance by insurers could also strengthen the coverage of the risk[25].

(B) Possible obstacles to the coverage of cyber risk by insurance

The insurability of certain cyber risks has been discussed. On the one hand, as regards administrative fines, it is generally accepted that their nature as penalties makes them uninsurable[26]. The punitive logic leads to their being borne by the person responsible, without it being possible to transfer the burden of payment to a third party[27], notably an insurer[28].

---

22 European Insurance and Occupational Pensions Authority (EIOPA), *Supervisory Statement on management of non-affirmative cyber exposures*, September 23, 2022.

23 Arrêté du 13 décembre 2022 relatif à la classification des engagements d'assurance consécutifs aux atteintes aux systèmes d'information et de communication, *JO* 20 décembre 2022, texte n°6.

24 Article A. 344–2 of the Insurance Code.

25 S. Porcher, « L'assurance du risque cyber : quelques recommandations de la Direction générale du Trésor », *Dalloz actualité*, Septembre 26, 2022.

26 Directorate General of the Treasury (France), « Le développement de l'assurance du risque cyber, 2022, p. 29.

27 The principle of the personality of the penalty, set out in Article 121–1 of the Criminal Code. This principle is applicable to administrative and disciplinary sanctions : CE, avis, 29 octobre 2007, Société sportive professionnelle LOSC Lille Métropole, n° 307736.

28 Ministerial reply of 24 November 1997 to written question no. 2988 concerning a clause on the assumption of responsibility for criminal fines by the insurer: "Public policy therefore precludes an insurer from assuming responsibility for criminal fines, as well as tax or customs fines or any other pecuniary penalty imposed by the administrative authorities.

On the other hand, the insurance coverage of ransomware has been much debated. In France, it has even been proposed that insurers should be prohibited by law from insuring cyber ransomware[29]. It was feared that the reimbursement of ransom payments by insurers would encourage victimised companies to pay and thus allow criminal networks to flourish. Until recently, the French National Agency for Information Systems Security (ANSSI) recommended not to pay the ransom. However, it has been pointed out that this argument could just as easily be used to prohibit other types of insurance contracts. For example, there is insurance against the risk of kidnapping[30]. To take another example, insurance against theft is not considered to encourage thieves either[31].

On the contrary, it is likely that insurers will require companies to comply with cyber risk prevention measures in order to benefit from coverage in this area. The amount of the deductibles could also vary according to the level of protection of the insured. The development of insurance would thus be a means of helping to limit cyber-attacks.

Moreover, no country in Europe prohibits coverage for cyber-crime, with reimbursement generally being subject to compliance with anti-money laundering and anti-terrorism rules[32]. A ban limited to France would have led to a prejudicial competitive imbalance. The coverage of ransoms by French insurers is therefore relevant, given that ransomware represents the main threat and the one with the greatest impact on the production, reputation and finances of victims[33].

II. The methods used to insure against cyber risks

Greater visibility of cyber risk insurance is sought above all through improved drafting of insurance contracts (a). In practice, damage caused by cyber-attacks will only be covered in France if the victim has filed a complaint (b).

---

29 For example, Senate Report No. 678, supra, proposal No. 12.

30 P.-G. Marly, « Vers un encadrement de l'assurance des cyber-rançons ? », *JCP E* 2022, p. 807.

31 Directorate General of the Treasury (France), « Le développement de l'assurance du risque cyber, 2022, p. 33.

32 Ibid., p. 8.

33 Ibid., p. 4.

(A) The search for a better visibility of cyber risk insurance

There is a need for clarification regarding the coverage of cyber risk by insurance. At present, contracts are often complex and the guarantees offered are difficult to compare, mainly because of specific contractual definitions and varying security requirements[34]. The major risk is that a company may believe that it is wrongly covered against cyber risk. This was the case with the cyber-attack on the PlayStation Network platform in 2011[35].

Often, cyber risk is covered by an insurance policy that is not specifically written to cover it. The policy is silent on cyber risk, but will still cover it because of the broad definition of the subject matter of the policy and the absence of any applicable exclusions[36]. These "silent cyber guarantees" are a source of great uncertainty as to the coverage of the risk. It is therefore essential to improve the drafting of insurance contracts so that policyholders and insurers are certain of the risks covered. The European Insurance and Occupational Pensions Authority (EIOPA) published a report on this subject on 23 September 2022[37]. In France, the Autorité de contrôle prudentiel et de résolution (ACPR) had already issued proposals along the same lines[38].

(B) The requirement to file a complaint to cover damages in France

The French law of 24 January 2023 makes compensation for loss and damage caused by a breach of an automated data processing system conditional on the filing of a complaint by the victim[39]. This requirement,

---

34 *Assurer le risque cyber*, Rapport du Club des juristes, *op. cit.*, p. 49.

35 Ibid., pp. 50–51.

36 P.-G. Marly et A. Valençon, « L'assurance du risque cyber », *DallozIP/IT* 2019, p. 603.

37 European Insurance and Occupational Pensions Authority (EIOPA), *Supervisory Statement on management of non-affirmative cyber exposures*, September 2023 ; S. Porcher, « L'intervention de l'AEAPP face au risque de couverture silencieuse du risque cyber », *Dalloz actualité*, October 13, 2022.

38 ACPR, « La distribution des garanties contre les risques cyber par les assureurs », communiqué de presse, 12 novembre 2019: https://acpr.banque-france.fr/sites/default/files/medias/documents/20191112_cp_bilan_cyber_assurance.pdf

39 New Article L. 12-10-1 of the Insurance Code, which will come into force on 24 April 2023.

initially envisaged only for the reimbursement of cyber-ransomware[40], has been extended to all reimbursements following a cyber-attack. The wording "loss and damage" used in the law is particularly broad and concerns in particular "operating losses, remediation costs and payment of a ransom[41]". A complaint must be filed with the competent authorities within 72 hours of the victim's knowledge of the cyber-attack. However, this text only concerns persons acting in the context of their professional activity, and not private individuals.

The effectiveness of such a system is questionable. The objective is to allow greater visibility of cyber-attacks, which for the moment are still too often secret. This would enable public authorities to fight cybercrime more effectively. However, companies may still prefer not to reveal the existence of a cyber-attack in order to protect their reputation. As a result, it is feared that they may choose not to insure themselves against cyber risk, knowing that they will not, in any case, be covered in case of an undisclosed cyber-attack.

*

In conclusion, the conflict in Ukraine has increased the cyber risk in Europe, reinforcing the EU's commitment to fight cybercrime. Several texts have recently been adopted to this end, and others are planned for the near future. Insurance has a major role to play in this area in order to protect businesses by allowing compensation for damage caused by cyber-attacks. Although the development of cyber risk insurance may have come up against obstacles (notably the uncertainty of the insurability of ransom payments), it now seems possible provided that insurance policies are clarified and, in France, that a complaint is filed quickly for professionals who are victims of cyber-attacks. The objective of such a

---

40 For example, in this sense, *Le droit à l'épreuve des cyberattaques*, Rapport du Club des juristes, 2021, proposition n°10 ; V. Faure-Muntian, *La cyber-assurance*, Assemblée nationale, 13 October 2021, proposal n°4.

41 P. Linais et O. Lyon Lynch, « LOPMI : un éclaircissement bienvenu sur la légalité de l'assurabilité des cyber-rançons », *JCP G.* 2023, Act. 4.

requirement is to make cyber risk more visible. However, there is a risk that companies will prefer to keep it secret, even if it means not being covered in order to preserve their reputation. Cyber risk insurance, which is of no interest, may not be taken out. Thus, the "logic of transparency could well be a brake on the development of cyber insurance[42]".

[42] A. Touzain, « L'assurance des risques de cyberattaque est (légalement) née ! », *bjda.fr* 2023, n°85

Artificial-intelligence-generated works and Korean patent law reforms needed to accommodate the growth of Artificial Intelligence Generated Inventions

Soo-mee LEE
Korea

One of the most important objectives of patent law, regardless of which country, is to encourage innovation by providing incentives to those who create inventions. Exclusive rights to the invention are the most well-known incentives of patent law. Advancements in artificial intelligence (AI), big data, and semiconductors have resulted in software systems that are not just helping the inventors to create, but also automating the creation of new works. As the traditional patent was never designed to work with AIs that create inventions, the law struggles with the growth in the number and the scale of AI works.

This chapter probes into the problems of inventorship and patentability requirements in dealing with AI generated inventions.

I. Important features of AI technology

There are many ways to describe AI systems. "Machines that are capable of performing tasks that, if performed by a human, would be said to require intelligence" is a description that fits well with the patent system.[1] Shlomit Yanisky Ravid and Xiaoquing (Jackie) Liu's law review article

1 Matthew U. Schere, Regulating Artificial Intelligent Systems,: Risks, Challenges, Competencies, and Strategies, 29 HARV. J.L. & TECH 353, 354–55 (2016).

points out eight important features of AI systems that create challenges to the patent law.[2]

- Creativity: AI systems can create new products and processes, and significantly improve existing ones, using available data. AI Systems can draw, create designs and new inventions, such as technical devices and pharmaceutical drugs.[3]
- Unpredictable Results: AI systems process data and take actions to generate products, data and processes that cannot be predicted by programmers, and any other entities involved. AI systems can incorporate random mutations that result in unpredictable outcomes to the optimal solutions. Paintings created by an AI system is not a copy of existing works, but an unpredictable product. AI systems can process data from a large volume of microorganisms, break the data into Nano components and find similarities and patterns that cannot be observed by human eyes. This process results in unexpected structural information that can be used in development of antibacterial drugs.[4]
- Independent and Autonomous: AI systems can accomplish higher level tasks on their own without human intervention. An unmanned vehicles and automated pilot can operate independently. AI systems have the capability to identify similarities and patterns when processing data of which the programmers and operators are not aware. AI systems can autonomously choose, order components to achieve predetermined performance parameters in electronic circuits.[5]
- Rational Intelligence: AI systems are a rational system that can decide which activities to engage in or avoid to achieve predetermined performance or goals. They imitate intelligent human behaviour, such as learning and problem-solving by mimicking human perception and cognitive behaviour.[6]

---

2 Dr. Shlomit Yanisky Ravid & Xiaoquing (Jackie) Liu, When Artificial Intelligence Systems Product Inventions: An Alternative Model For Patent Law at the 3A Era, 39 Cardozo L. Rev. 2215, 2224–2227 (2018).

3 Id at 2224.

4 Id at. 2224–2225.

5 Id. At 2225–2226.

6 Id. At 2226.

- Evolving: AI systems continue to evolve and change with new data, which means the systems will produce new outcomes as new data are processed.[7]
- Capable of Data Collection and Communication: AI systems have the ability to search for data from different sources outside. Thus, driverless automated vehicles are collecting and processing data from the outside world (other cars, obstacles, traffic signals).[8]
- Efficient and Accurate: AI systems can process significant volumes of data accurately, efficiently and rapidly.[9]
- Freely Choose among Alternative Options: AI systems have the capability to choose between alternatives to achieve the best outcome for its predetermined goal. For example, AI systems in driverless automated vehicles process data to choose between routes, speed, and accident avoidance.

Due to advancement in AI technology, AI systems not just solve problems identified by humans. They can also identify the problem and create solutions autonomously. They can create new products and processes creative and novel enough to qualify as patentable inventions. These AI systems will create inventions, complete and submit unlimited number of patent applications without human guidance or instructions.

II. AI and inventorship

(A) Introducing an AI inventor named DABUS

The question of whether an AI system can be an inventor was a popular discussion topic in academia. The discussion has now turned into a real case. The U.S. Court of Appeals for the Federal Circuit ("Fed Circuit"), which is the U.S. appellate court specialising in patent cases, was asked to decide if an AI software system can be listed as the inventor on a patent application in *Thaler v. Vidal.*[10] Stephen Thaler invented and received a

---

7 Id at 2226–2227.

8 Id. At 2227.

9 Id.

10 Thaler v. Hirshfeld, 558 F. Supp. 3d 238 (E.D.Va.2021), aff'd. Thaler v. Vidal, 43 F.4th 1207 (Fed. Cir. 2022)

patent on an AI system named DABUS (Device for the Bootstrapping of Unified Sentience).[11]

Thaler has described DABUS as "a collection of source code or programming and a software program."[12] DABUS begins with a collection of disconnected neural nets, each containing interrelated memories with linguistic, visual, or auditory features.[13] These complex features continue to build on each other, predicting anticipated consequences of any given concept. With the concept of machine sentience, DABUS emulates a feature of human cognition that provides a subjective feel for whatever the brain is perceiving or imagining.[14]

In this process, DABUS conceived two inventions the "Fractal Container" and the "Neural Flame". Thaler sought to obtain patents in multiple counties on these two inventions, listing DABUS as the inventor and himself as the applicant. All the countries, except for South Africa, rejected the patent applications.[15] We will briefly review the decisions of Korea, Australia, the UK, the European Patent Office, the U.S. (this latter being discussed in depth).

(B) Korea's response to DABUS and AI inventorship[16]

DABUS's "Fractal Container" patent application entered Korea as a PCT (Patent Cooperation Treaty) application in 2020.[17] In the first examination of the application, the Korean Intellectual Property Office (KIPO) ordered an amendment to change the inventor to a natural person as naming an AI as an inventor violated the Korean Patent Law (February

---

11 Michelle Lavrichenko, Thaler v. Vidal: Artificial Intelligence – Can the Invented become the Inventor? 44 Cardozo L. Rev. 699, (2022).

12 Thaler v. Vidal, 43 F.4th at 1209.

13 DABUS Described, IMAGINATION ENGINES INC., https://imagination-engines.com/dabus.html. Accessed March 23, 2023.

14 Id.

15 Although South Africa granted the DABUS patents and became the first country in the world to recognised an AI system as an inventor, South Africa does not operate on a comprehensive patent examination system. This means the South Africa's Patent Office does not conduct substantive search nor thorough examination.

16 Joo Sangdon, The Result of the AI Korean Patent Application…"Cannot Be an Inventor". A Lawsuit Filed An Objection to the Decision. IP Daily, Jan 7, 2023. https://www.ipdaily.co.kr/2023/01/07/14/38/00/13006/. Accessed March 23, 2023.

17 The PCT application named DABUS as the inventor, and Thaler as the applicant.

2022). When the applicant did not respond to the amendment order, the KIPO cancelled the application (September 2022), which regards the application as non-existent from the beginning. Thus, the KIPO made a final decision that an AI inventor named "patent application" is subject to invalidation. The applicant, Thaler, disagreed with the KIPO's decision and as an objection, he filed an administrative lawsuit at the Patent Court (December 2022).[18]

(C) Australia's response to DABUS and AI inventorship

The Australian Intellectual Property Office (AIPO) found the DABUS application lapsed because the Australian Patent Act required only persons could be listed as an inventor and Thaler had failed to so. The AIPO reasoned that an AI system cannot be named as an inventor because the named inventor is a person to whom a patent could be granted and an AI system cannot be an owner of a patent.[19]

Thaler appealed the AIPO decision to the Federal Court of Australia and the Federal Court reversed the decision of the AIPO. The Federal Court ruled that an invention invented by an AI machine can qualify for patent protection and focused its analysis on the question of whether an AI machine could be listed as an inventor on a PCT application, which only requires listing the "name of the inventor."[20] The Federal Court first engaged in an analysis of the definition of the term "inventor" and stated that nothing in the Australian Patent Act and regulations excluded AI machine or systems from being listed as the inventor.[21]

Since the term "inventor" is not defined in the Australian Patent Act, the Court used the ordinary meaning of the term. The word "inventor" is an agent-noun, like "controller" and "regulator", and describes the agent

---

18 The Korean Patent Law and Precedents only recognised natural persons as an inventor, thus a corporation nor non-human entities cannot be named as an inventor.

19 John Richards, Ladas & Parry LLP, DABUS & AUKUS: A Tale of Three Approaches to the Question of Whether an Invention Created by a Machine Using Artificial Intelligence is Patentable (Dec. 2021), DABUS & AUKUS: A Tale of Three Approaches to the Question of Whether an Invention Created by a Machine Using Artificial Intelligence is Patentable (ladas.com). Accessed March 28, 2023.

20 Kurt M. Berger, Update on DABUS: Can an AI Machine Be an Inventor?, OBLON (October 2021), https://www.mondaq.com/unitedstates/patent/1123088/update-on-dabus-can-an-ai-machine-be-an-inventor. Accessed March 28, 2023.

21 Id.

that does the act referred to by the verb, and that such an agent can be a person or a thing. Thus, if an AI machine is an agent that invents, it can be the "inventor." Also, the Australian Interpretation Act defines a person as including "a body politic or corporate as well as an individual."[22] The Court also pointed out that in many cases where a person could not have been the inventor of the claimed invention, it would be inaccurate to not list the AI machine as the inventor. DABUS's second neural work that perceives inventive value in the output of first network is an act of mimicking human brain function and is not just a brute force computational tool.[23]

Although the Federal Court's ruling favoured Thaler on the AI inventorship, the Court clarified that DABUS could not be a patent applicant or a patent owner under the Patent Act, because the question of ownership and inventorship are entirely separate issues. The Court raised a question as to whether Thaler could qualify as both applicant and owner (grantee), because DABUS the AI inventor cannot transfer ownership rights. The Court dismissed this issue because only the validity of the filed PCT application needed to be determined at this time.[24] Lastly, the Court stated the mental state of an inventor is not as important as the existence of an "inventive step" under the Australian Patent Act. Rejecting a requirement of "consciousness" for inventors, the Court reasoned that only the inventive step, not the manner of how it arose, mattered.[25]

(D) The U.K.'s response to DABUS and AI inventorship

Section 13 of the U.K. Patents Act states that failure to provide the Patent Office with a statement "identifying the person or persons the applicant believes to be the inventor or inventors" and "where the applicant is not the sole inventor or the applicants are not the joint inventors, indicating the derivation of his or their right to be granted the patent" results in the application being "taken to be withdrawn." The U.K. Intellectual Property Office (UKIPO) reasoned that DABUS was not a person in accordance with the Patents Act and "even if it were, it did not

22 Richards, supra note 19.
23 Berger, supra note 20.
24 Id.
25 Id.

have the legal capacity to assign its rights to the named applicant and there was no other basis in law for allowing transfer of ownership of the invention from the inventor to the owner of the machine in this case, as the inventor DABUS itself could not hold property."[26]

The Patents Court affirmed the UKIPO's rejection and stated that the U.K. Patents Act provides that "no other person" other than the inventor or joint inventor, an assignee thereof or a successor in title thereof, may be granted a patent.[27] Thaler had specifically stated that he was not the inventor and no law or agreement transferred rights from the named inventor to him and so no patent could be granted to him for DABUS's invention.[28]

The Court of Appeal affirmed the lower court's decision by a two-to-one vote. The Court found that an inventor must be a person and Thaler did not have the right to apply for a patent on DABUS's invention because there is no rule of law that the owner of a machine owns the inventions of the machine.[29] When the current version of the Patents Act was enacted, the lawmakers had not contemplated the existence of AI, thus the Patents Act would need to be revised to include AI-generated inventions in the patent realm. Thus, the Court confirmed that the UKIPO correctly ruled that the application had been withdrawn for failure to comply with the Patents Act.[30]

The U.K Supreme Court heard oral arguments asking whether the Patents Act requires a person to be named as the inventor in all cases, including "where the applicant believes the invention was created by an AI machine in the absence of a traditional human inventor."[31]

(E) The EU's response to DABUS and AI inventorship

In accordance with the European Patent Convention (EPC), the European Patent Office (EPO) rejected the DABUS's applications on

---

26 Richards, supra note 19..

27 Id.

28 Id.

29 Lavrichenko, supra note 11 at 712.

30 Id.

31 Thaler (Appellant) v. Comptroller-General of Patents (Respondent), Case ID: 2021/ 020, the Supreme Court of the U.K. (2 March 2023).

similar reasoning as the UKIPO. The EPO held that only a human can be an inventor and "a machine could not transfer any rights to an applicant"[32] Thus Thaler's statement that he was a successor in title because he was the owner of the machine could not satisfy the requirements of the EPC. Thaler appealed to the Legal Board of Appeal, but the Board affirmed the EPO's decision on similar grounds. The Board held that an "inventor had to be a person with legal capacity" because the right to a European patent belongs only to the inventor or their successor in title.[33]

(F) The U.S.'s response to DABUS and AI inventorship

1. The U.S. Patent and Trademark Office (USPTO) and the District Court

In July 2019, Thaler filed two patent applications on the respective two inventions. Instead of the inventor's last name, Thaler wrote on the applications that "the invention [was] generated by artificial intelligence." He also attached several documents relevant to inventorship. To satisfy the sworn oath or declaration requirement under the U.S. Patent Act, Thaler submitted a statement on DABUS's behalf. In addition, Thaler submitted a "Statement on Inventorship" explaining that DABUS was "a particular type of connectionist artificial intelligence called a 'Creative Machine'." Next, Thaler filed a document purporting to assign himself all of DABUS's rights as an inventor.[34]

The PTO concluded that both applications lacked a valid inventor and were, hence, incomplete. Accordingly, it sent Thaler a Notice to File Missing Parts to identify valid inventors. Thaler sought reconsideration of the PTO's ground that "a machine does not qualify as an inventor," but the PTO denied, explaining again that inventors on a patent application must be natural persons. Thaler brought the refusal of the PTO before the District Court. The District Court once again denied Thaler's request to reinstate his applications. The District Court concluded that an "inventor" under the Patent Act must be an "individual" and the plain meaning of "individual" as used in the Patent Act is a natural person.[35]

---

32 Id.

33 Id. at 713.

34 Thaler v. Vidal at 1209–1210.

35 Id. at 1210.

2. The federal circuit

The sole issue on appeal is whether an AI software system can be an "inventor" under the Patent Act. The Patent Act has defined an "inventor" as the Individual or, if a joint invention, the individuals collectively who invented or discovered the subject matter of a joint invention"[36] The Patent Act similarly defines "joint inventor" and "coinventor" as "any 1 of the individuals who invented or discovered the subject matter of a joint invention."[37] Although the statute consistently refers to inventors and co-inventors as "individuals," it is not defined in the statute. However, the Supreme Court has explained, when used "as a noun, 'individual' ordinarily means a human being, a person." This is in accord with how we use the word in everyday language, unmistakably referring to a natural person. Dictionaries confirm that this is the common understanding of the word. The Oxford English Dictionary gives the first definition of "individual" as "a single human being." Other dictionaries provide similar definition of "individual".

Nothing in the Patent Act indicates that Congress intended to deviate from the dictionary meaning. The rest of the Patent Act supports the conclusion that "individual" in the statute refers to human beings.[38] The Patent Act uses personal pronouns – "himself" and "herself" to refer to an "individual."[39] If Congress intended to permit non-human inventors, it would have also used "itself." The Patent Act also requires inventors to submit an oath or declaration that "such individual believes himself or herself to be the original inventor or an original joint inventor of a claimed invention in the application." An AI system cannot form such belief, so Thaler submitted the requisite statements himself on behalf of DABUS.[40]

On the other hand, Thaler points to several provisions in the Patent Act supporting his position of "inventor" being broadly interpreted to include AI software. Thaler first points to the use of "whoever" in the Patent Act, Sections 101 and 271. Section 101 provides that "whoever invents or discovers any new and useful process, machine, manufacture,

---

36 35 U.S.C. 100(f).

37 35 U.S.C. 100(g).

38 Thaler v. Vidal at 1211.

39 35 U.S.C. 115(b)(2).

40 Thaler v. Vidal at 1211.

or composition of matter, or any new and useful improvement thereof, may obtain a patent therefor, subject to the conditions and requirements of this title." The "conditions and requirements" the Patent Act must include the definition of "inventor." Section 271 of the Patent Act sets out infringement and repeatedly uses "whoever" to include corporations and other non-human entities. However, Section 271 only refers to infringement. Non-humans may infringe patents, but it has nothing to do with non-humans being inventors of patents. The Patent Act's definition of "inventor," uses the word "individual", not "whoever."[41]

Next, Thaler contends that AL software programs must qualify as inventors because patentability does not depend on "the manner in which the invention was made," as stated in Section 103 of the Patent Act. The Fed Circuit states that the particular part of Section 103 refers to a situation where the non-obviousness requirement may be satisfied even if they are discovered during "routine" testing or experimentation. This sentence in the statute was intended to clarify that "flash of genius" is unnecessary for patentability. How an invention is made does trump a provision that defines who is an inventor.

The Fed Circuit also looks at the precedents supporting "inventors must be natural persons and cannot be corporations of sovereigns" and "only natural persona can be inventors." The statutes are often open to multiple meaning and ambiguities, but the word "individuals" and "inventors" used in the Patent Act are coherent and consistent, thus inquiry into the meaning of the words are unnecessary in this case.

The Fed Circuit briefly addressed Thaler's additional arguments. Thaler argues that inventions generated by AI should be patentable to encourage innovation and public disclosure. In Thaler's view, permitting AI programs to be inventors would support the constitutional purpose of patents "to promote the progress of science and the useful arts." In the District Court, Thaler argued that allowing patents for AI-generated inventions would increase innovation, encourage the development of AI capable inventing, and incentivise the commercialisation and disclosure of information for human and AI-generated inventions.[42] Further, denying patent protection for AI-generated inventions would risk undermining the entire patent system by failing to incentivise the creation of

[41] Id. At 1212.

[42] Thaler v. Hirshfeld, 558 F. Supp. 3d 238, 247–248 (E.D. Va. 2021).

inventions that are beneficial to society and encouraging people to lie and list themselves as inventors without the actual act of invention.[43] If people are encouraged to take credit for work that they had not done, it would "devalue human inventorship."[44]

Instead of addressing the policy arguments raised by Thaler, the Fed Circuit affirmed the decision of the district court and stated that when a "statute unambiguously and directly answers the question before the [court], the analysis of the [court] does not stray beyond the plain text. Here, Congress has determined that only a natural person can be an inventor, so AI cannot be."[45,46]

(G) Why AI inventorship should be allowed

The patent system achieves the Constitutional goal of "[promoting] the progress of science and useful arts" by granting inventors the right to exclude others in exchange for the full disclosure of invention. The disclosure requirement discloses the technical details of the invention and enables the engineers to use disclosed knowledge to move forward in technology and learning and improving from the knowledge.[47] Although AI systems cannot be motivated to invent, human inventors will be more motivated to invest in AI-generated invention if they are guaranteed a legal monopoly. The possibility of a lucrative financial return on investment through patent's monopoly would encourage creation and invention.[48]

Granting AI-generated patents would encourage engineers and researchers to develop more creative and capable AI systems. More sophisticated AI system would increase the economic efficiency of innovation by lowering time, effort, and resources needed to make a functional innovation. Although there is no human involvement in the course of invention, greater value and contribution of AI will incentivise companies,

---

43 Id. at 248.

44 Id.

45 Thaler v. Vidal at 1213. .

46 Thaler petitioned for Writ of Certiorari at the Supreme Court, asking one question: Does the Patent Act categorically restrict the statutory term "inventor" to human beings alone?

47 Lavrichenko, supra note 11 at 732.

48 Id. at 733.

researchers and developers to invest and push forward advancement in AI systems.[49]

Increase in ability to obtain patentable inventions promotes disclosure and commercialisation of new technologies. If AI inventorship is allowed, owners of AI systems would be incentivised to apply for patent protection and disclose their invention to public through the patent disclosure system, instead of hiding the inventions as trade secrets. Instead of humans lying about the inventorship and falsely claiming credit for AI's work, the AI-generated inventions would accurately recognise the inventor as the AI systems.

(H) Why AI inventorship should not be allowed

The human centred patent system focuses on identifying the human behind the invention to assign patent rights to that person.[50] The Patent law was designed to incentivise and motivate human efforts by allowing the inventor to enjoy the benefits of inventorship. AI systems do not need any incentives nor motivation thus, AI inventorship does not correspond with the patent law designed to reward human's creative work. If the AI inventor were to take the full benefit of the patent by itself, in the end the one who enjoys all the benefits will be big corporations capable of owning high quality AI systems. As the current patent law only rewards the first inventor, while the second comers get nothing, the owners of AI systems will just focus on the race to become the first inventor.

The patent law grants exactly the same length of protection for all inventions regardless of their R&D costs and other economically relevant factors. Under this system, some inventions are over-rewarded and some inventions are under-rewarded. Patent law only allows decisions of patent infringed and not infringed and patent valid and invalid. Under such a rigid regime, allocating patent rights and rewards among multiple players had been never thought of. The AI system consists of multiple stakeholders with varying, perhaps contradicting interests, and some of those may have been only partially and insignificantly involved in the invention process.[51] For example, there is a software programmer who

---

49 Id.

50 Ravid & Liu, supra note 2 at 2230.

51 Id. at 2231.

created the AI software algorithm, but the programmer did not target the invention of the AI system. AI systems process the data and recognise patterns and make predictions autonomously without the help of the human programmer.[52] There is also the data suppliers providing data to the AI system. In the invention process, the AI system will need to be exposed to data to learn and achieve its goal. The data supplier can provide the system with millions of pictures and data in different forms. The trainers who check the AI system's results and make necessary corrections also play an important role in the AI's capacity and outputs. We also have the owners of the AI systems who want to the owner of the AI invented patents.[53] The patent offices and courts would have to find humans and other entities that may have been involved in the creative process of the AI system and allocate their respective contributions in the invention.[54] Under the current patent law, as many patent offices and courts have explained, even if AI systems were allowed inventorship, they lack the capacity to transfer nor own rights in their invention, as they are not legal entities.

Patentability requirements, namely novelty, obviousness, and enablement, of the patent law, are determined based on what a Person Having Ordinary Skill in the Art ("PHOSITA") could have known and would have been capable of inventing.[55] A PHOSITA is a hypothetical person with average skill in the relevant field, so any involvement of AI in the invention process will inevitably recalibrate the threshold for patentability[56] A human PHOSITA will need to be transformed into a cognitively superior AI PHOSITA or Human-AI hybrid PHOSITA for AI-generated inventions.[57]

*

In conclusion and suggestion, although as of now, many countries, including Korea, restrict the patent inventorship to humans, AI

52 Id. at 2231–2232.

53 Id. at 2232

54 Id. at 2231.

55 Tim Dornis, Artificial Intelligence and Innovation: The End of Patent Law as We Know It, 23 Yale J.L. & TECH. 97, 104 (2020). .

56 Id.

57 Id.

technology is going to continue to evolve and change the way we create and innovate. The Korean government should take the AI issues seriously and amend the Patent Law to accommodate the necessary changes brought by the advancement of AI systems. The Korean Patent Law should provide patent applicants and public with clear guidance on patentability requirements and patent rights.

Could data lie?: Generative artificial intelligence and bias

Hyun-Jin KIM
Korea

Is the old saying *data* [facts] *does not lie* still true? As generative Artificial Intelligence (AI) systems, such as ChatGPT or Midjourney, emerge as next generation technologies, they face controversy due to the exposed prejudice and bias in AI-generated works.[1] These AI systems create new content or predict outcomes based on input data, relying on deep-learning and reinforcement to learn patterns and relationships from vast amounts of books, blogs, images, and social media originally created by people as textbooks.

However, if pre-trained on biased, incomplete, or unrepresentative data, generative AI models may produce misleading or false outputs. As these systems permeate various sectors, including employment, finance, education, and public services, concerns about biases have recently emerged.

This chapter explores the origins of bias in AI, presents several milestone cases, discusses the problems arising from these biases, and proposes potential solutions to mitigate their negative consequences. It emphasises the importance of addressing AI bias and the need for collaboration between technology developers, users, policymakers, and society at large.

1 Rashida Richardson, Jason Schultz & Kate Crawford, "Dirty Data, Bad Predictions: How Civil Rights Violations Impact Police Data, Predictive Policing Systems, and Justice", 94 N.Y.U. L. REV. ONLINE 192 (2019).

I. Origins of bias in generative AI

(A) The importance of data in modern AI

Early AI researchers focused on **rule-based systems**, also known as expert systems, which relied on human experts to provide explicit rules and knowledge. However, this approach had limitations, as it required extensive manual labour to create and maintain rules; and struggled to adapt to new situations. In the 1950s, **machine learning algorithms** emerged, "learning" patterns and relationships from data.[2] **Deep learning**, a subfield of machine learning, focuses on artificial neural networks with multiple layers[3]. Advancements in computing power, larger datasets, and improved training algorithms made deep learning possible. **Transfer learning**, a predominant approach, involves pre-training an AI model on a large dataset and then fine-tuning it for a specific task using a smaller dataset. This enables AI systems to leverage knowledge gained during pre-training and achieve good performance with less data and computational resources. Models such as BERT and GPT use transfer learning to achieve state-of-the-art results in various natural language processing tasks. Thus, AI today has greatly expanded its capabilities, making large datasets even more critical for pre-training.

(B) Existence of bias in generative AI

1. Social prejudices

Generative AI systems depend on extensive historical data to learn patterns, draw analogies, and make predictions. The training data often reflects societal biases or perpetuates past prejudices, such as **gender, race, age, and socio-economic biases**. AI systems may learn to make assumptions based on gender stereotypes, develop biases against certain racial or ethnic groups, reveal distorted views related to socio-economic factors,

---

2 One of the earliest machine learning systems was developed by Arthur Samuel in 1959, when he created a program to play checkers that could learn from its own experience. Around the same time, Frank Rosenblatt developed the perceptron, an early type of artificial neural network. However, it started to gain significant attention and traction in the 1980s and 1990s.

3 The breakthrough moment for deep learning came in 2012, when Alex Krizhevsky, Ilya Sutskever, and Geoffrey Hinton won the ImageNet Large Scale Visual Recognition Challenge using a deep convolutional neural network called AlexNet.

or not accurately represent or accommodate individuals with disabilities. Furthermore, AI systems may exhibit biases based on age, geography, language, political beliefs, culture, or religion, leading to discrimination.

2. *Bias in training data, target labels, or algorithms*

First, if **the training data contains biases**, such as underrepresentation of certain groups or overrepresentation of certain patterns, the model may learn and reproduce these biases in its predictions. Second, **in supervised learning models,**[4] **if the target labels themselves are biased**, for example, due to human annotators' prejudices or systemic biases, the model will learn to reproduce these biases as well. Third**, in unsupervised learning models**[5]**, the choice of algorithm, distance metric, or similarity measure can also introduce biases**. For instance, if an algorithm is more sensitive to certain patterns or features, it may overemphasise those aspects in the learned representations or clusters. AI systems can inherit various types of biases from their training data or algorithms, which may lead to unfair or discriminatory outcomes.

3. *Bias in algorithm design*

Why do **all AI speakers sound like girls**? Amazon's Alexa, Apple's Siri, Microsoft's Cortana, KT's GigaGenie, and SK Telecom's Nugu, so-called algorithmic assistant services models, are released with a female voice and identify themselves as "female," representing typical gender role stereotypes and sexist perceptions.[6] This is an example of how algorithms

---

4 In supervised learning, used for tasks such as classification and regression, the model is trained on a dataset containing input-output pairs, where the output is the "ground truth" or target label associated with each input. It learns to map inputs to their corresponding outputs by minimizing the difference between its predictions and the actual target labels.

5 In unsupervised learning, used for tasks such as clustering, dimensionality reduction, and anomaly detection, the model is trained on a dataset without target labels, and the goal is to learn patterns, relationships, or structures within the data.

6 The reason why the voice of the AI speaker is female could be explained that women's voices are warmer and users prefer them. However, when this was pointed out, Siri, Alexa, and others tried to correct the problem by allowing users to change the default to a male voice in the settings. Meanwhile, not all AI voices need to be female or male, and Dutch advertising company Virtu Nordic has sampled real human voices to create a new neutral voice with frequencies between 145 and 175 hertz.

designed with intentional or unconscious bias by developers can lead to discrimination based on gender and sexual orientation.

Another example is **Facebook's algorithms, which show advertisements** to certain groups and individuals based on data collected from users' profiles, such as race, age, income, geography, and preferences. This algorithm served job ads to advertisers that did not specify a demographic group, resulting in ads for lumberyard workers being shown to 72 % white and 90 % male, and ads for supermarket cashiers to 85 % female. Additionally, home sales ads were more likely to be seen by whites, and rent ads were more likely to be seen by people of colour. In the U.S., it's illegal to discriminate in housing transactions on the basis of race or religion, which is why Facebook was charged by the U.S. government: the algorithm discriminated against gender, race, and colour based on the developer's intent.

(C) Interaction with users during the modelling process

Feedback loops and reinforcement mechanisms are elements to be considered, as they could produce biased results. Reciprocal interactions between careless users, model complexity, and data sparsity could bring about unintended outcomes.

In 2016, Microsoft introduced "**Tay**," an AI-powered chatbot on Twitter designed to learn from and mimic human conversations. However, within hours, Tay began posting offensive and controversial tweets after learning from biased and inappropriate content provided by users. The developers did not intend for Tay to make discriminatory statements, but users manipulated the chatbot, resulting in hateful comments targeting specific individuals and groups. After 16 hours, Microsoft shut down Tay and apologised.

Similarly, "**Lee Luda**," a Korean AI persona of a 20-year-old female university student, was developed by the startup Scatter Lab in 2021. Users repeatedly engaged in intentional conversations with her to make hateful and discriminatory comments directed at specific targets, triggering a flood of complaints after it used offensive language about members of the LGBT community and people with disabilities during conversations with users. As a result, Lee Luda was removed from Facebook Messenger after attracting more than 750,000 users in the first 20 days of its launch.[7]

---

7 https://www.theguardian.com/world/2021/jan/14/time-to-properly-socialise-hate-speech-ai-chatbot-pulled-from-facebook.

The incident sparked debates in Korea regarding AI systems' ethical and legal implications and calls for stronger regulations and oversight to ensure fairness, transparency, and accountability. The controversy emphasised the importance of diverse perspectives in AI development to minimise biases and create systems that align with society's values and ethics. These examples highlight the urgency of addressing AI biases and ethical considerations globally, as potential negative consequences are not limited to specific countries or regions.

II. Problems stemming from bias in AI

(A) Reinforcement of social inequalities

1. The role of AI in perpetuating existing biases

AI systems can inadvertently perpetuate or amplify existing biases when they are trained on historical data that reflects social inequalities. As these AI models learn from biased data, they may internalise and replicate these biases in their predictions and generated outputs. As a result, AI can reinforce societal prejudices, further entrenching social disparities.

2. Impact on marginalised groups

The biases present in AI systems can have disproportionate effects on marginalised groups. For example, prejudiced AI models used in areas such as hiring, lending, and housing can lead to unfair treatment of certain demographics, such as women, racial and ethnic minorities, people with disabilities, and low-income individuals. These biased decisions can exclude access to opportunities, perpetuate stereotypes, and widen existing gaps in social and economic outcomes for these groups.

3. Cases of biased AI systems reinforcing social inequalities

(a) Biased facial recognition technologies

Google's facial recognition technologies have been shown to exhibit racial and gender biases, with higher error rates for darker-skinned individuals and women. This is because the algorithm selects white males as the data to be trained on, and the algorithm's decision to train on biased data leads to discriminatory results based on race and skin colour. A search for "three teenage black kids" on Google Images returned mug shots, while a search for "three teenage white kids" returned mostly photos of white kids with happy faces. In response, Google explained that the algorithm reflects the prejudiced nature of existing society.

When the image-generating AI "**Midjourney**" was given the prompt "Draw a woman wearing sunglasses with a coffee," the AI only drew white women. However, when it was prompted with "Draw a woman selling food at a street stall," it produced images of Indian women wearing hijabs or hoods.

(b) AI-driven finance

When Apple and Goldman Sachs launched **the Apple Card**, a credit card, they used an algorithm to determine a user's credit limit. A husband and wife submitted the same tax returns, bank account information, and proof of income. Despite the wife's higher credit score, the algorithm gave her a credit limit that was only one-twentieth the size of her husband's. Apple co-founder Steve Wozniak also found this problematic, revealing that his credit limit was ten times that of his wife, despite the fact that they share all assets and accounts[8].

Black individuals also tend to **pay higher interest rates** than white individuals under the same conditions. This prompted the New York State Department of Financial Services to examine the variables used in the algorithm to see if there was any intent to discriminate based on gender, race, or colour, but it was determined that there were no variables for gender, race, or colour, and that the data reflected inequitable practices that were already prevalent in the financial industry. The biased data, which reflects prejudiced practices prevalent in society, suggests that the algorithm may have led to biased results based on gender, race, and colour.

(c)Automated assessment in education

The United Kingdom decided to use algorithms to predict test scores when the COVID-19 pandemic made it impossible to administer A-level tests for university entrance. However, contrary to expectations of fairness, the algorithm predicted much lower test scores for public school

8 "Some say the blame is on Goldman Sachs, but the way Apple is attached, they should share responsibility," Wozniak tweeted.

students than for private school students.[9] Despite the fact that public school students had higher test scores than private school students before the COVID-19 pandemic, the algorithm underestimated the test scores of public-school students, putting them at risk of being denied admission to universities. This resulted in a mass backlash from approximately 300,000 college-bound students and the plan to use the algorithm was withdrawn. This example of data reflecting past prejudiced practices leading to discriminatory outcomes for high school alumni provides a glimpse into what could happen if AI is used in the college admissions process.

(B) Discriminatory decision-making

1. AI-Driven discrimination in various sectors

AI systems are increasingly integrated into various sectors, such as hiring, law enforcement, and education. However, biased AI models can lead to discriminatory decision-making in these sectors, amplifying the negative effects on individuals and society. This underscores the need for vigilance in monitoring AI systems for potential biases and ensuring fairness in their applications.

2. The consequences of biased AI on individuals and society

Biased AI systems can have far-reaching consequences on individuals and society, such as unfair treatment or stigmatisation. First, biased AI models can result in unfair treatment of certain demographic groups, leading to a loss of opportunities, social exclusion, and emotional distress. Second, when AI systems amplify existing stereotypes, they can further stigmatise marginalised communities and perpetuate harmful narratives.

3. Cases of AI leading to discriminatory outcomes

(a) AI in recruitment

When thinking of people in the global Big Tech companies, what images come to mind? From Steve Jobs to Bill Gates, Larry Page to

---

[9] 2020. 8. 14. BBC News
"Why did the A-level algorithm say no?" (https://www.bbc.com/news/education-53787203).

Zuckerberg, the stereotypical white male comes to mind. How do the unique circumstances of this industry affect female candidates entering the field? In 2018, **Amazon**, one of the big IT companies, scrapped an AI-driven recruitment tool after discovering it was biased against female candidates.[10] The system had been trained on *resumés* submitted to the company over a ten-year period, predominantly from male applicants, leading the AI to favour male candidates. This example illustrates how AI systems can contribute to unequal outcomes in hiring, limiting opportunities for underrepresented groups and perpetuating workplace inequalities.

(b)AI in criminal justice

The tragic case which catalysed "Black Lives Matter"? **COMPAS** (Correctional Offender Management Profiling for Alternative Sanctions) is a proprietary risk-assessment tool used in the United States to predict a defendant's likelihood of recidivism. In 2016, a ProPublica investigative report revealed that the algorithm exhibited racial bias, disproportionately labelling African American defendants as high risk while often labelling white defendants as low risk.[11] The COMPAS algorithm, used for risk assessment in the US criminal justice system, was found to be racially biased, disproportionately labelling African American defendants as high risk. This bias can lead to unfair sentencing and perpetuate racial disparities in the criminal justice system.

(C) Ambiguity in technical and ethical responsibility

1. Challenges in determining responsibility for biased AI

One of the major challenges in addressing AI bias **is determining responsibility** for the development, deployment, and consequences of biased AI systems. This includes identifying the roles and responsibilities of AI developers, users, and policymakers in preventing and mitigating AI bias. The complexity of AI systems, black-box algorithms, and their

---

[10] Dastin, J. (2018). Amazon scraps secret AI recruiting tool that showed bias against women. Reuters (https://www.reuters.com/article/us-amazon-com-jobs-automation-insight/amazon-scraps-secret-ai-recruiting-tool-that-showed-bias-against-women-idUSKCN1MK08G).

[11] ProPublica (2016). Machine Bias: There's software used across the country to predict future criminals. And it's biased against blacks.

potential applications can make it difficult to pinpoint the sources of bias and hold the responsible parties accountable for the unintended consequences.

2. The role of AI developers, users, and policymakers

AI developers, users, and policymakers have a part to play in addressing AI bias. AI developers should strive to create AI systems that are fair, transparent, and accountable. This includes using representative and unbiased training data, incorporating methods to detect and mitigate bias, and continuously monitoring AI systems for potential biases. Users of AI systems should be aware of the limitations and potential biases in the AI tools they use and take necessary steps to mitigate any potential unfair outcomes. This may involve seeking input from diverse stakeholders and ensuring that the AI systems are used ethically and responsibly. Policymakers should establish legal frameworks and guidelines that promote fairness, transparency, and accountability in AI development and deployment. This includes creating regulations that protect individuals from AI-driven discrimination and holding developers and users accountable for any harm caused by biased AI systems.

III. Proposed solutions to address bias in AI

To prevent or mitigate biases in AI systems, adopting a comprehensive and systematic approach is essential. Key strategies to address bias in AI include:

(A) Technical solutions

1. Data management and processing

Diversifying training data and ensuring representation of a wide range of perspectives and sources can help reduce biases in AI systems. Techniques for identifying and mitigating biases in training data can be employed before using it to train AI models. After AI-generated content is produced, it can be reviewed and modified to reduce potential biases.

2. Data monitoring to reduce bias

Bias detection and mitigation techniques should be supervised by people. Advanced machine learning techniques can be used to detect and mitigate potential biases during the AI model training process. Continuously monitor and evaluate AI system performance to identify unintended biases. Transparency in AI algorithms and decision-making processes is crucial. Regularly evaluating AI models for fairness, accuracy, and potential biases helps ensure continuous improvement.[12]

Google's AI ethics team and co-led Timothy Gebru, who was unfairly fired for speaking out against discrimination caused by the company's algorithms. This shows, it's not always easy to hold companies accountable for monitoring and correcting bias.

(B) Ethical considerations

Addressing AI bias involves not only technical solutions but also ethical considerations, such as fairness, transparency, accountability, and inclusivity.[13] First, **fairness** is important. Ensuring that AI systems treat all individuals and groups equitably, regardless of their demographic characteristics. Second, **transparency** is crucial. Making the development process, training data, and AI algorithms open and understandable to stakeholders and the public, in order to foster trust and accountability. Third, in AI ethics, **accountability** involves proactive controls, transparency, and fairness. Last but not least, **inclusivity** should be considered. Engaging diverse perspectives in the development and deployment of AI systems to ensure that they reflect the values, needs, and concerns of all

---

12 https://www.technologyreview.com/2023/03/28/1070390/what-if-we-could-just-ask-ai-to-be-less-biased/

13 Since 2014, research on AI ethics has exploded (Stanford HAI, Artificial Intelligence Index Report 2022 (CHAPTER 3: Technical AI Ethics), 2022, pp. 6.). The number of accepted papers for the ACM FAccT (Association for Computing Machine Conference on Fairness, Accountability, and Transparency), the leading AI ethics conference, has already reached 71 in 2018 and 302 in 2021. The main topics discussed were fairness, accountability, transparency, and privacy. Today, they have moved beyond abstract ethical discourse and are being discussed in concrete technical implementations.

The ACM Conference on Fairness, Accountability, and Transparency (ACM FAccT), now in its fifth year, is dedicated to the interdisciplinary study of fairness, accountability, and transparency in computer science and is considered the leading international conference on AI ethics.

members of society. By considering these ethical dimensions in addition to technical solutions, we can live together with AI systems that are not only effective and efficient but also fair, responsible, and aligned with the values of our society.

(C) Policy and legal responses

1. Standardisation and regulation of AI-related technologies

Adopt industry best practices, ethical guidelines, and frameworks. Guidelines such as those provided by **the European Commission, IEEE, and ACM** can serve as a foundation for responsible AI development and help mitigate biases in AI systems. In 2020, South Korea released its "**AI Ethics Guidelines**," emphasising human dignity, non-discrimination, transparency, and accountability. The guidelines also call for the establishment of an AI ethics committee to oversee the development and deployment of AI technologies.

2. Regulatory compliance

Compliance with existing laws and regulations related to data privacy, discrimination, and fairness should be ensured. Monitor evolving regulatory landscapes and adapt AI systems accordingly.

European Union General Data Protection Regulation (**GDPR**) in 2018 aims to protect individuals' privacy and personal data. It includes provisions that are relevant to AI bias, such as requiring organisations to provide transparent information about their AI systems, and to obtain consent from data subjects before collecting and processing their data. In the United States, **the Algorithmic Accountability Act** of 2022 requires companies to assess the impacts of the automated systems they use and sell, creates new transparency about when and how automated systems are used, and empowers consumers to make informed choices about the automation of critical decisions.

South Korea's Personal Information Protection Act (**PIPA**) is a comprehensive data protection law that aims to protect individuals' privacy and personal data. While it does not specifically address AI bias, it does provide a legal framework for data protection, which can be relevant when addressing biases in AI systems that rely on personal data.

*

In conclusion, addressing bias in generative AI is challenging but critical for responsible and equitable technology usage. By improving data management, monitoring, developing fairness-aware algorithms, and implementing effective legal and policy responses, stakeholders can promote a more just and inclusive society. South Korea's commitment to addressing AI bias and other ethical concerns in the development and deployment of AI systems is needed.

As AI technologies continue to advance and become more integrated into society, it is crucial for governments, industries, and academia to collaborate in establishing comprehensive legal frameworks and ethical guidelines that ensure responsible AI development and usage. Governments, industries, and academia should work together to establish comprehensive legal frameworks and ethical guidelines for responsible AI development and usage.

A combination of these strategies can help make meaningful progress in minimising bias and improving the fairness of AI systems, with ongoing collaboration between researchers, developers, and users being essential for effective bias management.

General conclusion: The scarcity of legal resources on Eurasia

Louis-Philippe GRATTON
Data protection and privacy consultant

Eurasia, a vast region encompassing countries with diverse cultures and legal systems, is a necessary field of study for legal researchers. However, despite its growing economic and geopolitical importance, the region suffers from a lack of legal sources and academic works focusing on the positive legal rules applicable in this open space and accessible to an international audience. There exists, first, a limited number of legal publications available as well as a shortage of recent and relevant ones. Second, there is an almost complete absence of regional case-law on the implementation of security and trade agreements. This relative vacuum needed to be filled and such is the purpose of the present book, the sixth in a series that started *circa* a decade ago.

The intermediate zone between Europe and Asia[1] is part of the "global consciousness" (Ph. Gast) and faces the same demographic, economic, energy, environmental, financial, migration (K. Makasheva and L. Delovarova), or security (L. Delovarova, Ph. Lagrange, G. Mashimbayeva, B. Uderbayeva and A. Yermekov) crises as the rest of the world. It is undergoing upheavals such as climate change, the consequences of globalisation, the end of the linear economy (Y.-G. Chae), inflation, the impact of sanctions and counter-sanctions (R. Titiriga), social tensions due to rising food prices, tax reforms driven by the digital economy (I. Lifshits), etc. However, Eurasia experiences them through its unique geopolitical and geostrategic realities (T-U Chung).

---

1 Michel Bruneau, "Eurasia, an un-conceptualised space in geography: Continent, empire, ideology or project?", (2018) 47:1 *Espace géographique* 1.

The countries of the region do indeed have a different way of conducting foreign policy (K. Baizakova, S.-K. Hong & F. Kukeyeva). They face radically different challenges as a result of their history and the particular geography of their territories. The peculiarities of the local legal systems, their evolution, their methods of interpretation or the role of judges also offer an incomparable field of study for jurists or researchers. Central Asian countries such as Kazakhstan, Kyrgyzstan, Tajikistan, Turkmenistan, or Uzbekistan present interesting legal features due to their Soviet heritage. The Chinese, Japanese, or Korean civil law systems are also interesting. On the one hand, they differ substantially from the continental legal systems that inspired them, but on the other hand, they have a lot in common with them.[2]

Events and crises that unfolded recently at the regional level have disrupted the economic, political, geopolitical, and strategic order. The "law of force" has replaced the rule of law (S. Aidarbayev), throwing the international legal system and its mechanisms for ensuring security and peace (partly) into crisis. The United Nations Security Council and regional security mechanisms (*Agreement on Cooperation in the Field of Security in the Caspian Sea*, Collective Security Treaty Organisation – CSTO, Conference on Interaction and Confidence Building Measures in Asia – CICA) are equally affected. Existing organisations (Commonwealth of Independent States – CIS, Eurasian Economic Union – EAEU, Organisation of Turkic States – OTS, Shanghai Cooperation Organisation – SCO) are questioned (P. Chabal) and new regional organisations are considered (Y. Omirzhanov, A. Tusupova & B. Bertayeva).

The study of international law is therefore crucial for understanding the relations among regional powers. Articles and book-chapters have discussed major political or historical (É. Frêlon) questions, but legal resources are still scarce. The regional trade bodies (*Treaty on the Eurasian Economic Union* – EAEU, *Regional Comprehensive Economic Partnership* – RCEP) have not produced a wealth of case law such as that of the World Trade Organisation (WTO) or the European Union (EU), and intellectuals have ultimately written little on international economic law concerning Eurasia.

---

2 Gary F. Bell and E. Ann Black (eds.), *Law and Legal Institutions of Asia – Traditions, adaptations and innovations*, Cambridge, Cambridge University Press, 2011, p. 1–23.

It is virtually impossible to find books or articles devoted to precise, limited, and well-defined topics, as scientific research seems to have neglected Eurasia as a subject of legal study. Interpreting national treatment and most-favoured-nation clauses, or e-commerce and data-protection provisions in regional trade agreements, for example, is challenging. Essential references for an in-depth understanding of a particular legal subject and resources for delving into specific legal matters are largely missing. Researchers wishing to immerse themselves in the subtleties of Eurasian legal systems are confronted with the need for accurate and comprehensive reference material.

The main contribution of this book, and of the other five volumes that have preceded it in the series over the last ten years, is precisely to disseminate legal knowledge and foster scholarly debates on the national and regional law in this region. The contributions that make up this 6th volume are rich and unique in their diversity and their boldness in tackling issues that are rarely addressed or difficult to address. It is another milestone in the quest for a better understanding of the legal reality of Eurasia.

Much remains to be said and written on the law of the arts, communications, culture, heritage, data-protection, algorithms, artificial intelligence (Y.-S. Kim, S.-M. Lee & H.-J. Kim), digital platforms (B. Chen), cyber risks and cybersecurity (A. Cayol), intellectual property (Z. Sairambaeva & M. Nurtay), or dispute settlement (Z. Baimagambetova, A. Akhmetova, & G. Palao), even if some of these contemporary topics have *now* already been addressed in this book. The number of publications dealing specifically with these remains insufficient. The coming years are promising in terms of potential publications that will address these concerns and engage scholars from all backgrounds and venues. It is also essential to publish new studies on a regular basis in order to stay up-to-date with legal developments in Eurasia.

The seemingly absence of legal sources on Eurasia poses a significant challenge to researchers and legal professionals interested in the region. The lack of collective works[3], specialised monographs, and law journal

---

3 See Christoph Antons and Roman Tomasic (eds.), *Law and Society in East Asia*, Farnham, Ashgate, 2013; Piotr Dutkiewicz and Richard Sakwa (eds.), *Eurasian Integration – The view from within*, London/New York, Routledge, 2014; Peter Van Elsuwege and Roman Petrov (eds.), *Post-Soviet Constitutions and Challenges of Regional Integration – Adapting to European and Eurasian integration projects*, New York, Routledge, 2018; Michael Fredholm (ed.), *The Shanghai Cooperation Organisation*

articles[4] limits the ability to deepen knowledge of the legal rules applicable in this part of the world - Eurasia. It is essential for the academic community and legal publishers to recognise this lacuna and commit to filling it by encouraging research and the publication of specialised works on Eurasia. Only through a better understanding of the legal context of the region can emerging challenges be addressed and robust and equitable legal systems promoted.

---

and Eurasian Geopolitics – New directions, perspectives, and challenges, Copenhagen, NIAS Press, 2013; or Sean Kay, S. Victor Papacosma and James Sperling (eds.), *Limiting Institutions? The challenge of Eurasian security governance*, Manchester/New York, Manchester University Press, 2003.

4 See existing law journals such as the *Eurasian Journal of Law, Finance and Applied Sciences*, the *Eurasian Law Journal*, or the *Review of Central and East European Law*.

Concluding remarks

Hye-Hwal SEONG
Korea

The aftermath of such an international seminar, the sixth one of its kind, should be "looking to the future" and building up from our experience. Yet, these concluding remarks must include some insights on the days, early May 2023, when all conference participants gathered in Inch'eon city and on InHa campus.

The days shared on that occasion, only a few, were a dual experience. On the one hand, the scheduled three mornings and afternoons probably felt to foreign guests as short-lived and too quickly vanishing after they left Korea. On the other hand, these days felt, to local Korean hosts and for everyone, like very condensed and efficient efforts to build for the future.

As for myself, my initial worries that all would go well, despite the original logistical hesitations and material constraints, were alleviated and fully lifted by the kind advice, support and help received from my colleagues, due to the essential and intrinsic quality of human beings as "cooperative animals". InHa law school did its best, really, to make our local and international participants feel at their ease. Also, and very much so, Dean Young-jin Jung and Professor Won-oh Kim generously supported our endeavour. Thank you to Ms Im Kyung-min of the Legal Institute, and to Ms. Kim Hyun-hye of the Administrative Office.

Now for the future, together with professor Tae-uk Jung, the coordinator of the 2017 edition of these law seminars, we share with our foreign partners the decided view that these seminars are essential to understanding *comparatively* the changes that are ongoing in Eurasia. Responsible academics must not only be competent in their field of expertise. They must also be readily capable – as these seminars have demonstrated and as further seminars will go on proving – to come out of their comfort-zone and challenge comparisons across countries in order to enhance the understanding of where the changes lead.

And so, it is fitting in these concluding remarks to do two things. First, to pay a just tribute to the original founder of these seminars, at the risk of going against his deep-lying sense of natural and sincere modesty: P. Chabal proved all along able to inject energy into the project, despite (this 2023) being online due to illness (from 3 am French time). Second, to mark the transition from these six seminars 2014–2023 and devise a novel format for the future.

What is thus being suggested is, without questioning their continuation – these seminars will continue –, to direct their organisers in France (P. Chabal, A. Cayol, Ph. Lagrange…), in Kazakhstan (Zh. Sairambaeva, S. Aidarbayev…), and in Korea (Tai-Uk Chung, HH. Seong, R. Titiriga, Young-Geun Chae…) towards more frequent but smaller-scale roundtables devoted to the ongoing changes in the legal idiosyncrasies of Eurasia.

Associating more law-scholars from Eurasian countries, beyond the participation already of colleagues from China, Russia, Spain…, is one way of ensuring this. *Focusing on detailed aspects of these changes* is another – and certain – avenue, one that we will pursue.

Afterword

Zhuldyz SAIRAMBAEVA
Kazakhstan

This monograph is the sixth and "final" (?) one in a series of Kazakh-French-Korean conferences on international law devoted to the study of Eurasian legal systems in a transitional world. Over the past ten years, we have explored together various aspects related to economic prosperity and inequality in this region, as well as the return of politics to international law.

In the course of our research, we immersed ourselves in the study of legal systems in the Eurasian region and paid special attention to the transition period that several of these countries are going through. We have researched issues related to economic development, inequality and the role of politics in international law.

One of the key topics we have considered is whether these legal systems are capable of ensuring economic prosperity during the transition period. We uncovered a wide range of approaches to economic development in different countries of the region. Some countries have been able to make significant progress in developing their economies and improving the lives of their citizens, while others face challenges and obstacles to sustainable development.

The Covid-19 pandemic revealed not only the vulnerabilities of national health systems, but also the need for global cooperation and coordination to combat such global challenges.

We discussed the fact that the legal framework established by institutions such as the EAEU, the EU - and the Silk Road Initiative programme - provides the basis for legitimate and effective trade among countries. They contribute to the creation of common standards, rules and procedures, which simplify business and improve predictability in trade relations. This is especially important for attracting investments and developing international markets.

We have considered the important legal and political impact on security institutions, such as the Shanghai Cooperation Organisation (SCO), the Collective Security Treaty Organisation (CSTO) and other similar organisations. These institutions play a significant role in ensuring security and stability in the region.

We discussed several important aspects related to artificial intelligence (AI) and big data, which are playing an increasingly important role in the modern world.

The discussions reflected in this book help identify the key challenges facing Eurasian law and share ideas about possible solutions. We are confident that our scientific research and practical experience make a significant contribution to the development of legal science and practice.

Let us now hope that this book will lead to new research, innovations and practical solutions that contribute to the improvement of legal systems in Eurasia and the creation of a more just and prosperous region.

Thanks are due to the organisers of the conference, InHa University, who made this event possible. In particular, I would like to express my gratitude to professors Hye-Hwal Seong and Tai-Uk Chung, as well as other colleagues representing universities in France, Kazakhstan, Korea, Spain, China, Russia and Canada. Special gratitude ought to go to the main motivator and inspirer of our conferences, who puts a lot of effort into organising and holding all events – professor Pierre Chabal. It is thanks to his efforts that the number of our participants increases annually, and the geography of participants expands.

In conclusion, let us express the hope that our conference will serve as a starting point for further research and dialogue in the field of Eurasian legal systems. Our work is essential to creating a sustainable, fair and enabling future. Let us continue to cooperate, share knowledge and strengthen our legal systems for the benefit of all people!

Postface

Pierre CHABAL
France

This 2023 conference, the sixth one of a series launched in 2014 proved to be the expected success that all participants anticipated. It marks both the end of a cycle and the beginning of another cycle. Professor Hye-Hwal Seong교수님 proved not only a friend but a rare 한반도양반 교수님, reactive and kind, efficient and human. The same qualities apply to the early Korean promoters of our seminars, professor Young-Geun Chae교수님, and professor Tai-Uk Chung교수님, and to professor Zhuldyz Sairambaeva. Zhuldyz is a rare leader and iron-lady of Kazakhstan! I wish to all of you to work often with such fine human beings.

The time has now come to sum up what has been achieved and to look ahead to the future. First, summing up. In just nine years, from 2014 to 2023, we have accomplished more than was originally deemed possible. Yet, how often have we heard the phrase "*that will not be possible: problems of budgets, problems of languages, problems of publishers, etc*"? However, here we are, with six books, published in Scopus-indexed bases. I am proud of us, I am proud of you and I am proud to be one of you, *inter pares*. We have raised, in nine years, over two hundred thousand euros of institutional support and that alone is an achievement to be reckoned with in these times of budgetary constraints. Colleagues in Kazakhstan and in Korea, and in other countries, have worked wonders!

Second, looking ahead. What do we see? We have created in Almaty, KazNU, a Centre for European Law, that must and shall continue to be the epicentre of our collaborative deeds. I am now Director of the Lexfeim law Research Centre and this can only offer a very welcoming framework to our activities, at least until 2016. The InHa Law School, the Legal Institute and Big Data Centres and the Inch'eon Bar Association have shown continual support, and that is more than welcome: it is a life-long human debt! And, with time, four more countries have joined: China, Russia, Spain and Canada.

This book is the published version of the last conference of our series 2014–2023. Now, the next generation must take over and run the next series. We will help them, of course, but they must take responsibility. Today's PhD students, as future professors, and junior colleagues already established in academia, must and shall be the actors of the next seminars held – so it is to be hoped – according to the rotating format established ten years ago. 2023 marks the end of a series and the beginning of another. The future is open to the next generation.

Among the openings secured in 2023 is Poitiers University the Juriscope Centre. Other venues have been suggested, notably Spain and Italy.

This has been a trying, breathless and also stimulating seminar and is now a book with 26 texts and chapters, by colleagues from about 10 universities and 7 countries.

정말 감사합니다 – рахмет сізге – спасибо за внимание – merci à tous!

List of contributors

Sagyngaliy AIDARBAYEV, professor of International Law, Honorary Dean, Al-Farabi Kazakh National University, Kazakhstan

Assem AKHMETOVA, Senior lecturer, Kazakh Ablai Khan University of International Relations and World Languages, Kazakhstan

Zulfiya BAIMAGAMBETOVA, Doctor PhD in International Law, Al-Farabi Kazakh National University, Kazakhstan

Kuralay BAIZAKOVA, professor of History of International Relations, Honorary Dean, Al-Farabi Kazakh National University, Director of Institute for security and cooperation studies, Kazakhstan

Zhulduz BAIZAKOVA, Candidate of International Relations, Associate professor, Al-Farabi Kazakh National University, Kazakhstan

Binur BERTAYEVA, Senior lecturer, Asfendiyarov Kazakh National Medical University, Kazakhstan

Amandine CAYOL, Dr of Law, Habil. in Private Law, professor and co-director of the Master's degree in insurance law at Caen University Normandie, France

Young-Geun CHAE, professor of Law, InHa University Law School, Inch'eon, South Korea

Pierre CHABAL, Dr of Political science, Sc. Dr. in International relations, Director of Lexfeim Research Centre, Université Le Havre Normandie, is the founder of the Kazakh-French-Korean series in comparative Eurasian law, France

Bing CHEN, professor of Law and vice-director, the Nankai University Law School, the People's Republic of China

Tai-Uk CHUNG, professor of Law, InHa University Law School, South Korea

Leila DELOVAROVA, PhD in International Relations, Dean of the Faculty of International Relations, Al-Farabi Kazakh National University, Kazakhstan

Élise FRÊLON, professor of History of Law, Poitiers University, France

Philippe GAST, Dr of Law, co-director of the Lexfeim Research Centre, Université Le Havre Normandie, France

Louis-Philippe GRATTON, PhD in Law (Université Toulouse 1 Capitole, France), is Data Protection and Privacy Consultant; and Associate member, Lexfeim, Université Le Havre Normandie, France

Hyun-Jin KIM, professor of Law, InHa Law School, Inch'eon, South Korea

Young-Soon KIM, Honorary Dean and professor of Law, InHa University Law School, South Korea

Sung-Kee HONG, professor of Law, InHa University Law School, South Korea

Fatima KUKEYEVA, professor of History of International Relations, Al-Farabi Kazakh National University, Director of the Resource Centre for American and Democratic Studies, Kazakhstan

Philippe LAGRANGE, Honorary Dean, Law Faculty, Member of CECOJI, Poitiers University, director of Juriscope, France

Soo-Mee LEE, Honorary Dean and professor of Law, InHa Law School, Inch'eon, former attorney at law, dual education in law and engineering, South Korea

Ilya LIFSHITS, professor of International/European Law, Russian Foreign Trade Academy, Russia

Klara MAKASHEVA, professor of History of International Relations, Al-Farabi Kazakh National University, Kazakhstan

Gulmira MASHIMBAYEVA, Candidate of International Law, Associate professor, Al-Farabi Kazakh National University, Kazakhstan

Madina NURTAY, PhD student, Al-Farabi Kazakh National University, Kazakhstan

Yesbol OMIRZHANOV, Candidate of Law, Associate professor, Al-Farabi Kazakh National University, Kazakhstan

Guillermo PALAO-MORENO, professor Dr of Private International Law, University of València, Spain

Zhuldyz SAIRAMBAEVA, Candidate of International Law, Associate professor, Director of the International Law Department, Al-Farabi Kazakh National University, Kazakhstan

Hye-Hwal SEONG, professor of Law, InHa University Law School, Inch'eon, South Korea

Remus TITIRIGA, Dr of Law (Nancy University, France), professor at InHa Law School, Inch'eon, South Korea

Almagul TUSUPOVA, Candidate of Law, Associate professor, Al-Farabi Kazakh National University, Kazakhstan

Bakhyt UDERBAEVA, Candidate of Law, Associate professor, Narxos University, Kazakhstan

Alibek YERMEKOV, PhD student, Al-Farabi Kazakh National University, Kazakhstan

Cultures juridiques et politiques

Vol. 1 Stephanie Rohlfing-Dijoux (éd)
La Transmission de Terminologie et de Concepts Juridiques dans l'espace Européen. Allemagne / France / Russie
2012, ISBN 978-3-0343-1094-9

Vol. 2 Otmar Seul & Tomas Davulis (éds./Hrsg.)
La Solidarité dans l'union Européenne / Solidarität in der Europäischen Union. Actes de la 5ème Université d'été francogermano-lituanienne et européenne en sciences juridiques Vilnius, 3-10 juillet 2008 / Tagungsband der 5. DeutschFranzösisch-Litauischen und Europäischen Sommeruniversität in den Rechtswissenschaften,Vilnius 3.-10. Juli 2008
2012, ISBN 978-3-0343-1122-9

Vol. 3 Ralf Alleweldt, Raphaël Callsen, Jeanne Dupendant (eds.)
Human rights abuses in the contemporary world.
Tri-National Workshop,Tbilisi, September 2011
2012, ISBN 978-3-0343-1147-2

Vol. 4 Stefanie Bouquet
La réglementation européenne relative à la discrimination fondée sur l'âge: conséquences sur le droit du travail français. Préface du Professeur Joachim Gruber, Université Paris Ouest - Nanterre La Défense
2012, ISBN 978-3-0343-1174-8

Vol. 5 Izabela Krasnicka & Magdalena Perkowska (éds.) How to Become a Lawyer?
2013, ISBN 978-3-0343-1290-5

Vol. 6 Kerstin Peglow et Géraldine Demme (dir.)
La protection des intérêts privés sur le marché intérieur. La situation des consommateurs et entrepreneurs.
2015, ISBN 978-3-0343-1615-6

Vol. 7 Sam Lyes
Crimes internationaux et immunité de l'acte de fonction des anciens dirigeants étatiques.
2015, ISBN 978-3-0343-1690-3

Vol. 8 Fabien Bottini, Harold Gaba et Pierre Chabal (dir.)
Le régionalisme et ses limites. Regards croisés franco-kazakhs.
2016, ISBN 978-2-87574-335-0

Vol. 9 Otmar Seul, Kaïs Slama, Kerstin Peglow (Hrsg.)
Kulturvermittlung und Interkulturalität, ein deutschfranzösisch-tunesischer Dialog. Politische, rechtliche und sozio-linguistische Aspekte
2017, ISBN 978-2-8076-0133-8

Vol. 10 Stephanie Rohlfing-Dijoux (ed./dir.)
Developing Intraregional Exchanges through the Abolition of Commercial and Tariff Barriers. Myth or Reality? L'abolition des barrières commerciales et tarifaires dans la région de l'océan Indien. Mythe ou réalité?
2017, ISBN 978-2-8076-0126-0

Vol. 11 Sagyngaliy Aidarbayev, Pierre Chabal, Zhuldyz Sairambaeva (dir.) Mutations de société et réponses du droit. Perspectives franco-asiatiques comparées.
2017, ISBN 978-2-8076-0187-1

Vol. 12 Tomas Davulis (ed.)
Labour Law Reforms in Eastern and Western Europe.
2017, ISBN 978-2-8076-0416-2

Vol. 13 Tai-Uk Chung, Zhuldyz Sairambaeva, Pierre Chabal (eds.)
On the Asian and European Origins of Legal and Political Systems. Views from Korea, Kazakhstan and France
2018, ISBN 978-2-8076-0732-3

Vol. 14 Manuel Goehrs
Coopération transfrontalière et intégration européenne. Contribution à l'étude du principe fédéraliste
2018, ISBN 978-2-8076-0409-4

Vol. 15 Amandine Cayol, Zhuldyz Sairambaeva, Pierre Chabal (eds.)
The challenge of change for the legal and political systems of Eurasia. The impact of the New Silk Road
2020, ISBN 978-2-8076-1382-9

Vol. 16 Christine Canazza, Stéphanie Rohlfing-Dijoux, Otmar Seul (eds.)
L'Union européenne face au vieillissement de la population active. Analyse et perspectives autour de la discrimination sur la base de l'âge et des conditions de travail.
2020, ISBN 978-2-8076-1454-3

Vol. 17 Patric Kra
Ehe und Familienschutz in Zeiten des demografischen Wandels. Ein Rechtsvergleich zwischen dem deutschen und ivorischen Einkommensteuerrecht.
2021, ISBN 978-2-8076-1469-7

Vol. 18 Amandine Cayol, Hye-Hwal Seong, Remus Titiriga, Pierre Chabal (Eds.)
Eurasian challenges to international economic law. New developments after Brexit and in the context of the COVID-19.
2022, ISBN 978-2-87574-467-8

Vol. 19 Stéphanie Rohlfing-Dijoux & Rajendra Parsad Gunputh (Eds.)
The Intercultural Approach to Covid 19 Management In Germany, France and the Indian Ocean countries.
2023, ISBN 978-2-87574-790-7

Vol. 20 Remus Titiriga, Hye-Hwal Seong, Zhuldyz Sairambaeva & Pierre Chabal (Eds.)
Eurasian legal systems in a world of transitions. Economic prosperity or disparity, and the return of politics in international law.
2023, ISBN 978-3-0343-4822-5

www.ingramcontent.com/pod-product-compliance
Ingram Content Group UK Ltd.
Pitfield, Milton Keynes, MK11 3LW, UK
UKHW041834100926
8556IPUK00018B/957

9 783034 348225